FRENCH-ENGLISH
ENGLISH-FRENCH
DICTIONARY

THE NEW INTERNATIONAL
WEBSTER'S

ENGLISH/FRENCH
DICTIONARY

FRANÇAIS/ANGLAIS
DICTIONNAIRE

Trident Press International

2004 EDITION

THE NEW INTERNATIONAL
WEBSTER'S

ENGLISH/FRENCH
DICTIONARY

FRANÇAIS/ANGLAIS
DICTIONNAIRE

Published by
Trident Press International

801 12th Avenue South, Suite 400, Naples Florida 34102
www.trident-international.com • email: sales@trident-international.com

2004 Edition

ISBN 1-58279-615-7

Printed in Canada

ENGLISH-FRENCH

DICTIONARY

ABBREVIATIONS

adj. adjective
adv. adverb
art. article
conj. conjunction
dem. demonstrative
f. feminine
fig. figurative
impers. impersonal
inf. infinitive
int. interjection
m. masculine
pers. person
pl. plural
poss. possessive
pp. past participle

pron. pronoun
qch. quelque chose
qn. qulqu'un
rel. relative
s. substantive
sing. singular
s.o. someone
sth. something
v.a. active verb
v.a. & n. active and neuter verb
v. aux. auxiliary verb
v.n. neuter verb
* irregular verb
prep. preposition

Pronunciation

We give below a short, simple guide to French pronunciation, giving the French sounds and their description. Vowels or consonants that are equivalent to the English ones are not indicated in this list.

Letters	French key word	Description
a, à, â	la, là, bâtir	between *bag* and *bug*
ai, aî	chaise, maîtr	resembles *ai* in *chair*
an	dans	between the vowels of *ah* and *oh* with n nasalised
au	pause	as in *oh* but with no final *u*
c	a) café	before *a, o, u* pronounced as *k*
	b) ici	before *e, i, y* pronounced *s* as in *say*
ç	français	as *s* in *say*
ch	chambre	as *sh* in *she*
e	a) le, petit	as the unstressed vowel of *the, standard*
	b) derriere, m	(in a closed syllable) as *e* in *deck*
é	été	as in *day* but with no final *i*

è, ê	père, fête	resembles the vowels in *pear* or *mare* without diphthongization
eau	eau	as in *oh* but with no final *u*
en	enfant	between *ah* and *oh* with *n* nasalized
er	donner	as in *day* but with no final
eu	jeudi, leur	closer than *earth* or *sir* pronounced with the lips pouted
g	a) rouge	before *e, i, y* pronounced as *s* in *measure, usual*
	b) grand	as *g* in *grand, good*
gn	signe	as in *new* or *lenient*
h	homme	it is never pronounced in French
i	a) ici	tenser than English short *i*
	b) mise	as *ee* in *meet*
î	île	as *ee* in *meet*
ille	fille	as in *key* with *y* at the end
in	vin	resembles the sound in *tan* pronounced through the nose
o	jour	as *s* in *usual*
jô	mot, côte	as in *oh* but with no final *u*
œ	œil	closer than *earth* pronounced with the lips pouted
oi	moi	as in *memoir* (memwaa')
on	non, son	between *ah* and *oh* with *n* nasalized
ou, oû	rouge, goûter	short or long *oo* as in *foot* or
qu	quand, question	as *k* in English
r	rare	as a slightly rolled English *r*
s	a) son	usually *s* as in *say*
	b) maison	(between two vowels) *z* as in *zero*
th	thé	as *t* in English
tion	nation	always *sio*+nasal *n*
u, û	sur, sûr	no equivalent in English: round lips for *oo* and try to pronounce *ee*
un	brun	the vowel of *her, earth* with a nasal *n*
w	wagon	as *v* in English
x	a) deuxième	as *z* in *zero*
	b) six	as *s* in *say*
y	y	as short *i* in English

FRENCH GRAMMAR

L i a i s o n.—Final consonants are not usually pronounced, but in most cases, when a word begins with a vowel (or the mute *h*), it is linked with the last consonant of the preceding word. In such cases final *c* and *g* are pronounced as *k*, final *s* and *x* as *z*, e.g. les‿Anglais (lezangle).

S t r e s s.—In polysyllabic words stress usually falls on the last pronounced syllable, e.g. plusieurs, le docteur, la société.

The Article

The definite article is *le* (m.), *la* (f.), *les* (m. f. pl.). *Le, la* are shortened to *l'* before a vowel or mute *h*.

The indefinite article is *un* (m.), *une* (f.).

The Noun

The p l u r a l is generally formed in *s*. Nouns in *s*, *x*, and *z* do not change in the plural. Nouns in *au* and *eu* form their plurals in *x*, e.g. *joyau, joyaux, jeu, jeux*. Nouns in *al*, form their plurals in *aux*, e.g. *cheval, chevaux*.

There are two *genders* in French. Nearly all nouns ending in *e* mute are feminine, except those in *isme*, *age* and *iste*. Nearly all nouns ending in a consonant or a vowel other than *e* mute are masculine, except nouns in *tion* and *té*. Nouns in *er* form their f. in *ère* e.g. *laitier, laitière*. Nouns in *en, on* form their f. in *enne, onne*, e.g. *chien, chienne, lion, lionne*. Nouns in *eur* form their 'f. in *euse* except those in *ateur* which have *atrice*, e.g. *admirateur, admiratrice*.

The Adjective

The p l u r a l is generally formed in *s*. Adjectives in *s* or *x* do not change. Those in *al* usually form their plurals in *aux*, e.g. *principal, principaux*.

The f e m i n i n e-is generally formed by adding *e* to the masculine form, e.g. *élégant, élégante*. Adjectives in *f* change *f* into *ve*, e.g. *vif, vive*. Those in *x* change *x* into *se*, e.g. *heureux, heureuse*. Adj. in *er* form their f. in *ère*, e.g. *amer, amère*. Those in *el, eil, en, et, on* double the final consonant before adding *e*, e.g. *bel, belle, bon, bonne*.

C o m p a r a t i v e.—'more . . . than' or '. . . er than' is to be translated by 'plus . . . que'; 'less . . . than' by 'moins . . . que'.

S u p e r l a t i v e.—'the most . . . ' or 'the . . . st' is to be translated by 'le plus . . .', 'la plus . . . ' or 'les plus . . . '

The Pronoun

P e r s o n a l p r o n o u n s: je, tu, il, elle; nous, vous, ils, elles.—*Accusative:* me, te, le, la; nous, vous, les. *Dative:* me, te, lui; nous, vous, leur.—

After prep.. moi, toi, lui, elle; nous, vous, eux, elles.

Reflexive pronouns:
me, te, se; nous, vous, se.

Possessive pronouns: le mien (la mienne, les miens, les miennes), le tien (la tienne, les tiens, les tiennes), le sien (la sienne, les siens, les siennes); le nôtre (la nôtre, les nôtres), le vôtre (la vôtre, les vôtres), le leur (la leur, les leurs).

Relative pronouns: who = qui, whom = que, whose = dont, which = qui or que, to whom = a qui.

Interrogative pronoun: who, whom = qui; what = que.

The Adverb

Most French adverbs are formed by adding *ment*, to the feminine form of the corresponding adjective, e.g. *facile*, *facile+ment*, *heureux*, *heureuse + ment*. Those in *ant* and *ent* form their adverbs in *amment* and *emment*, respectively, e.g. *patient—patiemment*.

The Verb

We give here the conjugation of the two auxilliaries (*avoir*, *être*) and of the verbs in -er, -ir, and -re, giving only the principal simple forms:

avoir *Pres. Ind.* j'ai, tu as, il a, nous avons, vous avez, ils ont; *Impf.* j'avais, tu avais, il avait, nous avions, vous aviez, ils avaient; *Fut.* j'aurai, tu auras, il aura, nous aurons, vous aurez, ils auront; *Cond.* j'aurais, tu aurais, il aurait, nous aurions, vous auriez, ils auraient; *Pres. Subj.* que j'aie, que tu aies, qu'il ait, que nous ayons, que vous ayez, qu'ils aient; *Imp.* aie, ayons, ayez; *Pres. Part.* ayant; *Past.Part.* eu.

être *Pres. Ind.* je suis, tu es, il est, nous sommes, vous êtes, ils sont; *Impf.* j'étais, tu étais, il était, nous étions, vous étiez, ils étaient; *Fut.* je serai, tu seras, il sera, nous serons, vous serez, ils seront; *Cond.* je serais, tu serais, il serait, nous serions, vous seriez, ils seraient; *Pres. Subj.* que je sois, que tu sois, qu'il soit, que nous soyons, que vous soyez, qu'il soient; *Imp.* sois, soyons, soyez; *Pres. Part.* étant; *Past. Part.* été.

donner *Pres. Ind.* je donne, tu donnes, il donne, nous donnons, vous donnez, ils donnent; *Impf.* je donnais, tu donnais, il donnait, nous donnions, vous donniez, ils donnaient; *Fut.* je donnerai, tu donneras, il donnera, nous donnerons, vous donnerez, ils donneront; *Cond.* je donnerais, tu donnerais, il donnerait, nous donnerions, vous donneriez, ils donneraient; *Pres. Subj.* que je donne, que tu donnes, qu'il donne, que nous donnions, que vous donniez, qu'ils donnent; *Imp.* donne, donnons, donnez; *Pres. Part.* donnant; *Past. Part.* donné.

finir *Pres. Ind.* je finis, tu finis, il finit, nous finissons,

vous finnissez, ils finissent;
finis, il finit, nous finissons,
vous finissez, ils finissent;
Impf. je finissais, tu finissais, il finissait, nous finissions, vous finissiez, ils
finissaient; *Fut.* je finirai,
tu finiras, il finira, nous
finirons, vous finirez, ils
finiront; *Cond.* je finirais, tu
finirais, il finirait, nous
finirions, vous finiriez, ils
finiraient; *Pres. Subj.* que je
finisse, que tu finisses, qu'il
finisse, que nous finissions,
que vous finissiez, qu'ils
finissent; *Imp.* finis, finissons, finissez; *Pres. Part.*
finissant; *Past Part.* fini.

rendre *Pres. Ind.* je rends, tu
rends, il rend, nous rendons,
vous rendez, ils rendent;
Impf. je rendais, tu rendais,
il rendait, nous rendions,
vous rendiez, ils rendaient;
Fut. je rendrai, tu rendras,
il rendra, .nous rendrons,
vous rendrez, ils rendront;
Cond. je rendrais, tu rendrais, il rendrait, nous rendr-
ions, vous rendriez, ils
rendraient; *Pres. Subj.* que
je rende, que tu rendes, qu'il
rende, que nous rendions,
que vous rendiez, qu'ils
rendent; *Imp.* rends, rendons, rendez; *Pres. Part.*
rendant; *Past. Part.* rendu.

Irregular Verbs

Verbs in *-ger* add *e* before
endings in *a* and *o*. Verbs in
-eler, *-eter* double the *l* or *t*
before a mute *e*. Verbs having
an acute *é* in the last syllable
but one change for a grave *e*
when the ending begins with a
mute *e*. Verbs in *-yer* change *y*
into *i* before a mute *e*.

In the following list of the
most frequent French irregular verbs (the root verbs only)
the numbers indicate the principal tenses and forms in a
fixed order: **1.** Present Indica-
tive; **2.** Imperfect; **3.** Future;
4. Present Subjunctive; **5.** Imperative; **6.** Present Participle; **7.** Past Participle. (+
être, if *être* is used to form
the past tenses e.g. je suis
allé.)

absoudre 1. j'absous, tu
absous, il absout, nous ab-
solvons, vous absolvez, ils
absolvent; **2.** j'absolvais;
3. j'absoudrai; **4.** que
j'absolve; **5.** absous, absol-
vons, absolvez; **6.** absol-
vant; **7.** absous, absoute.

acquérir 1. j'acquiers, tu acquiers, il acquiert, nous
acquérons, vous acquérez,
ils acquièrent; **2.** j'acquér-
ais; **3.** j'acquerrai; **4.** que
j'acquière; **5.** acquiers, acquérons, acquérez; **6.** ac-
quérant; **7.** acquis.

aller 1. je vais, tu vas, il va,
nous allons, vous allez, ils
vont; **2.** j'allais; **3.** j'irai;
4. que j'aille, que nous all-
ions, qu'ils aillent; **5.** va,
allons, allez; **6.** allant; **7.**
allé (être).

assaillir 1. j'assaille, tu
assailles, il assaille, nous
assaillons, vous assaillez, ils
assaillent; **2.** j'assaillais;
3. j'assaillerai; **4.** que
j'assaille; **5.** assaille, assaillons, assaillez; **6.** assaillant;
7. assailli.

asseoir 1. j'assieds, tu assieds, il assied, nous asseyons, vous asseyez, ils asseyent *or* j'assois, tu assois, il assoit, nous assoyons, vous assoyez, ils assoient; **2.** j'assayais *or* j'assoyais; **3.** j'assiérai *or* j'assoierai; **4.** que j'asseye *or* que j'assoie; **5.** assieds, asseyons *or* assoyons, asseyez *or* assoyez; **6.** asseyant or assoyant; **7.** assis.

atteindre *as* **peindre.**

battre 1. je bats, tu bats, il bat, nous battons, vous battez, ils battent; **2.** je battais; **3.** je battrai; **4.** que je batte; **5.** bats, battons, battez; **6.** battant; **7.** battu.

boire 1. je bois, tu bois, il boit, nous buvons, vous buvez, ils boivent; **2.** je buvais; **3.** je boirai; **4.** que je boive; **5.** bois, buvons, buvez; **6.** buvant; **7.** bu.

bouillir 1. je bous, tu bous, il bout, nous bouillons, vous bouillez, ils bouillent; **2.** je bouillais; **3.** je bouillirai; **4.** que je bouille; **5.** bous, bouillons, bouillez; **6.** bouillant; **7.** bouilli.

clore 1. je clos, tu clos, il clôt; **3.** je clorai; **4.** que je close; **7.** clos.

concevoir 1. je conçois, tu conçois, il conçoit, nous concevons, vous concevez, ils conçoivent; **2.** je concevais; **3.** je concevrai; **4.** que je conçoive; **5.** conçois, concevons, concevez; **6.** concevant; **7.** conçu.

conclure 1. je conclus, tu conclus, il conclut, nous concluons, vous concluez, ils concluent; **2.** je concluais; **3.** je conclurai; **4.** que je conclue; **5.** conclus, concluons, concluez; **6.** concluant; **7.** conclu.

conduire 1. je conduis, tu conduis, il conduit, nous conduisons, vous conduisez, ils conduisent; **2.** je conduisais; **3.** je conduirai; **4.** que je conduise; **5.** conduis, conduisons, conduisez; **6.** conduisant; **7.** conduit.

connaître 1. je connais, tu connais, il connaît, nous connaissons, vous connaissez, ils connaissent; **2.** je connaissais; **3.** je connaîtrai; **4.** que je connaisse; **5.** connais, connaissons, connaissez; **6.** connaissant; **7.** connu.

conquérir *as* **acquérir.**

construire *as* **conduire.**

contraindre 1. je contrains, tu contrains, il contraint, nous contraignons, vous contraignez, ils contraignent; **2.** je contraignais; **3.** je contraindrai; **4.** que je contraigne; **5.** contrains, contraignons, contraignez; **6.** contraignant; **7.** contraint.

coudre 1. je couds, tu couds, il coud, nous cousons, vous cousez, ils cousent; **2.** je cousais; **3.** je coudrai; **4.** que je couse; **5.** couds, cousons, cousez; **6.** cousant; **7.** cousu.

courir 1. je cours, tu cours, il court, nous courons, vous courez, ils courent; **2.** je courais; **3.** je courrai; **4.** que je coure; **5.** cours, courons, courez; **6.** courant; **7.** couru.

couvrir *as* **ouvrir.**

croire 1. je crois, tu crois, il croit, nous croyons, vous croyez, ils croient; **2.** je croyais; **3.** je croirai; **4.** que je croie; **5.** crois, croyons, croyez; **6.** croyant; **7.** cru.

croître 1. je crois, tu crois, il croit, nous croissons, vous croissez, ils croissent; **2.** je croissais; **3.** je croîtrai; **4.** que je croisse; **5.** crois, croissons, croissez; **6.** croissant; **7.** crû, crue.

cueillir 1. je cueille, tu cueilles, il cueille, nous cueillons, vous cueillez, ils cueillent; **2.** je cueillais; **3.** je cueillerai; **4.** que je cueille; **6.** cueillant; **7.** cueilli.

cuire 1. je cuis, tu cuis, il cuit, nous cuisons, vous cuisez, ils cuisent; **2.** je cuisais; **3.** je cuirai; **4.** que je cuise; **5.** cuis, cuisons, cuisez; **6.** cuisant; **7.** cuit.

déchoir 1. je déchois, tu déchois, il déchoit, nous déchoyons, vous déchoyez, ils déchoient; **2.** je déchoyais; **3.** je décherrai; **4.** que je déchoie; **7.** déchu.

déconfire *as* **confire.**

découvrir *as* **ouvrir.**

déduire, détruire *as* **conduire.**

devoir 1. je dois, tu dois, il doit, nous devons, vous devez, ils doivent; **2.** je devais; **3.** je devrai; **4.** que je doive; **5.** dois, devons, devez; **6.** devant; **7.** dû, due.

dire 1. je dis, tu dis, il dit, nous disons, vous dites, ils disent; **2.** je disais; **3.** je dirai; **4.** que je dise; **5.** dis, disons, dites; **6.** disant **7.** dit.

dissoudre 1. je dissous, tu dissous, il dissout, nous dissolvons, vous dissolvez, ils dissolvent; **2.** je dissolvais; **3.** je dissoudrai; **4.** que je dissolve; **5.** dissous, dissolvons, dissolvez; **6.** dissolvant; **7.** dissous, dissoute.

dormir 1. je dors, tu dors, il dort, nous dormons, vous dormez, ils dorment; **2.** je dormais; **3.** je dormirai; **4.** que je dorme; **5.** dors, dormons, dormez; **6.** dormant; **7.** dormi.

échoir *or* **écheoir 1.** il échoit *or* il échet, ils échoient; **2.** il échoyait; **3.** il écherra, ils écherront; **4.** qu'il échoie; **6.** échéant; **7.** échu.

écrire 1. j'écris, tu écris, il écrit, nous écrivons, vous écrivez, ils écrivent; **2.** j'écrivais; **3.** j'écrirai; **4.** que j'écrive; **5.** écris, écrivons, écrivez; **6.** écrivant; **7.** écrit.

envoyer, 1. j'envoie, tu envoies, il envoie, nous envoyons, vous envoyez, ils envoient; **2.** j'envoyais; **3.** j'enverrai; **4.** que j'envoie; **5.** envoie, envoyons, envoyez; **6.** envoyant; **7.** envoyé.

éteindre *as* **peindre.**

étreindre *as* **peindre.**

exclure *as* **conclure.**

faire 1. je fais, tu fais, il fait, nous faisons, vous faites, ils font; **2.** je faisais; **3.** je ferai; **4.** que je fasse; **5.** fais, faisons, faites; **6.** faisant; **7.** fait.

13.

falloir 1. il faut; **2.** il fallait; **3.** il faudra; **4.** qu'il faille; **7.** fallu.

feindre *as* **peindre.**

frire 1. je fris, tu fris, il frit; **3.** je frirai; **5.** fris; **7.** frit.

fuir 1. je fuis, tu fuis, il fuit, nous fuyons, vous fuyez, ils fuient; **2.** je fuyais; **3.** je fuirai; **4.** que je fuie; **5.** fuis, fuyons, fuyez; **6.** fuyant; **7.** fui.

gésir 1. il git, nous gisons, vous gisez, ils gisent; **2.** je gisais; **6.** gisant.

haïr 1. je hais, tu hais, il hait, nous haïssons, vous haïssez, ils haïssent; **2.** je haïssais; **3.** je haïrai; **4.** que je haïsse; **5.** hais, haïssons, haïssez; **6.** haïssant, **7.** haï.

instruire *as* **conduire.**

joindre 1. je joins, tu joins, il joint, nous joignons, vous joignez, ils joignent; **2.** je joignais; **3.** je joindrai; **4.** que je joigne; **5.** joins, joignons, joignez; **6.** joignant; **7.** joint.

lire 1. je lis, tu lis, il lit, nous lisons, vous lisez, ils lisent; **2.** je lisais; **3.** je lirai; **4.** que je lise; **5.** lis, lisons, lisez; **6.** lisant; **7.** lu.

luire *as* **nuire.**

maudire 1. je maudis, tu maudis, il maudit, nous maudissons, vous maudissez, ils maudissent; **2.** je maudissais; **3.** je maudirai; **4.** que je maudisse; **5.** maudis, maudissons. maudissez; **6.** maudissant; **7.** maudit.

mentir *as* **sentir.**

mettre 1. je mets, tu mets, il met, nous mettons, vous mettez, ils mettent; **2.** je mettais; **3.** je mettrai; **4.** que je mette; **5.** mets, mettons, mettez; **6.** mettant; **7.** mis.

moudre 1. je mouds, tu mouds, il moud, nous moulons, vous moulez, ils moulent; **2.** je moulais; **3.** je moudrai; **4.** que je moule; **5.** mouds, moulons, moulez; **6.** moulant; **7.** moulu.

mourir 1. je meurs, tu meurs, il meurt, nous mourons, vous mourez, ils meurent; **2.** je mourais; **3.** je mourrai; **4.** que je meure; **5.** meurs, mourons, mourez; **6.** mourant; **7.** mort (être.)

mouvoir 1. je meus, tu meus, il meut, nous mouvons, vous mouvez, ils meuvent; **2.** je mouvais; **3.** je mouvrai; **4.** que je meuve; **5.** meus, mouvons, mouvez; **6.** mouvant; **7.** mû, mue.

naître 1. je nais, tu nais, il nait, nous naissons, vous naissez, ils naissent; **2.** je naissais; **3.** je naîtrai; **4.** que je naisse; **5.** nais, naissons, naissez; **6.** naissant; **7.** né, née (être.)

nuire 1. je nuis, tu nuis, il nuit, nous nouisons, vous nuisez, ils nuisent; **2.** je nuisais; **3.** je nuirai; **4.** que je nuise; **5.** nuis, nuisons, nuisez; **6.** nuisant; **7.** nui.

offrir *as* **ouvrir.**

ouvrir 1. j'ouvre, tu ouvres, il ouvre, nous ouvrons, vous ouvrez, ils ouvrent; **2.** j'ouvrais; **3.** j'ouvrirai; **4.** que j'ouvre; **5.** ouvre, ouvrons, ouvrez; **6.** ouvrant; **7.** ouvert.

paître 1. je pais, tu pais, il paît, nous paissons, vous paissez, ils paissent; **2.** je paissais; **3.** je paîtrai; **4.** que je paisse; **5.** pais, paissons, paissez; **6.** paissant.

paraître 1. je parais, tu parais, il paraît, nous paraissons, vous paraissez, ils paraissent; **2.** je paraissais; **3.** je paraîtrai; **4.** que je paraisse; **5.** parais, paraissons, paraissez; **6.** paraissant; **7.** paru.

partir 1. je pars, tu pars, il part, nous partons, vous partez, ils partent; **2.** je partais; **3.** je partirai; **4.** que je parte; **5.** pars, partons, partez; **6.** partant; **7.** parti (être.)

peindre 1. je peins, tu peins, il peint, nous peignons, vous peignez, ils peignent; **2.** je peignais; **3.** je peindrai; **4.** que je peigne; **5.** peins, peignons, peignez; **6.** peignant; **7.** peint.

plaire 1. je plais, tu plais, il plaît, nous plaisons, vous plaisez, ils plaisent; **2.** je plaisais; **3.** je plairai; **4.** que je plaise; **5.** plais, plaisons, plaisez; **6.** plaisant; **7.** plu.

pouvoir 1. je peux *or* je puis, tu peux, il peut, nous pouvons, vous pouvez, ils peuvent; **2.** je pouvais; **3.** je pourrai; **4.** que je puisse; **6.** pouvant; **7.** pu.

prendre 1. je prends, tu prends, il prend, nous prenons, vous prenez, ils prennent; **2.** je prenais; **3.** je prendrai; **4.** que je prenne; **5.** prends, prenons, prenez; **6.** prenant; **7.** pris.

prescrire *as* **écrire.**

produire *as* **conduire.**

proscrire *as* **écrire.**

recevoir *as* **concevoir.**

reconstruire *as* **conduire.**

réduire *as* **conduire.**

repartir *as* **partir.**

reproduire *as* **conduire.**

résoudre 1. je résous, tu résous, il résout, nous résolvons, vous résolvez, ils résolvent; **2.** je résolvais; **3.** je résoudrai; **4.** que je résolve; **5.** résous, résolvons, résolvez; **6.** résolvant; **7.** résolu.

restreindre *as* **peindre.**

rire 1. je ris, tu ris, il rit, nous rions, vous riez, ils rient; **2.** je riais; **3.** je rirai; **4.** que je rie; **5.** ris, rions, riez; **6.** riant; **7.** ri.

savoir 1. je sais, tu sais, il sait, nous savons, vous savez, ils savent; **2.** je savais; **3.** je saurai; **4.** que je sache; **5.** sais, sachons, sachez; **6.** sachant; **7.** sus.

sentir 1. je sens, tu sens, il sent, nous sentons, vous sentez, ils sentent; **2.** je sentais; **3.** je sentirai; **4.** que je sente; **5.** sens, sentons, sentez; **6.** sentant; **7.** senti.

servir 1. je sers, tu sers, ils sert, nous servons, vous servez, ils servent; **2.** je servais; **3.** je servirai; **4.** que je serve; **5.** sers, servons, servez; **6.** servant; **7.** servi.

sortir 1. je sors, tu sors, il sort, nous sortons, vous sortez, ils sortent; **2.** je sortais;'

3. je sortirai; **4.** que je sorte; **5.** sors, sortons, sortez; **6.** sortant; **7.** sorti (être).

souffrir as **ouvrir**.

se souvenir *as* **venir**.

suffire 1. je suffis, tu suffis, il suffit, nous suffisons, vous suffisez, ils suffisent; **2.** je suffisais; **3.** je suffirai; **4.** que je suffise; **5.** suffis, suffisons, suffisez; **6.** suffisant; **7.** suffi.

suivre 1. je suis, tu suis, il suit, nous suivons, vous suivez, ils suivent; **2.** je suivais; **3.** je suivrai; **4.** que je suive; **5.** suis, suivons, suivez; **6.** suivant; **7.** suivi.

surseoir 1. je sursois, tu sursois, il sursoit, nous sursoyons, vous sursoyez, ils sursoient; **2.** je sursoyais; **3.** je surseoirai; **4.** que je sursoie; **5.** sursois, sursoyons, sursoyez; **6.** sursoyant; **7.** sursis.

taire *as* **plaire**.

teindre *as* **peindre**.

tenir 1. je tiens, tu tiens, il tient, nous tenons, vous tenez, ils tiennent; **2.** je tenais; **3.** je tiendrai; **4.** que je tienne; **5.** tiens, tenons, tenez; **6.** tenant; **7.** tenu.

traduire *as* **conduire**.

traire 1. je trais, tu trais, il trait, nous trayons, vous trayez, ils traient; **2.** je trayais; **3.** je trairai; **4.** que je traie; **5.** trais, trayons, trayez; **6.** trayant; **7.** trait.

vaincre 1. je vaincs, tu vaincs, il vainc, nous vainquons, vous vainquez, ils vainquent; **2.** je vainquais: **3.** je vaincrai; **4.** que je vainque; **5.** vaincs, vainquons, vainquez; **6.** vaincant; **7.** vaincu.

valoir 1. je vaux, tu vaux, il vaut. nous valons, vous valez, ils valent; **2.** je valais, **3.** je vaudrai; **4.** que je vaille; **6.** valant; **7.** valu.

venir 1. je viens, tu viens, il vient, nous venons, vous venez, ils viennent; **2.** je venais; **3.** je viendrai; **4.** que je vienne; **5.** viens, venons, venez; **6.** venant; **7.** venu (être.)

vêtir 1. je vêts, tu vêts, il vêt, nous vêtons, vous vêtez, ils vêtent; **2.** je vêtais; **3.** je vêtirai; **4.** que je vête; **5.** vêts, vêtons, vêtez; **6.** vêtant; **7.** vêtu.

vivre 1. je vis, tu vis, il vit, nous vivons, vous vivez, ils vivent; **2.** je vivais; **3.** je vivrai; **4.** que je vive; **5.** vis, vivons, vivez; **6.** vivant; **7.** vécu.

voir 1. je vois, tu vois, il voit, nous voyons, vous voyez, ils voient; **2.** je voyais; **3.** je verrai; **4.** que je voie; **5.** vois, voyons, voyez; **6.** voyant; **7.** vu.

vouloir 1. je veux, tu veux, il veut, nous voulons, vous voulez, ils veulent; **2.** je voulais; **3.** je voudrai; **4.** que je veuille, que nous voulions; **5.** veuille, veuillions, veuillez *or* voulez; **6.** voulant; **7.** voulu.

PHRASES

Good morning. Good evening. Good-bye.
Bonjour. Bonsoir. Au revoir.

I beg your pardon. Excuse me.
Je vous demande pardon. Pardon.

How are you? Very well — and you?
Comment allez-vous? Très bien — et vous?

How do you do (delighted to meet you).
Enchanté (de faire votre connaissance) monsieur (madame, mademoiselle).

Allow me! You are very kind.
Permettez-moi! Vous êtes très gentil.

It's all the same to me.
Cela m'est égal.

Your good health.
A votre santé.

Allow me to introduce you to . . .
Permettez-moi de vous présenter à . . .

It is fine (bad) weather.
Il fait beau (mauvais) temps.

You are right. You are wrong.
Vous avez raison. Vous avez tort.

It is not my fault.
Ce n'est pas ma faute.

To do one's best.
Faire son possible.

It is very annoying.
C'est très ennuyeux.

You're pulling my leg.
Vous vous moquez de moi.

So much the better (worse).
Tant mieux (pis).

He's a jolly nice fellow.
C'est un chic type.

To put one's foot in it.
Mettre les pieds dans le plat.

Things are going badly.
Rien ne va bien. Tout va mal.

I am an Englishmen (Englishwoman).
Je suis anglais (anglaise).

I cannot speak French.
Je ne parle pas français.

I am looking for . . .
Je cherche . . .

I don't understand you.
Je ne vous comprends pas.

Please speak slowly!
Parlez lentement, s'il vous plaît!

Is there anyone here who speaks English?
Y-a-t-il quelque'un qui parle anglais?

Where is the British Consulate?
Où est le consulat britannique?

It is wonderful, splendid!
C'est épatant, formidable!

No . . . Trespassers will be prosecuted.
Défense de . . . sous peine d'amende.

No entry.	Entrée interdite.
Lavatory.	Les toilettes, les lavabos, les cabinets.
What time is it?	Quelle heure est-il?
It is five past one.	Il est une heure cinq.
We are in a hurry.	Nous sommes pressés.
How long does it take to . . . ?	Combien de temps faut-il pour . . . ?
This evening, tonight. Last night.	Ce soir. Hier soir.
How long have you been here?	Depuis quand êtes-vous ici?
I have been here a month.	Je suis ici depuis un mois.
Can we lunch (dine) here?	Est-ce qu'on peut déjeuner (dîner) ici?
There are four of us.	Nous sommes quatre.
We only want a snack.	Nous voudrions seulement un casse-croûte.
Please give us the menu.	Voulez-vous nous donner le menu, s'il vous plaît.
Bring us the wine list, please.	Apportez-nous la carte des vins, s'il vous plaît.
We would like black coffee (white coffee).	Nous voudrions du café noir (café au lait).
The bill, please.	L'addition, s'il vous plaît.
I want some petrol (oil, water).	Je voudrais de l'essence (de l'huile, de l'eau).
I have had a breakdown.	Je suis en panne.
My car is on the road two kilometres from here.	Mon auto est sur la route à deux kilomètres d'ici.
Do you know the road to . . . ?	Connaissez-vous a route de . . . ?
Is the post office (bank) near here?	Y a-t-il un bureau de poste (bureau de change) près d'ici?
Are there any letters for me?	Y a-t-il des lettres pour moi?
Do you sell . . . ?	Est-ce que vous vendez . . . ?
You have given me the wrong change.	Vous vous êtes trompé en me rendant la monnaie
Have you anything to declare?	Avez-vous quelque chose à déclarer?
I cannot find my ticket.	Je ne peux pas trouver mon billet.
I have left something in the train.	J'ai laissé quelque chose dans le train.
I have a train to catch.	J'ai un train à prendre.
What time is the first (last) train for . . . ?	A quelle heure est le premier (dernier) train pour . . . ?

From which platform?	Sur quel quai?
Where do I change for ...?	Où est-ce que je change pour ...?
Is there a hotel where I can stay the night?	Est-ce qu'il y a un hôtel où je peux passer la nuit?
The last train has gone	Le dernier train est parti.
I do not feel well.	Je ne me sens pas bien.
I want to get off at ...	Je veux descendre à ...
Do you go near ...?	Allez-vous près de ...?
Can I have a room for the night?	Puis-je avoir une chambre pour la nuit?
I am only staying for two or three days.	Je reste deux ou trois jours seulement.
I want a room with a double bed.	Je désire une chambre avec un grand lit.
Can you put me up for the night?	Pouvez-vous me donnez une chambre pour la nuit?
I shall be back at three.	Je serai de retour à trois heures.
Have you any English newspapers?	Avez-vous des journaux anglais?
What does it cost to send a letter to ...?	Combien met-on sur une lettre pour ...?
Where can I buy ...?	Où puis-je acheter ...?
Will you reserve this place for me?	Voulez-vous me reserver cette place?
Will you take a traveller's cheque?	Acceptez-vous un cheque de voyage?
Will you have letters sent on to this address?	Voulez-vous faire suivre mon courrier à cette adresse?
I need a guide who speaks English.	J'ai besoin d'un guide qui parle anglais.
Is this the right road for ...?	Est-ce bien la route pour ...?
How far is it from here to ...?	Combien de kilomètres d'ici à ...?
Have you any post-cards?	Avez-vous des cartes postales?
Have you a map (plan)?	Avez-vous une carte (un plan)?
Do you know what is on at the cinema (theatre)?	Savez-vous ce qu'on donne au cinéma (Théatre)?
Where does this road lead?	Ce chemin, ou mène-t-il?

Can you recommend a cheap restaurant?	Pouvez-vous recommander un restaurant pas trop cher?
It is too dear. Have you anything cheaper?	C'est trop cher. Avez-vous quelque chose de meilleur marché?
We are lost.	Nous sommes perdus.
Have you any identification papers?	Avez-vous une pièce d'identite?
Have you a carrier bag?	Avez-vous un sac en papier?
Here is my address.	Voici mon adresse.
That's all right.	Je vous en prie.
Don't mention it.	Il n'y a pas de quoi.
Take my seat, madame.	Prenez ma place, madame.
Can I help you?	Puis-je vous aider?
Am I disturbing you?	Est-ce que je vous dérange?
I am terribly sorry.	Je suis navré (désolé).
Thank you for your hospitality.	Je vous remercie de votre hospitalité.
We had a very good time.	Nous nous sommes bien amusés.
It's too much. It's too dear.	C'est trop. C'est trop cher.
Look out!	Attention!
You are right. You are wrong.	Vous avez raison. Vous avez tort.
Listen. Look.	Ecoutez. Regardez.
What is the matter?	Qu'est-ce qu-il y a?
Please speak slowly.	Parlez lentement, s'il vous plaît.
Wait, I am looking for the phrase in this book.	Attendez, je cherche la phrase dans ce livre.
I have already paid you.	Je vous ai déjà payé.
It's terribly funny.	C'est tordant, c'est rigolo.
You don't say!	Sans blague!
You are joking. Joking apart.	Vous plaisantez. Blague à part.
Agreed. O.K.	Entendu. D'accord.
What a pity!	Quel dommage!
Do not touch.	Ne pas toucher.
Wet paint.	Prenez garde à la peinture.
You have plenty of time.	Vous avez tout le temps.
I have no time.	Je n'ai pas le temps.
The day before yesterday.	Avant-hier.
The day after tomorrow.	Après-demain.

Waiter, bring us some bread, please.	Garçon apportez-nous du pain, s'il vous plaît.
A little more ...	Encore un peu de ...
What would you like to drink?	Que désirez-vous boire (comme boisson)?
Is the service (the cover charge) included?	Le service (le couvert), est-il compris?
Keep the change.	Vous pouvez garder la monnaie.
There is a mistake in the bill.	Il y a une erreur dans l'addition.
Please don't mention it.	Je vous en prie.
Is the garage open all night?	Est-ce que le garage est ouvert la nuit?
I want to leave early tomorrow.	Je veux partir demain de bonne heure.
How long shall I have to wait?	Combien de temps faut-il attendre?
Can you lend me ... ?	Pouvez-vous me prêter ...?
How much do I owe you?	Combien est-ce que je vous dois?
I have two first class (second class) seats reserved.	J'ai deux places réservées en première (en seconde).
Excuse me, sir, that seat is mine.	Pardon monsieur, cette place est à moi.
Porter I want to put this luggage in the cloakroom (left-luggage office).	Porteur, je veux mettre ces bagages à la consigne.
I am coming with you.	Je vous suis.
Is there a porter from the ... Hotel here?	Est-ce qu'il y a un porter de l'hôtel ... ici?
Where is the enquiry office?	Où est le bureau de renseignements?
When do we get to ... ?	A quelle heure arrive-t-on à ...?
How long does the train stop here?	Combien de temps le train s'arrête-t-il ici?
The plane for ... is twenty minutes late already.	L'avion pour ... a déjà vingt minutes de retard.
The ... plane is announced.	L'avion de ... est signalé.
Where is the Airline Office?	Où est le bureau de la compagnie aérienne?
I want to reserve a seat on the plane leaving tomorrow for ..	Je voudrais réserver une place dans l'avion qui part demain pour ..

Is there a plane for . . . today?	Est-ce qu'il y a un avion pour . . . aujourd'hui?
I do not feel well.	Je ne me sens pas bien.
Bring me some coffee (brandy, a glass of water), please.	Apportez-moi du café (cognac, un verre d'eau), s'il vous plait.
Put out your cigarettes and fasten your seat-belts, please.	Eteignez vos cigarettes et attachez vos ceintures, s'il vous plaît.
Call me a taxi.	Appelez-moi un taxi.
Go quickly, I am in a great hurry.	Dépêchez-vous, je suis très pressé.
Please wait here for a few minutes.	Attendez-moi ici quelques minutes, s'il vous plaît.
Where is the office?	Où est le bureau?
Have you a room with a private bathroom?	Avez-vous une chambre avec salle de bains?
What is the price of a room per night?	Quel est le prix d'une chambre par nuit?
I am expecting a gentleman (a lady, a young lady).	J'attends un monsieur (une dame, une demoiselle).
Give me two 25 centime stamps and two at 15 centimes.	Donnez-moi deux timbres de vingt-cinq centimes et deux de quinze.
I want to send a telegram.	Je voudrais envoyer une dépêche.
Have you the time-table of trains for . . . ?	Avez-vous l'horaire des trains pour . . . ?
Can we have an English breakfast?	Peut-on avoir un petit déjeuner anglais?
Order a taxi for 9.30, please.	Commandez un taxi pour neuf heures et demie, s'il vous plaît.
Please have my bill made out.	Préparez la note, s'il vous plaît.
We want to be together.	Nous voudrions être ensemble.
How far it to . . . ?	Quelle distance d'ici à . . . ?
What is the name of this town (village)?	Quel est le nom de cette ville (ce village)?
Where is the market place?	Où est le marché?
Weather permitting, we hope to leave at dawn.	Si le temps le permet, nous comptons partir à l'aube.
Get me Molitor 44—94,	Voulez-vous me demander

please.	Molitor quarante-quatre, quatre-vingt quatorze, s'il vous plait.
How much do I owe you for the call?	Combien vous dois-je pour la communication?
Can I make an appointment?	Puis-je prendre un rendezvous?
Can I have something to read?	Puis-je avoir de la lecture?
Can you make up this prescription, please?	Pouvez-vous faire cette ordonnance, s'il vous plaît?
Can you give me something for insect (ant, mosquito) bites?	Pouvez-vous me donner quelque chose pour les piqûres d'insects (de fourmis, de moustiques)?
My skin is smarting; have you anything to soothe it?	La peau me cuit; avez-vous quelque-chose de calmant?
For external use.	Pour l'usage externe.
I want a reversal (negative) colour film.	Je voudrais un film en couleur inversible (negatif).
Do you sell . . .?	Est-ce que vous vendez . . .?
Have you anything cheaper (better)?	Avez-vous quelque chose de moins cher (de meilleure qualité)?
I want something like this (that).	Je voudrais quelque chose comme ceci (cela).
Can you order it for me?	Pouvez-vous le (la) commander?
Will you send it to this address?	Voulez-vous l'envoyer à cette adresse?
That's exactly what I want.	Voilà ce qu'il me faut.
You have given me the wrong change.	Vous vous êtes trompé en me rendant la monnaie.
Can you change it?	Pouvez-vous le changer?
Do you sell English cigarettes (tobacco)?	Est-ce que vous vendez des cigarettes anglaises (du tabac anglais)?
There has been an accident.	Il y a eu un accident.
Is there a doctor near here?	Y a-t-il un médecin près d'ici?
Welcome to England (France).	Je vous souhaite la bienvenue en Angleterre

(France).	
Avez-vous fait un bon voyage?	Did you have a good journey?
A quelle heure est le petit déjeuner (le déjeuner, le goûter, le diner)?	What time is breakfast (lunch, tea, dinner)?

NUMBERS

1 *one*, un.	1st *first*, premier.
2 *two*, deux.	2nd *second*, deuxième.
3 *three*, trois.	3rd *third*, troisième.
4 *four*, quatre.	4th *fourth*, quatrième.
5 *five*, cinq.	5th *fifth*, cinquième.
6 *six*, six.	6th *sixth*, sixième.
7 *seven*, sept.	7th *seventh*, septième.
8 *eight*, huit.	8th *eighth*, huitième.
9 *nine*, neuf.	9th *ninth*, neuvième.
10 *ten*, dix.	10th *tenth*, dixième.
11 *eleven*, onze.	11th *eleventh*, onzième.
12 *twelve*, douze.	12th *twelfth*, douzième.
13 *thirteen*, treize.	13th *thirteenth*, treizième.
14 *fourteen*, quatorze.	14th *fourteenth*, quatorzième.
15 *fifteen*, quinze.	15th *fifteenth*, quinzième.
16 *sixteen*, seize.	16th *sixteenth*, seizième.

A

a, an, *art.* un, -e.

abandon, *v. a.* abandonner.

abate, *v. a. & n.* diminuer; se calmer, s'apaiser.

abbey, *s.* abbaye *f.*

abbot, *s.* abbé *m.*

abbreviate, *v. a.* abréger.

abbreviation, *s.* abréviation *f.*

abdicate, *v.a. & n.* abdiquer.

abdomen, *s.* abdomen *m.*

abhor, *v. a.* détester, abhorrer.

ability, *s.* capacité *f.*, habilité *f.*

able, *adj.* capable.

aboard, *adv.* à bord.

abode, *s.* demeure *f.*

abolish, *v.a.* abolir; supprimer.

abominable, *adj.* abominable.

abound, *v.n.* abonder (de).

about, *adv. & prep.* autour (de); environ, presque; au sujet de.

above, *adv. & prep.* audessus (de); *(in book)* ci-dessus.

abroad, *adv.* à l'étranger.

absence, *s.* absence *f.*, éloignement *m.*

absent, *adj.* absent.

absolute, *adj.* absolu.

absolve, *v.a.* absoudre; relever de; remettre, pardonner.

absorb, *v. a.* absorber.

abstain, *v.n.* s'abstenir de.

abstract, *adj.* abstrait.

abstraction, *s.* abstraction *f.*

absurd, *adj.* absurde; ridicule.

abundance, *s.* abondance *f.*

abundant, *adj.* abondant.

abusive, *adj.* abusif; injurieux; offensant.

academic, *adj.* académique.

academy, *s.* académie *f.*

accelerate, *v.a.* accélérer; *v.n.* s'accélérer.

accent, *s.* accent *m.*

accept, *v.a.* accepter

access, *s.* accès *m.*

accessible, *adj.* accessible.

accessory, *s. & adj.* accessoire *(m.)*.

accident, *s.* accident *m.*

accidental, *s.* accidentel.

accommodate, *v.a.* accommoder; loger; ~ oneself *to* s'accommoder à.

accommodation, *s.* ajustement *m.*, adaptation *f.*; commodité *f.*; logement *m.*

accompany, *v.a.* accompagner.

accomplish, *v.a.* accomplir, achever.

accomplishment, *s.* accomplissement *m.*; talent *m.*

accord, *s.* accord *m.*, consentement *m.*

according: ~ *to* selon, d'après.

accordingly, *adv.* donc; en conséquence.

account, *s.* compte *m.*; *(narration)* récit *m.*; *on* ~ *of* à cause de; *on no* ~ dans aucun cas; *take into* ~ tenir compte de; — *v.n.* ~ *for* expliquer; rendre compte de.

accuracy, *s.* exactitude *f.*

accusation, *s.* accusation *f.*

accuse, *v.a.* accuser; incriminer.

accustom, *v.a.* accoutumer (à).

ache, *s.* douleur *f.*

achieve, *v.a.* accomplir, achever; atteindre.

acknowledge, *v.a.* reconnaître; accuser réception de.

acquaint, *v.a.* informer (de); faire part à.

acquaintance, *s.* connaissance *f.*

acquire, *v.a.* acquérir.

acre, *s.* arpent *m.*

across, *prep.* à travers; en croix.

act, *s.* action *f.*; *(law)* loi *f.*; *(theatre)* acte *m.*; — *v.n.* agir; *v.a.* jouer.

action, *s.* action *f.*; acte *m.*; *(war)* combat *m.*

active, *adj.* actif.

activity, *s.* activité *f.*

actor, *s.* acteur *m.*

actress, *s.* actrice *f.*

actual, *adj.* réel.

actually, *adv.* en fait.

adapt, *v.a.* adapter.

add, *v.a.* ajouter; additionner.

addition, *s.* addition *f.*; *in ~ to* en plus de.

additional, *adj.* additionnel; supplémentaire.

address, *s.* adresse *f.*; — *v.a.* adresser.

adequate, *adj.* suffisant.

adjust, *v.a.* ajuster, régler.

administer, *v.a. & n.* administrer.

administration, *s.* administration *f.*

admirable, *adj.* admirable.

admiral, *s.* amiral *m.*

admiration, *s.* admiration *f.*

admire, *v.a.* admirer.

admission, *s.* admission *f.*; entrée *f.*

admit, *v.a.* admettre; laisser entrer.

adopt, *v.a.* adopter.

adoption, *s.* adoption *f.*

adore, *v.a.* adorer.

adult, *adj. & s.* adulte *(m.f.)*

advance, *v. n.* avancer; — *s.* avance *f.*; progrès *m.*

advantage, *s.* avantage *m.*

adventure, *s.* aventure *f.*

adversary, *s.* adversaire *m.*

adverse, *adj.* adverse.

adversity, *s.* adversité *f.*

advertise, *v.a.* annoncer; faire de la réclame (pour).

advertisement, *s.* annonce *f.*; réclame *f.*

advice, conseil *m.*; avis *m.*

advise, *v.a.* conseiller.

aerial, *s.* antenne *f.*

aerodrome, *s.* aérodrome *m.*

aeroplane, *s.* avion *m.*

affair, *s.* affaire *f.*

affect, *v.a.* affecter.

affection, *s.* affection *f.*

affectionate, *adj.* affectueux.

affirmative, *adj.* affirmatif; — *s.* affirmative *f.*

afford, *v.a.* donner, fournir, accorder; *can ~* avoir les moyens de.

afraid, *adj.* effrayé; *be ~ of* avoir peur de.

African, *adj.* africain; — *s.* Africain, -e.

after, *prep. & adj.* après.

afternoon, *s.* après-midi *m.* or *f.*

afterwards, *adv.* après, ensuite.

again, *adv.* encore une fois, de nouveau.

against, *prep.* contre.

age, *s.* âge *m.*

agency, s. agence f.

agent, s. agent m.

aggression, s. agression f.

ago, adv. il y a.

agony, s. agonie f.

agree, v.n. s'accorder, être d'accord; ~ (up-) on convenir sur; ~ to consentir à; ~ with entrer dans les idées de.

agreeable, adj. agréable.

agreement, s. accord m.

agricultural, adj. agricole.

agriculture, s. agriculture f.

ahead, adv. en avant.

aid, s. aide f.; — v.a. aider, assister.

aim, s. but m.; objectif m.; visée f.; — v.a. & n. viser.

air. s. air m.

air-conditioning, s. conditionnement d'air m.; climatisation f.

aircraft, s. avion m.

air-line, s. ligne f. aérienne.

air-mail s. poste aérienne; by ~ par avion.

airport, s. aéroport m.,

alarm, v.a. alarmer; —s. alarme f.

alcoholic, adj. alcoolique.

ale, s. bière (f.) anglaise.

alike, adj. semblable; — adv. également.

alive, adj. vivant.

all, pron. s., adv. & adj. tout; not at ~ pas du tout.

allege, v.a. alléguer.

alley, s. ruelle f.

allow, v.a. permettre; laisser; admettre.

allude, v.n. faire allusion.

ally, v.a. allier; v.n. s'allier; — s. allié, -e.

almost, adv. presque; à peu près.

alone, adj. & adv. seul.

along, prep. le long de.

aloud, adv. à haute voix.

already, adv. déjà.

also, adv. aussi.

altar, s. autel m.

alter, v.a.&n. changer.

alternate, adj. alternatif; — v.n. alterner.

although, conj. quoique; bien que.

altitude, s. altitude f., élévation f.

altogether, adv. tout à fait; entièrement.

always, adv. toujours.

amaze, v.a. frapper d'étonnement, frapper de stupeur.

amazing, adj. étonnant.

ambassador, s. ambassadeur m.

ambassadress, s. ambassadrice f.

ambition, s ambition f.

ambitious, adj. ambitieux.

ambulance, s. ambulance (automobile) f.

amend, v.a. amender.

amends: make ~ for dédommager de.

American, adj. américain; — s. Américain, -e.

among, prep. parmi; chez.

amount, s. somme f.; (total) montant m.; — v.n. ~ to monter à.

ample, adj. ample.

amplifier, s. amplificateur m.

amuse, v.a. amuser; divertir.

amusement, s. amusement m.; divertissement m.

an see a.

analogy, s. analogie f.

analyse, *v.a.* analyser.
analysis, analyse *f.*
anarchy, *s.* anarchie *f.*
anatomy, *s.* anatomie *f.*
ancestor, *s.* ancêtre *m. f.*
anchor, *s.* ancre *f.*
ancient, *adj.* ancien; antique.
and, *conj.* et.
anecdote, *s.* anecdote *f.*
angel, *s.* ange *m.*
anger, *s.* colère, *f.*
angle, *s.* angle *m.*
angler, *s.* pêcheur *m.*

Anglican, *adj.* anglican.
angry, *adj.* fâché, irrité.
animal, *s.* animal *m.* *(pl.* -aux).
ankle, *s.* cheville *f.*
anniversary, *s.* anniversaire *m.*
announce, *v.a.* annoncer.
announcement, *s.* annonce.
announcer, *s.* speaker *m.*
annoy, *v.a.* ennuyer; contrarier; gêner.
annoying, *adj.* contrariant; ennuyeux.
annual, *adj.* annuel.
annul, *v.a.* annuler.
another, *pron.* & *adj.* un autre, une autre.
answer, *s.* réponse *f.;* — *v.a.&n.* répondre.
ant, *s.* fourmi *f.*
antelope, *s.* antilope *f.*
antibiotic, *s.* antibiotique *m.*
anticipate, *v.a.* anticiper.
antipathy, *s.* antipathie *f.*
antiquated, *adj.* vieilli.
antiquity, *s.* antiquité *f.*
anvil, *s.* enclume *f.*
anxiety, *s.* anxiété *f.*
anxious, *adj.* inquiet; désireux; be ~ to désirer faire qch.
any, *adj.* & *pron.* quelque; *(at all)* n'importe quoi/qui/quel; *(some, in*

question) du, de la; *have you* ~? en avez vous; *not* ~ ne ... pas de; ~ *more* encore du.
anybody, *pron.* quelqu'un; *(at all)* n'importe qui.
anyhow, *adv.* n'importe comment.
anyone *see* anybody.

anything, *pron.* quelque chose; *(at all)* n'importe quoi.
anyway, *see* anyhow.
anywhere, *adv.* n'importe où.
apart, *adv.* à part; de côté; ~ *from* en dehors de.
apartment, *s.* logement *m.;* appartement *m.*
apologize, *v.n.* faire des excuses, s'excuser.
apology, *s.* excuse *f.*
apostle, *s.* apôtre *m.*
appalling, *adj.* épouvantable.
apparatus, *s.* appareil *m.*
apparent, *adj.* manifeste.
appeal, *s.* appel *m.;* — *v.n.* en appeler (à).
appear, *v.n.* (ap)paraître; *(seem)* sembler.
appearance, *s.* apparition *f.;* *(look)* air *m.*
appendicitis, *s.* appendicite *f.*
appendix, *s.* appendice *m.*
appetite, *s.* appétit *m.*
applaud, *v.n.* applaudir.
applause, *s.* applaudissement *m.*

apple, *s.* pomme *f.*
appliance, *s.* appareil *m.*
applicant, *s.* postulant, -e.
application, *s.* demande *f.;* *(use)* application *f.*
apply, *v.a.* appliquer; — *v.n.* avoir rapport à; ~ *for* solliciter.
appoint, *v.a.* nommer; désigner.

appointment, s. nomination f.; emploi m.; rendez-vous m.

appreciate, v.a. apprécier.

appreciation, s. appréciation f.

apprehend, v.a. appréhender; (understand) comprendre.

apprentice, s. apprenti m.

approach, s. approche f.; — v. a. & n. (s')approcher (de).

appropriate, adj. approprié, convenable.

approval, s. approbation f.

approve, v.a. & n. approuver.

approximate, adj. approximatif.

approximation, approximation f.

apricot, s. abricot m.

April, s. avril m.

apron, s. tablier m.

aptitude, s. aptitude f.

Arab, s. Arabe m.

Arabian, adj. arabe.

arbitrary, adj. arbitraire.

arcade, s. arcade f.

arch, s. arche f.; arc m.

archaeology, s. archéologie f.

archbishop, s. archevêque m.

architect, s. architecte m.

architecture, s. architecture f.

area, s. surface f.; aire f.

Argentine, adj. argentine.

argue, v.n. argumenter; v.a. discuter.

argument, s. argument m.; discussion f.

arise, v. n. se lever; (emerge) surgir; (come from) résulter de.

aristocratic, adj. aristocratique.

arm[1], s. bras m.

arm[2], s.(pl). arme(s) f.

armament, s. armement m.

armchair, s. fauteuil m.

armour, s. armure f.

army, s. armée f.

around, adv. & prep. autour (de).

arouse, v.a. réveiller.

arrange, v.a. arranger.

arrangement, s. arrangement m.; ～s mesures f. pl.

array, s. ordre m.

arrears, s. pl. arriéré m.

arrest, v.a. arrêter; — s. arrestation f.

arrival, s. arrivée f.

arrive, v.n. arriver.

arrow, s. flèche f.

art, s. art m.

artery, s. artère f.

article, s. article m.

artificial, adj. artificiel.

artillery, s. artillerie f.

artist, s. artiste m.

artistic, adj. artistique.

as, adv. & conj. comme; (like a) en; (when) comme; ～ ... ～ aussi ... que.

ascend, v.n. monter.

ash(es), s. (pl.) cendre f.

ashamed, adj. honteux; be ～ of avoir honte de.

ashore, adv. à terre.

ash-tray, s. cendrier m.

Asiatic, adj. asiatique.

aside, adv. de côté.

ask, v. a. demander (à + qn., de + inf.); ～ about se renseigner sur; ～ for demander.

asleep, adj. endormi; fall ～ s'endormir.

aspect, s. aspect m.; (look) air m.

aspire, v.n. aspirer à.

ass, *s.* âne *m.*
assail, *v. a.* assaillir.
assault, *s.* assaut *m.*
assemble, *v. a.* assembler;
   v.n. s'assembler.
assembly, *s.* assemblée *f.;*
   ~ *hall* halle *f.* de
   montage; ~ *line* chaîne
   f. de montage.
assert, *v.a.* affirmer.
assess, *v.a.* cotiser.
assets, *s. pl.* actif *m.*
assign, *v. a.* assigner;
   céder.
assignment, *s.* cession *f.*
assist, *v.a.* aider.
assistance, *s.* aide *f.*
associate, *v.a.* associer;
   — *s.* associé, -e *m. f.*
association, *s.* association
   f.
assume, *v.a.*   prendre;
   assumer; supposer.
assumption, *s.* supposition *f.*
assurance, *s.* assurance *f.*
assure, *v.a.* assurer.
astonish, *v. a.* étonner.
astonishment, *s.* étonnement *m.*
astronomy, *s.* astronomie
   f.
at, *prep. (place, time)* à;
   (house, shop) chez.
athletic, *adj.* athlétique.
athletics, *s.* athlétisme *m.*
at-home, *s.* réception *f.*
atlas, *s.* atlas *m.*
atmosphere, *s.* atmos-
   phère *f.*
atom, *s.* atome *m.*
atomic, *adj.* atomique; ~

   bomb bombe *f.* atomique; ~ *energy* énergie
   f. atomique.
attach, *v.a.* attacher.
attaché, *s.* attaché *m.;*
   ~ *case* petite valise *f.*
attachment, *s.* attache-
   ment *m.*
attack, *v.a.* attaquer; —

   s. attaque *f.*
attain, *v.a.* atteindre.
attainment, *s.*   réalisation *f.;* connaissances
   f. pl.
attempt, *s.* tentative *f.;*
   — *v.a.* tenter; entreprendre.
attend, *v.a.* suivre; *(look
   after)* soigner; — *v.i.*
   faire attention à; as-
   sister.
attendance, *s.* présence *f.;*
   (persons present) assistance *f.*
attendant, *s.* serviteur *m.;*
   employé *m.;* ouvreuse
   f.
attention, *s.* attention *f.*
attitude, *s.* attitude *f.*
attorney, *s.* avoué *m.*
attract, *v.a.* attirer.
attraction, *s.* attraction *f.*
attractive, *adj.* attrayant.
attribute, *v.a.* attribuer.
auction, *s.* vente *f.*
audience, *s.* auditoire *m.*
audio-visual, *adj.* audiovisuel.
auditorium, *s.* salle *f.* (de
   cours).
August, *s.* août *m.*
aunt, *s.* tante *f.*
Australian, *adj.* australien
   — *s.* Australien, -ne *m.*
   f.
Austrian, *adj.* autrichien;
   — *s.* Autrichien, -enne
   m. f.
authentic, *adj.* authentique.
author, *s.* auteur *m.*
authority, *s.* autorité *f.*
authorize, *v.a.* autoriser·
automatic, *adj.* automatique.
autonomy, *s.* autonomie
   f.
autumn, *s.* automne *m.*
avail, *s. be of no* ~ ne
   servir à rien; — *v.a.*

~ *oneself of* profiter
de.
available, *adj.* disponible;
sous la main.
avalanche, *s.* avalanche *f.*
avenge, *v.a.* venger.
avenue, *s.* avenue *f.*
average, *s.* moyenne *f.;*
— *adj.* moyen.
aversion, *s.* aversion *f.*
avoid, *v.a.* éviter.
await, *v.a.* attendre.
awake, *v. a.* éveiller; *v. n.*
s'éveiller; — *adj.* éveil-
lé.
awaken, *v.a.* éveiller.
award, *v.a.* accorder.
aware, *adj. be* ~ *of* avoir
conscience de, savoir
bien.
away, *adv.* (au) loin;
carry ~ enlever; *go* ~
partir.
awful, *adj.* terrible.
awhile, *adv.* pendant quelque temps, un moment.
awkward, *adj. (pers.)*
gauche; maladroit;
(things) gênant, embar-
rassant.
axe, *s.* hache *f.*
axis, *s.* axe *m.*

axle, *s.* essieu *m.*

B

babble, *s.* babil *m.;* —
v.n. babiller.
baby, *s.* bébé *m.*
baby-sitter, *s.* garde-bébé
m.
bachelor, *s.* célibataire;
(arts) licencié *m.*
back, *s.* dos *m.; (hand)*
revers *m.; (football)*
arrière *m.;* — *adj.* de
derrière; arriéré; —
adv. en arrière; *be* ~
être de retour; — *v.a.*
soutenir, seconder;
(bet) parier pour; *v.ŋ.*

reculer.
background, *s.* fond *m.;*
arrière-plan *m.*
backstairs, *s. pl.* escalier
m. de service.
backward, *adj.* arriéré.
backwards, *adv.* en arrière; à reculons.
bacon, *s.* lard *m.*
bad, *adj.* mauvais.
badge, *s.* insigne *m.*
badger, *s.* blaireau *m.*
badly, *adv.* mal.
bag, *s.* sac *m.; (large)*
valise *f.*
baggage, *s.* bagage *m.*
bait, *s.* amorce *f.*
bake, *v.a.* cuire; faire
cuire.
baker, *s.* boulanger *m.*
bakery, *s.* boulangerie *f.*
balance, *s. (weighing,*
account) balance *f.;*
(bank) solde *m.; (equi-*
librium) équilibre *m.;*
— *v.a.* balancer; *v.n.* se
balancer.
balcony, *s.* balcon *m.*
bald, *adj.* chauve; plat.
ball, *s. (games)* balle *f.*
ballon *m.; (bowl)* boule
f.; (dance) bal *m.*
ball-bearings, *s. pl.* roulement *m.* à billes.
ballet, *s.* ballet *m.*
balloon, *s.* ballon *m.*
ball(-point) pen, *s.* stylo
m. à bille.
bamboo, *s.* bambou *m.*
banana, *s.* banane *f.*
band, *s. (people)* troupe
f.; bande *f.;* orchestre
m.; (ribbon, tie) ruban
m.; lien *m.*
bandage, *s.* bandage *m.*
bandit, *s.* bandit *m.*
bang, *s.* coup *m.;* claquement *m.*
banish, *v.a.* bannir.
banister, rampe *f.*
bank[1], *s. (river)* rive *f.;*

(earth) talus *m.*
bank³, *s.* banque *f.*
bank-holiday, *s.* (jour *m.* de) fête *f.* légale.
banknote, *s.* billet *m.* (de banque).
bankruptcy, *s.* banqueroute *f.;* faillite *f.*
banner, *s.* bannière *f.*
banquet, *s.* banquet *m.*
baptism, *s.* baptême *m.*
baptize, *v.a.* baptiser.
bar, *s. (iron, tribunal, music)* barre *f.; (railway)* barrière *f.; (obstacle)* obstacle *m.; (lawyers)* barreau *m.; (counter place for drink)* comptoir *m.,* débit *m.* (de boissons), bar *m.*
barber, *s.* coiffeur *m.*
bare, *adj.* nu; *(mere)* seul.
barefoot, *adj.* nu-pieds.
barely, *adv.* à peine.
bargain, *s.* marché *m.;* — *v.n.* marchander.
bark, *s.* aboiement *m.;* — *v.n.* aboyer.
barley, *s.* orge *f.*
barmaid, *s.* demoiselle *f.* de comptoir, barmaid *f.*
barman, *s.* garçon *m.* de comptoir, barman *m.*
barn, *s.* grange *f.*
barometer, *s.* baromètre *m.*
baron, *s.* baron *m.*
baroness, *s.* baronne *f.*
barracks, *s. pl.* caserne *f.*
barrel, *s.* tonneau *m.*
barren, *adj.* stérile.
barrier, *s.* barrière *f.*
barrister, *s.* avocat *m.*
bartender *see* barman.
barter, *s.* échange *m.;* — *v.a.* échanger.
base, *s.* fondement *m.;* base *f.*
basement, *s.* sous-sol *m.*
bashful, *adj.* timide.
basic, *adj.* fondamental;

basique.
basin, *s.* bassin *m.;* cuvette *f.*
basis, *s.* base *f.*
basket, *s.* panier *m.*
basket-ball, *s.* basket-ball *m.*
bass, *s.* basse *f.*
bat¹, *s.* chauve-souris *f.*
bat², *s.* batte *f.*
bath, *s.* bain *m.; (tub)* baignoire *f.*
bathe, *v.n.* se baigner; *v.a.* baigner.
bathing-costume, *s.* costume *m.* de bain(s).
bathroom, *s.* salle *f.* de bain.
battery, *s. (military)* batterie *f.; (electr.)* pile *f.*
battle, *s.* bataille *f.*
bay, *s.* baie *f.*
be, *v. n.* être; *(be situated)* se trouver; *there is* il y a.
beach, *s.* plage *f.*
bead, *s. (string of)* collier *m.*
beak, *s.* bec *m.*
beam, *s. (timber)* poutre *f.; (light)* rayon *m.*
bean, *s.* fève *f.*
bear¹, *s.* ours *m.*
bear², *v.a.* porter; soutenir; supporter.
beard, *s.* barbe *f.*
bearing, *s.* rapport *m.*
beast, *s.* bête *f.*
beat, *v.a.* battre; frapper; — *s.* battement *m.*
beautiful, *adj.* beau, bel, belle.
beauty, *s.* beauté *f.*
beaver, *s.* castor *m.*
because, *conj.* parce que; ~ *of* à cause de.
beckon, *v.n.* faire signe (à).
become, *v. n.* devenir.
bed, *s.* lit *m.*
bed-clothes, *s. pl.* cou-

vertures *f. pl.*
bedroom, *s.* chambre *f.* à coucher.
bee, *s.* abeille *f.*
beech, *s.* hêtre *m.*
beef, *s.* bœuf *m.*
beef-steak, *s.* bifteck *m.*
beer, *s.* bière *f.*
beetle, *s.* scarabée *m.*
beetroot, *s.* betterave *f.*
before, *prep.(time)* avant; *(space)* devant; — *adv.* avant; *(in front)* en avant.
beforehand, *adv.* d'avance; en avance.
beg, *v.a.* demander, prier; *v. n.* mendier; *I ~ your pardon!* excusez-moi!; pardon!
beget, *v.a.* engendrer.
beggar, *s.* mendiant, -e.
begin, *v. a. & n.* commencer.
beginner, *s.* commençant, -e *m. f.*
beginning, *s.* commencement *m.*
behalf, *s. on ~ of* de la part de; *in ~ of* en faveur de.
behave, *v.n.* se conduire.
behaviour, *s.* conduite *f.*
behind, *prep.* derrière.
Belgian, *adj.* belge; — *s.* Belge *m. f.*
belief, *s.* croyance *f.*
believe, *v.a. & n.* croire.
bell, *s.* cloche *f.*
belly, *s.* ventre *m.*
belong, *v.n. ~ to* appartenir à.
belongings, *s. pl.* effets *m.; biens m.*
below, *adv.* au-dessous; en bas; — *prep.* au-dessous de.
belt, *s.* ceinture *f.*
bench, *s.* banc *m.; (working)* établi *m.*
bend, *v. a.* courber; tendre

fléchir; *v.n.* se courber; — *s.* courbure *f.; (road)* tournant *m.*
beneath *see below.*
benefit, *s.* bienfait *m.; (gain)* bénéfice *m.*
bent, *s.* penchant *m.*
berry, *s.* baie *f.; (coffee)* grain *m.*
berth, *s.* couchette *f.; (for ship)* mouillage *m.*
beseech, *v. a.* supplier.
beside, *prep.* auprès de, à côté de.
besides, *adv.* en outre.
best, *adj.* le meilleur; *do one's ~* faire tout son possible (pour).
bestow, *v. a.* conférer (à).
bet, *v.a.* parier.
betray, *v. a.* trahir.
better, *adj.* meilleur; *adv.* mieux.
between, *prep* entre.
beyond, *prep.* au delà de.
bias, *s.* biais *m.; (fig.)* préjugé *m.*
Bible, *s.* bible *f.*
bibliography, *s.* bibliographie *f.*
bicycle, *s.* bicyclette *f.*
big, *adj.* grand; gros.
bill, *s. (hotel)* note *f.; (restaurant)* addition *f.; (invoice)* facture *f.; (of exchange)* lettre *f.* de change; *(of fare)* carte *f.,* menu *m.; (poster)* affiche *f.;(parliament)* projet *m.* de loi.
bin, *s.* huche *f.,* coffre *m.*
bind, *v.a.* lier; *(book)* relier.
biological, *adj.* biologique.
biology, *f.* biologie *f.*
birch, *s.* bouleau *m.*
bird, *s.* oiseau *m.*
birth, *s.* naissance *f.*
birthday, *s.* anniversaire *m.*

birth-place, *s.* lieu *m.* de naissance.

biscuit, *s.* biscuit *m.*

bishop, *s.* évêque *m.*

bit¹, *s.* morceau *m.*; *(drill)* mèche *f.*; *a ~* un peu (de).

bit², *s. (horse)* mors *m.*

bite, *v. a. & n.* mordre.

bitter, *adj.* amer; mordant; *(cold)* âpre.

bitterness, *s.* amertume *f.*

black, *adj.* noir.

blackbird, *s.* merle *m.*

blackmail, *s.* chantage *m.*

blacksmith, *s.* forgeron *m.*

bladder, *s.* vessie *f.*

blade, *s.* lame *f.*

blame, *s.* blâme *m.*; — *v. a.* blâmer, accuser qn.

blameless, *adj.* innocent.

blank, *adj.* blanc; nu; — *s.* blanc *m.*

blanket, *s.* couverture *f.*

blast, *s.* rafale *f.*; coup *m.* de vent; souffle *m.*; — *v.a.* faire sauter; détruire.

blaze, *s.* flamme *f.*; — *v.n.* flamber.

bleak, *adj.* lugubre.

bleed, *v.a. & n.* saigner.

blend, *s.* mélange *m.*; — *v.a.* fondre; mêler.

bless, *v.a.* bénir.

blessing, *s.* bénédiction *f.*

blind¹, *adj.* aveugle.

blind², *s.* store *m.*

blindness, *s.* cécité *f.*

blink, *v. n.* clignoter.

bliss, *s.* félicité *f.*

blister, *s.* ampoule *f.*

block, *s.* bloc *m.*; *(wood)* billot *m.*; *(buildings)* pâté *m.*; *(traffic)* encombrement *m.*

blond *adj.* blond.

blood, *s.* sang *m.*

bloody, *adj.* sanglant.

bloom, *s.* fleur *f.*; — *v. n.* fleurir.

blossom, *s.* fleur *f.*

blot, *s.* tache *f.*; pâté *m.*

blouse, *s.* blouse *f.*

blow¹, *v. a. (trumpet)* sonner; *(glass)* souffler; *~ out* éteindre; *~ up* faire sauter; *v.n. (wind)* souffler.

blow², *s.* coup *m.*

blue, *adj.* bleu.

blunder, *s.* bévue *f.*; — *v. n.* faire une bévue

blunt, *adj.* émoussé; *(person)* brusque.

blush, *v.n.* rougir.

board, *s.* planche *f.*; *(meals)* pension *f.*; *(council)* conseil *m.*; *(paper)* carton *m.*; *(theatre) ~s* planches; *~ and lodging* pension *f.* et chambre(s); *on ~ (ship)* à bord d'un navire; — *v.n.* prendre pension chez; *v.a.* monter à bord de.

boarder, *s.* pensionnaire *m. f.*

boarding-house, *s.* pension *f.*

boarding-school, *s.* pensionnat *m.*

boast, *s.* vanterie *f.*; — *v. n.* se vanter (de).

boat, *s.* bateau *m.*

body, *s.* corps *m.*

bog, *s.* marécage *m.*

boil¹, *v.a.* faire bouillir; *(cook)* faire cuire; *v. n.* bouillir.

boil², *s.* furoncle *m.*

boiler, *s.* chaudière *f.*

bold, *adj.* hardi; effronté.

boldness, *s.* hardiesse *f.*; effronterie *f.*

bolt, *s.* verrou *m.*; — *v. a.* verrouiller; *v. n.* filer.

bomb, *s.* bombe *f.*

bond, *s.* lien *m.*

bone, *s.* os *m.*; *(fish)*

arête *f.*

bonnet, *s.* chapeau *m.;* bonnet *m.; (motor)* capot *m.*

bony, *adj.* osseux; maigre.

book, *s.* livre *m.; — v.a.* prendre (un billet); retenir.

bockcase, *s.* bibliothèque *f.*

booking-office, *s.* guichet *m.*

book-keeper, *s.* teneur *m.* de livres.

book-keeping, *s.* comptibilité *f.*

booklet, *s.* livret *m.*

bookseller, *s.* libraire *m.*

bookshelf, *s.* rayon *m.*

bookshop, *s.* librairie *f.*

book-stall, *s.* bibliothèque (de gare) *f.*

boot, *s.* bottine *f.;* brodequin *m.*

booth, *s.* baraque *f.*

booty, *s.* butin *m.*

border, *s.* bord *m.;* frontière *f.*

bore, *v. a.* ennuyer, raser; *— s.* raseur *m.*

boring, *adj.* ennuyeux, assommant.

born, *pp.* né; *be ~* naître.

borrow, *v. a.* emprunter.

bosom, *s.* sein *m.*

boss, *s.* patron *m.*

botanical, *adj.* botanique.

botany, *s.* botanique *m.*

both, *pron. & adj.* l'un(e) et l'autre; tous (les) deux; *~ ... and* et ... et ...

bother, *v.a.* tracasser.

bottle, *s.* bouteille *f.*

bottom, *s.* bas *m.;* fond *m.;* derrière *m.*

bough, *s.* rameau *m.*

bound, *pp. ~ for* à destination de, en route pour.

boundary, *s.* borne *f.*

bounty, *s.* générosité *f.*

bouquet, *s.* bouquet *m.*

bow[1]**,** *s.* arc *m.; (violin)* archet *m.; (knot)* nœud *m.*

bow[2]**,** *v.a.* incliner; courber; *v.n.* s'incliner; se courber; *— s.* salut *m.; (ship)* avant *m.*

bowels, *s. pl.* entrailles *f.*

bowl, *s.* bol *m.,* jatte *f.*

box, *s.* boîte *f.,* caisse *f.; (horse)* stalle *f.; (theatre)* loge *f.; (on the ears)* soufflet *m.; — v. n.* boxer.

box-office, *s.* bureau *m.* de location.

boy, *s.* garçon *m.; ~ scout* boy-scout *m.,* éclaireur *m.*

bra, *s.* soutien-gorge *m.*

brace, *s.* couple *f.;* lien *m.; ~s* bretelles *f. pl.*

bracelet, *s.* bracelet *m.*

brain, *s.* cerveau *m.; ~s* cervelle *f.*

brainy, *adv.* intelligent.

brake, *s.* frein *m.*

branch, *s.* branche *f.*

brand, *s.* tison *m.;* marque *f.; — v.a.* marquer.

brandy, *s.* cognac *m.*

brass, *s.* cuivre jaune *m.*

brave, *adj.* brave.

brawl, *s.* querelle *f.*

bread, *s.* pain *m.*

breadth, *s.* largeur *f.*

break, *v.a.* briser, casser; *(law)* violer; *(promise)* manquer; *(news)* apprendre à; *v. n.* se casser; se briser; *~ down* abattre; s'effondrer; *(motor)* avoir une panne; *~ in* dresser; *~ up* lever; *— s.* interruption *f.;* pause *f.*

break-down, *s. (motor)* panne *f.; (health)* débâcle; ~ *lorry* dépanneuse *f.*

breakfast, *s.* déjeuner *m.*

breast, *s.* poitrine *f.*, sein *m.*

breath, *s.* haleine *f.;* souffle *m.*

breathe, *v.a.* & *n.* respirer.

breathless, *adj.* essoufflé; sans souffle.

breeches, *s. pl.* culotte *f.*

breed, *s.* race *f.;* — *v.a.* élever.

breeze, *s.* brise *f.*

breezy, *adj.* venteux.

brew, *v.a.* brasser.

bribe, *s.* pot-de-vin *m.;* — *v.a.* corrompre.

brick, *s.* brique *f.*

bricklayer, *s.* maçon *m.*

bride, *s.* mariée *f.*

bridegroom, *s.* marié *m.*

bridge, *s.* pont *m.*

bridle, *s.* bride *f.*

brief, *adj.* bref.

briefcase, *s.* serviette *f.*

briefly, *adv.* brièvement.

briefs, *s. pl.* slip *m.*

bright, *adj.* brillant; vif; clair; éclatant.

brighten, *v.a.* faire briller; égayer.

brightness, *s.* éclat *m.*

brilliant, *s.* brillant *m.*

brim, *s.* bord *m.*

bring, *v.a.* amener; apporter; ~ *about* amener; ~ *back* rapporter; ~ *forth* produire; ~ *up* élever.

brink, *s.* bord *m.*

brisk, *adj.* vif; actif.

bristle, *s. (brush)* poil *m.*

British, *adj.* britannique.

brittle, *adj.* cassant.

broad, *adj.* large; vaste.

broadcast, *v.a.* radiodiffuser.

broadcasting, *s.* radiodiffusion *f.*

broken, *adj.* brisé.

bronze, *s.* bronze *m.*

brooch, *s.* broche *f.*

brood, *s.* couvée *f.;* — *v.n.* couver.

brook, *s.* ruisseau *m.*

broom, *s.* balai *m.*

brother, *s.* frère *m.*

brother-in-law, *s.* beau-frère *m.*

brow, *s.* sourcil *m.*

brown, *adj.* brun.

bruise, *s.* contusion *f.;* — *v.a.* meurtrir.

brush, *s.* brosse *f.;* pinceau *m.;* balai *m.;* — *v.a.* brosser; ~ *up* donner un coup de brosse à.

brutal, *adj.* brutal, cruel.

brutality, *s.* brutalité *f.*

bubble, *s.* bulle *f.;* — *v. n.* bouillonner.

buck, *s.* daim *m.*

bucket, *s.* seau *m.*

buckle, *s.* boucle *f.*

bud, *s.* bourgeon *m.*

budget, *s.* budget *m.*

buffet, *s.* soufflet *m.*

bug, *s.* punaise *f.*

build, *v.a.* bâtir; construire; sur; ~ *up* établir.

builder, *s.* entrepreneur *m.* de bâtiments; constructeur *m.*

building, *s.* bâtiment *m.*

bulb, *s.* bulbe *m.; (lamp)* ampoule *f.*

bulge, *v.n.* bomber.

bulk, *s.* masse *f.;* volume *m.*

bull, *s.* taureau *m.*

bullet, *s.* balle *f.*

bulletin, *s.* bulletin *m.*

bump, *s.* bosse *f.;* collision *f.;* coup *m.*

bumper, *s.* pare-choc *m.*

bun, *s.* brioche *f.*

bunch, *s.* bouquet *m.;* botte *f.;* grappe *f.*

bundle, *s.* botte *f.;* paquet

m.; fagot *m.*

bunk, *s.* couchette *f.*

buoy, *s.* bouée *f.*

burden, *s.* charge *f.;* fardeau *m.*

burglar, *s.* cambrioleur *m.*

burial, *s.* enterrement *m.*

burn, *v.a.* & *n.* brûler.

bursary, *s.* bourse *f.*

burst, *v.n.* éclater; crever; exploser; *v.a.* faire éclater; rompre; crever; — *s.* éclat *m.;* explosion *f.*

bury, *v.a.* enterrer.

bus, *s.* autobus *m.*

bush, *s.* buisson *m.*

business, *s.* affaires *f. pl.;*

profession *f.;* on ∼ pour affaires; ∼ *hours* heures *(f. pl.)* d'ouverture.

businessman, *s.* homme *m.* d'affaires.

bus-stop, *s.* arrêt *m.* d'autobus.

busy, *adj.* occupé, affairé.

but, *conj.* mais.

butcher, *s.* boucher *m.;* ∼'s *(shop)* boucherie *f.*

butter, *s.* beurre *m.*

butterfly, *s.* papillon *m.*

buttock, *s.* fesse *f.*, derrière *m.*

button, *s.* bouton *m.*

buy, *v.a.* acheter.

buyer, *s.* acheteur *m.*

by, *prep.* par; *de;* ∼ *Monday* d'ici à lundi.

bystander, *s.* spectateur, -trice *m. f.*

C

cab, *s.* taxi *m.;* fiacre *m.*

cabbage, *s.* chou *m.*

cabin, *s.* cabane *f.; (ship)* cabine *f.*

cabinet, *s. (politics)* cabinet *m.*

cable, *s.* câble *m.*

cablegram. *s.* câblo-

gramme *m.*

café, *s.* café(-restaurant) *m.*

cage, *s.* cage *f.*

cake, *s.* gâteau *m.*

calculate, *v.a.&n.* calculer.

calculation, *s.* calcul *m.*

calendar, *s.* calendrier *m.*

calf, *s.* veau *m.; (leg)* mollet *m.*

call, *v. a.* & *n.* appeler; ∼ *for*, réclamer; ∼ *on* faire visite à; — *s.* appel *m.;* cri *m.; (visit)* visite *f.*

call-box, *s.* cabine *f.* téléphonique.

calm, *adj.* calme.

calorie, *s.* calorie *f.*

camel, *s.* chameau, -elle *m. f.*

camera, *s.* appareil *m.* (photographique).

camp, *s.* camp *m.*

campaign, *s.* campagne *f.*

camping, *s.* camping *m.*

can¹, *s.* broc *m.;* pot *m.*

can², *v. aux.* pouvoir; savoir.

canal, *s.* canal *m.*

canary, *s.* canari *m.*

cancel, *v.a.* annuler.

cancer, *s.* cancer *m.*

candle, *s.* chandelle *f.;* bougie *f.*

cannon, *s.* canon *m.*

canoe, e *s.* canoë *m.*

canteen, *s.* cantine *f.*

canvas, *s.* toile *f.*

cap, *s.* bonnet *m.;* casquette *f.*

capable, *adj.* capable (de).

capacity, *s.* capacité *f.*

cape, *s. (land)* cap *m.; (cloak)* pèlerine *f.;* cape *f.*

capital, *s. (city)* capitale *f.; (letter)* majuscule *f.* *(commerce)* capital *m;*

capsule, *s.* capsule *f.*

captain, s. capitaine m.
caption, s. sous-titre m.
captivate, v.a. captiver.
capture, v.a. capturer; —
s. capture f.
car, s. voiture f., auto f.
caravan, s. roulotte f.
(de camping), cara-
vane f.
carbon-paper, s. papier m.
carbone.
carburetter, s. carbura-
teur m.
card, s. carte f.
cardboard, s. carton m.
cardinal, adj. m. cardinal
m.
care, s. attention f.; soin
m.; souci m.; ~ of aux
bons soins de; take ~ of
prendre soin de; —
v.n. ~ for se soucier de;
~ to aimer.
career, s. carrière f.
careful, adj. soigneux.
careless, adj. insouciant,
négligent.
caress, v.a. caresser.
cargo, s. cargaison f.
caricature, s. caricature f.
carnation, s. œillet m.
carpenter, s. charpentier
m.
carpet, s. tapis m.
carriage, s. voiture f.;
(transport) transport
m.
carriage-way, s. chaussée
f.
carrier, s. voiturier m.
carrot, s. carotte f.
carry, v.a. porter; transporter; ~ on exercer;
~ out mettre à exécu-
tion.
cart, s. charrette f.
cartridge, s. cartouche f.
carve, v. a.& n. sculpter;
(meat) découper.
case, s. (box) étui m.,
caisse f.; (instance) cas

m.; cause f.
casement, s. croisée f.
cash, s. espèces f. pl.
cash-book, s. livre m. de
caisse.
cashier, s. caissier, -ère
m. f.
cash-register, s. caisse
f. enregistreuse.
cask, s. tonneau m.
cast, v.a. jeter; (metal)
fondre; — s. coup m.;
(theatre) distribution f.
castle, s. château m.
casual, adj. casuel.
casualty, s. accident m.
cat, s. chat, -te m. f.
catalogue, s. catalogue m.
catastrophe, s. catastrophe f.
catch, v.a. saisir; attra-
per; (eye) frapper; ~
up rattraper; — s.
prise f.; attrape f.
category, s. catégorie f.
cater, v.n. pourvoir à.
caterpillar, s. chenille f.
cathedral, s. cathédrale f.
catholic, adj. catholique.
catholicism, s. catholicisme m.
cattle, s. bétail m. (pl.
bestiaux).
cauliflower, s. chou-fleur
m.
cause, s. cause f.; motif m.; — v.a. causer.
caution, s. prudence f.
cautious, adj. prudent.
cave, s. caverne f.
cavity, s. cavité f.
cease, v.a. & n. cesser.
ceiling, s. plafond m.
celebrate, v.a. célébrer.
celebration, s. célébration
f.; commémoration f.
celery, s. céleri m.
cell, s. cellule f.
cellar, s. cave f.
cello, s. violoncelle m.
cellophane, s. cellophane

f.

cement, *s.* ciment *m.;* — *v.a.* cimenter.

cemetery, *s.* cimetière *m.*

centenary, *s.* centenaire *m.*

central, *adj.* central.

centre, *s.* centre *m.*

century, *s.* siècle *m.*

cereal, *s.* céréale *f.*

ceremony, *s.* cérémonie *f.*

certain, *adj.* certain.

certainly, *adj.* certainement; sans doute

certainty, *s.* certitude *f.*

certificate, *s.* certificat *m.*

certify, *v.a.* certifier.

chain, *s.* chaîne *f.*

chair, *s.* chaise *f.; (professorship)* chaire *f.;* *take the* ~ présider.

chairman, *s.* président *m.*

chalk, *s.* craie *f.*

challenge, *s.* défi *m.;* — *v.a.* défier; provoquer.

chamber, *s.* chambre *f.;* ~s étude *f.;* appartement *m.*

champagne, *s.* champagne *m.*

champion, *s.* champion *m.*

championship, *s.* championnat *m.*

chance, *s.* chance *f.;* *by* ~ par hasard.

chancellor, *s.* chancelier *m.*

chancery, *s.* chancellerie *f.*

change, *s.* changement *m.; (money)* monnaie *f.;* — *v.a.&n.* changer.

channel, *s.* canal *m.; the English Channel* la Manche.

chap, *s.* type *m.*

chapel, *s.* chapelle *f.*

chaplain, *s.* chapelain *m.*

chapter, *s.* chapitre *m.*

character *s.* caractère *m.; (theatre)* personnage

m.

characteristic, *adj.* caractéristique; — *s.* trait *m.* caractéristique.

charcoal, *s.* charbon *m.* de bois

charge, *s.* charge *f.; (price)* prix *m.; (accusation)* accusation *f.;* — *v.a.* charger (de); *(price)* demander; faire payer; *(accuse)* accuser (de).

charity, *s.* charité *f.*

charm, *s.* charme *m.*

charming, *adj.* charmant.

chart, *s.* carte *f.* marine.

charter, *s.* charte *f.*

charwoman, *s.* femme *f.* de ménage.

chase, *v.a.* chasser; poursuivre; — *s.* chasse *f.*

chassis, *s.* châssis *m.*

chat, *s.* causette *f.;* — *v. n.* causer.

chatter, *v.n.* babiller; *(teeth)* claquer.

cheap, *adj.* bon marché.

cheat, *v.a.* tromper; tricher; — *s.* tromperie *f.;* tricherie; *(pers.)* fourbe *m.*

check, *v.a.* contrôler, vérifier; *(stop)* arrêter; — *s.* vérification *f.,* contrôle *m.*

checkmate, *s.* échec et mat *m.*

check-up, *s.* examen *m.* médical.

cheek, *s.* joue *f.*

cheeky, *adj.* impertinent.

cheer, *v.a.* réjouir, encourager; acclamer; *v.n.* ~ up reprendre sa gaieté; courage!; — *s.* joie *f.;* ~s acclamations *f.*

cheerful, *adj.* joyeux.

cheese, *s.* fromage *m.*

chemical, *adj.* chimique.

chemist, *s.* chimiste *m.;*

pharmacien *m.;* ~'s
(shop) pharmacie *f.*
chemistry, *s.* chimie *f.*
cheque, *s.* chèque *m.;*
traveller's ~ chéque
m. de voyage.
cheque-book, *s.* carnet
m. de chèques.
cherish, *v. a.* soigner;
(hope) caresser.
cherry, *s.* cerise *f.*
chess, *s.* échecs *m. pl.*
chess-board, *s.* échiquier
m.
chest, *s.* coffre *m.; (part
of body)* poitrine *f.;*
~ of drawers commode
f.
chestnut, *s.* châtaigne *f.*
chew, *v.a.* mâcher.
chicken, *s.* poulet *m.*
chief, *adj.* principal; —
s. chef *m.*
chiefly, *adv.* principa-
lement.
child, *s.* enfant *m.f.*
childhood, *s.* enfance *f.*
childish, *adj.* enfantin.
childless, *adj.* sans enfant.
chill, *s.* coup *m.* de
froid; — *v.a.* refroi-
dir, glacer.
chilly, *adj. (weather)* frais;
(un peu) froid.
chimney, *s.* cheminée *f.*
chin, *s.* menton *m.*
china, *s.* porcelaine *f.*
Chinese, *adj.* chinois; —
s. Chinois, -e.
chip, *s.* éclat *m.;* copeau
m.; ~s frites *f. pl.*
chirp, *v.n.* gazouiller.
chisel, *s.* ciseau *m.;* —
v.a. ciseler.
chivalry, *s.* chevalerie *f.*
chocolate, *s.* chocolat *m.*
choice, *s.* choix *m.*
choir, *s.* chœur *m.*
choke, *v.a. & n.* étouffer.
choose, *v.a.* choisir.
chop, *s.* côtelette *f.*

chorus, *s.* chœur *m.*
Christian, *adj.* chrétien;
~ name prénom *m.*
Christianity, *s.* christianisme *m.*
Christmas, *s.* Noël *m.;*
~ eve veille *f.* de Noël.
chuckle, *v.n.* rire tout
bas; — *s.* rire étouffé.
church, *s.* église *f.*
churchyard, *s.* cimetière
m.
cider, *s.* cidre *m.*
cigar, *s.* cigare *m.*
cigarette, *s.* cigarette *f.*
cigarette-case, *s.* étui *m.*
à cigarettes.
cigarette-holder, *s.* porte-
cigarette *m.*
cinders, *s.pl.* cendres *f.*
cine-camera, *s.* camera *f.*
cinema, *s.* cinéma *m.*
cinerama, *s.* cinérama *m.*
circle, *s.* cercle *m.*
circuit, *s.* circuit *m.;*
détour *m.;* tournée *f.*
circular, *adj.* circulaire.
circulate, *v.n.* circuler;
v.a. faire circuler.
circulation, *s.* circulation
f.
circumstance, *s.* circonstance *f.*
circus, *s.* cirque *m.*
cistern, *s.* citerne *f.*
citation, *s.* citation *f.*
cite, *v. a.* citer.
citizen, *s.* citoyen, -ne
m. f., habitant *m.*
citizenship, *s.* droit *m.*
de cité.
city, *s.* ville *f.; the City*
Cité *f.*
civil, *adj.* civil; (polite)
poli; ~ servant fonc-
tionnaire *m.*
civilization, *s.* civilisation *f.*
civilize, *v.a.* civiliser.
claim, *s.* demande *f.,*
réclamation *f.;* droit
m.; — *v.a.* revendi-

quer, réclamer.

clamp, *s.* crampon *m.*

clang, *s.* bruit *m.* métallique; — *v.n.* retentir.

clap, *s.* battement *m.;* applaudissements *m. pl.;* — *v.n.* applaudir.

clash, *v.a.* choquer; *v.n.* s'entre-choquer.

clasp, *s.* agrafe *f.;* fermoir *m.;* — *v.a.* agrafer; joindre.

class, *s.* classe *f.*

classic(al), *adj.* classique.

classify, *v.a.* classifier.

class-room, *s.* classe *f.*

clatter, *s.* bruit *m.;* fracas *m.;* — *v.n.* faire du bruit.

clause, *s.* clause *f.,* article *m.*

claw, *s.* griffe *f.;* serre *f.;* ongle *m.*

clay, *s.* glaise *f.;* argile *f.*

clean, *adj.* propre; blanc; pur; — *v.a.* nettoyer.

cleanse, *v.a.* nettoyer.

clear, *adj.* clair; — *v.a.* déblayer; éclaircir; *v.n.* s'éclaircir; ~ *away* enever; ~ *out* filer.

clearly, *adv.* clair, clairement; évidemment.

cleave, *v.a.* fendre; *v.n.* se fendre.

clergy, *s.* clergé *m.*

clergyman, *s.* ministre *m.*

clerk, *s.* employé *m.,* commis *m.*

clever, *adj.* habile, adroit; intelligent.

client, *s.* client *m.*

cliff, *s.* falaise *f.*

climate, *s.* climat *m.*

climb, *v.a. & n.* grimper.

cling, *v.n.* ~ *to* se cramponner à.

clinic, *s.* clinique *f.*

clip, *s.* pince; — *v.a.* tondre; couper; rogner; *(tickets)* poinconner.

cloak, *s.* manteau *m.*

cloak-room, *s.* consigne *f.;* vestiaire *m.*

clock, *s.* horloge *f.;* pendule *f.; it is 10 o'clock* il est dix heures.

close, *v.a. (shut)* fermer; *(end)* terminer; *v.n.* (se) fermer; se terminer; — *adj.* fermé; *(narrow)* étroit; *(relations)* proche; intime; — *adv.* tout près; — *s.* enclos *m.; (end)* fin *f.*

closely, *adv.* de près; étroitement.

closet, *s.* cabinet *m.;* armoire *f.*

cloth, *s.* drap *m.; (table)* nappe *f.*

clothe, *v.a.* vêtir.

clothes, *s.pl.* habits *m.pl.*

clothing, *s.* vêtements *m. pl.*

cloud, *s.* nuage *m.*

cloudy, *adj.* couvert.

clover, *s.* trèfle *m.*

club, *s. (stick)* massue *f.; (people)* cercle *m.,* club *m.,* société *f.; (cards)* trèfle *m.*

clue, *s.* fil *m.; (crossword)* définition *f.*

clumsy, *adj.* gauche.

cluster, *s.* grappe *f.*

clutch, *v.a.* empoigner; *m.* pour empoigner; *(motor)* embrayage *m.*

coach, *s.* voiture *f.;* wagon *m.;* autocar *m.; (sports)* entraîneur *m.*

coal, *s.* charbon *m.*

coal-mine, *s.* mine *f.* de houille.

coarse, *adj.* grossier; vulgaire.

coast, *s.* côte *f.*

coat, *s. (jacket)* veston *m.; (top)* pardessus *m.,* manteau *m.*

cock, *s.* coq *m.,* mâle *m.; (gun)* chien *m.; (tap)* robinet *m.*

cocktail, *s.* cocktail *m.*

cocoa, *s.* cacao *m.*

cod, *s.* morue *f.*

code, *s.* code *m.*

coffee, *s.* café *m.*

coffee-pot, *s.* cafetière *f.*

coffin, *s.* cercueil *m.*

cog-wheel, *s.* roue *f.* dentée.

coil, *s.* rouleau *m.;* bobine *f.;* — *v.a.* lover; enrouler.

coin, *s.* pièce *f.*

coincidence, *s.* coïncidence *f.*

coke, *s.* coke *m.*

cold, *adj.* froid; be ~ *(pers.)* avoir froid; *(weather)* faire froid; — *s.* froid *m.; (in the head)* rhume *m.; catch a* ~ s'enrhumer.

collaborate, *v. n.* collaborer.

collaborator, *s.* collaborateur, -trice *m.f.*

collapse, *v.n.* s'effondrer; *(pers.)* s'affaisser; — *s.* effondrement *m.; (pers.)* affaissement *m.* subit.

collar, *s.* col *m.;* collet *m.*

colleague, *s.* collègue *m. f.*

collect, *v.a.* rassembler; recueillir.

collection, *s.* collection *f.;* collecte *f.; (mail)* levée *f.*

college, *s.* collège *m.*

collide, *v.n.* se heurter (contre), entrer en collision.

colliery, *s.* houillère *f.;* mine *f.*

collision, *s.* collision *f.*

colon, *s.* deux points *m. pl.*

colonel, *s.* colonel *m.*

colony, *s.* colonie *f.*

colour, *s.* couleur *f.*

colourful, *adj.* coloré.

colourless, *adj.* terne, pâle.

column, *s.* colonne *f.*

comb, *s.* peigne *m.;* — *v.a.* peigner.

combat, *s.* combat *m.*

combination, *s.* combinaison *f.*

combine, *v.a.* combiner.

come, *v.n.* venir, arriver; ~ *across* rencontrer; ~ *back* revenir; ~ *by* obtenir; passer; ~ *down* descendre; ~ *in* entrer; ~ *off* avoir lieu; se détacher; ~ *out* sortir; ~ *up* monter.

comedian, *s.* comédien *m.*

comedy, *s.* comédie *f.*

comely, *adj.* avenant, bienséant.

comfort, *s.* consolation *f.;* bien-être *m.;* — *v.a.* consoler.

comfortable, *adj.* confortable; commode; be ~ être à l'aise.

comic, *adj.* comique.

comma, *s.* virgule *f.*

command, *s.* ordre *m.;* — *v.a.* commander.

commander, *s.* commandant *m.*

commandment, *s.* commandement *m.*

commemorate, *v.a.* commémorer.

commence, *v.a.& n.* commencer.

commend, *v.a.* recommander; louer.

comment, *s.* commentaire *m.; — v.n.* commenter.

commentary, *s.* commentaire *m.*

commerce, *s.* commerce *m.*

commercial, *adj.* commercial; ~ *traveller* voyageur *m.* de commerce.

commission, *s.* commission *f.;* commande *f.*

commissioner, *s.* commissaire *m.*

commit, *v.a.* commettre; confier; ~ *oneself* se compromettre.

commitment, *s.* engagement *m.*

committee, *s.* comité *m.*

commodity, *s.* marchandise *f.,* article *m.*

common, *adj.* commun.

commonwealth, *s. the British Commonwealth* commonwealth *m.*

communicate, *v. a. & n.* communiquer.

communication, *s.* communication *f.*

communication-cord, *s.* signal *m.* d'alarme.

communion, *s.* communion *f.*

communiqué, *s.* communiqué *m.*

community, *s.* communauté *f.*

compact, *s.* pacte *m.;* poudrier *m.; — adj.* compact; concis.

companion, *s.* compagnon, -agne *m. f.*

company, *s.* compagnie *f.;* société *f.*

comparatively, *adv.* comparativement.

compare, *v.a.* comparer

(to à, *with* avec).

comparison, *s.* comparaison *f.*

compartment, *s.* compartiment *m.*

compass, *s. (mariner's)* boussole *f.; (pair of)* ~*es* compas *m.*

compassion, *s.* compassion *f.*

compel, *v.a.* forcer.

compete, *v.n.* faire concurrence (à); concourir.

competence, *s.* compétence *f.;* capacité *f.*

competent, *adj.* capable.

competition, *s.* concurrence *f.;* concours *m.;* compétition *f.*

competitor, *s.* concurrent *m.*

compilation, *s.* compilation *f.*

compile, *v.a.* compiler.

complain, *v.n.* se plaindre

complaint, *s.* plainte *f.;* maladie *f.;* réclamation *f.*

complement, *s.* complément *m.*

complete, *v.a.* compléter, achever; — *adj.* complet.

complicated, *adj.* compliqué.

complication, *s.* complication *f.*

compliment, *s.* compliment *m.*

comply, *v.n.* ~ *with* se conformer à.

component, *adj. & s.* composant *(m.).*

compose, *v.a.* composer; *be* ~*d of* se composer de.

composer, *s.* compositeur *m.*

composition, *s.* composition *f.;* dissertation *f.*

compound, *s. & adj.* composé *(m.); — v.a.* composer.

comprehend, *v.a.* comprendre.

comprehension, *s.* compréhension *f.*

compress, *v.a.* comprimer.

compromise, *s.* compromis *m.;* — *v.a.* compromettre.

compulsory, *adj.* obligatoire.

compute, *v.a.* calculer, computer.

computer, *s.* calculateur *m.* (électronique).

comrade, *s.* camarade *m.*

conceal, *v. a.* cacher.

conceit, *s.* vanité *f.*

conceive, *v.a.* concevoir.

concept, *s.* concept *m.*

concern, *v.a.* concerner; regarder; *be ~ed (in, with)* s'intéresser (à); *(about)* s'inquiéter (de); — *s.* affaire *f.;* entreprise *f.;* anxiété *f.*

concerning, *prep.* concernant.

concert, *a.* concert *m.*

concession, *s.* concession *f.*

conciliation, *s.* réconciliation *f.*

concise, *adj.* concis.

conclude, *v.a. &n.* conclure.

conclusion, *s.* conclusion *f.; in ~* pour conclure.

concrete, *s.* béton *m.;* — *adj.* concret.

condemn, *v.a.* condamner.

condense, *v.a.* condenser.

condition, *s.* condition *f.;* état *m.; on ~ that* à condition que.

conduct, *s.* conduite *f.;* — *v. a.* conduire; diriger.

conductor, *s.* receveur *m.;* chef *m.* d'orchestre.

cone, *s.* cône *m.*

confederacy, *s.* confédération *f.*

confer, *v.a. & n.* conférer.

conference, *s.* conférence *f.*

confess, *v.a.* avouer; confesser.

confession, *s.* confession *f.*

confidence, *s.* confiance *f.*

confident, *adj.* confiant.

confidential, *adj.* confidentiel.

confine, *v.a.* confiner, enfermer; *be ~d to bed* être alité.

confirm, *v. a.* confirmer.

confirmation, *s.* confirmation *f.*

conflict, *s.* conflit *m.*

confound, *v. a.* confondre.

confront, *v.a.* être en face; confronter.

confuse, *v.a.* brouiller, mettre en désordre.

confusion, *s.* confusion *f.*

congratulate, *v.a.* féliciter (de).

congratulation, *s.* félicitations *f. pl.*

congregation, *s.* assemblée *f.*, congrégation *f.*

congress, *s.* congrès *m.*

conjunction, *s.* conjonction *f.*

connect, *v.a.* joindre, lier; associer.

connection, *s.* connexion *f.;* rapport *m.; (railw.)* correspondance *f.*

conquer, *v.a.* vaincre; conquérir.

conqueror, *s.* vainqueur *m.;* conquérant *m.*

conscience, *s.* conscience *f.*

conscious *adj. be ~* (*= not fainting)* avoir connaissance; *be ~ of* avoir la conscience de.

consciousness, *s.* connaissance *f.;* conscience *f.*

conscript, *adj. & s.* conscrit *(m.).*

consent, *s.* consentement; — *v.n.* consentir.

consequence, *s.* consé-
quence *f.*

consequent, *adj.* consé-
quent.

consequently, *adv.* par
conséquent.

conservation, *s.* conservation *f.*

consider, *v.a.* considérer.

considerable, *adj.* considérable.

considerate, *adj.* attentif; réfléchi.

consideration, *s.* considération *f.; (money)*
rémunération *f.*

consign, *v.a.* livrer; consigner, expédier.

consignment, *s.* expédi-
tion *f.;* envoi *m.*

consist, *v. n.* ~ *of* se composer de, consister en.

consistent, *adj.* consé-
quent.

consolation, *s.* consolation *f.*

consonant, *s.* consonne *f.*

conspicuous, *adj.* en vue;
frappant.

conspiracy, *s.* conspiration *f.*

conspire, *v. a. & n.* conspirer.

constable, *s.* agent *m.*
(de police).

constant, *adj.* continuel;
constant.

constipation, *s.* constipation *f.*

constitute, *v.a.* constituer.

constitution, *s.* constitution *f.*

constrain, *v.a.* contraindre (à).

constraint, *s.* contrainte *f.*

construct, *v. a.* construire.

construction, *s.* construction *f.*

consul, *s.* consul *m.*

consulate, *s.* consulat *m.*

consult, *v.a. & n.* con-
sulter.

consultation, *s.* consultation *f.;* ~ *room* cabi-
net *m.* (de consultation).

consume, *v.a. (destroy)*
consumer; *(use up)* con-
sommer.

consumer, *s.* consomma-
teur, -trice *m.f.;* ~
goods articles *m.* de
grande consommation.

consumption, *s.* consom-
mation *f.; (disease)*
phtisie *f.,* tuberculose *f.*

contact, *s.* contact *m.;*
— *v.a.* entrer en rela-
tions avec.

contain, *v.a.* contenir.

container, *s.* récipient *m.*

contemplate, *v.a.* con-
templer; projeter.

contemplation, *s.* con-
templation *f.*

contemporary, *adj. & s.*
contemporain *(m.).*

contempt, *s.* mépris *m.*

contemptuous, *adj.* mé-
prisant.

contend, *v.n.* lutter contre (pour).

content, *s.* contentement
m.; ~*s* contenu *m.; table
of* ~*s* table *f.* des matières; — *adj.* content.

contest, *s.* lutte *f.; (sport)*
rencontre *f.,* match *m.;*
(dispute) contestation
f.; — *v. a.* contester.

continent, *s.* continent *m.*

continental, *adj.* continental.

continual, *adj.* continuel.

continuation, *s.* conti-
nuation *f.;* suite *f.*

continue, *v.a. & n.* continuer.

continuous, *adj.* continu.

contract, *s.* contrat *m.;*
— *v.a.* contracter.

contractor, *s.* entrepreneur *m.*

contradiction, *s.* contradiction *f.*

contrary, *adj.* contraire; — *adv.* contrairement.

contrast, *s.* contraste *m.;* — *v.a.* mettre en contraste.

contribute, *v. a. & n.* contribuer.

contribution, *s.* contribution *f.;* article *m.*

contributor, *s.* contribuant *m.;* collaborateur *m.*

contrive, *v.a.* inventer.

control, *s.* autorité *f.;* maîtrise *f.;* direction *f.,* commande *f.;* — *v.a.* gouverner, commander, maîtriser, diriger; contrôler.

controversy, *s.* polémique *f.,* controverse *f.*

convenience, *s.* commodité *f.,* convenance *f.;* *public* ~ cabinets *m. pl.* d'aisances.

convenient, *adj.* commode; *be* ~ *to s.o.* convenir à qn.

conversation, *s.* conversation *f.*

converse, *v.n.* converser; causer.

convert, *v.a.* convertir.

convey, *v.a.* transporter; transmettre; présenter.

conveyance, *s.* transport *m.;* voiture *f.,* véhicule *m.*

conveyer, *s.* porteur *m.;* ~ *belt* bande *f.* transporteuse.

convict, *s.* forçat *m.;* — *v.a.* convaincre (de), condamner.

convince, *v. a.* convaincre (de).

convoy, *s.* convoi *m.*

cook, *s.* cuisinier, -ière *m. f.; head* ~ chef *m.;*

— *v.a.* faire cuire; *v.n.* cuire.

cooking, *s.* cuisine *f.*

cool, *adj.* frais *(f.* fraîche); *(fig.)* calme; — *v.a.* rafraîchir.

co-operate, *v.n.* coopérer.

co-operation, *s.* coopération *f.*

copper, *s.* cuivre *m.*

copy, *s.* copie *f.;* exemplaire *m.;* numéro *m.* — *v. a.* copier.

copy-book, *s.* cahier *m.*

copyright, *s.* droit *m.* d'auteur.

coral, *s.* corail *m.*

cord, *s.* corde *f.*

cordial, *adj.* cordial.

cork, *s.* bouchon *m.*

corkscrew, *s.* tire-bouchon *m.*

corn, *s.* grain *m.;* grains *m. pl.; (wheat)* blé *m.; (maize)* maïs *m.*

corner, *s.* coin *m.*

corporal, *adj.* corporel; — *s.* caporal *m.*

corporation, *s.* corporation *f.*

corps, *s.* corps *m.*

corpse, *s.* cadavre *m.*

correct, *adj.* correct; exact; — *v.a.* corriger, rectifier.

correction, *s.* correction *f.;* rectification *f.*

correspond, *v.n.* correspondre; être conforme (à).

correspondence, *s.* correspondance *f.*

correspondent, *s.* correspondant *m.*

corresponding, *adj.* correspondant.

corridor, *s.* corridor *m.;* couloir *m.*

corridor-train, *s.* train *m.* à couloir.

corrupt, *adj.* corrompu

cosmetics, *s. pl.* cosmétiques *m. pl.*, produits *m.pl.* de beauté.

cosmonaut, *s.* cosmonaute *m.*

cost, *s.* coût *m.*, frais *m. pl.*; prix *m.*; ~ *of living* coût de la vie; *at the* ~ *of* au prix de; — *v.n.* coûter.

costly, *adj.* coûteux.

costume, *s.* costume *m.*

cosy, *adj.* confortable.

cottage, *s.* chaumière *f.*

cotton, *s.* coton *m.*

couch, *s.* canapé *m.*, divan *m.*

cough, *s.* toux *f.*; — *v.n.* tousser.

council, *s.* conseil *m.*

councillor, *s.* conseiller *m.*

counsel, *s.* conseil *m.*; avocat *m.*

count[1], *s.* compte *m.*; *(title)* comte *m.*

count[2], *v.a.* & *n.* compter.

countenance, *s.* visage *m.*; air· *m.*

counter, *s.* comptoir *m.*, guichet *m.*; jeton *m.*

counterfoil, *s.* souche *f.*

countersign, *v.a.* contresigner.

countess, *s.* comtesse *f.*

countless, *adj.* innombrable.

country, *s.* pays *m.*; *(not town)* campagne *f.*

countryman, *s.* campagnard *m.*

countryside, *s.* (les) campagnes *f.pl.*

countrywoman, *s.* paysanne *f.*

county, *s.* comté *m.*

couple, *s.* couple *f.*

courage, *s.* courage *m.*

courageous, *adj.* courageux.

course, *s.* cours *m.*; route *f.*; *(meal)* service *m.*, plat *m.*; *of* ~ bien entendu.

court, *s.* cour *f.*; tribunal *m.*; court *m.* (de tennis); — *v.a.* faire la cour à.

courteous, *adj.* courtois.

courtesy, *s.* courtoisie *f.*

courtship, *s.* cour *f.*

courtyard, *s.* cour *f.*

cousin, *s.* cousin, -e *m. f.*

cover, *s.* couverture *f.*; couvercle *m.*; *(meal)* couvert *m.*; *(post)* enveloppe *f.*; — *v.a.* couvrir.

cow, *s.* vache *f.*

coward, *s.* & *adj.* lâche *m.*

crab, *s.* crabe *m.*

crack, *s.* craquement *m.*; — *v.a.* faire craquer; *v.n.* craquer; se fêler.

cradle, *s.* berceau *m.*

craft, *s.* habileté *f.*; embarcation *f.*; métier *m.*; profession *f.*

craftsman, *s.* artisan *m.*

cram, *v.a.* fourrer; bourrer.

crane, *s.* grue *f.*

crash, *s.* fracas *m.*; débâcle; atterrissage brutal, collision; *v.n*, tomber avec fracas; s'écraser sur le sol.

crash-helmet, *s.* serretête *m.*

crave, *v.n.* ~ *for* désirer ardemment.

crawl, *v.n.* ramper; *(pers.)* se traîner.

crayon, *s.* crayon *m.*

craze, *s.* manie *f.*

crazy, *adj.* fou, toqué.

creak, *s.* cri *m.*, grincement *m.*; — *v. n.* crier, grincer.

cream, *s.* crème *f.*

crease, *s.* (faux) pli *m.*

create, *v.a.* créer.

creation, s. création f.

creature, s. créature f.

credit, s. crédit m.; mérite m.; honneur m.; on ~ à terme: give ~ to ajouter foi à; — v.a. ajouter foi à, créditer.

creditor, s. créancier m.

creek, s. crique f.

creep, v.n. ramper; se glisser.

crew, s. équipage m.; équipe f.

crib, s. mangeoire f.; lit m. d'enfant; berceau m.

cricket, s. (game) cricket m.

crime, s. crime m.

criminal, adj. & s. criminel, -elle.

cripple, s. estropié m.

crisis, s. crise f.

crisp, adj. croquant, croustillant; (air) vif.

critic, s. critique m.

critical, adj. critique.

criticize, v.a. critiquer.

critique, s. critique f.

croak, v.n. croasser.

crochet, s. crochet m.

crop, s. récolte f.; cueillette f.

cross, s. croix f.; — v.a. croiser, traverser.

crossing, s. passage m.; (sea) traversée f.; level ~ passage à niveau.

cross-question, s. contre-interrogatoire m.; — v.a. contre-interroger.

cross-reference, s. renvoi m.

crossroad, s. chemin m. de traverse; ~s carrefour m.

cross-section, s. coupe f. en travers.

cross-word (puzzle) s. mots m.pl. croisés.

crouch, v. n. se blottir.

crow, s. corneille f.

crowd, s. foule f.; tas m.

crowded, adj. encombré, comble.

crown, s. couronne f ; — v.a. couronner.

crucial, adj. décisif.

crude, adj brut; cru; grossier.

cruel, adj. cruel.

cruelty, s. cruauté f.

cruet, s. burette f.

cruise, v.n. croiser; — s. voyage m.

cruising, adj. ~ speed vitesse f. de croisière.

crumb, s. mie f.; miette f.

crumble, v.a. émietter; v.n. s'émietter.

crusade, s. croisade f.

crush, s. écrasement m.; cohue f.; — v.a. écraser.

crust, s. croûte f.

crutch, s. béquille f.

cry, s. cri m.; — v.a. crier; ~ down décrier; v.n. crier; (weep) pleurer.

crystal, s. cristal m.

cub, s. petit m.; (boy scout) louveteau m.

cube, s. cube m.

cuckoo, s. coucou m.

cucumber, s. concombre m.

cue, s. réplique f.

cuff, s. poignet m., manchette f.

cuff-links, s. pl. boutons m.pl. de manchette.

culminate, v.n. se terminer.

culprit, s. accusé, -e m. f.

cultivate, v.a. cultiver.

cultural, adj. cultural.

culture, s. culture f.

cunning, s. ruse f., finesse f.; — adj. rusé.

cup, s. tasse f.; gobelet m.

cupboard, s. armoire f.; placard m.

curate, s. vicaire m.

curb, s. gourmetté f.

curd, s. (lait) caillé m.

curdle, v.a. cailler; v.n. se cailler.

cure, s. guérison f.; cure f.; remède m.; — v.a. guérir.

curiosity, s. curiosité f.

curious, adj. curieux.

curl, s. boucle f.; — v.a. & n. boucler, friser; ~ up s'enrouler.

curly, adj. bouclé, frisé.

currant, s. black ~ cassis m.; red ~ groseille f. rouge.

currency, s. circulation f., cours m.; terme m. d'échéance; unité f. monétaire, monnaie f.; foreign ~ monnaie étrangère.

current, adj. courant, en cours; in ~ use d'usage courant; ~ events actualités f.; ~ account compte m. courant; — s. courant m.; cours m.

curse, s. malédiction f.; — v.a. maudire; v.n. blasphémer.

curtain, s. rideau m.

curve, s. courbe f.

cushion, s. coussin m.

custom, s. coutume f.; ~s douane f.; ~s duties droits m. de douane; ~s declaration déclaration f. de douane; ~s formalities la visite de la douane.

customary, adj. coutumier; accoutumé.

customer, s. client m., acheteur m.

custom-house, s. douane f.; ~ officer douanier m.

cut, v.a. couper; trancher; tailler; hacher; ~ down abattre, couper; réduire; ~ off couper; ~ out tailler; ~ up couper, débiter; — s. (knife) coup m.; (wound) coupure f.; (clothes) coupe f.; (meat) morceau m.; (in wages) réduction f.

cutlery, s. coutellerie f.

cutlet, s. côtelette f.

cutter, s. tailleur m.; coupeur m.

cycle, s. cycle m.; bicyclette f.; — v.n. pédaler.

cycling, s. cyclisme m.

cylinder, s. cylindre m.

cynic, adj. & s. cynique m.

Czech, adj. tchèque; — s. Tchèque m.

D

dad, daddy, s. papa m.

dagger, s. poignard m.

daily, adj. journalier, quotidien; — s. (journal) quotidien m.

dainty, adj. friand, délicat; gentil; — s. friandise f.

dairy, s. laiterie f.

daisy, s. marguerite f.

dam, s. barrage m.; digue f.

damage, s. dommage m.; préjudice m.; ~s dommages-intérêts m.

damn, v.a. condamner; — s. juron m.

damp, adj. humide; — s. humidité f.; — v. a mouiller, humecter.

dance, s. danse f.; bal m.; v.n. & a. danser.

dancer, s. danseur, -euse m. f.

dancing-hall, s. salle f. de danse; dancing m.

dancing-shoes, s.pl. souliers m. de bal, escarpins m.

Dane, s. Danois, -e m. f.

danger, s. danger m.

dangerous, adj. dangereux.

Danish, adj. danois; — s. (language) danois m.

dare, v. aux. & a. oser.

daring, adj. audacieux.

dark, adj. obscur, sombre; (colour) foncé; (fig.) triste; be ~ faire sombre; — s. obscurité f.; in the ~ dans l'obscurité.

darken, v.a. obscurcir.

darkness, s. obscurité f.

darling, adj. & s. chéri, -e.

darn, v.a. repriser.

darning, s. reprise f.

dart, s. dard m.; ~s (game) fléchettes f.pl.

dash, v.a. lancer; flanquer (par terre); ~ to pieces briser en morceaux; v.n. ~ against se heurter contre; ~ at se précipiter sur — s. (with pen) trait m., tiret m.; (vigour) élan m., fougue f.; attaque f. soudaine.

dash-board, s. tablier m; tableau m. de bord.

data, s. pl. données f.

date¹, s. date f.; millésime m.; be up to ~ être à la page; — v.a. & n. dater.

date², s. datte f.

daughter, s. fille f.

daughter-in-law, s. belle-fille f.

dawn, s. point m. du jour; aube f.

day, s. jour m.; (whole day) journée f.

daylight, s. jour m.

daytime, s. jour m., journée. f.

daze, v.a. étourdir; éblouir.

dazzle, v.a. éblouir.

deacon, s. diacre m.

dead, adj. mort; the ~ les morts m.pl.

deadly, adj. mortel.

deaf, adj. sourd; ~ and dumb sourd-muet.

deal, v.a. ~ out distribuer; donner; v.n. ~ with traiter qn; commercer, traiter avec qn; traiter (d'un sujet); ~ in commercer de; — s. (cards) donne f.; (commerce) affaire f.; a good ~, a great ~ beaucoup (de).

dealer, s. marchand m. (in de).

dean, s. doyen m.

dear, s. & adj. cher m., chère f.

death, s. mort f.

debate, s. débat m., discussion f.; — v.a. discuter, mettre en discussion.

debt, s. dette f.

debtor, s. débiteur, -trice m. f.

decay, s. décadence f.; — v.n. tomber en décadence; pourrir.

decease, s. décès m.; — v.n. décéder.

deceit, s. déception f.; tromperie f.

deceive, v.a. tromper; décevoir.

December, s. décembre m.

decent, adj. décent; assez bon.

deception, s. déception f.

decide, v.a. décider.

decision, s. décision f.

decisive, *adj.* décisif.

deck, *s.* pont *m.*

deck-chair, *s.* transatlantique *f.*

declaration, *s.* déclaration *f.*

declare, *v.a.* déclarer.

decline, *s.* décadence *f.;* — *v.a.* décliner; *v.n.* baisser.

decorate, *v.a.* décorer (de).

decoration, *s.* décoration *f.*

decrease, *v.a. & n.* diminuer; — *s.* diminution *f.*

decree, *s.* décret *m.*

dedicate, *v.a.* dédier.

deed, *s.* action *f.;* acte *m.*

deem, *v.a.* juger.

deep, *adj.* profond; *ten feet ~* dix pieds de profondeur.

deer, *s.* cerf *m.*

deface, *v.a.* défigurer.

defeat, *s.* défaite *f.;* — *v.a.* vaincre.

defect, *s.* défaut *m.*

defence, *s.* défense *f.*

defend, *v.a.* défendre.

defender, *s.* défenseur *m.*

defer, *v.a.* retarder, ajourner; *~ to* déférer à.

defiance, *s.* défi *m.; set at ~* défier.

deficiency, *s.* manque *m.*

deficient, *adj.* insuffisant.

defile, *s.* défilé *m.;* — *v.n.* défiler; *v.a.* souiller.

define, *v.a.* définir.

definite, *adj.* déterminé, défini.

definition, *s.* définition *f.*

defy, *v.a.* défier; braver.

degrade, *v.a.* dégrader.

degree, *s.* degré *m.; (university)* grade *m.;* diplôme *m.*

delay, *s.* retard *m.,* délai *m.;* — *v.a.* retarder; différer; *v.n.* tarder.

delegate, *s.* délégué *m.*

delegation, *s.* délégation *f.*

deliberate, *adj.* délibéré; — *v.a. & n.* délibérer.

delicacy, *s.* délicatesse *f.*

delicate, *adj.* délicat.

delicious, *adj* délicieux.

delight, *v.a. be ~ed at* être enchanté de.

delightful, *adj.* délicieux.

delinquent, *s.* délinquant *m.*

deliver, *v.a. (letters)* distribuer, *(goods etc.)* livrer; *(message)* remettre; *(speech)* faire, prononcer; *(free)* délivrer; *be ~ed of* accoucher de.

delivery, *s. (letters)* distribution *f., (message)* remise *f., (goods)* livraison *f.; (speech)* prononciation *f.,* débit *m.*

delusion, *s.* illusion *f.*

demand, *s.* demande, *f.* réclamation *f.;* — *v. a.* demander, réclamer.

democracy, *s.* démocratie *f.*

democrat, *s.* démocrate *m.*

democratic, *adj.* démocratique.

demolish, *v.a.* démolir.

demonstrate, *v.a.* démontrer.

demonstration, *s.* démonstration *f.*

den, *s.* antre *m.; repaire m.*

denial, *s.* dénégation *f.*

denomination, *s.* dénomination *f.; secte f.*

denote, *v.a.* dénoter.

denounce, *v.a.* dénoncer.

dense, *adj.* dense, épais.

density, *s.* densité *f.*

dentist, *s.* dentiste *m.*

denture, *s. (artificial)* dentier *m.*

deny, *v.a.* nier.

depart, *v.n.* partir.

department, *s.* départe-
ment *m.*

departure, *s.* départ *m.*

depend, *v.n.* dépendre
(de), compter (sur).

dependence, *s.* dépendance *f.*

dependent, *adj.* dépen-
dant.

deplore, *v.a.* déplorer.

deposit, *s.* dépôt *m.;* —
v.a. déposer.

depot, *s.* dépôt *m.*

depression *s.* abattement
m.

deprive, *v.a.* priver (de).

depth, *s.* profondeur *f.*

deputy, *s.* délégué *m.;*
vice-, sous-.

derive, *v.a.* retirer (de);
be ~d from dériver de.

descend, *v.n.* descendre.

descendant, *s.* descen-
dant, -e *m. f.*

descent, *s.* descente *f.*

describe, *v.a.* décrire.

description, *s.* description *f.;* sorte *f.*

desert, *s.* désert *m.;* —
v.a. déserter.

deserve, *v.a.* mériter.

design, *s.* dessein *m.;*
projet *m.;* dessin *m.;*
— *v.a.* dessiner.

desirable, *adj.* désirable.

desire, *s.* désir *m.;* — *v.a.*
désirer.

desk, *s.* bureau *m.*

desolation, *s.* désolation *f.*

despair, *s.* désespoir *m.;*
— *v.n.* désespérer.

despatch *see* dispatch.

desperate, *adj.* désespéré.

despise, *v.a.* mépriser.

despite, *prep.* ~ *(of)* en
dépit de.

dessert, *s.* dessert *m.*

destination, *s.* destination *f.*

destine, *v.a.* destiner.

destiny, *s.* destin *m.*
destinée *f.*

destroy, *v.a.* détruire.

destruction, *s.* destruction
f.

detach, *v.a.* détacher.

detachment, *s.* détache-
ment *m.*

detail, *s.* détail *m.*

detain, *v.a.* retenir;
détenir.

detect, *v.a.* découvrir.

detective, *s.* détective *m.*

detention, *s.* détention *f.*

detergent, *s.* détergent *m.*

deteriorate, *v.n.* se dé-
tériorer.

determination, *s.* détermination *f.*

determine, *v.a. & n.* déterminer, décider.

detrimental, *adj.* pré-
judiciable.

develop, *v.a.* développer;
v.n. se développer.

development, *s.* développe-
pement *m.*

deviation, *s.* déviation *f.*

device, *s* expédient *m.;*
invention *f.*

devil, *s.* diable *m.*

devilish, *adj.* diabolique.

devise, *v.a.* combiner;
tramer.

devote, *v.a.* consacrer.

devoted, *adj.* dévoué.

devotion, *s.* dévotion *f.;*

dévouement *m.*

devour, *v.a.* dévorer.

dew, *s.* rosée *f.*

diagnosis, *s.* diagnostic *m.*

diagram, *s.* diagramme *m.*

dial, *s.* cadran *m.;* —
v.a. composer un
numéro.

dialogue, *s.* dialogue *m.*

diameter, *s.* diamètre *m.*

diamond, *s.* diamant *m.;*
(cards) carreau *m.*

diaper, *s.* couche *f.*

diarrhoea, *s.* diarrhée *f.*
diary, *s.* journal *m.;* agenda *m.*
dictate, *v.a.* dicter; *v.n.*
~ *to* donner des ordres à.
dictation, *s.* dictée *f.*
dictator, *s.* dictateur *m.*
dictionary, *s.* dictionnaire *m.*
die¹, *s.* dé *m.*
die², *v.n.* mourir.
Diesel engine, *s.* moteur *m.* Diesel; diesel *m.*
diet, *s.* alimentation *f.;* régime *m.*
differ, *v.n.* différer.
difference, *s.* différence *f.*
different, *adj.* différent.
difficult, *adj.* difficile.
difficulty, *s.* difficulté *f.*
diffuse, *adj.* diffus.
dig, *v.a.* bêcher.
digest, *v.a.* digérer.
digestion, *s.* digestion *f.*
dignity, *s.* dignité *f.*
diligent, *adj.* diligent.
dim, *adj.* faible, pâle, obscur.
dimension, *s.* dimension *f.*
diminish, *v. a. & n.* diminuer.
dimple, *s.* fossette *f.*

dine, *v.n.* dîner.
dining-car, *s.* wagon-restaurant *m.*
dining-hall, *s.* salle *f.* à manger; réfectoire *m.*
dining-room, *s.* salle *f.* à manger.
dinner, *s.* dîner *m.*
dinner-jacket, *s.* smoking *m.*

dip, *v.a. & n.* plonger.
diploma, *s.* diplôme *m.*
diplomacy, *s.* diplomatie *f.*
diplomat, *s.* diplomate *m.*
diplomatic, *adj.* diplomatique.

direct, *adj.* direct; — *v. a.* diriger; commander; adresser.
direction, *s.* direction *f;* instructions *f. pl.*
directly, *adv.* directement; tout de suite.
director, *s.* directeur *m.*
directory, *s.* annuaire *m.;* Bottin *m.*
dirt, *s.* saleté *f.;* boue *f.,* crotte *f.;* crasse *f.*
dirty, *adj.* sale; crotté; crasseux.
disadvantage, *s.* désavantage *m.*
disagree, *v.n.* différer; se brouiller; ne pas convenir (à).
disagreeable, *adj.* désagréable.
disappear, *v. n.* disparaître
disappearance, *s.* disparition *f.*
disappoint, *v.a.* désappointer; tromper.
disappointment, *s.* désappointement *m.*

disapprove, *v.n.* ~ *of* désapprouver qch.
disaster, *s.* désastre *m.*
disastrous, *adj.* désastreux.

disc *see* disk.
discern, *v.a.* discerner.
discharge, *v. a.* décharger; *(employee)* congédier; renvoyer; *(prisoner)* élargir; *(gas)* dégager; *(debt)* liquider; *(duty)* s'acquitter de; — *s.* décharge *f.; (employee)* congé *m.; (prison)* élargissement *m.*

discipline, *s.* discipline *f.*
disclose, *v.a.* découvrir.
discontented, *adj.* mécontent (de).
discourage, *v. a.* décourager.
discouragement, *s.* décou-

ragement *m.*
discourse, *s.* discours *m.*
discover, *v.a.* découvrir.
discovery, *s.* découverte *f.*
discredit, *s.* discrédit *m.;*
— *v.a.* discréditer.
discreet, *adj.* discret.
discretion, *s.* discrétion
f.; prudence *f.*
discuss, *v.a.* discuter.
discussion, *s.* discussion *f.*
disdain, *v.a.* dédaigner;
— *s.* dédain *m.*
disease, *s.* maladie *f.*
disembark *v.a. & n.* débarquer.
disgrace, *s.* disgrâce *f.;*
— *v.a.* disgracier.
disgraceful, *adj.* honteux.
disguise, *s.* déguisement;
— *v.a.* déguiser.
disgust, *s.* dégoût *m.;*
— *v.a.* dégoûter.
disgusting, *adj.* dégoûtant
dish, *s.* plat *m.;* mets *m.;*
wash up the ~es laver la
vaisselle.
dishonest, *adj.* malhonnête.
dishonour, *s.* déshonneur
m.; — *v.a.* déshonorer
(bill) ne pas honorer.
disinfect, *v.a.* désinfecter.
disk, *s.* disque *m.*
dislike, *s.* aversion *f.,*
dégoût *m.;* — *v.a.* ne
pas aimer.
dismal, *adj.* lugubre, sombre.
dismay, *s.* consternation
f.
dismiss, *v.a.* congédier;
bannir, écarter.
disobedience, *s.* désobéissance *f.*
disobedient, *adj.* désobéissant.
disobey, *v. a.* désobéir (à).
disorder, *s.* désordre *m.*
dispatch, *s.* expédition
f.; dépêche *f.*

dispensary, *s.* pharmacie
f.
dispense, *v.a.* dispenser;
préparer; *v.n.* ~ *with*
se disposer de.
disperse, *v.a.* disperser.
displaced, *adj.* ~ *person*
personne *f.* déplacée.
displacement, *s.* déplacement *m.*
display, *v.a.* exposer;
étaler; déployer, faire
preuve de; — *s.* exposition *f.;* étalage *m.;*
parade *f.*
displease, *v.a.* déplaire à
disposal, *s. at s.o.'s* ~
à la disposition de qn.
dispose, *v.n.* ~ *of* disposer de; vendre.
disposition, *s.* disposition
f.
dispute, *s.* dispute *f.* discuission *f.;* — *v.a* discuter; *v. n.* se disputer.
disqualify, *v.a.* disqualifier.
dissatisfy, *v.a.* mécontenter.
dissolve, *v.a.* dissoudre;
v.n. se dissoudre.
distance, *s.* distance *f.*
distant, *adj.* lointain; éloigné.
distil, *v. a. & n.* distiller.
distinct, *adj.* distinct (de);
marqué.
distinction, *s.* distinction
f.
distinguish, *v.a.* distinguer.
distract, *v.a.* distraire.
distraction, *s.* distraction
f.; confusion *f.*
distress, *s.* détresse *f.;*
— *v.a.* affliger.
distribute, *v. a.* distribuer.
distribution, *s.* distribution *f.*
district, *s.* région *f.,*
contrée *f.;* district *m.*

disturb, *v.a.* troubler; déranger.

disturbance, *s.* trouble *m.*, dérangement *m.*

ditch, *s.* fossé *m.*

dive, *v.n.* plonger *(into dans).*

diver, *s.* plongeur *m.*, scaphandrier *m.*

divergent, *adj.* divergent.

diversion, *s.* déviation *f.*

divide, *v.a.* diviser.

dividend, *s.* dividende *m.*

divine, *adj.* divin.

divinity, *s.* théologie *f.*

division, *s.* division *f.*

divorce, *s.* divorce *m.;* — *v. a.* divorcer (d'avec).

dizzy, *adj.* *feel* ~ avoir le vertige.

do, *v. a.* faire; finir; ~ *away with* supprimer; ~ *up* envelopper; ~ *with* se contenter de.

dock, *s.* bassin *m.*

doctor, *s.* docteur *m.;* médecin *m.*

doctrine, *s.* doctrine *f.*

document, *s.* document *m.*

dog, *s.* chien *m.*

dogma, *s.* dogme *m.*

doll, *s.* poupée *f.*

dollar, *s.* dollar *m.*

domestic, *adj. & s.* domestique *(m. f.).*

domicile, *s.* domicile *m.*

dominate, *v.a. &. n.* dominer.

dominion, *s.* domination *f.;* ~*s* colonies *f.*

donkey, *s.* âne *m.*

doom, *s.* sentence *f.;* — *v.a.* condamner; ~*ed to* voué à.

door, *s.* porte *f.; (vehicle)* portière *f.*

dormitory, *s.* dortoir *m.*

dose, *s.* dose *f.*

dot, *s.* point *m.*

double, *adj. & s.* double *(m.).*

doubt, *s.* doute *m.; no* ~ sans doute; — *v.a. & n.* douter.

doubtful, *adj.* douteux.

doubtless, *adj.* sans doute.

dough, *s.* pâte *f.*

dove, *s.* colombe *f.*

down, *adv.* à bas, en bas, par en bas; *be* ~ *with (illness)* être au lit avec; *fall* ~ tomber à terre; *go* ~ aller en bas; — *prep.* le long de; ~ *the river* en aval; ~ *the street* plus bas dans la rue.

downhill, *s.* pente *f.;* — *adv.* en pente, en descendant.

downstairs, *adv.* en bas.

downwards, *adv.* en bas.

dozen, *s.* douzaine *f.*

draft, *s.* projet *m.; (letter)* minute *f.; (troops)* détachement *m.; (drawing)* esquisse *f.*

drag, *v.a.* traîner; tirer.

drain, *s.* égout *m.*, canal *m.;* — *v.a.* drainer; vider.

drama, *s.* drame *m.;* théâtre *m.*

dramatic, *àdj.* dramatique.

draper, *s.* marchand *m.* d'étoffes, (marchand) drapier *m.;* ~'s magasin *m.* de nouveautés.

draught, *s.* tirage *m.; (drink)* trait *m.; (air)* courant *m.* d'air.

draw, *v.a. (pull)* tirer, traîner; *(tooth)* arracher; *(sketch)* dessiner; ~ *down* baisser; ~ *on* tirer; ~ *out* prolonger; — *v. n.* tirer; ~ *near* s'approcher.

drawer, s. tiroir m.

drawing, s. dessin m.

drawing-pin, s. punaise f.

drawing-room, s. salon m.

dread, v.a. redouter.

dreadful, adj. redoutable.

dream, s. rêve m.; — v.a. & n. rêver.

dress, s. habits m.pl.; robe f.; — v. a. habiller; v.n. s'habiller; ~ a wound panser.

dress-circle, s. (premier) balcon m.

dressing-gown, s. (woman) peignoir m., (man) robe f. de chambre.

dressmaker, s. couturière f.

drift, v.n. flotter; dériver; — s. dérive f.; amoncellement m.

drill, s. foret m.; (soldiers) exercice m.

drink, s. boisson f.; — v.a. boire.

drip, v.n. dégoutter.

drive, v.a. conduire; ~ in (nail) enfoncer; v.n. conduire; aller en voiture.

driver, s. (engine) mécanicien m.; (bus) conducteur m.; (car) chauffeur m.

driving, s. conduite f.; ~ licence permis m. de conduire.

drop, s. goutte f.; — v.a. laisser tomber; abandonner; v.n. (dé)goutter; ~ in entrer en passant.

drown, v.a. noyer; v.n. se noyer.

drug, s. drogue f.

druggist, s. droguiste m.

drum, s. tambour m.

drunk, adj. ivre.

dry, adj. sec, sèche; aride; tari; — v.a. sécher.

dry-clean, v.a. nettoyer à sec.

dual, adj. double.

dub, v.a. doubler.

duchess, s. duchesse f.

duck, s. cane f.; canard m.

due, adj. (proper) dû; (owing) exigible; échéant, payable; in ~ form en bonne et due forme; in ~ time en temps voulu; ~ to causé par, par suite de; the train is ~ at le train arrive à; — s. dû m.; droit m.

duke, s. duc m.

dull, adj. borné; ennuyeux; (colour) terne; (weather, sad) triste.

dumb, adj. muet.

dummy, s. mannequin m.; (cards) mort m.

dung, s. fumier m.

dupe, s. dupe f.; — v.a. duper.

duplicate, s. duplicata m.; — adj. en double; — v.a. faire en double.

during, adv. pendant, au cours de.

dusk, s. crépuscule m.

dust, s. poussière f.

dustbin, s. poubelle f.

dusty, adj. poussiéreux, poudreux.

Dutch, adj. hollandais.

Dutchman, s. Hollandais m.

duty, s. devoir m.; (customs) droit m.; (task) tâche f., fonction(s) f.(pl.); be on ~ être de service.

duty-free, adj. exempt de droits, en franchise.

dwarf, s. nain, -e m. f.

dwell, v.n. habiter; ~ (up)on s'appesantir sur.

dwelling, s. habitation f.

dwelling-house *s.* maison *f.* d'habitation.

dwindle, *v.n.* diminuer.

dye, *s.* teinte *f.*, teinture *f.*; — *v.a.* teindre.

dynasty, *s.* dynastie *f.*

E

each, *pron.* chacun, -e; ~ *other* l'un l'autre; — *adj.* chaque.

eager, *adj.* ardent.

eagle, *s.* aigle *m.*

ear, *s.* oreille *f.*

earl, *s.* comte *m.*

early, *adv.* de bonne heure — *adj.* précoce; premier.

earn, *v. a.* gagner; mériter

earnest, *adj.* sérieux.

earnings, *s.pl.* salaire *m.*

earth, *s.* terre *f.*

earthenware, *s.* poterie *f.*

earthquake, *s.* tremblement *m.* de terre.

ease, *s.* aise *f.*; repos *m.*; *at one's* ~ à son aise; *with* ~ avec facilité.

east, *s.* est *m.*; — *adj.* d'est, de l'est; — *adv.* à l'est (de).

Easter, *s.* Pâques *m. pl.*

eastern, *adj.* (de l')est, oriental.

eastwards, *adv.* vers l'est.

easy, *adj.* facile.

easy-chair, *s.* fauteuil *m.*

easy-going, *adj.* nonchalant.

eat, *v.a.* manger; ~ *up* finir; dévorer.

ebb, *s.* reflux *m.*

ecclesiastic, *adj. & s.* ecclésiastique *(m.).*

economic, *adj.* économique.

economical, *adj.* économe

economics, *s.* économie *f.* politique.

economize, *v.n.* faire des économes.

economy, *s.* économie *f.*

ecstasy, *s.* extase *f.*

edge, *s.* tranchant *m.*, fil *m.*; bord *m.*

edition, *s.* édition *f.*

editor, *s.* rédacteur *m.*

editorial, *s.* article *m.* de fond.

educate, *v.a.* élever.

education, *s.* éducation *f.*

effect, *s.* effet *m.*

effective, *adj.* efficace; effectif.

efficiency, *s.* efficacité *f*

efficient, *adj.* capable.

effort, *s.* effort *m.*

egg, *s.* œuf *m.*; *boiled* ~ œuf à la coque; *fried* ~ œuf sur le plat.

Egyptian, *adj.* égyptien; — *s.* Egyptien, -enne *m. f.*

eight, *adj. & s.* huit.

eighteen, *adj. & s.* dix-huit.

eighteenth, *adj.* dix-huitième.

eighth, *adj.* huitième.

eighty, *adj.&s.* quatre-vingt(s).

either, *pron. & adj.* l'un ou l'autre; chacun; chaque; ~ ... *or* ou ... ou.

elaborate, *v.a.* élaborer; — *adj.* minutieux.

elastic, *adj.* élastique.

elbow, *s.* coude *m.*

elderly, *adj.* d'un certain âge.

elect, *v.a.* choisir; élire.

election, *s.* élection *f.*

electric(al), *adj.* électrique; ~*al engineer* (ingénieur) électricien *m.*

electricity, s. électricité f.
electron, s. électron m.
electronic, adj. électronique.
elegance, s. élégance f.
elegant, adj. élégant.
element, s. élément m.
elementary, adj. élémentaire.
elephant, s. éléphant m.
elevate, v.a. élever.
eleven, adj. & s. onze.
eleventh, adj. onzième.
elm, s. orme m.
else, adj. autre; *anything ~, madam?* encore quelque chose, Madame?; — *adv. or ~* ou bien, autrement.
elsewhere, adv. ailleurs.
embankment, s. remblai m.
embark, v.a. embarquer; v.n. s'embarquer.
embarrass, v.a. embarrasser.
embassy, s. ambassade f.
embrace, v.a. embrasser.
embroidery, broderie f.
emerge, v.n. émerger; apparaître.
emergency, s. circonstance f. critique; *in case of ~* en cas d'accident *or* d'urgence; *~ exit* sortie f. de secours.
emigrant, s. émigrant, -e m. f.
emigrate, v.n. émigrer.
emigration, s. émigration f.
eminent, adj. éminent.
emit, v.a. émettre.
emotion, s. émotion f.
emphasis, s. accent m., force f.; *lay ~ on* appuyer sur.
emphasize, v. a. appuyer sur.
empire, s. empire m.
employ, v.a. employer.

employee, s. employé m.
employer, s. employeur m.
employment, s. emploi m.
empty, adj. vide.
enable, v. a. rendre capable.
enclose, v.a. entourer (de); joindre (à une lettre).
encounter, v.a. affronter; rencontrer.
encourage, v.a. encourager.
encouragement, s. encouragement m.
encyclopaedia, s. encyclopédie f.
end, s. bout m.; fin f.; — v.a.&n. finir; *~ in* finir en.
endeavour, s. effort m.; — v. n. s'efforcer (à *or* de).
ending, s. terminaison f.; fin f.
endless, adj. sans fin.
endorse, v.a. endosser.
endorsement, s. endossement m.
endow, v.a. doter (de).
endure, v.a. supporter, endurer.
enemy, s. ennemi, -e m. f.
energetic, adj. énergique.
energy, s. énergie f.
enforce, v.a. imposer; *(law)* faire exécuter.
engage, v.a. engager; fiancer; *be ~d* être occupé; être fiancé(e).
engagement, s. engagement m.; fiançailles f. pl.
engine, s. machine f.
engine-driver, s. mécanicien m.
engineer, s. ingénieur m.
English, adj. anglais.
Englishman, s. Anglais m.

Englishwomen, s. Anglaise f.

enjoy, v. a. jouir de; trouver bon; ~ oneself s'amuser.

enjoyment, s. jouissance f.

enlarge, v.a. agrandir.

enlist, v.a. enrôler.

enormous, adj. énorme.

enough, adj. & adv. assez (de).

enquire see inquire.

enrage, v.a. exaspérer.

enrol(l), v.a. enrôler.

ensign, s. (flag) drapeau m., pavillon m.; (pers.) porte-drapeau m.

ensue, v.n. s'ensuivre.

enter, v.a. entrer (dans); (in list) inscrire.

enterprise, s. entreprise f.

entertain, v.a. amuser; recevoir; avoir (une opinion).

entertainment, s. divertissement m.; amusement m.; hospitalité f.

enthusiasm, s. enthousiasme. m.

enthusiastic, adj. enthousiaste.

entire, adj. entier.

entirely, adv. entièrement.

entitle, v.a. be ~d to avoir droit à.

entrance, s. entrée f.; ~ examination examen d'entrée m.

entreat, v.a. supplier.

entry, s. entrée f.; inscription f.

enumerate, v.a. énumérer.

envelope, s. enveloppe f.

envious, adj. envieux (de).

enviromment, s. milieu m.

envy, s. envie f.; — v.a. envier.

epidemic, s. épidémie f.

equal, adj. égal.

equality, s. égalité f.

equation, s. équation f.

equip, v.a. équiper.

equipment, s. équipement m.

erase v.a. effacer.

erect, adj. droit ; — v.a. dresser; ériger.

err, v.n. errer.

error, s. erreur f.

escalator, s. escalator m., escalier m. roulant.

escape, v. n. (s')échapper; — s. fuite f.

escort, s. escorte f.; — v.a. escorter.

essay, s. essai m., composition f.

essential, adj. essentiel.

establish, v.a. établir.

establishment, s. établissement m.

estate, s. propriété f.; biens m. pl.

esteem, s. estime f.; — v.a. estimer.

estimate, s. estimation f.; évaulation f.; — v.a. estimer.

eternal, adj. éternel.

eucharist, s. eucharistie f.

European, adj. européen.

evacuate, v.a. évacuer.

even, adj. uni; égal; pair; — adv. même; ~ if même si.

evening, s. soir m.; (party) soirée f.

event, s. événement m.

eventual, adj. éventuel.

ever, adv. toujours; (any time) jamais.

evermore, adv. toujours.

every, adj. (all) tous; (each) chaque; ~ day tous les jours.

everybody, pron. tout le monde.

everyday, adj. de tous les jours.

everyone see everybody.

everything, pron. tout m.

everywhere, *adv*. partout.
evidence, *s*. évidence *f*.
evident, *adj*. évident.
evil, *s*. mal *m.;* — *adj*. mauvais.
evolution, *s*. évolution *f*.
ewe, brebis *f*.

exact, *adj*. exact.
exactly, *adv*. exactement.
exaggerate, *v.a*. exagérer.
exaggeration, *s*. exagération *f*.
examination, *s*. examen *m*.
examine, *v.a*. examiner; vérifier; *(customs)* visiter.
example, *s*. example *m.; for* ~ par exemple.
excavation, *s*. fouille *f*.
exceedingly, *adv*. excessivement.
excel, *v. a*. surpasser; *v. n*. exceller à.
excellent, *adj*. excellent.
except, *v.a*. excepter; — *prep*. excepté; sauf; ~ *for* exception faite pour.
exception, *s*. exception *f*.
exceptional, *adj*. exceptionnel.
excess, *s*. excès *m.;* ~ *luggage* excédent *m*. de bagages.
excessive, *adj*. excessif.
exchange, *s*. échange *m.; (telephone)* bureau central *m.; foreign* ~ change *m.;* — *v.a*. échanger.
excite, *v.a*. exciter.
excitement, *s*. excitation *f*.
exclaim, *v.n*. s'écrier.
exclamation, *s*. exclamation *f*.
exclude, *v.a*. exclure.
exclusive, *adj*. exclusif.
excursion, *s*. excursion *f*.
excuse, *s*. excuse *f.;* — *v.a*. excuser.

execute, *v.a*. exécuter.
execution, *s*. exécution *f*.

executive, *adj. & s*. exécutif *m.;* agent *m*. d'exécution
exempt, *adj*. exempt (de); *v.a*. exempter (de).
exercise, *s*. exercice *m.;* — *v.a*. exercer.
exertion, *s*. effort *m*.
exhaust, *v.a*. épuiser.
exhaust-pipe, *s*. tuyau *m*. d'échappement.
exhibit, *v. a*. présenter, exhiber; exposer.
exhibition, *s*. exhibition *f.;* exposition *f*.
exist, *v.n*. exister.
existence, *s*. existence *f*.
exit, *s*. sortie *f*.
expand, *v.a*. étendre; dilater.
expansion, *s*. expansion *f*.
expect, *v.a*. attendre, s'attendre à; *(think)* croire.
expedient, *s*. expédient *m*.
expedition, *s*. expédition *f*.
expel, *v.a*. expulser.
expense, *s*. dépense *f*.
expensive, *adj*. coûteux, cher.
experience, *s*. expérience *f.;* — *v.a*. éprouver.
experiment, *s*. expérience *f.;* — *v.n*. faire des expériences, expérimenter.
experimental, *adj*. expérimental.
expert, *s*. expert *m*.
expire, *v.n*. expirer.
explain, *v.a*. expliquer.
explanation, *s*. explication *f*.
exploration, *s*. exploration.
explore, *v.a*. explorer.

explosion, *s*. explosion *f*.
export, *s*. exportation *f.;* ~*s* articles *m.pl*. d'ex-

portation; — *v.a.* exporter.

exporter, *s.* exportateur *m.*

expose, *v.a.* exposer.

exposure, *s.* exposition *f.*; révélation *f.*

express, *adj.* exprès; formel; exact; ~ *letter* lettre *f.* par exprès; — *s.* (*train*) express *m.*; — *v.a.* exprimer.

expression, *s.* expression *f.*

exquisite, *adj.* exquis.

extend, *v.a.* étendre; prolonger.

extension, *s.* extension *f.*; prolongation *f.*

extensive, *adj.* étendu, vaste.

extent, *s.* étendue *f.*

extinguish, *v.a.* éteindre.

extra, *adj.* supplémentaire.

extract, *s.* extrait *m.*; — *v.a.* extraire.

extraordinary, *adj.* extraordinaire.

extravagant, *adj.* extravagant.

extreme, *adj.* & *s.* extrême (*m.*).

extremely, *adv.* extrêmement.

extremity, *s.* extrèmité *f.*

eye, *s.* œil *m.*

eyebrow, *s.* sourcil *m.*

eyelid, *s.* paupière *f.*

eyepiece, *s.* oculaire *m.*

F

fable, *s.* fable *f.*

fabric, *s.* tissu *m.*; textile *m.*

face, *s.* visage *m.*; face *f.*; figure *f.*; *in* ~ *of* devant; — *v.a.* affronter, faire face à, braver.

facility, *s.* facilité *f.*

fact, *s.* fait *m.*; *in* ~ de fait; en effet.

factor, *s.* facteur *m.*; élément *m.*

factory, *s.* fabrique *f.*; usine *f.*

faculty, *s.* faculté *f.*

fade, *v.n.* se faner; ~ *away* s'évanouir.

fail, *v.n.* manquer (de); (*not succeed*) échouer, (*in an exam*) être refusé.

failure, *s.* insuccès *m.*

faint, *v.n.* s'évanouir.

fair, *adj.* beau; bel, belle; (*hair*) blond; (*just*) juste; (*weather*) clair; ~ *play* jeu loyal *m.*

fairly, *adv.* assez bien.

faith, *s.* foi *f.*

faithful, *adj.* fidèle.

falcon, *s.* faucon *m.*

fall, *v.n.* tomber; baisser; ~ *back on* avoir recours à; ~ *in* s'effondrer; ~ *off* se déprécier; ~ *under* être compris dans; — *s.* chute *f.*; baisse *f.*

false, *adj.* faux; artificiel.

falter, *v.n.* hésiter.

fame, *s.* réputation *f.*; renommée *f.*

familiar, *adj.* familier, intime (avec).

family, *s.* famille *f.*

famous, *adj.* célèbre, fameux.

fan[1], *s.* éventail *m.*; ventilateur *m.*

fan[2], *s.* passionné, -e *m. f.*, fervent *m.*

fancy, *s.* fantaisie *f.*, imagination *f.*

fantastic, *adj.* fantastique; fantasque.

far, *adv.* loin; ~ *off* au loin; *as* ~ *as* autant que; *by* ~ de beaucoup; *how* ~ *is it?* à

quelle distance est-ce?;
— *adj.* lointain.
fare, *s.* prix de (la) place
m.; (taxi) prix de la
course *m.; (food)* chère *f.*
farewell, *s.* adieu *m.; bid*
~ *to* dire adieu à.
farm, *s.* ferme *f.*
farmer, *s.* fermier *m.*
farming, *s.* agriculture *f.*
farmyard, *s.* cour *f.* de
ferme.
farther, *adv.* plus loin
(que).
fashion, *s.* mode *f.;*
manière *f.*
fashionable, *adj.* élégant.
fast, *adj.* vite, rapide;
be ~ *(clock)* avancer;
— *adv.* vite.
fasten, *v.a.* attacher.
fastener, *s.* attache *f.;*
agrafe *f.; zip* ~ ferme-
ture éclair *f.*
fat, *adj.* gros, gras; — *s.*
gras *m.;* graisse *f.*
fatal, *adj.* fatal.
fate, *s.* destin *m.,* sort *m.*
father, *s.* père *m.*
father-in-law, *s.* beau-
père *m.*
fatigue, *s.* fatigue *f.*
fault, *s.* défaut *m.;* faute
f.
faultless, *adj.* sans faute.
faulty, *adj.* défectueux.
favour, *s.* faveur *f.; in* ~
of en faveur de; *do a* ~
rendre un service (à).
favourable, *adj.* favorable.
favourite, *adj.* favori.
fear, *s.* crainte *f.;* —
v.a.& n. craindre.
fearful, *adj.* affreux,
effrayant.
feast, *s.* fête *f.;* festin *m.*
feat, *s.* exploit *m.*
feather, *s.* plume *f.*
feature, *s.* trait *m.;* caractéristique *f.;* ~ *film* le

grand film.
February, *s.* février *m.*
federal, *adj.* fédéral.
federation, *s.* fédération *f.*
fee, *s.* honoraires *m. pl.;*
(school) ~s frais *m. pl.*
feeble, *adj.* faible.
feed, *v. a.* nourrir; paître.
feel, *v.n.&a.* (se) sentir;
éprouver, ressentir,
(with hand) toucher;
tâter; ~ *cold* avoir
froid.
feeling, *s.* sentiment *m.*
fellow, *s.* camarade *m.;*
compagnon *m.;* gar-
çon *m.; (of a society)*
membre *m., (univer-
sity)* agrégé *m.*
fellowship, *s.* camaraderie
f.; communauté *f.*
female, *adj.* féminin;
(animal) femelle; — *s.*
femme *f.;* femelle *f.*
feminine, *adj.* féminin.
fence, *s.* clôture *f.;* pa-
lissade *f.;* — *v.a.*
enclore; *v. n.* faire de
l'escrime.
fencing, *s.* escrime *f.*
fender, *s.* pare-choc(s) *m.*
ferry, *s.* (passage *m.* en)
bac *m.*
ferry-boat, *s.* bac *m.*
fertile, *adj.* fertile.
fertilize, *v.a.* fertiliser.
festival, *s.* festival *m.*
fetch, *v.a.* aller chercher;
apporter.
feudal, *adj.* féodal.
fever, *s.* fièvre *f.*
few, *pron. & adj.* peu
(de); *a* ~ quelques-
(-uns).
fiancé, -e, *s.* fiancé, -e
m. f.
fibre, *s.* fibre *f.*
fiction, *s.* fiction *f.;*
(novels) romans *m. pl.*
field, *s.* champ *m.;*
(sport) terrain *m.*
fierce, *adj.* cruel, violent,

féroce.

fiery, *adj*. de feu; ardent.

fifteen, *adj*. & *s*. quinze *(m.)*.

fifteenth, *adj*. quinzième.

fifth, *adj*. cinquième; cinq.

fiftieth, *adj*. cinquantième.

fifty, *adj*. & *s*. cinquante *(m.)*.

fig, *s*. figue *f*.

fight, *s*. combat *m.;* lutte *f*.

fighter, *s*. combattant *m.;* avion *m*. de chasse.

figure, *s*. figure *f.; (arithm.)* chiffre *m*.

file[1], *s. (tool)* lime *f.;* − *.a*. limer.

file[2], *s*. classeur *m*., dossier *m.;* liasse *f.; (people)* file *f.;* − *v.a*. classer; enregistrer.

filing-cabinet, *s*. cartonnier *m*., fichier *m*.

fill, *v.a*. remplir; occuper; ∼ *in, up* remplir.

film, *s. (photo)* pellicule *f.; (cinema)* film *m*.

filter, *s*. filtre *m.;* − *v.a*. filtrer.

filthy, *adj*. sale; *(fig.)* obscène.

fin, *s*. nageoire *f*.

final, *adj*. final.

finally, *adv*. enfin.

finance, *s*. finance *f*.

financial, *adj*. financier.

find, *v.a*. trouver; ∼ *out* inventer, découvrir.

fine[1], *s. (penalty)* amende *f.;* − *v.a*. mettre à l'amende.

fine[2], *adj*. fin; beau.

finger, *s*. doigt *m.; first* ∼ index *m*.

finger-print, *s*. empreinte *f*. digitale.

finish, *v. a*. finir; terminer.

Finnish, *adj*. finlandais.

fir, *s*. sapin *m*.

fire, *s*. feu *m.; on* ∼ en feu; − *v.a*. mettre feu à; *(gun)* tirer; *v.n*. tirer.

fire-arm, *s*. arme *f*. à feu.

fire-brigade, *s*. les pompiers *m. pl*.

fire-engine, *s*. pompe *f*. à incendie.

fire-escape, *s*. escalier *m*. de sauvetage.

fireplace, *s*. cheminée *f*.

fire-station, *s*. poste *m*. d'incendie.

fireworks, *s.pl*. feu *m*. d'artifice.

firm[1], *s*. maison *f*. (de commerce).

firm[2], *adj*. ferme.

firmament, *s*. firmament *m*.

firmness, *s*. fermeté *f*.

first, *adj*. premier; − *adv*. premièrement; d'abord; *(railway)* en première; *at* ∼ d'abord.

firstly, *adv*. premièrement.

first-rate, *adj*. de premier ordre.

fish, *s*. poisson *m.;* − *v. a*. & *n*. pêcher.

fisher(man), *s*. pêcheur *m*.

fishmonger, *s*. poissonnier *m*.

fist, *s*. poing *m*.

fit[1], *s*. attaque *f.;* accès *m*.

fit[2], *adj*. convenable, bon, propre; en état (de), capable (de).

five, *adj*. & *s*. cinq *(m.)*.

fix, *v.a*. fixer; ∼ *up* arranger.

flag, *s*. drapeau *m.; (navy)* pavillon *m*.

flagrant, *adj*. flagrant.

flake, *s*. flocon *m*.

flame, *s.* flamme *f.*
flannel, *s.* flanelle *f.*
flap, *s.* coup *m.*, tape *f.*
flare, *v.n.* flamboyer.
flash, *s.* éclair *m.;* —
v.n. jeter des éclairs,
étinceler.
flashlight, *s.* flash (électronique) *m.*
flat¹, *adj.* plat; insipide;
(postitive) formel, net;
— *s.* plat *m.; (music)*
bémol *m.*
flat², *s.* appartement *m.;*
étage *m.*
flatter, *v.a.* flatter.
flattery, *s.* flatterie *f.*
flavour, *s.* saveur *f.*,
goût *m.*, arome *m.*
flax, *s.* lin *m.*
flea, *s.* puce *f.*
flee, *v.a.* & *n.* fuir, se
sauver.
fleece, *s.* toison *f.*
fleet, *s.* flotte *f.*
flesh, *s.* chair *f.;* viande *f.*
flexible, *adj.* flexible.
flight, *s.* vol *m. (birds,
stairs)* volée *f.; (fleeing)* fuite *f.*
flimsy, *adj.* ténu; fragile;
frivole.
fling, *v.a.* jeter.
flirt, *s.* coquette *f.;* —
v.n. flirter.
float, *v.n.* flotter; *v.a.*
faire flotter.
flock, *s.* troupeau *m.*,
troupe *f.*
flood, *s.* inondation *f.;
(tide)* flux *m.;* — *v.a.*
inonder.
flood-light, *v.a.* illuminer
par projecteurs.
floor, *s.* plancher *m.*,
parquet *m.; (storey)*
étage *m.*
flour, *s.* farine *f.*
flourish, *v.n.* fleurir;
prospérer.
flow, *v.n.* couler, s'écouler; — *s.* flux *m.;* cours

m.
flower, *s.* fleur *f.*
flower-bed, *s.* plate-bande
f.
flu, *s.* grippe *f.*
flue, *s.* tuyau *m.*
fluent, *adj.* facile, cou-
lant.
fluid, *adj.* & *s.* fluide *(m.)*.
fluorescent, *adj.* ~ *lamp*
tube *m.* fluorescent.
flush, *v.a.* inonder; nettoyer avec une chasse
d'eau; *v. n.* rougir.
flute, *s.* flûte *f.*
flutter, *s.* voltigement *m.;*
— *v. a.* agiter; *v. n.* voltiger.
fly¹, *s.* mouche *f.*
fly², *v.n.* voler; prendre
l'avion (pour).
foam, *s.* écume *f.; (beer)*
mousse *f.*
focus, *s.* foyer *m.*
fodder, *s.* fourrage *m.*
fog, *s.* brouillard *m.*
foil¹, *s.* feuille *f.;* tain *m.*
foil², *s. (fencing)* fleuret
m.
fold, *s.* pli *m.;* — *v.a.*
plier; envelopper;
(arms) croiser; ~ *up*
replier.
folding, *adj.* pliant.
foliage, *s.* feuillage *m.*
folk, *s.* gens *m. pl.*
follow, *v.a.* suivre; accompagner; *v.n.* sui-
vre; s'ensuivre; *as* ~s
comme suit.
follower, *s.* suivant *m.*,
compagnon *m.*, parti-
san *m.*
following, *adj.* suivant;
the ~ ce qui suit.
folly, *s.* sottise *f.*
fond, *adj. be* ~ *of* aimer.
food, *s.* nourriture *f.*,
aliments *m. pl.*
fool, *s.* sot *m.*
foolish, *adj.* sot; fou.

foot, *s.* pied *m.; on* ~ à pied.

football, *s.* football *m.;* ballon *m.*

foot-brake, *s.* frein *m.* à pied

foot-note, *s.* note *f.* (au bas de la page).

footstep, *s.* pas *m.*

for[1], *prep.* pour; *(in exchange for)* contre; *(because of)* à cause de; *(time)* pendant; *(in spite of)* malgré.

for[2], *conj.* car.

forbid, *v.a.* défendre; interdire.

force, *s.* force *f.;* violence *f.;* — *v.a.* forcer.

forearm, *s.* avant-bras *m.*

forecast, *s.* prévision *f.;* — *v.a.* prévoir.

forefinger, *s.* index *m.*

foreground, *s.* premier plan *m.*

forehead, *s.* front *m.*

foreign, *adj.* étranger.

foreigner, *s.* étranger, -ère *m. f.*

foremost, *adj.* premier; — *adv. first and* ~ tout d'abord.

foresee, *v.a.* prévoir.

forest, *s.* forêt *f.*

foretell, *v.a.* prédire.

foreword, *s.* avant-propos *m.*

orge, *v.a.* forger.

forgery, *s.* contrefaçon *f.;* faux *m.*

forget, *v.a.* oublier.

forgetful, *adj.* oublieux.

forgive, *v.a.* pardonner.

fork, *s.* fourchette *f.; (hay)* fourche *f.*

form, *s.* forme *f.; (bench)* banc *m.; (class)* classe *f.; (paper)* formule *f.;* ~ *of government* régime *m.;* — *v.a.* former.

formal, *adj.* formel.

formality, *s.* formalité *f.*

former, *pron.* le premier, la première; celui-là, celle-là; — *adj.* premier, -ère; précédent.

formerly, *adv.* autrefois.

formula, *s.* formule *f.*

forsake, *v. a.* abandonner.

fortieth, *adj.* quarantième.

fortification, *s.* fortification *f.*

fortify, *v.a.* fortifier.

fortnight, *s.* quinze jours *m. pl.*

fortress, *s.* forte sse *f.*

fortunate, *adj.* ureux.

fortunately *ad* heureusement

fortune, *s.* fortune *f*

forty, *adj. & s.* quarante *(m.).*

forward, *adv.* en avant; *go* ~ (s')avancer; — *adj.* avancé; — *v.a.* faire suivre; expédier.

forwarding, *s.* expédition *f.;* ~ *agency* entreprise *f.* de transport.

forwards, *adv.* en avant.

foul, *adj.* sale; impure; *(language)* ordurier.

found, *v. a.* fonder.

foundation, *s.* fondation *f.*

founder, *s.* fondateur *m.*

fountain, *s.* fontaine *f.*

fountain-pen, *s.* stylo-(graphe) *m.*

four, *adj. & s.* quatre *(m.).*

fourteen, *adj. & s.* quatorze *(m.).*

fourth, *adj.* quatrième; quatre.

fowl, *s.* poule *f.*

fox, *s.* renard *m.*

fraction, *s.* fraction *f.*

fracture, *s.* fracture *f.*

fragile, *adj.* fragile.

fragment, *s.* fragment *m.*

fragrant, *adj.* parfumé.

frame, *s.* *(picture)* cadre *m.; (structure)* charpente *f.; (window)* châssis *m.*

framework, *s.* charpente *f.*

frank, *adj.* franc.

frankness, *s.* franchise *f.*

fraud, *s.* fraude *f.*

free, *adj.* libre; ~ *of, from* exempt de.

freedom, *s.* liberté *f.*

freely, *adv.* librement; gratis.

freeze, *v.a.* geler.

freight, *s.* fret *m.*

French, *adj.* français; — *s. (language)* le français; *the* ~ les Français *m. pl.*

French-bean(s), *s. (pl.)* haricots *m.pl.* verts.

Frenchman, *s.* Français *m.*

Frenchwoman, *s.* Française *f.*

frequent, *adj.* fréquent; — *v. a.* fréquenter.

frequently, *adv.* fréquemment.

fresh, *adj.* frais, fraîche; nouveau, nouvel, -elle.

friar, *s.* moine *m.*

fricassee, *s.* fricassée *f.*

friction, *s.* friction *f.*

Friday, *s.* vendredi *m.*

fridge, *s.* frigo *m.*

friend, *s.* ami, -e *m. f.*

friendly, *adj.* aimable; ami; amical.

friendship, *s.* amitié *f.*

fright, *s.* peur *f.; take* ~ prendre peur.

frighten, *v.a.* effrayer.

frightful, *adj.* affreux; effrayant.

frock, *s.* robe *f.*

frog, *s.* grenouille *f.*

frolic, *s.* ébats *m. pl.; — v.n.* folâtrer, gambader.

from, *prep. (place)* de; *(time)* depuis; *(separation)* de, à; *(change)* de.

front, *s.* front *m.; devant m.; façade f.; in* ~ *of* en face de, en avant de; — *adj.* de devant.

front-door, *s.* porte *f.* d'entrée.

frontier, *s.* frontière *f.*

frost, *s.* gelée *f.*

frosty, *adj.* de gelée; *fig.* froid.

frown, *v.a. & n.* froncer les sourcils.

frozen, *adj.* gelé.

fruit, *s.* fruit *m.*

fruitful, *adj.* fructueux.

fruit-tree, *s.* arbre fruitier *m.*

frustrate, *v.a.* déjouer; décevoir; contrecarres.

fry, *v. a. & n.* (faire) frire.

frying-pan, *s.* poêle (à frire) *f.*

fuel, *s.* combustible *m.*

fulfil, *v.a.* accomplir.

full, *adj.* plein; complet; ~ *name* les nom et prénoms *m. pl.;* ~ *stop* point *m.*

full-time, *adj.* de toute la journée.

fully, *adv.* pleinement.

fume, *s.* fumée *f.*

fun, *s.* amusement *m.; for* ~ pour rire.

function, *s.* fonction *f.*

fund, *s.* fonds *m.*

fundamental, *adj.* fondamental.

funeral, *s.* funérailles *f. pl.*

funnel, *s.* entonnoir *m.; (steamer)* cheminée *f.*

funny, *adj.* drôle.

fur, *s.* fourrure *f.*

fur-coat, *s.* manteau *m.* de fourrure.

furious, *adj.* furieux.

furnace, *s.* fourneau *m.*

furnish, *v. a.* pourvoir (de), fournir; meubler (de).

furniture, *s.* meubles *m. pl.,* ameublement *m.;*

piece of ~ meuble *m.*
furrier, *s.* fourreur *m.*
furrow, *s.* sillon *m.*
further, *adv.* plus loin;
(any longer) davanta-
ge; — *adj.* ultérieur;
autre; plus lointain;
supplémentaire, nou-
veau.
furthermore, *adv.* en
outre, de plus.
fury, *s.* fureur *f.; (pers.)*
furie *f.*
fuss, *s.* embarras *m.;*
bruit *m.; make a* ~
faire des embarras; —
v. n. faire des embarras;
~ *about* faire l'affairé.
future, *s.* avenir *m.;*
(gramm.) futur *m.; in
the* ~ à l'avenir; — *adj.*
futur.

G

gain, *s.* gain *m.;* — *v.a.*
gagner.
gait, *s.* allure *f.*
gala, *s.* gala *m.*
gale, *s.* grand vent *m.*
gall, *s.* bile *f.;* fiel *m;*
amertume *f.*
gallant, *adj.* brave; galant.
gallery, *s.* galerie *f.*
gallon, *s.* gallon *m.*
gallop, *s.* galop *m.;* —
v.n. galoper.
gamble, *v. n.* jouer; — *s.*
jeu *m.*
game, *s.* jeu *m.;* partie *f.;*
(animal) gibier *m.*
gamekeeper, *s.* garde-
chasse *m.*
gang, *s.* bande *f.;* équipe *f.*
gangway, *s.* passage *m.*
gaol *see* **jail.**
gap, *s.* trou *m.;* brèche *f.;*
vide *m.*
gape, *v.n.* bâiller; *stand
gaping* gober des mou-
ches; ~ *at* regarder
bouche bée.
garage, *s.* garage *m.*

garden, *s.* jardin *m.*
gardener, *s.* jardinier *m.*
garlic, *s.* ail *m.*
garment, *s.* vêtement *m.*
garnish, *s.* garniture *f.;* —
v.a. garnir.
garter, *s.* jarretière *f.*
gas, *s.* gaz *m.*
gasp, *s.* soupir *m.*
gas-works, *s. pl.* usine *f.*
à gaz.
gate, *s.* porte *f.*
gateway, *s.* portail *m.*
gather, *v.a.* réunir; amasser; cueillir; *(under-
stand)* conclure; *v.n.*
s'assembler.
gathering, *s.* rassemble-
ment *m.;* abcès *m.*
gauge, *s.* jauge *f.;* calibre
m.; indicateur *m.;* —
v.a. jauger; calibrer.
gauze, *s.* gaze *f.*
gay, *adj.* gai.
gear, *s.* attirail *m.,* appareil *m.; (motorcar)*
vitesse *f.*
gear-box, *s.* boîte *f.* des
vitesses.
gear-lever, *s.* levier *m.* dès
vitesses.
general, *adj.* général; — *s.*
général *m. (pl.* géné-
raux).
generation, *s.* génération *f.*
generator, *s.* générateur
m.
generosity, *s.* générosité *f.*
generous, *adj.* généreux.
genial, *adj.* doux, douce;
bienfaisant.
genius *s.* génie *m.*
gentle, *adj.* doux, douce.
gentleman, *s.* gentleman
m.
genuine, *adj.* authentique; vrai.
geographical, *adj.* géographique.
geography, *s.* géographie *f*
geology, *s.* géologie *f.*
geometric(al), *adj.* géomé-

trique.

geometry, *s.* géométrie *f.*

germ, *s.* germe *m.*

German, *adj.* allemand; — —*s.* Allemand, -e *m.f.*

gesticulate, *v.n.* gesticuler.

gesture, *s.* geste *m.*

get, *v.a.* obtenir, procurer, trouver, recevoir; — *v.n.* arriver; *(become)* devenir; ~ *at* parvenir (à); ~ *in* entrer; ~ *off* partir; ~ *on* prospérer; *(agree)* s'accorder (avec); ~ *out of* sortir (de); ~ *over* surmonter; *(illness)* se remettre; ~ *up* se lever.

geyser, *s.* chauffe-bain *m.*

ghost, *s.* esprit *m.;* revenant *m.,* fantôme *m.*

giant, *s.* géant *m.*

gift, *s.* don *m.*

gifted, *adj.* bien doué.

gills, *s. pl.* ouïes *f.*

gin, *s.* genièvre *m.;* gin *m.*

giraffe, *s.* girafe *f.*

girdle, *s.* ceinture *f.;* — *v.a.* ceinturer.

girl, *s.* jeune fille *f.*

give, *v. a.* donner; ~ *up* renoncer à; livrer; *v.n.* ~ *in* céder (à).

glacier, *s.* glacier *m.*

glad, *adj.* heureux; content; joyeux.

gladness, *s.* joie *f.*

glance, *s.* coup *m.* d'œil,; — *v. n.* ~ *at* jeter un regard sur.

glare, *s.* lumière *f.* éblouissante; clinquant *m.;* — *v.n.* briller d'un éclat éblouissant.

glass, *s.* verre *m.;* *(pane)* vitre *f.;* ~*es* lunettes *f. pl.*

glazier, *s.* vitrier *m.*

gleam, *s.* lueur *f.;* — *v. n.* luire.

glide, *v. n.* glisser; planer.

glider, *s.* planeur *m.*

glimmer, *s.* lueur *f.;* — *v.n.* jeter une lueur faible.

glimpse, *s.* coup *m.* d'œil (rapide).

glitter, *v.n.* étinceler.

globe. *s.* globe *m.*

gloomy, *adj.* sombre.

glorious, *adj.* glorieux.

glory, *s.* gloire *f.*

glove, *s.* gant *m.*

glow, *v.n.* luire rouge; *(joy)* rayonner; *(coal)* être rouge; — *s.* chaleur *f.;* lumière *f.; fig.* ardeur *f.*

glue, *s.* colle (forte) *f.;* — *v.a.* coller.

gnat, *s.* cousin *m.;* moustique *f.*

gnaw, *v.a. & n.* ronger.

go, *v. n.* aller; ~ *away* s'en aller; ~ *back* retourner; ~ *back on one's word* reprendre sa parole; ~ *down* descendre; baisser; ~ *in for* s'occuper de, s'adonner à, faire (de); ~ *into* entrer dans; ~ *off* s'en aller; ~ *on* continuer; *(happen)* se passer; ~ *out* sortir; ~ *over, through* traverser; *(read)* parcourir; ~*up* monter; ~ *with* accompagner; ~ *without* se passer de; *let* ~ lâcher prise.

goal, *s.* but *m.*

goalkeeper, s. gardien (de but) *m.*

goat, *s.* bouc *f.,* chèvre *f.*

God, *s.* Dieu *m.*

god-child, *s.* filleul, -e *m. f.*

godfather, *s.* parrain *m.*

godmother, *s.* marraine *f.*

goggles, *s. pl.* bésicles *f.*

gold, *s.* or *m.*

golden, *adj.* d'or, en or.

golf, *s.* golf *m.*

good, *adj.* bon; ~ *evening!* bonsoir!; ~ *morning!* bonjour!; *be so ~ as to* avoir la bonté de; *make* ~ remplir; indemniser de; — *s.* bien *m.;* ~*s* marchandise *f.;* ~*s station* gare *f.* de marchandises; ~*s train* train *m.* de marchandises.

good-bye, *int.* & *s.* adieu *(m.).*

good-looking, *adj.* de belle mine, beau.

goodness, *s.* bonté *f.*

good-tempered, *adj.* de caractère facile, de bonne humeur.

goodwill, *s.* bonne volonté *f.*

goose, *s.* oie *f.*

gooseberry, *s.* groseille *f.* à maquereau.

gospel, *s.* évangile *m.*

gossip, *s.* bavardage *m.;* racontar *m.,* cancan *m.; (pers.)* compère *m.;* commère *f.;* — *v.n.* bavarder.

Gothic, *adj.* gothique.

govern, *v.a.* & *n.* gouverner.

governess, *s.* gouvernante *f.*

government, *s.* gouvernement *m.*

governor, *s.* gouverneur *m.*

gown, *s.* robe *f.*

grace, *s.* grâce *f.*

graceful, *adj.* gracieux.

gracious, *adj.* gracieux.

grade, *s.* grade *m.;* classe *f.*

gradual, *adj.* graduel.

graduate, *s.* gradué, -e *m. f.;* — *v.a.* graduer;

v.n. prendre ses diplômes.

grain, *s.* grain *m.*

grammar, *s.* grammaire *f.*

grammar-school, *s.* lycée *m.,* collège *m.*

grammatical, *adj.* grammatical.

gram(me), *s.* gramme *m.*

gramophone, *s.* gramophone *m.,* phonographe *m.*

gramophone-record, *s.* disque *m.*

grand, *adj.* grand; magnifique; ~ *stand* tribune *f.*

grandchild, *s.* petit-fils *m.,* petite-fille *f. (pl.* petits-enfants *m.)*

granddaughter, *s.* petite-fille *f.*

grandfather, *s.* grand-père *m.*

grandmother, *s.* grand' mère *f.*

grandson, *s.* petit-fils *m.*

granite, *s.* granit *m.*

granny, *s.* grand'maman *f.*

grant, *v.a.* accorder, concéder; accéder; ~ *that* admettre que; — *s.* don *m.,* concession *f.;* subside *m.*

grape, *s.* grain *m.* de raisin; *bunch of* ~*s* grappe *f.* de raisin.

grape-fruit, *s.* pamplemousse *f.*

graph, *s.* graphique *m.,* courbe *f.*

graphic, *adj.* graphique.

grasp, *v.a.* saisir; comprendre; — *s.* prise *f.,* étreinte *f.*

grass, *s.* herbe *f.;* gazon *m.*

grasshopper, *s.* sauterelle *f.*

grate, *s.* grille *f.;* — *v.a.*

râper; faire grincer; v.n. grincer.

grateful, *adj.* reconnaissant (à).

gratitude, *s.* reconnaissance *f.*

grave[1], *s.* tombe *f.*, tombeau *m.*

grave[2], *adj.* grave.

gravel, *s.* gravier *m.*

gravy, *s.* jus *m.*

gray, *adj.* gris.

graze, *v.n.* paître.

grease, *s.* graisse *f.*; — *v.a.* graisser.

great, *adj.* grand; *a* ~ many beaucoup (de).

greatly, *adj.* très; beaucoup.

greatness, *s.* grandeur *f.*

greed, *s.* avidité *f.*

greedy, *adj.* avide.

Greek, *adj.* grec, grecque; —*s.* Grec *m.*, Grecque *f.*

green, *adj.* vert.

greengrocer, *s.* fruitier, -ère *m. f.*

greenhouse, *s.* serre *f.*

greet, *v.a.* saluer.

greeting, *s.* salutation *f.*

grey, *adj.* gris.

grief, *s.* chagrin *m.*

grieve, *v.a.* affliger; *v.n.* s'affliger.

grill, *s.* gril *m.*; — *v.a.* griller.

grim, *adj.* sévère, menaçant. sinistre.

grin, *v.n.* grimacer; ~ *at* faire des grimaces à; — *s.* rire *m.*; grimace *f.*

grind, *v.a.* moudre.

grinder, *s.* (*tooth*) molaire *f.*

grindstone, *s.* meule *f.*

grip, *s.* étreinte *f.*; prise *f.*; — *v.a.* saisir, étreindre.

groan, *v. n.* gémir; — *s.* gémissement *m.*

grocer, *s.* épicier, -ère *m.*

f.; ~'s (*shop*) épicerie *f.*

grocery, *s.* épicerie *f.*

groove, *s.* rainure *f.*

gross, *adj.* gros; grossier; (*weight*) brut.

ground, *s.* terre *f.*; terrain *m.*; (*reason*) raison *f.*; ~s jardins *m. pl.*; — *v.a.* fonder.

group, *s.* groupe *m.*

grow, *v.a.* cultiver; *v.n.* (*pers.*) grandir; (*plant*) croître; (*become*) devenir.

growl, *s.* grondement *m.*; — *v.n.* gronder.

grown-up, *s.* grande personne *f.*

growth, *s.* croissance *f.*; culture *f.*; récolte *f.*

grudge, *s.* rancune *f.*; — *v.a.* donner à contrecœur à.

grumble, *v.n.* grommeler; — *s.* grognement *m.*

grunt, *s.* grognement *m.*; — *v.n.* grogner.

guarantee, *s.* garantie *f.*; (*pers.*) garant, -e *m. f.*; — *v.a.* garantir.

guard, *s.* garde *f.*; (*train*) conducteur *m.*; — *v.a.* garder; *v.n.* ~ *against* se garder.

guardian, *s.* gardien, -enne *m. f.*

guess, *v.a. & n.* deviner; conjecturer; — *s.* conjecture *f.*

guest, *s.* invité *m.*, convive *m.*; hôte, -esse *m. f.*

guide, *s.* guide *m.*; — *v. a.* guider.

guide-book, *s.* guide *m.*

guilt, *s.* culpabilité *f.*

guilty, *adj.* coupable (de).

guitar, *s.* guitare *f.*

gulf, *s.* golfe *m.*

gull, *s.* mouette *f.*

gullet, *s.* gosier *m.*

gum¹, *s.* gomme *f.;* — *v.a.* gommer.

gum², *s. (teeth)* gencive *f.*

gun, *s.* fusil *m.;* canon *m.*

gush, *v.i.* jaillir; — *s.* jaillissement *m.*

gutter, *s. (street)* ruisseau *m.*

gymnasium, *s.* gymnase *m.*

gymnastics, *s.* gymnastique *f.*

H

haberdashery, *s.* mercerie *f.*

habit, *s.* habitude *f.*

hail, *s.* grêle *f.;* — *v.n.* grêler.

hair, *s. (single)* cheveu *m.; (whole)* cheveux *m. pl.; (animal)* poil *m.*

hairdresser, *s.* coiffeur, -euse *m. f.*

half, *s.* moitié *f.;* demi *m.;* — *adj.* demi; ~ *an hour* une demi-heure *f.*

half-time, *s.* mi-temps *m.*

half-way, *adv.* à mi-chemin; à moitié chemin; à mi-distance.

hall, *s. (grande)* salle *f.; (college)* réfectoire *m.; (house)* vestibule *m.; (hotel)* hall *m.*

halt, *s.* halte *f.; v.a.* faire arrêter; *v.n.* faire halte; boiter.

ham, *s.* jambon *m.*

hammer, *s.* marteau *m.*

hand, *s.* main *f.; (pers.)* ouvrier *m.; (clock)* aiguille *f.; on the one* ~ ...*on the other* d'une part ... d'autre part.

handbag, *s.* sac (à main) *m.*

handbook, *s.* manuel *m.*

handkerchief, *s.* mouchoir *m.*

handle, *s.* manche *m.,* anse *f.;* poignée *f.;* bras *m.;* — *v.a.* manier; traiter.

hand-made, *adj.* fait à la main.

handsome, *adj.* joli.

handwriting, *s.* écriture *f.*

handy, *adj. (pers.)* adroit; *(thing)* commode.

hang, *v.a.* pendre; *(with tapestry)* tendre; ~ *up* accrocher; *v. n.* pendre; dépendre (de).

hanger, *s.* crochet *m.;* cintre *m.*

happen, *v.n.* arriver; se trouver; *I* ~*ed to be present* je me trouvais là par hasard.

happiness, *s.* bonheur *m.*

happy, *adj.* heureux.

harbour, *s.* port *m.*

hard, *adj.* dur; difficile; sévère; ~ *up* gêné; — *adv.* durement; *work* ~ travailler dur.

hardly, *adv.* à peine.

hardware, *s.* quincaillerie *f.*

hare, *s.* lièvre *m.*

harm, *s.* mal *m.;* tort *m.; do* ~ *to* nuire à.

harmful, *adj.* nuisible.

harmless, *adj.* inoffensif.

harmony, *s.* harmonie *f.*

harness, *s.* harnais *m.*

harp, *s.* harpe *f.*

harsh, *adj.* revêche; âpre; rigoureux.

hart, *s.* cerf *m.*

harvest, *s.* moisson *f.; (crop)* récolte *f.*

haste, *s.* hâte *f.; make* ~ se dépêcher.

hasten, *v.a.* hâter; *v. n.* se dépêcher.

hasty, *adj.* précipité.

hat, *s.* chapeau *m.*

hate, *v: a.* haïr; — *s.* haine *f.*

hateful, *adj.* odieux.
hatred, *s.* haine *f.*
haul, *v.a.* traîner; haler;
— *s.* traction *f.*
haulage, *s.* roulage *m.*;
frais *m.pl.* de roulage.
haunch, *s.* hanche *f.*
haunt, *v.a.* fréquenter;
hanter.
have, *v.a.* avoir; *(food)*
prendre; ~ *to* il faut
que, il faut (+ *inf.*);
had rather préférer
(+ *inf.*); ~ *on*
(clothes) porter.
haversack, *s.* havresac *m.*
hawk, *s.* faucon *m.*
hay, *s.* foin *m.*
hazard, *s.* hasard *m.*
hazy, *adj.* brumeux; *(fig.)*
vegue.
he, *pron.* il, *(alone)* lui;
~ *who* celui qui
head, *s.* tête *f.; chief)*
chef *m.: (river)* source
f.; — *v.a.* être en tête
de; — *adj.* principal.
headache, *s.* mal *m.* de
tête.
heading, *s.* en-tête *m.*
headlight, *s.* phare *m.*,
projecteur *m.*
headline, *s.* manchette *f.*
headmaster, *s.* directeur
m.
headquarters, *s. pl.* quartier *m.* général.
heal, *v.a.* guérir; *v.n.* se
guérir.
health, *s.* santé *f.*
healthy, *adj.* bien por-
tant; sain.
heap, *s.* amas *m.*, tas *m.*;
— *v.a.* ~ *up* entasser.
hear, *v.a.* entendre;
(listen to) écouter; *v. n.*
entendre; ~ *from* rece-
voir une lettre de; ~ *of*
avoir des nouvelles de;
entendre parler de.
heart, *s.* cœur *m.; by* ~
par cœur.

hearth, *s.* foyer *m.*
hearty, *adj.* cordial.
heat, *s.* chaleur *f.; (anger)*
colère *f.;* — *v.a.&n.*
chauffer.
heating, *s.* chauffage *m.*
heave, *v.a.* lever; pousser; jeter; *v.n.* se soulever.
heaven, *s.* ciel *m.*
heavy, *adj.* pesant; lourd.
hedge, *s.* haie *f.*
hedgehog, *s.* hérisson *m.*
heed, *s.* attention *f.; take*
~ *to* faire attention à.
heedless, *adj.* insouciant;
inattentif.
heel, *s.* talon *m.*
height, *s.* hauteur *f.*
heir, *s.* héritier *m.*
heiress, *s.* héritière *f.*
helicopter, *s.* hélicoptère
m.
hell, *s.* enfer *m.*
hello, *int.* allô!
helm, *s.* barre (du gouvernail) *f.*
helmet, *s.* casque *m.*
help, *v.a.* aider; secourir;
~ *oneself* se servir; — *s.*
aide *f.*
helpful, *adj. (pers.)* ser-
viable; *(thing)* utile.
helping, *s.* portion *f.*
helpless, *adj.* sans se-
cours.
hem, *s.* ourlet *m.; bord m.*
hen, *s.* poule *f.*
hence, *adv. (place, time)*
d'ici; *(reason)* de là.
her, *pron. (acc.)* la; *(dat.)*
lui; *(alone)* elle.
herb, *s.* herbe *f.*
herd, *s.* troupeau *m.*
here, *adv.* ici; *from* ~
d'ici; *look* ~! dites
donc!; ~ *he is!* le voici!
heritage, *s.* héritage *m.*
hermit, *s.* ermite *m.*
hero, *s.* héros *m.*
heroic, *adj.* héroïque.
heroine, *s.* héroïne *f.*

herring, *s.* hareng *m.*

hers, *pron.* à elle; le sien, la sienne, les siens, les siennes.

herself, *pron.* elle-même; *(reflex.)* se.

hesitate, *v.n.* hésiter.

hew, *v.a.* couper.

hiccough, hiccup, *s.* hoquet *m.*

hide, *v.a.* cacher; *v.n.* se cacher.

hideous, *adj.* hideux; horrible.

high, *adj.* haut; *(speed)* grand; *(price)* élevé; — *adv.* haut.

highness, *s.* altesse *f.*

highroad, highway, *s.* grande route *f.*

hike, *v.n.* faire du tourisme à pied.

hiker, *s.* touriste *f.*, randonneur, -euse (à pied) *m. f.*

hill, *s.* colline *f.*

hilly, *adj.* montueux.

him, *pron. (acc.)* le; *(dat.)* lui; *(alone)* lui.

himself, *pron.* lui-même; *(reflex.)* se; *by* ~ tout seul.

hinder, *v.a.* empêcher.

hindrance, *s.* empêchement *m.*

hinge, *s.* gond *m.*; charnière *f.*; — *v.n.* tourner (sur).

hint, *s.* allusion *f.*; avis *m.*; — *v.n.* ~ *at* faire allusion à.

hip, *s.* hanche *f.*

hire, *s.* louage *m.*; *for* ~ à louer; — *v.a. & n.* louer.

his, *pron.* son, sa; ses.

hiss, *s.* sifflement *m.*; — *v. a. & n.* siffler.

historic(al), *adj.* historique.

history, *s.* histoire *f.*

hit, *v.a.* frapper; at-

teindre; trouver; — *s.* coup *m.*; succès *m.*

hitch-hike, *v.n.* faire de l'auto-stop.

hive, *s.* ruche *f.*

hoard, *s.* magot *m.*, amas *m.*; — *v. a.* thésauriser; entasser.

hoarse, *adj.* raque.

hobby, *s.* dada *m.*

hockey, *s.* hockey *m.*

hoe, *s.* houe *f.*

hog, *s.* porc *m.*

hoist, *v.a.* hisser; —*s.* monte-charge *m.*

hold, *v.a.* tenir; retenir; maintenir; contenir; *(consider)* tenir (pour); ~ *back* retenir; ~ *out* tendre; offrir : ~ *that* soutenir que; — *v.n.* tenir; *(be true)* être vrai; ~ *on* ne pas lâcher prise; ~ *out* durer.

holder, *s.* possesseur *m.*

hole, *s.* trou *m.*

holiday, *s.* fête *f.*, jour *m.* férié; *(holidays)* vacances *f. pl.*, congé *m.*; *be on* être en congé, en vacance(s).

hollow, *adj.* reux, -euse; *fig.* faux, fausse.

holy, *adj.* saint; bénit.

home, *s.* foyer *m.*, demeure *f.*; *at* ~ chez soi, à la maison; — *adv.* chez soi; *come, go* ~ rentrer; — *adj.* domestique; de l'intérieur.

homeless, *adj.* sans asile.

homely, *adj.* simple; modeste.

homesickness, *s.* mal du pays *m.*

homeward, *adv.* vers la maison; ~ *bound* en retour.

honest, *adj.* honnête.

honesty, *s.* honnêteté *f.*

honey, *s.* miel *m.*

honeymoon, s. lune f. de miel.

honour, s. honneur m.; — v.a. honorer.

hood, s. capuchon m.; capeline f.; (motor) capote f.

hoof, s. sabot m.

hook, s. crochet m., croc m.; (fishing) hameçon m.

hoop, s. cercle m.

hoot, v.a. huer; v.n. corner; — s. huée f.

hooter, s. sirène f.; corne f., trompe f.

hop, v.n. sautiller.

hope, s. espérance f.; espoir m.; — v.n. espérer.

hopeful, adj. plein d'espoir.

hopeless, adj. sans espoir

horizon, s. horizon m.

horizontal, adj. horizontal.

horn, s. corne f.; trompe f.

horrible, adj. affreux, -euse.

horse, s. cheval m. (pl. chevaux).

horseback: on ~ à cheval.

horseman, s. cavalier m.

horse-race, s. course f. de chevaux.

horseshoe, s. fer m. à cheval.

hose, s. bas m. pl.

hospitable, adj. hospitalier.

hospital, s. hôpital m.

hospitality, s. hospitalité f.

host, s. hôte m.

hostel, s. pension f. pour étudiants, hôtellerie f.

hostess, s. hôtesse f.

hostile, adj. hostile (à).

hostility, s. hostilité f.

hot, adj. chaud.

hotel, s. hôtel m.

hour, s. heure f.

house, s. maison f.; (theatre) salle f.

household, s. ménage m.

housekeeper, s. gouvernante f.

housekeeping, s. ménage m.

housewife, s. ménagère f.

housework, s. travaux (m. pl.) domestiques; do the ~ faire le ménage.

how, adv. comment; ~ many, much? combien de?; ~ long? combien de temps?; ~ are you? comment allez-vous?

however, adv. de quelque manière que...; toutefois, cependant.

howl, v. a. & n. hurler; — s. hurlement m.

hue, s. couleur f.; cri m.

hug, v.a. serrer dans les bras.

huge, adj. énorme.

hullo, int. holà; allô!

hum, v. n. bourdonner; — s. bourdonnement m.

human, adj. humain.

humanity, s. humanité f.

humble, adj. humble.

humorous, adj. amusant; humoristique; drôle.

humour, s. humour m.; be in a ~ to être d'humeur à.

hundred, s. cent m.

hundredth, adj. centième.

hundredweight, s. quintal m.

Hungarian, adj. hongrois; — s. Hongrois, -e m. f.

hunger, s. faim f.; — v.n. avoir faim.

hungry, adj. affamé; be ~ avoir faim.

hunt, v.a. & n. chasser; (with hounds) chasser à courre; — s. chasse (à courre) f.

hunter, s. chasseur m.

hurl, *v.a.* jeter; lancer.

hurry, *s.* hâte; *be in a ~ to* être pressé de; — *v.n.* se presser; *~ up!* pressez-vous!; *v.a.* presser, hâter.

hurt, *v.a.* faire mal à; blesser; *(feelings)* froisser.

husband, *s.* mari *m.*

hush, *int.* chut!; — *s.* calme *m.;* — *v.a.* calmer.

husk, *s.* cosse *f.;* glume *f.;* — *v. a.* écosser, monder.

hut, *s.* cabane *f.*

hydrogen, *s.* hydrogène *m.*

hygiene, *s.* hygiène *f.*

hymn, *s.* hymne *m.*

hyphen, *s.* trait d'union *m.*

hypnotize, *v.a.* hypnotiser.

hypocrisy, *s.* hypocrisie *f.*

hysterical, *adj.* hystérique.

I

I, *pron.* je; moi.

ice, *s.* glace *f.*

ice-cream, *s.* glace *f.*

icy, *adj.* glacial.

idea, *s.* idée *f.*

ideal, *adj. & s.* idéal *(m.).*

identical, *adj.* identique.

identity, *s.* identité *f.; ~ card* carte *f.* d'identité.

idle, *adj.* désœuvré; *(lazy)* paresseux; — *v.a. ~ away* perdre.

idleness, *s.* oisiveté *f.;* paresse *f.*

if, *conj.* si; *as ~* comme si.

ignition, *s.* ignition *f.; (motor)* allumage *m.*

ignorant, *adj.* ignorant; *be ~ of* ignorer.

ignore, *v.a.* refuser de connaître.

ill, *adj.* malade; *(bad)* mauvais; *be taken ~* tomber malade; *~ luck* malheur *m.;* — *adv.* mal; — *s.* mal *m.*

illegal, *adj.* illégal.

illegitimate, *adj.* illégitime.

illicit, *adj.* illicite.

illness, *s.* maladie *f.*

illusion, *s.* illusion *f.*

illustrate, *v.a.* illustrer.

illustration, *s.* illustration *f.;* exemple *m.*

image, *s.* image *f.*

imagination, *s.* imagination *f.*

imagine, *v. a.* imaginer; se figurer.

imitate, *v.a.* imiter.

immediate, *adj.* immédiat.

immense, *adj.* immense.

immigrant, *adj. & s.* immigrant, -e *(m. f.).*

immigrate, *v. n.* immigrer

immigration, *s.* immigration *f.*

immoral, *adj.* immoral.

immortal, *adj.* immortel.

impatience, *s.* impatience *f.*

impatient, *adj.* impatient.

impediment, *s.* obstacle *m.*

impel, *v.a.* forcer; pousser.

imperfect, *adj. & s.* imparfait *(m.).*

imperial, *adj.* impérial.

impertinent, *adj.* impertinent.

implement, *s.* outil *m.,* ustensile *m.*

implication, *s.* implication *f.*

implore, *v.a.* implorer.

imply, *v.a.* impliquer; donner à entendre.

import, *v.a.* importer; *(mean)* signifier; — *s.* *(usu. pl.)* importation(s) *f.*

importance, *s.* importance *f.*

important, *adj.* important.

importer, *s.* importateur *m.*

impose, *v.a.* imposer (à).

impossibility, *s.* impossibilité *f.*

impossible, *adj.* impossible.

impression, *s.* impression *f.*

imprison, *v.a.* emprisonner.

imprisonment, *s.* emprisonnement.

improbable, *adj.* improbable.

improper, *adj.* impropre; inconvenant.

improve, *v.a.* améliorer; perfectionner; *v.n.* s'améliorer.

improvement, *s.* amélioration *f.; progrès m.*

impulse, *s.* impulsion *f.*

in, *prep.* dans; en; à; ~ *the morning* le matin; ~ *the evening* le soir; ~ *time* à temps; ~ *spring* au printemps.

inadequate, *adj.* insuffisant.

incapable, *adj.* incapable (de).

incense, *s.* encens *m.*

inch, *s.* pouce *m.*

incident, *s.* incident *m.*

incidental, *adj.* fortuit; incidental.

incline, *v. a. & n.* incliner.

include, *v.a.* comprendre; renfermer.

inclusive, *adj.* inclusif; ~ *of* y compris.

income, *s.* revenu *m.*

income-tax, *s.* impôt *m.* sur (le) revenu.

incompatible, *adj.* incompatible.

incompetent, *adj.* incom-

pétent.

inconsistent, *adj.* inconséquent.

inconvenient, *adj.* incommode, gênant.

increase, *v.a.&n.* augmenter; — *s.* augmentation *f.*

incredible, *adj.* incroyable.

incur, *v. a.* contracter; encourir; s'attirer.

incurable, *adj.* incurable.

indebted, *adj.* endetté.

indeed, *adv.* de fait; vraiment.

independence, *s.* indépendance *f.*

independent, *adj.* indépendant.

index, *s.* index *m.; (on dial)* aiguille *f.; (math.)* exposant *m.;* ~ *finger* index *m.*

Indian, *adj.* indien; des Indes; ~ *corn* maïs *m.* — *s.* Indien, -enne *m. f.*

india-rubber, *s.* gomme *f.*

indicate, *v.a.* indiquer.

indicator, *s.* indicateur *m.*

indifference, *s.* indifférence *f.*

indifferent, *adj.* indifférent (à).

indigestion, *s.* indigestion *f.*

indignant, *adj.* indigné.

indirect, *adj.* indirect.

indiscreet, *adj.* indiscret.

indiscretion, *s.* indiscrétion *f.;* imprudence *f.*

indispensable, *adj.* indispensable.

individual, *adj.* individuel; — *s.* individu *m.*

indoor, *adj.* d'intérieur.

indoors, *adv.* à la maison; *stay* ~ ne pas sortir.

induce, *v.a.* persuader; *(cause)* occasionner.

inducement, *s.* encouragement *m.* ~s attraits

m. pl.

indulge, v. a. se livrer (à); caresser; v.n. ~ in s'abandonner à; se laisser aller à.

indulgence, s. indulgence f.; laisser-aller m.

industrial, adj. industriel.

industrious, adj. travailleur.

industry, s. industrie f.

inefficient, adj. incapable; inefficace.

inestimable, adj. inestimable.

inevitable, adj. inévitable.

inexpensive, adj. peu coûteux, peu cher, bon marché.

inexperienced, adj. inexpérimenté.

inexplicable, adj. inexplicable.

infallible, adj. infaillible.

infamous, adj. infâme.

infant, s. enfant m. f.

infantry, s. infanterie f.

infant-school, s. école f. maternelle.

infection, s. infection f.

infer, v.a. conclure, déduire.

inferior, adj. inférieur.

infinitive, s. infinitif m.

infirm, adj. infirm.

infirmary, s. infirmerie f.

inflame, v.a. enflammer

inflammable, adj. inflammable.

inflate, v.a. gonfler.

inflexion, s. inflexion f.

inflict, v.a. infliger; imposer à.

influence, s. influence f.; — v.a. influencer.

influenza, s. grippe f.

inform, v.a. informer.

informal, adj. sans cérémonie.

information, s. information f.; renseignements

m. pl.

ingenious, adj. ingénieux.

ingenuity, s. ingéniosité f.

ingredient, s. ingrédient m.

inhabit, v.a. habiter.

inhabitant, s. habitant m.

inherit, v.a. & n. hériter (de).

inheritance, s. héritage m.

initial, s. initiale f.

initiative, s. initiative f.

injection, s. injection f.

injure, v.a. nuire à; blesser.

injury, s. préjudice m.; dommage m.; blessure f.

injustice, s. injustice f.

ink, s. encre f.

inland, s. & adj. intérieur (m.).

inn, s. auberge f.; taverne f.

inner, adj. intérieur.

innocence, s. innocence f.

innocent, adj. innocent.

innumerable, adj. innombrable.

inoculate, v.a. inoculer.

inquire, v.n. ~ about s'enquérir, se renseigner sur; ~ after demander après, demander des nouvelles de.

inquiry, s. demande f.; recherche f.; make inquiries about s'informer de; ~ office bureau m. des renseignements.

insane, adj. fou, fol, folle.

inscription, s. inscription f

insect, s. insecte m.

insecure, adj. peu sûr, mal assuré.

insensible, adj. sans connaissance; insensible.

inseparable, adj. inséparable.

insert, v. a. insérer (dans).

inside, s. & adj. intérieur

(m.); — adv. à l'inté-
rieur.

insignificant, adj. insignifiant.

insist, v.n. insister (on
sur).

insistence, s. insistance f.

inspect, v.a. inspecter.

inspection, s. inspection
f.

inspector, s. inspecteur m.

inspiration, s. inspiration f.

inspire, v.a. inspirer.

install. v.a. installer.

instalment, s. fraction f.,
acompte m.

instance, s. exemple m.;
cas m.; for ~ par
exemple.

instant, adj. urgent; — s.
instant m.

instead, adv. ~ of au lieu
de.

instinct, s. instinct m.

institute, s. institut m.;
— v.a. instituer.

institution, s. institution f.

instruct, v. a. instruire.

instruction, s. instruction f.

instructive, adj. instructif.

instrument, s. instrument
m.

instrumental, adj. instrumental.

insufficiency, s. insuffisance f.

insufficient, adj. insuffisant.

insult, s. insulte f.; —
v.a. insulter.

insurance, s. assurance f.

insure, v. a. (faire) assurer.

integral, adj. intégral; —
s. intégrale f.

integrity, s. intégrité f.

intellectual, adj. intéllec-
tuel.

intelligence, s. intelligence f.; (information)
renseignements m.pl.

intelligent, adj. intelligent.

intend, v. a. avoir l'intention de (faire qch.), se
proposer de; destiner
qn., qch. (à); vouloir
dire.

intense, adj. intense.

intensity, s. intensité f.

intent, s. intention f.; —
adj. ~ on absorbé dans.

intention, s. intention f.

intercontinental, adj. intercontinental.

interest, s. intérêt m.; —
v.a. intéresser.

interesting, adj. intéressant.

interfere, v. n. intervenir;
~ with gêner; se mêler
de.

interior, adj. & s. intérieur (m.).

intermediate, adj. intermédiaire.

intermission, s. interruption f., pause f.

internal, adj. interne; intérieur.

international, adj. international.

interpret, v.a. interpréter.

interpretation, s. interprétation f.

interpreter, s. interprète m.

interrogation, s. interrogation f.

interrupt, v.a. interrompre.

interruption, s. interruption f.

interval, s. intervalle m.

intervention, s. intervention f.

interview, entrevue f.;
interview m. f.

intimate, adj. intime.

into, prep. dans; en.

intolerable, adj. intolérable.

introduce, v.a. introduire; (pers.) présenter.

introduction, *s.* introduction *f.; (pers.)* présentation *f.*

invade, *v.a.* envahir.

invalid¹, *s.* malade *m. f.*

invalid², *adj.* invalide.

invasion, *s.* invasion *f.*

invent, *v.a.* inventer.

invention, *s.* invention *f.*

inverted, *adj.* ~ *commas* guillemets *m.*

invest, *v.a.* *(money)* placer.

investigate, *v.a.* rechercher.

investigation, *s.* investigation *f.*

investment, *s.* placement *m.*

invisible, *adj.* invisible.

invitation, *s.* invitation *f.*

invite, *v.a.* inviter.

invoice, *s.* facture *f.*

involuntary, *adj.* involontaire.

involve, *v.a.* envelopper (dans); impliquer (dans); entraîner.

inward, *adj.* intérieur; interne.

inwards, *adv.* intérieurement; en dedans.

Irish, *adj.* irlandais

iron, *s.* fer *m.* — *v.a.* repasser.

ironical, *adj.* ironique.

ironware, *s.* quincaillerie *f.*

ironworks, *s.* ferronnerie *f.*

irony, *s.* ironie *f.*

irregular, *adj.* irrégulier.

irrelevant, *adj.* non pertinent; hors de la question; inapplicable (à).

irresolute, *adj.* irrésolu.

irritate, *v.a.* irriter.

island, *s.* île *f.; (street)* refuge *m.*

isle, *s.* île *f.*

isolate, *v.a.* isoler.

isotope, *s.* isotope *m.*

issue, *s.* *(way out)* sortie *f.; (end)* issue *f.*, fin *f.*, résultat *m.; (publication)* publication *f.*, édition, *(paper)* numéro *m.*, *(money)* émission *f.;* — *v. a.* émettre; publier.

it, *pron.* il, elle; *(acc.)* le, la; *of it* en; *to* ~ y.

Italien, *adj.* italien; — *s.* Italien, -enne *m.f.*

itch, *s.* démangeaison *f.;* — *v.n.* démanger.

itchy, *adj.* galeux.

item, *s.* article *m.*, détail *m.*

its, *pron.* son, sa, *pl.* ses.

itself, *pron.* lui-même, elle-même; se; *(emphatic)* même.

ivory, *s.* ivoire *m.*

ivy, *s.* lierre *m.*

J

jack, *s.* *(cards)* valet *m.;* *(lifting)* cric *m.*, lève-auto *m.*

jackal, *s.* chacal *m.*

jacket, *s.* veston *m.*

jail, *s.* prison *f.*

jam¹, *s.* confiture *f.*

jam², *v.a.* serrer; coincer; encombrer; — *s.* encombrement *m.*

January, *s.* janvier *m.*

Japanese, *adj.* japonais.

jar, *s.* jarre *f.;* bocal *m.*

javelin, *s.* javeline *f.*

jaw, *s.* mâchoire *f.*

jealous, *adj.* jaloux.

jealousy, *s.* jalousie *f.*

jelly, *s.* gelée *f.*

jerk, *s.* saccade *f.;* secousse *f.*

jersey, *s.* jersey *m.*

jet, *s.* jet *m.;* *(gas)* bec *m.;* ~ *plane* avion *m.* à réaction.

Jew, *s.* Juif *m.*

jewel, *s.* bijou *m.*

jeweller, *s.* bijoutier *m.;* ~'s shop bijouterie *f.*

jewellery, *s.* bijouterie *f.*

jib, *s.* foc *m.*

job, *s.* tâche *f.;* travail *m. (pl. -aux);* emploi *m.; odd* ~s petits travaux *m.*

join, *v.a.* joindre; unir; se joindre (à); *v.n.* se joindre; s'unir; ~ *in* prendre part à.

joiner, *s.* menuisier *m.*

joint, *s.* joint *m.;* articulation *f.; (meat)* gros morceau *m.;* — *adj.* commun; indivis; co-; ~-stock company société *f.* par actions.

joke, *s.* plaisanterie *f.*

jolly, *adj.* joyeux; jovial.

journal, *s.* journal *m. (pl. -aux).*

journalist, *s.* journaliste *m.*

journey, *s.* voyage *m.*

joy, *s.* joie *f.*

joyful, *adj.* joyeux.

judge, *s.* juge *m.;* — *v.a.&n.* juger.

judg(e)ment, *s.* jugement *m.*

jug, *s.* cruche *f.;* pot *m.*

juggler, *s.* jongleur *m.*

Jugoslav, *adj.* yougoslave.

juice, *s.* jus *m.*

July, *s.* juillet *m.*

jump, *s.* saut *m.;* — *v.n. & a.* sauter.

junction, *s.* jonction *f.;* (gare *f.* d')embranchement. *m.*

June, *s.* juin *m.*

jungle, *s.* jungle *f.*

junior, *adj.* jeune.

jury, *s.* jury *m.*

juryman, *s.* juré *m.*

just, *adj.* juste; — *adv. (exactly)* juste; *(barely)* à peine; ~ *now* il n'y a qu'un instant; ~ *so* précisément.

justice, *s.* justice *f.*

justification, *s.* justification *f.*

justify, *v.a.* justifier.

jut, *v.n.* ~ *out* faire saillie.

juvenile, *adj.* juvénile; d'enfants.

K

kangaro, *s.* kangourou *m.*

keel, *s.* quille *f.*

keen, *adj.* aigu; tranchant; *(mind)* pénétrant; *be* ~ *on* être enthousiaste de, avoir la passion de.

keep, *v.a.* tenir; garder; maintenir; observer; ~ *back* retenir; ~ *up* soutenir; — *v. n.* rester; ~ *on* continuer à.

keeper, *s.* gardien *m.*

kerb, *s.* bordure *f.*

kernel, *s.* amande *f.*

kettle, *s.* bouilloire *f.*

key, *s.* clé *f.; (piano)* touche *f.; (music)* ton *m.*

keyboard, *s.* clavier *m.*

kick, *v.a.* donner un coup de pied (à); *v.n.* ruer; — *s.* coup *m.* de pied.

kid, *s.* chevreau *m.; (child)* gosse *m. f.*

kidney, *s.* rein *m.; (food)* rognon *m.*

kill, *v.a. & n.* tuer; abattre.

kilogram(me), *s.* kilogramme *m.*

kilometre, *s.* kilomètre *m.*

kind, *adj.* bon; bienveillant; aimable.

kindle, *v.a.* allumer; exciter; enflammer; *v.n.* s'enflammer.

kindly, *adj.* bon; doux.
kindness, *s.* bonté *f.;*
bienveillance *f.*
kindred, *s.* parenté *f.;*
parents *m.pl.*
king, *s.* roi *m.*
kingdom, *s.* royaume *m.*
kinsman, *s.* parent *m.*
kiss, *s.* baiser *m.; v.a.*
embrasser; baiser.
kit, *s.* fourniment *m.*
kitchen, *s.* cuisine *f.*

kite, *s.* cerf-volant *m.*
kitten, *s.* petit chat *m.*
knapsack, *s.* havresac *m.*
knee, *s.* genou *m. (pl.*
-x).
kneel, *v.n.* s'agenouiller;
~ *down* se mettre à
genoux.
knife, *s.* couteau *m.*
knight, *s.* chevalier *m.;*
(chess) cavalier *m.*
knit, *v. a.* tricoter; *(brow)*
froncer.
knob, *s.* bosse *f.;* bouton
m.
knock, *s.* coup *m.;* —
v.a. & *n.* frapper; ~
down renverser.
knocker, *s.* marteau *m.*
knot, *s.* nœud *m.;* —
v.a. nouer;*v.n.* se nouer.
know, *v.a.* savoir; con-
naitre; reconnaitre;
~*n for* connu pour; —
v.n. savoir; ~ *of* avoir
connaissance de; *let* ~
prévenir.
knowledge, *s.* connaissance *f.; (acquired)*
savoir *m.*
knuckle, *s.* articulation
f. de doigt.

L

label, *s.* étiquette *f.;* —
v.a. étiqueter.
laboratory, *s.* laboratoire

m.
labour, *s.* travail *m.;*
~ *(e)exchange* bureau
m. de placement; —
v.n. travailler.
labourer, *s.* travailleur *m.*
lace, *s.* dentelle *f.*
lack, *s.* manque; — *v.a.*
& *n.* ~ *(for)* manquer
(de).
lad, *s.* jeune garçon *m.*
ladder, *s.* échelle *f.*
lading, *s.* chargement *m.*
ladle, *s.* louche *f.*
lady, *s.* dame *f.; young* ~
jeune dame *f.;* de-
moiselle *f.,* jeune fille *f.*
lag, *v.n.* ~ *behind* rester
en arrière.
lake, *s.* lac *m.*
lamb, *s.* agneau *m.*
lame, *adj.* boiteux.
lamp, *s.* lampe *f.*
lamp-shade, *s.* abat-jour
m.
land, *s. (not sea)* terre *f.;*
(country) pays *m.;* —
v.n. & *a.* débarquer;
(plane) atterrir.
landing, *s.* débarquement
m.; (plane) atterris-
sage *m.*
landing-strip, *s.* piste *f.*
d'atterrissage.
landlady, *s.* propriétaire
f.; aubergiste *f.*
landlord, *s.* propriétaire
m.; aubergiste *m.*
landscape, *s.* paysage
m.
lane, *s.* ruelle *f.;* chemin
m.
language, *s.* langue *f.;*
(expression) langage *m.*
lap¹, *s.* genoux *m. pl.;*
(coat) pan *m.; (sports)*
tour (de piste) *m.*
lap², *v. a.* envelopper (de);
laper.
lapse, *s.* faute *f.;* chute
f.; lapsus *m.; (time)*
laps *m.;* — *v.n.* re-

tomber (dans); *(time)* s'écouler; *(fail)* faire un faux pas.

lard, *s.* saindoux *m.*

larder, *s.* dépense *f.*

large, *adj.* gros, grand; considérable; *at* ~ en liberté, en général.

lark, *s.* alouette *f.*

last, *adj.* dernier; — *adv.* dernièrement, en dernier lieu; — *v.n.* durer.

lasting, *adj.* durable.

latch, *s.* loquet *m.*

latch-key, *s.* clef *f.* de porte.

late, *adj.* tardif; *be* ~ être en retard; — *adv.* tard; ~*r on* par la suite; plus tard.

lately, *adv.* dernièrement, recemment.

latest, *adj.* récent, le dernier; *at (the)* ~ au plus tard.

lathe, *s.* tour *m.*

lather, *s.* mousse *f.*

Latin, *adj.* latin; — *s.* latin *m.*

latter, *adj.* dernier; *the* ~ ce dernier; celui-ci, celle-ci, ceux-ci.

laugh, *v.n.* rire *(at* de); — *s.* rire *m.*

laughter, *s.* rire *m.*

launch, *v.a.* lancer.

launching, *adj.* ~ *site* rampe *f.* à fusées.

laundry, *s.* buanderie *f.,* blanchisserie *f.*

lavatory, *s.* lavabo *m.* cabinet *m.* de toilette,

lavish, *adj.* prodigue (de). — *v.a.* prodiguer.

law, *s.* loi *f.;* droit *m.*

law-court, *s.* cour *f.* de justice, tribunal *m.*

lawful, *adj.* légal; permis; légitime.

lawn, *s.* pelouse *f.*

lawn-mower, *s.* tondeuse *f.*

lawsuit, *s.* procès *m.*

lawyer, *s.* homme *m.* de loi avoué *m.;* avocat *m.*

lay, *v.a.* coucher, poser, étendre; ~ *aside, by* mettre de côté; *(money)* réserver; ~ *down* poser; ~ *on* appliquer; *be laid up* être alité.

lay-by, *s.* refuge *m.,* garage *m.*

layer, *s.* couche *f.*

lazy, *adj.* paresseux.

lead¹, *s. (metal)* plomb *m.*

lead², *v.a. & n.* mener, conduire; ~ *the way* montrer le chemin.

leader, *s.* conducteur *m.; (newspaper)* éditorial *m.*

leadership, *s.* conduite *f.;* direction *f.*

leaf, *s.* feuille *f.; (book)* feuillet *m.;* page *f.*

leak, *s.* fuite *f.;* voie d'eau *f.;* — *v.n.* fuir.

lean, *adj.* maigre.

leap, *v. n. & a.* sauter; — *s.* saut *m.*

learn, *v.a. & n.* apprendre.

learning, *s.* savoir *m.,* science *f.*

leash, *s.* laisse *f.*

least, *adj.* le plus petit; le moindre; — *adv.* le moins; — *s.* moins *m.; at* ~ au moins, à tout le moins; *not in the* ~ pas le moins du monde.

leather, *s.* cuir *m.*

leave, *v. a.* laisser; quitter; *be left* rester; — *s.* permission *f.;* congé *m.; on* ~ en congé.

lecture, *s.* conférence *f. (on* sur); — *v.n.* faire des conférences.

lecturer, *s.* conférencier

m.; *(univ.)* professeur m. (de faculté).

left, *adj. & s.* gauche *(f.)*.

left-luggage office, *s.* consigne *f.*

leg, *s.* jambe *f.*; patte *f.*

legal, *adj.* légal.

legislature, *s.* législature *f.*

legitimate, *adj.* légitime.

leisure, *s.* loisir *m.; be at* ~ être de loisir.

lemon, *s.* citron *m.*

lemonade, *s.* limonade *f.*

lend, *v.a.* prêter.

length, *s.* longueur *f.; (time)* durée *f.*

lengthen, *v.a.* allonger; prolonger.

lens, *s.* lentille *f.*

leopard, *s.* léopard *m.*

less, *adj.* moindre; moins de; — *adv.* moins; ~ *than* moins de.

lessen, *v. a. & n.* diminuer.

lesson, *s.* leçon *f.*

lest, *conj.* de peur que.

let, *v.a.* laisser, permettre à; *(house)* louer; ~ *me go* laisse-moi aller; ~ *down* ~ laisser tomber (à); ~ *in* laisser entrer.

letter, *s.* lettre *f.;* ~*s* belles-lettres *f. pl.*

lettuce, *s.* laitue *f.*

level, *s.* niveau *m.;* — *adj.* uni; plat; horizontal; — *v.a.* niveler; pointer.

lever, *s.* levier *m.*

levy, *s.* levée *f.;* — *v.a.* lever.

lexicon, *s.* lexique *m.*

liability, *s.* responsabilité *f.; liabilities* passif *m.*

liable, *adj.* responsable (de); sujet (à).

liar, *s.* menteur, *m.*

liberal, *adj.* libéral; généreux.

liberty, *s.* liberté *f.*

librarian, *s.* bibliothécaire *m. f.*

library, *s.* bibliothèque *f.*

licence, *s.* permission *f.;* permis *m.*, patente *f.; (excess of liberty)* licence *f.*

license, *v.a.* accorder un permis (à).

lick, *v.a.* lécher.

lid, *s.* couvercle *m.*

lie¹, *s.* mensonge *m.;* — *v.n.&a.* mentir.

lie², *v.n.* être couché; *(dead)* reposer; *(be situated)* se trouver; ~ *down* se coucher; *it* ~*s with you* cela dépend de vous.

lieutenant, *s.* lieutenant *m.*

life, *s.* vie *f.*

life-insurance, *s.* assurance *f.* sur la vie.

lifeless, *adj.* inanimé.

lift, *v.a.* lever; *fig.* élever; ~ *up* soulever; — *s. (apparatus)* ascenseur *m.; give s. o. a* ~ faire monter qn (dans sa voiture).

light¹, *s.* lumière *f.;* éclairage *f.;* jour *m.;* lampe *f.; (fire)* feu *m.; come to* ~ se révéler; — *v. a.* allumer; éclairer; *v.n.* s'éclairer; — *adj.* clair; éclairé.

light², *adj.* léger; *make* ~ *of* faire peu de cas de.

lighten¹, *v.a.* éclairer; *v.n.* faire des éclairs.

lighten², *v.a.* alléger.

lighter, *s.* briquet *m.*

lighthouse, *s.* phare *m.*

lighting, *s.* éclairage *m.*

lightning, *s.* éclair *m.*

like¹, *adj.* semblable, pareil, ressemblant; — *prep.* comme.

like², *v.a.* aimer; *I should* ~ *to* je voudrais + *inf.*

likely, *adv.* probable.

likeness, *s.* ressemblance *f.;* portrait *m.*

lily, *s.* lis *m.*

limb, *s.* membre *m.*

limit, *s.* limite *f.; v.a.* limiter.

limited, *adj.* ~ *liability company* société anonyme *f.*

line, *s.* ligne *f.; (poetry)* vers *m.; railw.)* voie *f.;* — *v.a. (garment)* doubler; *v.n.* ~ *up* s'aligner; faire la queue.

linen, *s.* toile *f.;* ligne *m.*

lining, *s.* doublure *f.*

link, *s.* chaînon *m., fig.* lien *m.;* — *v.a.* lier; unir.

lion, *s* lion *m.*

lip, *s.* lèvre *f.*

lipstick, *s.* rouge *m.* à lèvres.

liquid, *adj..* & *s.* liquide *(m.)*

list, *s.* liste *f.;* — *v.a.* enregistrer.

listen, *v.n.* (also ~ *in)* écouter.

listener, *s.* auditeur, -trice *m. f.*

literary, *adj.* littéraire.

literature, *s.* littérature *f.*

litter, *s.* litière *f.*

little, *adj.* petit; peu de.

live, *v.n.* vivre; *(reside)* habiter, demeurer; ~ *on* vivre de.

lively, *adv.* vivant, gai.

liver, *s.* foie *m.*

living-room, *s.* salle *f.* de séjour.

load, *s.* charge *f.;* fardeau *m.;* — *v.a.* charger.

loaf, *s.* pain *m.*

loan, *s.* prêt *m.;* emprunt *m.*

loathe, *v.a.* détester.

lobby, *s.* couloir *m.,* vestibule *m.*

lobster, *s.* homard *m.*

local, *adj.* local.

location, *s.* emplacement *m.;* situation *f.*

lock[1], *s.* serrure *f.*

lock[2], *s. (hair)* boucle *f.*

locksmith, *s.* serrurier *m.*

lodger, *s.* locataire *m. f.*

lodging, *s.* logement *m.* *furnished* ~s garni *m.*

log, *s.* bûche *f.;* bille *f.*

logical, *adj.* logique.

loin, *s. (pork)* longe *f.; (beef)* aloyau *m.;* rein *m.*

lonely, *adj.* solitaire.

long[1], *adj.* long; *a* ~ *time (since)* depuis longtemps; *be* ~ *in* être long à; — *adv.* longtemps; *how* ~? combien de temps?; ~ *ago* il y a longtemps.

long[2], *v.n.* ~ *for* désirer qch., soupirer après.

long-distance, *adj.* à (longue) distance.

long-play(ing), *adj.* ~ *record* microsillon *m.*

look, *v. n.* & *a.* regarder; ~ *after* soigner; ~ *at* regarder; ~ *back* regarder en arrière; ~ *for* chercher; ~ *into* examiner; ~ *out* être sur ses gardes, *int.* gare!; ~ *over* parcourir; ~ *up* chercher; — *s.* regard *m.;* air *m.;* aspect *m.*

looking-glass, *s.* miroir *m.*

loom, *s.* métier *m.* de tisserand.

loop, *s.* boucle .

loose, *adj.* lâche; délié; détaché; vague.

loosen, *v.a.* desserrer.

lord, *s.* maître *m.;* seigneur *m.*

lorry, *s.* camion *m.*

lose, *v.a.* & *n.* perdre.

loss, s. perte f.

lot, s. sort m.; (portion) partage m.; a ~ of beaucoup de.

lottery, s. loterie f.

loud, adj. fort; bruyant.

loud-speaker, s. haut-parleur m.

lounge, s. (grand) vestibule m.; foyer m., hall m.; — v.n. flâner.

lounge-suit, s. complet veston m.

love, s. amour m.; — v.a. aimer.

lovely, adj. beau, bel, belle; charmant.

lover, s. amoureux m.; amant m.

low, adj. & adv. bas.

lower, adj. inférieur; (deck) premier (pont); — v.a. baisser; (flags, sails) amener.

loyal, adj. loyal; fidèle.

loyalty, s. loyauté f.

lubricate, v.a. lubrifier.

luck, s. chance f.; bad ~ malchance f.

lucky, adj. heureux.

luggage, s. bagages m. pl.

luggage-van, s. fourgon m. (aux bagages).

lump, s. morceau m.

lunch, s. déjeuner m.; — v.n. déjeuner.

lung, s. poumon m.

lute, s. luth m.

luxurious, adj. luxueux.

luxury, s. luxe m.

lyre, s. lyre f.

lyric, adj. lyrique.

M

machine, s. machine f.

machinery, s. machines f.pl.; fig. mécanisme m.

mackintosh, s. imperméable m.

mad, adj. fou, fol, folle.

madam, s. madame f.

magazine, s. revue f.; (rifle) magasin m.

magic, adj. magique.

magistrate, s. magistrat m.

magnet, s. aimant m.

magnetic, adj. magnétique.

magnificent, adj. magnifique.

maid, s. (jeune) fille f.; bonne f.

mail, s. courrier m.

mail-boat, s. paquebot-poste m.

mail-van, s. wagon-poste m.

main, adj. principal.

mainland, s. terre f. ferme.

mainly, adv. principalement.

mains, s. secteur (de courant) m.

maintain, v.a. maintenir; soutenir.

maintenance, s. entretien m.

majesty, s. majesté f.

major, s. commandant m.; — adj. majeur.

majority, s. majorité f.; plupart f.

make, v.a. & n. faire; rendre; ~ away with détruire; ~ for se diriger vers; ~ off décamper; ~ out comprendre; prouver; ~ over céder; ~ up (list) dresser; (invent) inventer; ~ up for compenser; — s. forme f., fabrication f.

male, adj. mâle; masculin; — s. mâle m.

malice, s. méchanceté

f.

man, *s.* homme *m.*

manage, *v. a.* conduire, diriger, gérer, gouverner; *I shall* ~ *it* j'en viendrai à bout.

management, *s.* direction *f.;* gérance *f.*

manager, *s.* directeur *m.;* gérant *m.*

manicure, *s.* manicure *n. f.*

manifest, *adj.* manifeste; — *v.a .* manifester.

manipulate, *v.a.* manipuler.

manner, *s.* manière *f.;* air *m.;* ~*s* manières *f. pl.;* *(morals)* mœurs *f. pl.*

manœuvre, *s.* manœuvre *f.;* — *v.a.* faire manœuvrer.

manor, *s.* manoir *m.*

manual, *adj. & s.* manuel *(m.).*

manufacture, *s.* manufacture *f.;* — *v.a.* fabriquer.

manufacturer, *s.* manufacturier *m.;* fabricant *m.*

manure, *s.* fumier *m.*

manuscript, *s.* manuscrit *m.*

many, *adj.* beaucoup de.

map, *s.* carte *f.* géographique.

marble, *s.* marbre *m.*

march, *s.* marche *f.;* — *v.n.* marcher.

March, *s.* mars *m.*

mare, *s.* jument *f.*

margarine, *s.* margarine *f.*

marine, *s.* marine *f.;* — *adj.* marin; maritime.

mariner, *s.* marin *m.*

mark, *s.* marque *f.; (aim)* but *m.; (school)* point *m.; (coin)* marc *m.;* — *v.a.* marquer; souligner.

market, *s.* marché *m.*

market-price, *s.* prix *m.* courant.

marmalade, *s.* marmelade *f.* (d'oranges).

marriage, *s.* mariage *m.*

married, *adj.* marié.

marry, *v. a.* épouser; *v. n. (get married)* se marier.

marsh, *s.* marais *m.*

marshal, *s.* maréchal *m.;* — *v.a.* ranger; conduire.

martial, *adj.* martial.

martyr, *s.* martyr *m.*

marvel, *s.* merveille *f.;* — *v.n.* s'étonner (de).

marvellous, *adj.* merveilleux.

masculine, *adj.* mâle; masculin.

mask, *s.* masque *m.*

mason, *s.* maçon *m.*

mass[1]**,** *s.* masse *f.;* majorité *f.*

mass[2]**,** *s. (eccles.)* messe *f.*

mast, *s.* mât *m.*

master, *s.* maître *m.;* — *v. a.* maîtriser

mat, *s. (door)* paillasson *m.; (table)* dessous de plat, *m.*

match[1]**,** *s.* égal, -e *m.f.,* pareil, -le *m. f.,* mariage *m.; (pers.)* parti *m.; (sport)* match *m.;* — *v.a.* assortir; *v.n.* s'assortir.

match[2]**,** *s.* allumette *f.*

mate, *s.* camarade *m.; (birds)* mâle *m.,* femelle *f.; (chess)* mat *m.; (ship)* second *m.;* — *v.a.* marier (à); *v.n.* s'accoupler.

material, *s.* matière *f.;* — *adj.* matériel.

maternal, *adj.* maternel.

mathematical, *adj.* mathématique.

mathematics, *s.* mathématiques *f. pl.*

matinée, *s.* matinée *f.*

matron, *s.* mère de famille, *f.; (hospital)* infirmière-en-chef *f.;* surveillante *f.*

matter, *s.* matière *f.;* affaire *f.;* sujet *m.;* chose *f.; as a ~ of fact* en fait; *what is the ~?* qu'est-ce qu'il y a?; — *v.n.* importer; *it does not ~* n'importe.

mattress, *s.* matelas *m.; spring ~* sommier *m.,* matelas *m.* à ressort.

mature, *adj.* mûr; — *v.a. & n.* mûrir.

maturity, *s.* maturité *f.*

May, *s.* mai *m.*

may, *v. aux.* pouvoir; *~ I?* vous permettez?

maybe, *adv.* peut-être.

mayor, *s.* maire *m.*

me, *pron. (acc.)* me; *(alone, with prep.)* moi.

meadow, *s.* pré *m.*

meal, *s.* repas *m.*

mean¹, *s.* moyen terme, *m.; (math.)* moyenne *f.; ~s* moyens *m. pl., (way to do)* moyen *m.; by ~s of* au moyen de: *by all ~s* mais certainement; *by no ~s* en aucune façon; — *adj.* moyen.

mean², *v.a. (signify)* vouloir dire, signifier: *(wish)* vouloir (faire), avoir l'intention (de); destiner; *what does that word ~?* que signifie ce mot?; *what do you ~ by that?* qu'entendez-vous par là?

mean³, *adj.* misérable, pauvre; bas, vil; ladre.

meaning, *s.* intention *f.;* sens *m.*

meantime, -while, *adv. (in the ~)* dans l'intervalle, pendant ce temps-là.

measure, *s.* mesure *f.;* — *v.a.* mesurer.

meat, *s.* viande *f.; (food)* nourriture *f.*

mechanic, *s.* artisan *m.,* mécanicien *m.*

mechanical, *adj.* mécanique.

mechanics, *s.* mécanique *f.*

mechanism, *s.* mécanisme *m.*

mechanize, *v.a.* mécaniser.

medal, *s.* médaille *f.*

medical, *adj.* médical; *~ student* étudiant *m.* en médecine.

medicine, *s.* médecine *f.*

meditate, *v.a.&n.* méditer.

medium, *s.* moyen terme *m.;* milieu *m.;* — *adj.* moyen.

meet, *v.a.* rencontrer (qn.), se rencontrer avec (qn.); *(face)* affronter; *(expenses)* faire face à; *~ sy at the station* aller recevoir qn. à la gare; — *v. n.* se rencontrer; *~ with* rencontrer; éprouver.

meeting, *s.* rencontre *f.;* réunion *f.*

mellow, *adj.* mûr; moelleux.

melody, *s.* mélodie *f.*

melon, *s.* melon *m.*

melt, *v.a.* fondre.

member, *s.* membre *m.*

memorial, *s.* monument *m.;* mémorial *m.*

memory, *s.* mémoire *f.;* souvenir *m.*

mend, *v. a.* raccommoder; réparer; corriger.

mental, *adj.* mental.

mention, *v. a.* mentionner; citer; *don't* ~ *it* il n'y a pas de quoi.

merchandise, *s.* marchandise *f.*

merchant, *s.* négociant *m.;* commerçant *m.*

merciful, *adj.* miséricordieux.

mercy, *s.* pitié *f.;* miséricorde *f.*

mere, *adj.* seul.

merely, *adv.* purement; simplement.

merit, mérite *m.;* — *v.a.* mériter.

merry, *adj.* gai.

mess, *s.* gâchis *m.; make a* ~ *of* gâcher.

message, *s.* message *m.*

messenger, *s.* messager *m.*

metal, *s.* métal *m.*

meteorology, *s.* météorologie *f.*

method, *s.* méthode *f.*

metre, *s.* mètre *m.*

microphone, *s.* microphone *m.*

microscope, *s.* microscope *m.*

middle, *s.* milieu *m.;* — *adj.* du milieu; moyen.

midnight, *s.* minuit *m.*

might, *s.* force *f.;* puissance *f.*

mighty, *adj.* fort; puissant

migrate, *v.n.* émigrer.

mild, *adj.* doux; bénin.

mile, *s.* mille *m.*

mileage, *s.* parcours *m.;* *(expense)* prix *m.* par mille.

military, *adj.* militaire.

milk, *s.* lait *m.*

milkman, *s.* laitier *m.*

mill, *s.* moulin *m.;* fabrique *f.*

miller, *s.* meunier *m.*

milliner, *s.* modiste *f.*

million, *s.* million *m.*

mince, *s.* hachis *m.;* —

v.a. hacher.

mind, *s.* esprit *m.;* *(remembrance)* souvenir *m.; (opinion)* pensée *f.,* avis *m.; change one's* ~ changer d'avis; *make up one's* ~ *to* se décider à, se résigner à; — *v.a.* faire attention à, prendre garde à; écouter; *(look after)* garder; *(trouble about)* s'inquiéter de; *do you* ~ *my smoking?* est-ce que cela vous gêne que je fume?; *I don't* ~ cela m'est égal; *never* ~ ça ne fait rien.

mine¹, *s.* mine *f.;* — *v.a.* miner.

mine², *pron.* à moi; le mien.

miner, *s.* mineur *m.*

mineral, *adj. & s.* minéral *(m.).*

minister, *s.* ministre *m.*

ministry, *s.* ministère *m.*

minor, *adj.* mineur.

minority, *s.* minorité.

mint, *s.* Hôtel *m.* de la Monnaie; *(plant)* menthe *f.*

minus, *adj.* en moins; — *adv.* moins.

minute, *s.* minute *f.;* petit moment, *m.;* ~ *hand* grande aiguille *f.*

miracle, *s.* miracle *m.*

mirror, *s.* miroir *m.*

miscarry, *v.n.* avorter.

miscellaneous, *adv.* divers.

mischief, *s.* mal *m.;* méchanceté *f.*

miser, *s.* avare *m.*

miserable, *adj.* misérable; malheureux.

misery, *s.* misère *f.*

misfortune, *s.* malheur *m.*

miss¹, *v.a.* manquer; ne pas entendre; ne pas voir; s'apercevoir de l'absence (de); ~ out omettre; *be ~ing* manquer.

miss², *s.* mademoiselle *f.*

missile, *s.* projectile *m.*

mission, *s.* mission *f.*

missionary, *s.* missionnaire *m. f.*

mist, *s.* brouillard *m.*, brume *f.*

mistake, *s.* erreur *f.*, méprise *f.*; faute *f.*; — *v.a.* se tromper de; ~ *for* prendre pour; *be ~n* se tromper.

mistress, *s.* maîtresse *f.* (de maison).

mistrust, *s.* méfiance *f.*

misty, *adj.* brumeux.

misunderstand, *v. a.* comprendre mal.

mitten, *s.* mitaine *f.*

mix, *v.a.* mêler; mélanger; *be ~ed up in* être mêlé à.

mixture, *s.* mélange *m.*; mixture *f.*

moan, *v.n.* gémir; — *s.* gémissement *m.*

mob, *s.* foule *f.*, populace *f.*

mobilization, *s.* mobilisation *f.*

mobilize, *v.a.* mobiliser.

mock, *s.* moquerie *f.*; — *adj.* faux; — *v.a.* railler.

mockery, *s.* moquerie *f.*

model, *s.* modèle *m.*

moderate, *adj.* modéré; — *v.a.* modérer.

moderation, *s.* modération *f.*

modern, *adj.* moderne.

modest, *adj.* modeste.

modesty *s.* modestie *f.*

modify, *v.a.* modifier.

moist, *adj.* moite, humide.

moisten, *v.a.* humecter.

moisture, *s.* humidité *f.*

molecule, *s.* molécule *f.*

moment, *s.* moment *m.*

momentary, *adj.* momentané.

monarch, *s.* monarque *m.*

monarchy, *s.* monarchie *f.*

Monday, *s.* lundi *m.*

money, *s.* argent *m.*; monnaie *f.*

money-order, *s.* mandat *m.*

monk, *s.* moine *m.*

monkey, *s.* singe *m.*

monopolize, *v.a.* monopoliser.

monopoly, *s.* monopole *m.*

monotonous, *adj.* monotone.

monstrous, *adj.* monstrueux.

month, *s.* mois *m.*

monthly, *adj.* mensuel; — *adv.* mensuellement.

monument, *s.* monument *m.*

monumental, *adj.* monumental.

mood, *s.* humeur *f.*; mode *m.*

moon, *s.* lune *f.*

moonlight, *s.* clair *m.* de lune.

moor, *s.* bruyère *f.*

mop, balai *m.*: — *v.a.* (also ~ *up*) éponger, essuyer.

moral, *s.* morale *f.*; ~*s* moeurs *f. pl.*; — *adj.* moral; de morale.

more, *adj. & pron.* plus de; davantage de; ~ *than* plus que; *some* ~ en ... davantage; *no* ~ n'en ... pas davantage, ne ... plus; — *adv.* plus; davantage; ~ *and* ~ de plus en plus.

moreover, *adv.* de plus.

morning, *s.* matin *m.*; *in the* ~ le matin; — *adj.* du matin.

mortal, *adj. & s.* mortel (*m., f.*).

mortality, *s.* mortalité *f.*

mortgage, *s.* hypothèque *f.;* — *v. a.* hypothéquer.

mosquito, *s.* moustique *f.*

moss, *s.* mousse *f.*

most, *adj. & pron.* le plus (de), la plupart (de); *at the* ~ tout au plus; ~ *people* la plupart des gens; *make the* ~ *of* tirer le meilleur parti de; — *adv.* très, fort, bien.

mostly, *adv.* pour la plupart; principalement; la plupart du temps.

motel, *s.* motel *m.*

moth, *s.* mite *f.*

mother, *s.* mère *f.*

mother-in-law, *s.* belle-mère *f.*

mother-tongue, *s.* langue *f.* maternelle.

motion, *s.* mouvement *m.;* signe *m.;* (*proposal*) motion *f.*

motionless, *adj.* immobile.

motive, *s.* motif *m.*

motor, *s.* moteur *m.*

motor-bus, *s.* autobus *m.*

motor-car, *s.* auto(mobile) *f.*

motor-coach, *s.* autocar *m.*

motor-cycle, *s.* motocyclette *f.*

motor-scooter, *s.* scooter *m.*

motorway,, *s.* autoroute *f.*

mould, *s.* moule *m.;* — *v.a.* mouler.

mount, *s.* mont *m.;* — *v.a. & n.* monter.

mountain, *s.* montagne *f.*

mountaineering, *s.* alpinisme *m.*

mountainous, *adj.* montagneux.

mourn, *v. n. & a.* pleurer, (se) lamenter.

mouse, *s.* souris *f.*

moustache, *s.* moustache *f.*

mouth, *s.* bouche *f.;* (*beast*) gueule *f.*

move, *s.* mouvement *m.;* (*chess*) coup *m.;* — *v.a.* remuer; déplacer; (*goods*) transporter; (*affect*) émouvoir; (*motion*) proposer ~ *house* (*also:* ~) déménager; — *v.n.* se mouvoir, se déplacer; s'avancer; (*chess*) jouer; ~ *forward* s'avancer; ~ *in* emménager; ~ *out* déménager; ~ *on* avancer; *int.* circulez!

movement, *s.* mouvement *m.*

mow, *v.a.* faucher; tondre.

mower, *s.* faucheur *m.;* faucheuse (à moteur) *f.*

much, *adj. & pron.* beaucoup; — *adv.* beaucoup; très; *too* ~ trop.

mud, *s.* boue *f.*

muddle, *s.* fouillis *m.;* — *v.a.* embrouiller.

muddy, *adj.* boueux.

mug, *s.* timbale *f.*

mule, *s.* mulet *m.,* mule *f.*

multiple, *adj.* multiple.

multiplication, *s.* multiplication *f.*

multiply, *v.a.* multiplier.

multitude, *s.* multitude *f.*

municipal, *adj.* municipal.

murder, *s.* meurtre *m.*

murderer, *s.* meurtrier *m.*

murmur, *s.* murmure

m.

muscle, s. muscle m.

museum, s. musée m.

mushroom, s. champignon m.

music, s. musique f.

musical, adj. musical; ~ instrument instrument m. de musique.

music-hall, s. café m. concert.

musician, s. musicien, -enne m. f.

must, v. aux. il faut que; devoir.

mustard, s. moutarde f.

mute, adj. muet.

mutter, s. murmure m.; — v. n. murmurer.

mutton, s. mouton m.

mutual, adj. mutuel.

my, pron. mon, ma; mes (pl.).

myself, pron. moi-même; by ~ seul.

mysterious, adj. mystérieux.

mystery, s. mystère m.

mystic, adj. mystique.

myth, s. mythe m.

N

nail, s. (to hammer) clou m.; (on fingers) ongle m.; — v.a. clouer.

nail-brush, s. brosse f. à ongles.

naked, adj. nu; dénudé.

name, s. nom m.; — v.a. nommer; désigner.

namely, adv. savoir.

nap, s. somme m.

napkin, s. serviette f.; (infant) couche f.

narrate, v. a. raconter.

narrow, adj. étroit.

nation, s. nation f.

national, adj. national.

nationality, s. nationalité

f.

nationalize, v.a. nationaliser.

native, adj. & s. natif, -ive (m. f.).

natural, adj. naturel.

naturalize, v.a. naturaliser.

nature, s. nature f.

naughty, adj. méchant.

nava l. adj. naval

navigate, v.n. naviguer.

navigator, s. navigateur m.

navy, s. marine f.

near, adv. près, proche; — prep. près de, auprès de; — adj. proche.

nearly, adv. (almost) presque.

neat, adj. propre; élégant.

necessary, adj. nécessaire.

necessity, s. néccesité f.

neck, s. cou m.

necklace, s. collier m.

necktie, s. cravate f.

need, s. besoin; — v.a. avoir besoin (de); demander.

needle, s. aiguille f.

needless, adj. inutile.

needy, adj. nécessiteux.

negative, adj. négatif; — s. négative f.; (photo) cliché m.; in the ~ négativement.

neglect, v. a. négliger (de).

negligence, s. négligence f.

negotiation, s. négociation f.

negro, -ess s. nègre m., négresse f.

neighbour, s. voisin, -e m. f.

neighbourhood, s. voisinage m.

neither, pron. & adj. ni l'un ni l'autre.

nephew, s. neveu m.

nerve, s. nerf m.

nervous, adj. nerveux.

nest, s. nid m.

net¹, s. filet m.
net², adj. net.
network, s. réseau m.
neutral, adj. neutre.
never, adj. (ne . . .) jamais..
nevertheless, adv. néan-
moins.
new, adj. neuf, neuve;
nouveau, -el, -elle; New
Year Nouvel An.
news, s. nouvelle f.
newspaper, s. journal
m.
next, adj. le plus proche;
prochain, suivant; ~
door to à côté de; adv.
ensuite, après; — prep.
~ to à côté de.
nice, adj. agréable, bon;
gentil.
niece, s. nièce f.
night, s. nuit f.; soir m.;
by ~ de nuit; good ~!
bonne nuit!
nightingale, s. rossignol
m.
nine, adj. & s. neuf (m.).
nineteen, adj. & s. dix-
neuf (m.).
ninety, adj. & s. quatre-
-vingt-dix (m.).
ninth, adj. neuvième;
neuf.
nip, v.a. pincer.
nitrogen, s. azote m.
no, adj. ne . . . pas (de),
ne . . . aucun.
noble, adj. noble.
nobleman, s. gentilhomme
m.
nobody, no one, pron.
personne ne (+ verb).
noise, s. bruit m.
noisy, adj. bruyant.
none, pron. ne . . . aucun;
personne ne (+ verb.)
nonsense, s. bêtise; m. no
~ pas de bêtises
non-smoker, s. compart-
ment m. pour non-
fumeurs.

non-stop, adj. & adv.
sans arrêt; sans escale.
noon, s. midi m.
nor, conj. ni; (and . . .
not) et ne . . . pas,
non plus.
normal, adj. normal.
north, s. nord m.; — adj.
du nord.
north-east, adj. & s.
nord-est m.
northern, adj. du nord.
north-west, adj. & s.
nord-ouest m.
nose, s. nez m.
nostril, s. narine f.
not, adv. ne . . . pas, ne
. . . point.
notable, adj. notable.
note, s. note f.; (letter
and money) billet m.;
(tone) ton m.; — v.a.
noter; remarquer.
note-book, s. carnet m.
noted, adj. distingué.
nothing, pron. rien; ne . . .
rien.
notice, s. avis m.; attention f.; connaissance
f.; take ~ of faire
attention à.
notify, v.a. avertir, noti-
fier.
notion, s. idée f.
noun, s. nom m.
nourish, v.a. nourrir.
novel, s. roman m.
novelist, s. romancier m.
novelty, s. nouveauté f.
November, s. novembre m.
now, adv. maintenant.
nowadays, adv. de nos
jours.
nowhere, adv. ne . . . nulle
part.
nuclear, adj. nucléaire; ~
energy énergie f. nu-
cléaire; ~ physics
physique f. nucléaire;
~ power station centrale
f. nucléaire.
nuisance, s. (pers.) peste

f.; (thing) ennui *m.*

number, *s.* nombre *m.,* numéro *m.*

number-plate, *s.* plaque *f.* matricule.

numerous, *adj.* nombreux.

nun, *s.* religieuse *f.*

nurse, *s.* nourrice *f.,* bonne (d'enfant) *f.; (hospital)* infirmier, -ère *m. f.; — v.a. (suckle)* allaiter; *(the sick)* soigner.

nursery, *s.* chambre *f.* des enfants.

nut, *s.* noix *f.,* noisette *f.*

nylon, *s.* nylon *m.; ~ stockings (or ~s)* bas nylons *m. pl.*

O

oak, *s.* chêne *m.*

oar, *s.* rame *f.*

oat(s) *s. (pl).* avoine *f.*

oath, *s.* serment *m.*

obedience, *s.* obéissance *f.*

obedient, *adj.* obéissant.

obey, *v.a. & n.* obéir (à)·

object, *s.* objet *m.;* but *m.; (gramm.)* régime *m.; — v.a.* objecter; *v.n.* s'opposer (à).

objection, *s.* objection *f.*

objective, *adj. & s.* objectif *(m.).*

obligation, *s.* obligation *f.*

oblige, *v.a.* obliger.

obscure, *adj.* obscur.

observation, *s.* observation *f.*

observe, *v.a.& n.* observer.

obstacle, *s.* obstacle *m.*

obstinate, *adj.* obstiné.

obtain, *v.a.* obtenir.

obvious, *adj.* évident.

occasion, *s.* occasion *f.*

occasional *adj.* occasionnel.

occasionally, *adv.* de temps en temps.

occupation, *s.* occupation *f.*

occupy, *v.a.* occuper; *~ oneself with* s'occuper de.

occur, *v.n.* arriver; se trouver; *it ~red to me* il m'est venu à l'idée que.

occurrence, *s.* événement *m.*

ocean, *s.* océan *m.*

October, *s.* octobre *m.*

odd, *adj.* impair; dépareillé, déparié; *(strange)* non usuel, bizarre.

odds, *s. pl.* avantage *m.;* chances *f. pl.*

of, *prep.* de.

off, *adv.* à . . . de distance; *be ~* s'en aller; *be well ~* être à l'aise; — *prep:* de.

offence, *s* offense *f.*

offend, *v. a. & n.* offenser.

offensive, *s.* offensive *f.*

offer, *s.* o.fre *f.; — v.a.* offrir.

office, *s.* bureau *m.; (of pers.)* charge *f.;* fonction *f.*

officer, *s.* officer *m.; (police)* agent *m.*

official, *adj.* officiel; — *s.* fonctionnaire *m. f.*

often, *adv.* souvent.

oil, *s.* huile *f.;* pétrole *m.*

ointment, *s.* onguent *m.*

old, *adj.* vieux, -eil, -eille; âgé; ancien; *how ~ are you?* quel âge avez-vous?; *~ age* vieillesse *f.; grow ~* vieillir.

old-fashioned, *adj.* à l'ancienne mode.

omission, *s.* omission *f.*

omit, *v.a.* omettre (de).

on, *prep.* sur; *(prep. omitted with days etc.); ~ Monday* lundi; *~*

time à la minute.
once, *adv.* une fois; autrefois; *at* ~ tout de suite.
one, *adj. & s.* un, une; — *pron.* (~, ~s *omitted if*

preceded by adj.); (people, they) on; *this* ~ celui-ci; *that* ~ celui-là; ~'s son, sa, ses; *which* ~? lequel ...?
oneself, *pron.* soi-même; *by* ~ tout seul.
onion, *s.* oignon *m.*
onlooker, *s.* spectateur, -trice *m. f.*
open, *adj.* ouvert; découvert; public; franc; — *v.a.* ouvrir; *v.n.* s'ouvrir.
opening, *s.* ouverture *f.*
opera, *s.* opéra *m.*
operate, *v.a. & n.* opérer; ~ *on* opérer (qn).
operating-theatre, *s.* salle *f.* d'opération.
operation, *s.* opération *f.*
operative, *adj.* actif.
opinion, *s.* opinion *f.*; *in my* ~ à mon avis.
opponent, *s.* adversaire *m.*
opportunity, *s.* occasion *f.*
oppose, *v.a.* s'opposer à; ~d *to* opposé à.
opposition, *s.* opposition *f.*
optional, *adj.* facultatif.
or, *conj.* ou; *whether* ... ~ ou ... ou.
oral, *adj.* oral.
orange, *s.* orange *f.*
orchard, *s.* verger *m.*
orchestra, *s.* orchestre *m.*
order, *s.* ordre *m.*; *(commerce)* commande *f.*; *(ruling)* règlement *m.*; — *v.a.* ordonner; *(goods)* commander.
order-form, *s.* bon *m.* commande.

ordinary, *adj.* ordinaire *m.*
ore, *s.* minerai *m.*
organ, *s.* organe *m.*; *(music)* orgue *m.*
organic, *adj.* organique.
organization, *s.* organisation. *f*
organize, *v.a.* organiser.
oriental, *adj.* oriental.
origin, *s.* origine *f.*
original, *adj.* original.
ornament, *s.* ornement *m.*; — *v.a.* orner.
ornamental, *adj.* ornemental.
orphan, *adj. & s.* orphelin, -e *(m. f.).*
other, *adj. & pron.* autre.
otherwise, *adv.* autrement.
ought, *v. aux.* devoir.
ounce, *s.* once *f.*
our, *adj.* notre, *(pl.)* nos.
ours, *pron.* le, la nôtre; les nôtres.
ourself, *pron.* nous(-mêmes); *ourselves* nous(-mêmes); *by ourselves* seul, -s.
out, *adv.* dehors; — *prep.* ~ *of* hors de.
outdoors, *adv.* dehors, en plein air.
outfit, *s.* trousseau *m.*
outing, *s.* excursion *f.*
outline, *s.* contour *m.*; aperçu *m.*; — *v.a.* esquisser.
outlive, *v.a.* survivre à.
outlook, *s.* perspective *f.*
output, *s.* production *f.*
outrageous, *adj.* outrageant; atroce.
outset, *s.* début *m.*; *at the* ~ dès le commencement.
outside, *adv.* au dehors; — *prep.* en dehors de; — *adj.* du dehors; — *s.* extérieur.
outskirts, *s. pl.* banlieue

f.; lisière f.

outstanding, *adj.* non réglé, à payer; saillant; éminent.

outward, *adj.* extérieur.

outwards, *adv.* à l'extérieur, en dehors.

oven, *s.* four *m.*

over, *prep.* au-dessus de; *(motion)* par dessus; *(superior)* sur; *(more than)* plus de; *(across)* par; — *adv. (more)* davantage; *(finished)* fini, passé; *(too)* trop.

overcoat, *s.* pardessus *m.*

overcome, *v.a.* surmonter; vaincre.

overcrowded, *adj.* surpeuplé.

overdo, *v.a.* faire trop cuire; exagérer.

overexpose, *v.a.* surexposer.

overflow, *s.* débordement *m.;* — *v.a.* inonder; *v.n.* déborder.

overlook, *v.a. (look on to)* avoir vue sur; *(neglect)* négliger; *(superintend)* surveiller.

overpower, *v.a.* accabler; subjuguer.

oversea, *adj.* d'outre-mer; ∼*s (adv.)* outre-mer.

oversight, *s.* inadvertence *f.*

overtake, *v.a.* rattraper; surprendre (par).

overthrow, *s.* renversement *m.;* — *v.a.* renverser.

overtime, *s.* heures *f. pl.* supplémentaires.

overwhelming, *adj.* accablant.

owe, *v.a.* devoir (à); être redevable (à).

owing, *adj.* ∼ *to* à cause de.

owl, *s.* hibou *m.*

own, *adj.* propre; *of my* ∼ à moi; — *v.a.* posséder.

owner, *s.* propriétaire *m. f.*

ox, *s.* bœuf *m.*

oxygen, *s.* oxygène *m.*

oyster, *s.* huître *f.*

P

pace, *s.* pas *m.;* *v.a.* arpenter; *v.n.* aller au pas.

pack, *s.* paquet; *(cards)* jeu *m.;* *(wool)* balle; *(hounds)* meute *f.;* — *v.a.* emballer; faire: ∼ *off* expédier.

package, *s.* colis *m.;* paquet *m.*

packet, *s.* paquet *m.*

pact, *s.* pacte *m.*

pad, *s.* bourrelet *m.;* tampon *m.;* bloc *m.;* *blotting* ∼ buvard *m.*

paddle, *v.n.* pagayer.

page, *s.* page *f.*

pail, *s.* seau *m.*

pain, *s.* douleur *f.;* *take* ∼*s* se donner de la peine.

painful, *adj.* douloureux.

paint, *s.* peinture *f.;* — *v. a.* peindre.

painter, *s.* peintre *m.*

painting, *s.* peinture *f.*

pair, *s.* paire *f.;* couple *m.*

palace, *s.* palais *m.*

palate, *s.* palais *m.*

pale, *adj.* pâle; *grow* ∼ pâlir.

palm, *s.* palme *f.*

pan, *s.* poêle *f.*

pane, *s.* vitre *f.*

panel, *s.* panneau *m.*

panorama, *s.* panorama *m.*

pansy, *s.* pensée *f.*

pantry, *s.* office *f.*

pants, *s.pl.* caleçon *m.;* pantalon *m.*

paper, *s.* papier *m.;*

(newspaper) journal *m.; (essay)* étude *f.; (exam)* composition *f.*

parade, *s.* parade *f.; — v.n.* parader.

paraffin, *s.* pétrole *m.*

paragraph, *s.* paragraphe *m.*

parallel, *s. (line)* parallèle *f.; (comparison)* parallèle *m.; — adj.* parallèle.

paralysis, *s.* paralysie *f.*

parcel, *s.* paquet *m.*

pardon, *s.* pardon *m.; I beg your ~* je vous demande pardon; *(I beg your) ~?* comment (dites-vous)?, pardon?; *— v.a.* pardonner.

parents, *s. pl.* père *m.* et mère *f.,* parents.

parish, *s.* paroisse *f.*

Parisian, *adj.* parisien; *— s.* Parisien, -enne *m.f.*

park, *s.* parc *m.; (car)* (parc de) stationnement *m.; — v.a.* garer; stationner; *no ~ing* stationnement interdit.

parliament, *s.* parlement *m.*

parliamentary, *adj.* parlementaire.

parlour, *s.* petit salon *m.*

parrot, *s.* perroquet *m.*

part, *s.* part *f.;* partie *f.; (theatre)* rôle *m.; (region)* région *f.; on my ~* de ma part; *take ~ in* prendre part à; *— v.a.* diviser; séparer; *v.n.* se diviser; *(pers.)* se séparer (de).

partial, *adj. (unfair)* partial; *(incomplete)* partiel.

participant, *s.* participant *m.*

participate, *v.n.* *~ in* prendre part à.

participation, *s.* participation *f.*

participle, *s.* participe *m.*

particular, *adj.* particulier; *— s.* détail *m.*

partly, *adv.* en partie.

partner, *s.* associé, -e *m. f.;* partenaire *m. f.*

partridge, *s.* perdrix *f.*

party, *s.* parti *m.;* partie *f.;* groupe *m.;* réception *f.,* soirée *f.*

pass, *v.a.* passer; dépasser; surpasser; *(law)* voter; *(resolution)* prendre; *(exam)* être reçu (à); *— v. n.* passer; *— s.* défilé *m.;* laisser-passer *m.*

passage, *s.* passage *m.;* couloir *m.*

passenger, *s.* voyageur, -euse *m. f.;* passager, -ère *m. f.*

passer-by, *s.* passant *m.*

passion, *s.* passion *f.*

passionate, *adj.* passionné.

passive, *adj. & s.* passif *(m.).*

passport, *s.* passeport *m.*

past, *adj.* passé; dernier; *— s.* passé *m.*

paste, *s.* pâte *f.*

pastime, *s.* passe-temps *m*

pastry, *s.* pâtisserie *f.*

patch, *s.* pièce *f.*

patent, *s.* brevet *m.* d'invention.

path, -way, *s.* sentier *m.*

patience, *s.* patience *f.*

patient, *s.* malade *m. f.; — adj.* patient.

patriot, *s.* patriote *m. f.*

patrol, *s.* patrouille; *— v.n.* aller en patrouille.

patron, *s.* patron *m.;* client *m.*

pattern, *s.* modèle *m.*

pause, *s.* pause *f.; — v.n.* faire une pause.

pave, *v.a.* paver.

pavement, *s.* trottoir *m.*

pavilion, s. pavillon m.
paw, s. patte f.
pay, v.a. payer; (visit) faire; ~ off acquitter; v.n. payer; — s. paye f., salaire m.
payable, adj. payable (à).
payment, s. payement m.
pea, s. pois m.
peace, s. paix f.
peaceful, adj. paisible.
peach, s. pêche f.
peacock, s. paon m.
peak, s. pic m., cime f.
pear, s. poire f.
pearl, s. perle f.

peasant, s. paysan, -anne m. f.
pebble, s. caillou m.
peck, s. coup m. de bec.
peculiar, adj. particulier.
pedestrian, s. piéton m.
peel, s. pelure f.; — v.a. peler.
peer, s. pair m.
peg, s. pince f.; piquet m.
pen, s. stylo m.
penalty, s. peine f.
pencil, s. crayon m.
penicillin, s. pénicilline f.
penknife, s. canif m.

penny, s. penny m.
pension, s. pension f.
people, s. peuple m.; gens m. pl. [f. with adj. before it]; famille f.
pepper, s. poivre m.
per, prep. par; ~ cent pour cent.
perceive, v.a. percevoir.
perch, s. perchoir m.; — v.n. se percher.
perfect, adj. parfait; — v.a. rendre parfait; achever.
perform, v.a. accomplir, exécuter.
performance, s. représentation f.
perfume, s. parfum m.

perhaps, adv. peut-être.
peril, s. péril m.
period, s. période f.
periodical, s. périodique m.
perish, v.n. périr.
perishable, adj. périssable.
permanent, adj. permanent.
permission, s. permission f.
permit, s. permis m.; — v.a. permettre.
persecution, s. persécution f.
Persian, adj. persan.
persist, v.n. persister.
person, s. personne f.
personal, adj. personnel.
personality, s. personnalité f.
perspiration, s. transpiration f.
persuade, v.a. convaincre (de), persuader.
pertain, v.n. appartenir (à).
pet, s. enfant m.f. gâté, -e; — adj. favori; ~ dog chien m. familier.
petrol, s. essence f.
petroleum, s. pétrole m.
petticoat, s. jupon m.
phase, s. phase f.
pheasant, s. faisan, -e m. f.
phenomenon, s. phénomène m.
philosopher, s. philosophe m.
philosophy, s. philosophie f.
phone, s. téléphone m.; — v.a. & n. téléphoner.
photo(graph), s. photographie f. — v.a. photographier.
phrase, s. phrase f.
physical, adj. physique.
physician, s. médecin m.
physicist, s. physicien m.

physics, *s.* physique *f.*
pianist, *s.* pianiste *m. f.*
piano, *s.* piano *m.*
pick, *v. a.* cueillir; picoter; *(teeth)* curer; *(bone)* ronger; *(choose)* choisir; ~ *out* choisir; ~ *up* ramasser; prendre.
pickle, *s.* marinade *f.* ~*s* pickles *m.*
picnic, *s.* pique-nique *m.*
picture, *s.* tableau *m.*; portrait *m.*; film *m.*; ~*s* cinéma *m.*
pie, *s.* pâté *m.*
piece, *s.* morceau *m.*; partie *f.*; pièce *f.*; ~ *of news* nouvelle *f.*; ~ *of work* ouvrage *m.*
pier, *s.* jetée *f.*
pierce, *v.a.* percer.
pig, *s.* cochon *m.*
pigeon, *s.* pigeon *m.*
pile¹, *s.* tas *m.*; — *v.a.* (also ~ *up*) entasser, amasser.
pile², *s.* pieu *m.*, pilot *m.*
pill, *s.* pillule *f.*
pillar, *s.* pilier *m.*
pillar-box, *s.* boîte *f.* aux lettres.
pillow, *s.* oreiller *m.*
pilot, *s.* pilote *m.*
pin, *s.* épingle *f.*
pinch, *v.a.* pincer.
pine, *s.* pin *m.*
pineapple, *s.* ananas *m.*
pink, *adj.* & *s.* rose *(m.).*
pint, *s.* pinte *f.*
pious, *adj.* pieux.
pipe, *s.* tuyau *m.*; *(smoking)* pipe *f.*
pistol, *s.* pistolet *m.*
pit, *s.* fosse *f.*; creux *m.*; *(theatre)* parterre *m.*
pitch, *s.* degré *m.*; ton *m.*; *v.a.* *(tent)* dresser; *(camp)* asseoir.
pity, *s.* pitié *f.*; dommage *m.*

place, *s.* lieu *m.*, endroit *m.*; place *f.*; emploi *m.*; — *v.a.* mettre.
plain, *adj.* uni; simple; évident; ordinaire.
plait, *s.* tresse *f.*
plan, *s.* plan *m.*; projet *m.*; — *v.a.* faire le plan (de).
plane, *s.* plan *m.*; *(tool)* rabot *m.*; *(aero-)* avion *m.*; — *v.a.* raboter.
planet, *s.* planète *f.*
plank, *s.* planche *f.*
plant, *s.* plante *f.*; *(works)* usine *f.*, fabrique *f.*; — *v.a.* planter.
plantation, *s.* plantation *f.*
plaster, *s.* (em)plâtre *m.*
plastic, *adj.* plastique; ~*s* plastiques *m. pl.*
plate, *s.* plaque *f.*; planche *f.*; *(china)* assiette *f.*; *(silver)* vaisselle *f.*
platform, *s.* quai *m.*
platinum, *s.* platine *m.*
platter, *s.* plat *m.*
play, *s.* jeu *m.*; pièce *f.* de théâtre; — *v.a.* & *n.* jouer.
player, *s.* joueur, -euse *m. f.*
playground, *s.* cour *f.* de récréation.
plea, *s.* excuse *f.*; défense *f.*
plead, *v.a.&n.* plaider
pleasant, *adj.* agréable.
please, *v.a.* & *n.* plaire (à); *be* ~*ed with, to* être content de; *as you* ~ comme vous voulez; *if you* ~ s'il vous plaît.
pleasure, *s.* plaisir *m.*
pledge, *s.* gage *m.*; — *v.a.* mettre en gage.
plenty, *s.* abondance *f.*; ~ *of* quantité de,

beaucoup de.

plot, s. (land) terrain m.; (story) intrigue f.; (conspiracy) complot m.; v.n. conspirer.

plough, s. charrue f.; — v.a.&n. labourer.

plug, s. tampon m.; prise f. de courant; — v.a. tamponner.

plum, s. prune f.

plume, s. plume f.; plumet m.

plunder, v.a. piller; — s. pillage m.

plunge, v.a. & n. plonger; — s. plongeon m.

plural, s. & adj. pluriel (m.).

plus, prep. plus.

ply, v.a. manier; s'appliquer (à); v.n. faire le service (entre).

pocket, s. poche f.

pocket-book, s. carnet m.; portefeuille m.

poem, s. poème m.

poet, s. poète m.

poetic(al), adj. poétique

poetry, s. poésie·f.

point, s. point m ; pointe f.; — v.a. & n. ~ out montrer du doigt; faire valoir (un fait); ~ to indiquer.

poison, s. poison m.; v.a. empoisonner.

poisonous, adj. vénéneux.

pole, s. pôle m.

Pole, s. Polonais, -e m. f.

police, s. police f.

policeman, -officer, s. agent (de police) m.

police-station, s. poste (de police) m.

policy, s. politique f.; (insurance) police f.

polish, s. poli m.; fig. politesse f.; — v. a. polir.

Polish, adj. polonais.

polite, adj. poli.

political, adj. politique.

politician, s. politique m.; politicien m.

politics, s. politique f.

poll, s. vote m.; liste f. (électorale); scrutin m.

pool[1], s. mare f.

pool[2], s. pool m.

poor, adj. pauvre; (bad) mauvais.

pope, s. pape m.

popular, adj. populaire.

popularity, s. popularité f.

population, s. population f.

pork, s. porc m.; ~ butcher charcutier m.

port, s. port m.; (ship) bâbord m.

portable, adj. portatif.

porter, s. portier m.; (railw.) porteur m.

portfolio, s. serviette f.

portion, s. portion f.; — v.a. partager.

portrait, s. portrait m.

Portuguese, adj. portugais; — s. Portugais, -e m. f.

position, s. position f.

positive, adj. & s. positif (m.).

possess, v.a. posséder.

possession, s. possession f.

possibility, s. possibilité f.

possible, adj. possible.

post[1], s. poteau m.; — v.a. afficher, placarder.

post[2], s. poste f.; courrier m. — v.a. mettre à la poste.

postage, s. port m., affranchissement; ~ paid port payé.

postal, adj. postal; ~ order mandat (de poste) m.

poster, s. affiche f.

post-free, *adj.* franco.

postman, *s.* facteur *m.*

post(-)office, *s.* bureau *m.* de poste

postpone, *v.a.* remettre.

postscript, *s.* post-scriptum *m.*

pot, *s.* pot *m.*

potato, *s.* pomme *f.* de terre.

pottery, *s.* poterie *f.*

pouch, *s.* blague *f.*

poultry, *s.* volaille *f.*

pound, *s.* livre *f.*

pour, *v.a.* verser.

pouring, *adj.* torrentiel.

poverty, *s.* pauvreté *f.*

powder, *s.* poudre *f.*

power, *s.* pouvoir *m.;* puissance *f.;* force *f.*

powerful, *adj.* puissant.

power-plant, -station, *s.* centrale *f.* électrique.

practical, *adv.* pratique.

practice, *s.* pratique *f.;* exercise *m.*

practise, *v.a.* pratiquer, exercer; étudier.

praise, *s.* louange *f.;* — *v.a.* louer.

pray, *v.a.* & *n.* prier.

prayer, *s.* prière *f.*

preach, *v.a.* & *n.* prêcher.

preacher, *s.* prédicateur *m.*

precede, *v.a.* précéder.

preceding, *adj.* précédent.

precious, *adj.* précieux.

precision, *s.* précision *f.*

predecessor, *s.* prédécesseur *m.*

predict, *v.a.* prédire.

prefabricated, *adj.* préfabriqué.

preface, *s.* préface *f.*

prefer, *v.a.* préférer *(to* à), aimer mieux.

preferable, *adj.* préférable (à).

preference, *s.* préférence *f.*

pregnant, *adj.* enceinte.

prejudice, *s.* préjugé *m.*

preliminary, *adj.* préliminaire.

premature, *adj.* prématuré.

premier, *s.* premier ministre *m., (in France)* président *m.* du conseil.

premises, *s. pl.* lieux *m. pl.;* local *m.,* immeuble *m.*

premium, *s.* prime *f.*

preparation, *s.* préparation *f.*

prepare, *v.a.* préparer, apprêter; — *v.n.* se préparer.

preposition, *s.* préposition *f.*

Presbyterian, *adj.* presbytérien.

prescribe, *v.a.* prescrire, ordonner; *v.n.* ~ *for* faire une ordonnance pour.

prescription, *s.* prescription *f.; (medical)* ordonnance *f.*

presence, *s.* présence *f.*

present[1], *adj.* présent; actuel; — *s.* présent *m.; at* ~ à présent.

present[2], *s. (gift)* cadeau *m.,* présent *m.; — v.a.* présenter; donner.

presently, *adv.* tout à l'heure.

preserve, *v.a.* préserver; *(fruits)* conserver; — *s.* confiture *f.;* conserve *f.*

president, *s.* président *m.*

press, *s.* presse *f.; — v.a.* presser; serrer.

pressure, *s.* pression *f.*

presume, *v.a.* présumer.

presumption, *s.* présomption *f.*

pretend, *v. a.* & *n.* feindre,

faire semblant; pré-
tendre (à).

pretention, *s.* prétension
f.

pretty, *adj.* joli.

prevail, *v.n.* prévaloir;
prédominer.

prevent, *v.a.* empêcher.

prevention, *s.* empêchement *m.*

previous, *adj.* antérieur
(à).

prey, *s.* proie *f.*

price, *s.* prix *m.;* cours *m.*

price-list, *s.* prix-courant
m., tarif *m.*

prick, *v.a.* piquer; —
s. piqûre *f.*

pride, *s.* orgueil *m.*

priest, *s.* prêtre *m.*

primary, *adj.* primaire.

prime, *adj.* ~ *minister*
see premier.

primitive, *adj.* primitif.

prince, *s.* prince *m.*

princess, *s.* princesse *f.*

principal, *adj.* principal;
— *s.* directeur *m.*,
patron, -ne *m.f.*, principal *m.*

principle, *s.* principe *m*

print, *s.* empreinte *f.;*
impression *f.; out of* ~
épuisé; — *v.a.* im-
primer; faire une em-
preinte (sur); *(photo)*
tirer; ~*ed matter* im-
primés *m. pl.*

printing-office, *s.* imprimerie *f.*

prison, *s.* prison *f.*

prisoner, *s.* prisonnier,
-ère *m. f.*

private, *adj.* particulier;
personel; privé.

privilege, *s.* privilège *m.*

prize, *s.* prix *m.*

probability, *s.* probabilité *f.*

probable, *adj.* probable.

probably, *adv.* probablement.

problem, *s.* problème *m.*

procedure, *s.* procédé *m.*

proceed, *v.n.* aller (à);
se mettre (à); avan-
cer; passer (à); pro-
céder; ~ *with* conti-
nuer.

process, *s.* développement *m.;* méthode *f.*,
procédé *m.;* — *v.n.*
aller en procession.

procession, *s.* cortège *m.;*
procession *f.*

proclaim, *v. a.* proclamer.

proclamation, *s.* proclamation *s.*

produce, *v.a.* produire.

producer, *s.* producteur,
-trice *m. f.*

product, *s.* produit *m.*

production, *s.* production
f.

profess, *v.a.* professer, déclarer.

profession, *s.* profession *f.*

professional, *adj.* professionnel; de profession.

professor, *s.* professeur *m.*

profit, *s.* profit *m.;* —
v.n. ~ *by* profiter de.

profitable, *adj.* profitable.

profound, *adj.* profond.

programme, *s.* programme *m.*

progress, *s.* progrès *m.;*
marche *f.;* — *v.n.*
s'avancer, faire des
progrès.

prohibit, *v.a.* défendre.

prohibition, *s.* prohibition *f.*, défense *f.*

project, *s.* projet *m.;*
— *v.a.* projeter; *v.n.*
saillir.

projector, *s.* projecteur
m.

prolong, *v.a.* prolonger.

prominent, *adj.* (pro)émi-
nent.

promise, *s.* promesse *f.;*
— *v.a.* promettre.

promote, *v.a.* donner de

l'avancement (à); encourager.

promotion, s. promotion f., avancement m.

prompt, adj. prompt; — v.a. (rheatre) souffler; inspirer.

pronoun, s. pronom m.

pronounce, v.a. prononcer.

pronunciation, s. prononciation f.

proof, s. preuve f.; épreuve f.

propeller, s. hélice f.

proper, adj. propre; convenable.

property, s. propriété f.

prophet, s. prophète m.

proportion, s. proportion f.

propose, v.a. proposer.

proposition, proposal, s. proposition f.

prose, s. prose f.

prospect, s. prospective f.

prospectus, s. prospectus m.

prosper, v.n. prospérer.

prosperity, s. prospérité f.

prosperous, adj. prospère.

protest, s. protestation f.; protêt m.; — v.a. protester.

Protestant, adj. & s. protestant, -e (m. f.).

proud, adj. fier, -ère.

prove, v.a. prouver; éprouver.

proverb, s. proverbe m.

provide, v.a. pourvoi de; fournir de; v.n. ~ for pourvoir à; ~d that pourvu que.

providence, s. prévoyance f.

province, s. province f.

provincial, adj. provincial.

provision, s. provision f.

provoke, v. a. provoquer (à).

prudent, adj. prudent.

psalm, s. psaume m.

psychological, adj. psychologique.

psychology, s. psychologie f.

public, adj. & s. public m.

publication, s. publication f.

publicity, s. publicité f.

publish, v.a. publier.

publisher, s. éditeur m.

pudding, s. pouding m.

pull, v.a. tirer; ~ down démolir; ~ out arracher; ~ up arrêter; v. n. tirer; ~ through s'en tirer; — s. traction f., tirage f.

pulpit, s. chaire f.

pulse, s. pouls m.

pump, s. pompe f.; — v. a. pomper.

punch[1], s. poinçon m.; — v.a. poinçonner, percer.

punch[2], s. punch m.

punctual, adj. ponctuel.

puncture, s. piaûre f.; (tyre) crevaison f.; — v.a.& n. crever.

punish, v.a. punir.

punishment,, s. punition f.

pupil[1], s. élève m. f.

pupil[2], s. (eye) pupille f.

puppy, s. petit chien m.

purchase, s. achat m.; — v.a. acheter.

pure, adj. pur.

purge, v.a. purger.

purify, v.a. purifier.

purity, s. pureté f.

purpose, s. but m.

purse, s. porte-monnaie m., bourse f.

pursue, v.a. (pour)suivre.

pursuit, *s.* poursuite *f.*

push, *v.a. & n.* pousser; ~ *back* repousser; ~ *on* faire avancer; pousser (jusqu'à); — *s.* poussé *f.;* allant *m.*

puss, *s.* minet *m.*

put, *v.a.* mettre; *(express)* dire; ~ *back* remettre; ~ *down* déposer; attribuer; inscrire; ~ *off* remettre; ôter; ~ *on* mettre; ~ *out* tendre; éteindre; ~ *up* ouvrir; loger; ~ *up with* s'accommoder.

puzzle, *v.a.* embarrasser.

pyjamas, *s. pl.* pyjama *m.*

pyramid, *s.* pyramide *f.*

Q

quadrangle, *s.* quadrilatère *m.;* cour *f.*

quake, *v.n.* trembler.

qualification, *s.* qualification *f.;* compétence *f.*

qualify, *v.a.* qualifier; *v.n.* ~ *for* passer l'examen de.

quality, *s.* qualité *f.*

quantity, *s.* quantité *f.*

quarrel, *s.* querelle *f.;* brouille *f.;* — *v.n.* se brouiller; ~ *with* se quereller avec.

quarter, *s.* quartier *m.;* quart *m.;* ~*s* quartiers *m.pl.*

quartet(te), *s.* quatuor *m.*

quay, *s.* quai *m.*

queen, *s.* reine *f.;* *(cards)* dame *f.*

queer, *adj.* bizarre.

quench, *v.a.* éteindre.

question, *s.* question *f.;* — *v.a.* interroger.

queue, *s.* queue *f.;* — *v.n.* ~ *up* faire (la) queue.

quick, *adj.* prompt, rapide; vif.

quick(ly), *adv.* vite.

quiet, *adj.* tranquille; calme; *be* ~ se taire.

quilt, *s.* courtepointe *f.*

quit, *v.a.* quitter.

quite, *adv.* tout à fait.

quiver, *v.n.* trembler.

quiz, *s.* mystification *f.;* persifleur *m.;* *v.a.* railler.

quotation, *s.* citation *f.*

quote, *v.a.* citer.

R

rabbi, *s.* rabbin *m.*

rabbit, *s.* lapin, -e *m. f.*

race¹, *s.* course *f.;* — *v.n.* faire la course; courir; lutter de vitesse.

race², *s.* race *f.*

rack, *s.* râtelier *m.*

racket, *s.* raquette *f.*

radiate, *v.n.* rayonner, irradier; *v.a.* dégager.

radiator, *s.* radiateur *m.*

radical, *adj.* radical.

radio, *s.* radio *f.*

radioactive, *adj.* radioactif.

radish, *s.* radis *m.*

rag, *s.* chiffon *m.*

rage, *s.* rage *f.*

raid, *s.* razzia *f.,* rafle *f.;* raid *m.*

rail, *s.* barre *f.,* rampe *f.;* rail *m.; by* ~ par chemin de fer.

railway, *s.* chemin *m.* de fer.

rain, *s.* pluie *f.;* — *v.n.* pleuvoir.

rainy, *adj.* pluvieux.

raise, *v.a.* lever, élever; soulever; *(plants)* faire pousser, cultiver.

rake, *s.* râteau *m.*

rally, *v.n.* se rallier; — *s.* ralliement *m.*

ramify, *v.n.* ramifier.

random, *s.* at ~ par hasard.

range, *s.* rangée *f.*; *(mountains)* chaîne *f.*; *(extent)* étendue *f.*; *(kitchen)* fourneau *m.*; — *v.a.* ranger.

rank, *s.* rang *m.*; grade *m.*

ransom, *s.* rançon *f.*; — *v.a.* payer rançon pour.

rap, *s.* tape *f.*; coup *m.*; — *v.a.* frapper.

rapid, *adj.* rapide.

rare, *adj.* rare.

rascal, *s.* coquin *m.*

rash, *adj.* téméraire; inconsidéré.

raspberry, *s.* framboise *f.*

rat, *s.* rat *m.*

rate, *s.* taux *m.*, cours *m.*, tarif *m.*; *(speed)* vitesse *f.*, allure *f.*; *(tax)* taxe *f.*; at the ~ of à la vitesse de; at any ~ en tout cas, quoi qu'il en soit; — *v.a.* estimer; taxer.

rather, *adv.* plutôt; un peu.

ratify, *v.a.* ratifier.

ration, *s.* ration *f.*

rational, *adj.* raisonnable.

rattle, *s.* bruit *m.*; — *v.n.* faire du bruit.

raven, *s.* corbeau *m.*

raw, *adj.* cru; ~ *material* matière *f.* première.

ray, *s.* rayon *m.*

razor, *s.* rasoir *m.*; *safety* ~ rasoir de sûreté;

electric ~ rasoir électrique.

razor-blade, *s.* lame *f.* de rasoir.

reach, *v.a.* arriver (à); atteindre; *v. n.* atteindre; parvenir (à); — *s.* étendue *f.*; portée *f.*; *within* ~ à portée.

react, *v.n.* réagir.

reaction, *s.* réaction *f.*

reactor, *s.* réacteur *m.*

read, *v.a.* lire; *(study)* étudier; ~ *for (exam)* préparer.

reader, *s.* lecteur, -trice *m. f.*

reading, *s.* lecture *f.*

ready, *adj.* prêt (à); prompt (à); près (de); *get* ~ (se) préparer.

real, *adj.* réel; véritable.

reality, *s.* réalité *f.*

realization, *s.* réalisation *f.*

realize, *v.a.* réaliser.

really, *adv.* vraiment.

realm, *s.* royaume *m.*; *fig.* domaine *m.*

reap, *v.a. & n.* moissonner.

reaper, *s.* moissonneur *m.*

rear, *adj.* de derrière; — *s.* arrière *m.*; queue *f.*; — *v.a.* élever; *v. n.* se cabrer.

reason, *s.* raison *f.*; — *v. a. & n.* raisonner.

reasonable, *adj.* raisonnable.

reasoning, *s.* raisonnement *m.*

rebellion, *s.* rébellion *f.*

rebuke, *s.* réprimande *f.*; — *v.a.* réprimander.

recall, *v.a.* rappeler; *(remember)* se rappeler.

receipt, *s.* reçu *m.*, quittance *f.*; recette *f.*

receive, *v.a.* recevoir.

receiver, s. destinataire m. f.; (phone, wireless) écouteur m., récepteur m., poste m.

recent, adj. récent.

recently, adv. récemment.

reception, s. réception f.

receptionist, s. portier m. d'auberge; employé à la réception.

recipe, s. recette f.

recital, s. récit m.; récital m.

recite, v.a. & n. réciter.

reckless, adj. insouciant.

reckon, v.a. compter.

recognize, v.a. reconnaître.

recollect, v. a. se rappeler.

recommend, v.a. recommander.

recommendation, s. recommandation f.

reconcile, v. a. réconcilier.

record, s. rapport m. officiel; souvenir m.; mention f.; archives f. pl.; (gramophone) disque m.; (sport) record m.; — v.a. enregistrer; rapporter.

recount, v.a. raconter.

recover, v.a. recouvrer; v.n. se remettre.

recreation, s. récréation f.

recruit, s. recrue f.; — v.a. recruter.

rectangle, s. rectangle m.

rector, s. recteur m.; curé m.

recur, v. n. revenir.

red, adj. rouge; roux.

redress, v.n. réparer; redresser.

reduce, v.a. réduire.

reduction, s. réduction f.

reed, s. roseau m.

reef, s. ris m.; récif m.

reel, s. dévidoir m.; bobine f.; — v.n. tourner.

refer, v.a. référer; renvoyer; v.n. ~ to se rapporter à, s'en rapporter à, se référer à.

referee, s. arbitre m.; — v.a. arbitrer.

reference, s. renvoi m., référence f.; rapport m.; allusion f.; with ~ to à propos de; have ~ to se rapporter à.

refill, s. recharge f.

reflect, v.a. réfléchir; v.n. méditer (sur).

reflection, s. réflexion f.; image f.

reform, s. réforme f.; — v.a. réformer.

Reformation, s. Réforme f.

refrain, v.n. ~ from se retenir de.

refresh, v.a. rafraîchir.

refreshment, s. rafraîchissement m.; ~ room buffet m.

refrigerator, s. réfrigérateur m.

refuge, s. refuge m.; take ~ se réfugier.

refugee, s. réfugié, -e m. f.

refusal, refus m.

refuse, v.a. refuser.

refute, v.a. réfuter.

regain, v.a. reconquérir; regagner; reprendre.

regard, s. égard m.; with ~ to à l'égard de; kind(est) ~s meilleurs amitiés f. pl.; — v.a. regarder; tenir compte (de); considérer.

regent, s. régent m.

regime, s. régime m.

regiment, s. régiment m.

region, s. région f.

register, v. a. enregistrer.

regret, *v.a.* regretter;
— *s.* regret *m.*
regular, *adj.* régulier.
regulate, *v.a.* régler.
regulation, *s.* ordonnance
f.; réglementation *f.*
rehearsal, *s.* répétition *f.*
rehearse, *v.a.* répéter.
reign, *s.* règne *m.;* — *v. a.*
régner
rein, *s.* rêne *f.*
reject, *v.a.* rejeter; refuser.
relate, *v.a.* raconter;
be ～*ed to* être appa-
renté à; *v.n.* ～ *to*
se rapporter à; *relat-
ing to* relatif à.
relation, *s.* relation *f.,*
rapport *m.* (à); *(rela-
tive)* parent, -e *m. f.*
relative, *s.* parent, -e
m. f.; — *adj.* relatif;
～ *to* au sujet de.
relax, *v.n.* se relâcher;
v. a. relâcher.
relay, *s.* relais *m.*
release, *s.* délivrance *f.;*
— *v.a.* libérer; dé-
charger (de).
reliable, *adj.* digne de
confiance.
relic, *s.* relique *f.*
relief[1], *s.* délivrance *f.;*
soulagement *m.;* se-
cours *m.*
relief[2], *s.* relief *m.*
relieve, *v.a.* soulager;
secourir; délivrer.
religion, *s.* religion *f.*
religious, *adj.* religieux.
rely, *v.n.* ～ *upon* compter sur.
remain, *v.n.* rester.
remark, *s.* remarque *f.;*
— *v.a.* remarquer;
v.n. faire une remar-
que.
remarkable, *adj.* remar-
quable.
remedy, *s.* remède *m.*
remember, *v.a.* se souve-

nir (de), se rappeler.
remembrance, *s.* souvenir
m.
remind, *v. a.* ～ *of* rappeler
(à), faire souvenir (de).
remit, *v.a.* remettre.
remittance, *s.* remise *f.*
remorse, *s.* remords *m.*
remote, *adj.* reculé.
removal, *s.* déménage-
ment *m.;* enlèvement;
(dismissal) renvoi *m.*
remove, *v.a.* déménager;
enlever; *(dismiss)* ren-
voyer, *(from school)*
retirer; *v.n.* démé-
nager; s'en aller.
Renaissance, *s.* Renais-
sance *f.*
render, *v.a.* rendre.
renew, *v.a.* renouveler.
renounce, *v.a.* renoncer
(à); dénoncer; répudier.
rent, *s. (house)* loyer
m.; — *v.a.* louer.
repair, *s.* réparation *f.;*
— *v.a.* réparer.
repay, *v.a.* rembourser.
repeat, *v.a.* répéter.
repentance, *s.* repentir *m.*
repetition, *s.* répétition *f.*
replace, *v.a.* replacer.
reply, *s.* réponse *f.;* —
v.a. & n. répondre.
report, *s.* rapport *m.,*
compte *m.* rendu; bruit
m.; bulletin *m.;* —
v.a. rapporter; rendre
compte (de).
reporter, *s.* reporter *m.*
represent, *v.a.* représenter.
representation, *s.* représentation *f.*
representative, *s.* re-
présentant *m.*
reproach, *s.* reproche *m.*
reproduce, *v.a.* repro-
duire.
reproduction, *s.* reproduction *f.*
reprove, *v.a.* répriman-

der.

republic, *s.* république *f.*

repulsion *s.* répulsion *f.*

repulsive, *adj.* repoussant.

reputation, **repute**, *s.* réputation *f.*

request, *s.* requête *f.*; — *v.a.* demander.

require, *v. a.* demander; exiger.

requirement, *s.* besoin *m.*; exigence *f.*

rescue, *s.* délivrance *f.*; secours *m.*; — *v.a.* délivrer; secourir.

research, *s.* recherche *f.*

resemble, *v.a.* ressembler (à).

resent, *v.a.* être froissé (de); ressentir.

reserve, *s.* réserve *f.*; — *v.a.* réserver.

reside, *v.n.* résider.

residence, *s.* résidence *f.*

resident, *s.* habitant *m.*; — *adj.* résidant.

resign, *v.a.* résigner, se démettre (de); *v.n.* donner sa démission.

resignation, *s.* résignation *f.*; démission *f.*

resist, *v. a.* résister (à).

resistance, *s.* résistance *f.*

resolution, *s.* résolution *f.*

resolve, *v.a.* résoudre; *v.n.* se résoudre (à), se décider (à faire).

resort, *s.* recours *m.*; ressource *f.*; — *v.n.* ~ *to* avoir recours à.

resource, *s.* ressource *f.*

respect, *s.* respect *m.*; rapport *m.*; *in this* ~ sous ce rapport; *with* ~ *to* concernant ... ; — *v.a.* respecter.

respectful, *adj.* respectueux.

respective, *adj.* respectif.

respond, *v.n.* répondre.

response, *s.* réponse *f.*

responsibility, *s.* responsabilité *f.*

responsible, *adj.* responsable (de).

rest[1], *s.* reste *m.*; *the* ~ les autres.

rest[2], *s.* repos *m.*; pause *f.*; — *v.n.* se reposer.

restaurant, *s.* restaurant *m.*

restless, *adj.* sans repos; inquiet; agité.

restoration, *s.* restauration *f.*

restore, *v.a.* restaurer.

restrain, *v. a.* retenir; ~ *from* empêcher de.

restraint, *s.* contrainte *f.*; retenue *f.*

restrict, *v.a.* restreindre.

restriction, *s.* restriction *f.*

result, *s.* résultat *m.*; — *v.n.* ~ *from* résulter de; ~ *in* avoir pour résultat.

resume, *v. a.* reprendre.

retain, *v.a.* retenir.

retire, *v. n.* se retirer.

retreat, *s.* retraite *f.*

return, *v.n.* revenir, retourner; *v.a.* rendre; renvoyer; *(answer)* faire; — *s.* retour *m* ; renvoi *m.*; ~ *ticket* billet *m.* d'aller et retour.

reveal, *v.a.* révéler.

revenge, *s.* vengeance *f.*; — *v.a.* venger.

revenue, *s.* revenu *m.*

reverend, *adj.* révérend.

reverse, *adj.* inverse; — *s.* revers *m.*

review, *s.* revue *f.*; *(of book)* compte *m.* rendu, critique *f.*; — *v.a.* revoir; *(book)* faire la critique (d'un livre).

revision, *s.* révision *f.*

revolt, *s.* révolte *f.*

revolution, *s.* révolution

f.; *(motor)* tour *m.*

reward, *s.* récompense *f.;* — *v.a.* récompenser.

rheumatism, *s.* rhumatisme *m.*

rhyme, *s.* rime *f.*

rhythm, *s.* rythme *m.*

rib, *s.* côte *f.*

rice, *s.* riz *m.*

rich, *adj.* riche.

rid, *v.a.* get ~ *of* se débarrasser de.

riddle, *s.* énigme *f.*

ride, *v.n.* monter; aller à cheval *or* à bicyclette; *(bus)* voyager; aller (en autobus); *v. a.* monter; — *s.* promenade *f.*

ridge, *s.* crête *f.*

ridiculous, *adj.* ridicule.

rifle, *s.* fusil *m.*

right, *adj.* droit; correct, exact; juste, bon; bien; ~ *side* endroit *m.; be* ~ avoir raison; *that's* ~ c'est ça; — *s.* droit *m.; (opposed to left)* droite *f.;* — *adv.* droit; bien; *(very)* très.

rim, *s.* bord *m.*

ring¹, *s.* anneau *m.;* cercle *m.; (sport)* ring *m.*

ring², *v.n. & a.* sonner; ~ *up* appeler (au téléphone); — *s.* son *m.;* coup *m.* de sonnette; *there is a* ~ *at the door* on sonne (à la porte).

rinse, *v.a.* rinser.

riot, *s.* émeute *f.*

rip, *v.a.* déchirer; ~ *up* arracher; *v.n.* aller à toute vitesse.

ripe, *adj.* mûr.

rise, *v. n.* se lever; *(revolt)* se soulever; *(prices)* hausser; *(originate)* naître (de); — *s.* montée *f.; (salary)* augmentation *f.; give* ~ *to* donner lieu à.

risk, *s.* risque *m.;* — *v.a.* risquer.

rival, *adj. & s.* rival, -e *(m. f.);* — *v.a.* rivaliser (avec).

rivalry, *s.* rivalité *f.*

river, *s.* fleuve *m.,* rivière *f.*

road, *s.* route *f.,* chemin *m.*

road-map, *s.* carte *f.* routière. *f.*

roar, *s.* rugissement *m.;* — *v.n.* rugir; hurler.

roast, *v.a. & n.* rôtir; — *s.* rôti *m.*

rob, *v.a.* voler.

robber, *s.* voleur *m.*

robbery, *s.* vol *m.*

robe, *s.* robe *f.*

robin, *s.* rouge-gorge *m.*

rock, *s.* rocher *m.,* roc *m.*

rocket, *s.* fusée *f.*

rocky, *adj.* rocheux.

rod, *s.* baguette *f.*

rogue, *s.* coquin, -e *m. f.*

roll, *s.* rouleau *m.;* liste *f.;* — *v. a.* rouler.

roller-towel, *s.* essuie-mains *m.* à rouleau.

Roman, *adj.* romain; — *s.* Romain, -e *m. f.*

romantic, *adj.* romanesque; romantique.

roof, *s.* toit *m.*

room, *s.* chambre *f.;* salle *f.; (space)* place *f.*

root, *s.* racine *f.;* source *f.*

rope, *s.* corde *f.*

rose, *s.* rose *f.*

rotten, *adj.* pourri, carié.

rough, *adj.* rude; grossier; brut; *(sea)* gros.

roughly, *adv.* approximativement.

round, *adj.* rond; — *adv.* de tour, en rond, autour; *hand* ~ faire circuler; *go* ~ tourner;

turn ~ tourner, se retourner; — *prep.* autour de; — *s.* rond *m.*, cercle *m.*; tournée *f.;* tour *m.*

rouse, *v.a.* réveiller.

route, *s.* route *f.*

routine, *s.* routine *f.*

row¹, *s.* rang *m.*, rangée *f.;* ligne *f.*

row², *v.n.* ramer; *v.a.* faire aller (à la rame); — *s.* promenade *f.* en canot.

row³, *s.* chahut *m.*, vacarme *m.*, querelle *f.;* réprimande *f.*

royal, *adj.* royal.

rub, *v.a.* frotter.

rubber, *s.* caoutchouc *m.*

rubbish, *s.* décombres *m. pl.;* ordure(s) *f. (pl)*, immondices *f. pl.*

ruby, *s.* rubis *m.*

rudder, *s.* gouvernail *m.*

rude, *adj.* rude.

ruffian, *s.* bandit *m.*

ruffle, *s.* ride *f.;* — *v.a.* rider; ébouriffer.

rug, *s.* couverture *f.;* tapis *m.*

ruin, *s.* ruine *f.;* — *v. a.* ruiner.

rule, *s.* autorité *f.;* règle *f.;* *(of the road)* code *m.;* as a ~ généralement; — *v.a.* gouverner; régler; guider; ~ *out* exclure.

ruler, *s.* gouverneur *m.*, souverain *m.;* *(for lines)* règle *f.*

rum, *s.* rhum *m.*

Rumanian, *adj.* roumain; — *s.* Roumain, -e *m. f.*

rumour, *s.* rumeur *f.*

run, *v.n.* courir; fuir, se sauver; *(flow)* couler; *(veh.)* marcher, faire le service; *(engine)* fonctionner; *(play in*

theatre) se jouer; *v.a.* faire fonctionner; mettre en service; faire marcher, faire aller; ~ *after* courir après; ~ *away* s'enfuir; ~ *down* descendre en courant; *(health)* s'affaiblir; ~ *in (motor)* roder; ~ *into* heurter, rencontrer; ~ *off* s'enfuir; s'écouler; ~ *out* se terminer; ~ *over* passer dessus; ~ *up (debts)* entasser; — *s.* course *f.;* voyage *m.*

runner, *s.* coureur, -euse *m. f.*

runway, *s.* piste (d'envol) *f.*

rupture, *s.* rupture *f.*

rural, *adj.* rural.

rush, *v.n.* se précipiter, se jeter; *v.a.* entraîner à toute vitesse; — *s.* ruée *f.*, hâte *f.;* ~ *hours* heures *f.pl.* d'affluence, coup *m.* de feu.

Russian, *adj.* russe; — *s.* Russe *m. f.*

rust, *s.* rouille *f.*

rustic, *adj.* rustique.

rustle, *s.* bruissement *m.*

rye, *s.* seigle *m.*

S

sabre, *s.* sabre *m.*

sack, *s.* sac *m.*

sacrament, *s.* sacrement *m.*

sacrifice, *s.* sacrifice *m.*

sad, *adj.* triste.

saddle, *s.* selle *f.*

sadness, *s.* tristesse *f.*

safe, *adj.* sûr, en sûreté. sans danger; — *s.* coffre-fort *m.*

safely, *adv.* sain et sauf;

en sûreté.
safety, s. sûreté f.
sail, s. voile f.; — v.n.
faire voile, naviguer.
sailor, s. marin m., matelot m.
saint, s. saint, -e m. f.
sake: for the ~ of pour l'amour de.
salad, s. salade f.
salary, s. traitement m., appointements m. pl.
sale, s. vente f.; (auction) vente f. aux enchères.
salesman, s. vendeur m.
saleswoman, s. vendeuse f.
salmon, s. saumon m.
saloon, s. salon m.; ~ bar bar m.
salt, s. sel m.
salt-cellar, s. salière f.
salvation, s. salut m.
same, adj. & pron. même.
sanatorium, s. sanatorium m.
sanction, s. sanction f.; — v.a. sanctionner.
sand, s. sable m.; the ~s la plage.
sandal, s. sandale f.
sandwich, s. sandwich m.
sanitary, adj. sanitaire.
sarcastic, adj. sarcastique.
sardine, s. sardine f.
Satan, s. Satan m.
satellite, s. satellite m.
satire, s. satire f.
satisfaction, s. satisfaction f.
satisfactory, adj. satisfaisant.
satisfy, v.a. satisfaire.
Saturday, s. samedi m.
sauce, s. sauce f.
sausage, s. saucisse f.
save, v. a. sauver; (spare) épargner, gagner; v.n. économiser.
savings-bank, s. caisse f. d'épargne.
Saviour, s. Sauveur m.

saw, s. scie f.; — v.a. & n. scier.
say, v. a. dire; that is to ~ c'est-à-dire.
scale¹, s. plateau (de balance) m.; (pair of) ~s balance f.; — v. a. peser.
scale², s. échelle f.; (music) gamme f.
scale³, s. (fish) écaille f.
scanty, adj. maigre.
scar, s. cicatrice f.
scarce, adj. rare.
scarcely, adv. à peine.
scare, s. panique f.; — v.a. effrayer.
scarf, s. écharpe f., foulard m.
scarlet, adj. écarlate.
scatter, v.a. disperser; éparpiller; dissiper.
scene, s. scène f.; behind the ~s dans les coulisses.
scenery, s. paysage m.; (theatre) décor m.
scent, s. odeur f.; parfum m.; (dog) flair m.
schedule, s. liste f.; cédule f.
scheme, s. plan m.; projet m.
scholar, s. (child) écolier, -ère m. f.; (learned) savant m.
scholarship, s. bourse f.
school, s. école f.; classe f.
schoolboy, -girl, s. écolier, -ère m. f.
schoolmaster, s. instituteur m., maître m. d'école.; (secondary) professeur m.
schoolmistress, s. maîtresse f. d'école; (secondary) professeur m.
schoolroom, s. (salle de) classe f.
science, s. science f.

scientific, *adj.* scientifique.

scientist, *s.* savant *m.*

scissors, *s. pl.* ciseaux *m. pl.*

scold, *v.a.* gronder.

scoop, *s.* écope *f.*

scooter, *s.* scooter *m.*

scope, *s.* portée *f.;* envergure *f.;* carrière *f.*

scorch, *v.a.* roussir, brûler.

score, *s.* entaille *f.; (sum)* compte *m.; (games)* points *m. pl.,* marque *f.,* score *m.; (twenty)* vingtaine *f.; (music)* partition *f.; — v.a.* marquer; ~ *out* rayer.

scorn, *s.* mépris *m.*

Scotch, Scottish, Scots, *adj.* écossais.

Scotsman, *s.* Écossais *m.*

scout, *s.* éclaireur *m.*

scrambled: ~ *eggs* œufs *m. pl.* brouillés.

scrap, *s.* morceau *m.;* bout *m.*

scrape, *v.a.* gratter; râcler; ~ *off* décrotter.

scratch, *v.a.* gratter; égratigner; *v. n.* griffer gratter; — *s.* égratignure *f.; m.* coup d'ongle.

scream, *v.n. & a.* crier; — *s.* cri *m.*

screen, *s.* écran *m.*

screw, *s.* vis *f.*

scrub, *v.a.* frotter; nettoyer à la brosse.

scrupulous, *adj.* scrupuleux.

sculptor, *s.* sculpteur *m.*

sculpture, *s.* sculpture *f.; — v.a.* sculpter.

scythe, *s.* faux *f.*

sea, *s.* mer *f.; by* ~ par (voie de) mer.

seal[1], *s. (animal)* phoque *m.*

seal[2], *s.* sceau *m.; — v.a.* sceller; cacheter.

seam, *s.* couture *f.*

seaport, *s.* port *m.* de mer.

search, *v.a.* chercher; — *s.* recherche *f.*

search-light, *s.* projecteur *m.*

seasickness, *s.* mal *m.* de mer.

seaside, *s.* bord *m.* de la mer.

season, *s.* saison *f.*

seat, *s.* siège *m.; — v.a.* asseoir; placer.

second, *adj.* second; deux; deuxième; — *s.* seconde *f.*

secondary, *adj.* secondaire; ~ *school* école *f.* secondaire.

second-hand, *adj.* de seconde main, d'occasion.

secret, *adj. & s.* secret *(m.).*

secretary, *s.* secrétaire *m. f.*

section, *s.* section *f.*

secular, *adj.* séculier.

secure, *adj.* en sûreté, sûr; — *v.a.* mettre en sûreté; obtenir; fixer.

security, *s.* sécurité *f.;* caution *f.;* sûreté *f.; securities* valeurs *f. pl.; social* ~ sécurité *f.* sociale.

sediment, *s.* sédiment *m.*

see, *v.a.* voir; *(understand)* comprendre; *(make sure)* s'assurer; *(accompany)* accompagner; ~ *about* s'occuper de; ~ *out* accompagner jusqu'à la porte; ~ *through* voir à travers, pénétrer; mener à bonne fin; ~ *to* veiller à, s'occuper de.

seed, s. semence f.; graine f.

seek, v.a. chercher.

seem, v.n. sembler, paraître.

seize, v.a. saisir; prendre.

seldom, adv. rarement.

select, v.a. choisir.

selection, s. choix m.

self, s. moi m.

self-conscious, adj. gêné.

self-control, s. maîtrise f. de soi-même.

selfish, adj. égoïste.

selfishness, s. égoïsme m.

self-respect, s. respect m. de soi.

self-service, adj. ~ restaurant restaurant à libre service.

sell, v.a. vendre; ~ out vendre tout son stock; v. n. se vendre.

seller, s. vendeur, -euse m. f.

semaphore, s. sémaphore m.

semicolon, s. point (et) virgule m.

senate, s. sénat m.

senator, s. sénateur m.

send, v.a. envoyer; (money) remettre; ~ back renvoyer; ~ for envoyer chercher; ~ forth exha er; ~ off expédier; ~ on faire suivre; ~ out lancer.

sender, s. expéditeur, -trice m. f.

sense, s. sens m.

senseless, adj. insensé; sans connaissance.

sensibility, s. sensibilité f.

sensible, adj. sensible; sensé, raisonnable.

sensitive, adj. sensible.

sensual, adj. sensuel.

sentence, s. jugement m.; sentence f.; phrase f.;

— v. a. condamner.

sentiment, s. sentiment m.

sentry, s. sentinelle f.

separate, adj. séparé; à part; — v.a. séparer; v.n. se séparer.

separation, s. séparation f.

September, s. septembre m.

serenade, s. sérénade f.

sergeant, s. sergent m.

series, s. série f.

serious, adj. sérieux.

sermon, s. sermon m.

servant, s. serviteur, -vante m. f.; domestique m. f.

serve, v. a. & n. servir.

service, s. service m.; utilité f.

service-station, s. station-service f.

session, s. séance f., session f.

set, v.a. mettre, placer; (limb) remettre; (fashion) donner; (jewels) monter; (watch) régler; (problem) donner; (appoint) fixer; (trap) tendre; — v.n. (sun) se coucher; — ~ about se mettre à; ~ aside mettre de côté; ~ down déposer; noter; ~ forth exposer; ~ in commencer; ~ off, out partir; ~ on pousser (à); ~ up dresser; établir; ~ up for se donner pour. — s ensemble m., assortiment m., collection f.; (tea) service m.; (radio) poste m.; (ornaments) garniture f.; (tennis) set m.; (gang) bande f.; ~ of furniture ameublement m.; ~ of false teeth dentier m.

setting, s. mise f., pose f.; montage m.; installation f.; coucher m.

settle, *v. a.* fixer; arranger; régler, payer; décider, résoudre; *v.n.* s'établir; se poser (sur); se décider à; ~ *down* s'établir.

settlement, *s.* colonie *f.*

seven, *adj. & s.* sept.

seventeen, *adj.* dix-sept.

seventh, *adj.* septième.

seventy, *adj. & s.* soixante-dix.

several, *adj.* plusieurs; différent.

severe, *adj.* sévère.

sew, *v.a.* coudre.

sewing-machine, *s.* machine *f.* à coudre.

sex, *s.* sexe *m.*

sexual, *adj.* sexuel.

shabby, *adj.* usé, râpé.

shade, *s.* ombre *f.;* ombrage *m.;* — *v.a.* ombrager.

shadow, *s.* ombre *f.*

shady, *adj.* ombreux.

shaft, *s.* bois *m.;* trait *m.;* flèche *f.;* arbre *m.*

shake, *v.a.* secouer; ébranler; *(hands)* serrer; *v.n.* trembler; s'ébranler; — *s.* secousse *f.*

shaky, *adj.* tremblant, branlant; cassé; faible.

shall, *(future see Grammar); (command)* vouloir; *(duty)* devoir.

shallow, *adj.* peu profond.

shame, *s.* honte *f.*

shameless, *adj.* éhonté; honteux.

shampoo, *s.* shampooing *m.*

shank, *s.* jambe *f.*

shape, *s.* forme *f.;* — *v. a.* façonner; former; diriger; *v.n.* se développer; promettre.

shapeless, *adj.* sans forme.

share, *s.* part *f.;* action *f.; have a* ~ *in* contribuer (à); *go* ~*s (in)* partager; — *v. a. & n.* partager.

shareholder, *s.* actionnaire *m. f.*

sharp, *adj.* tranchant; aigu; aigre; piquant; perçant; — *s. (music)* dièse *m.;* — *adv.* net; *9.0* ~ 9 heures précises.

sharpen, *v.a.* aiguiser; tailler.

shatter, *v.a.* fracasser; déranger.

shave, *v.a.* raser; *v.n.* se raser.

shawl, *s.* châle *m.*

she, *pron.* elle.

shear, *v.a.* tondre; couper; — *s. (pair of)* ~*s* cisailles *f. pl.*

sheath, *s.* étui; fourreau *m.*

shed, *v.a.* verser; *(light)* répandre.

sheep, *s.* mouton *m.*

sheer, *adj.* pur; perpendiculaire.

sheet, *s.* drap *m.;* *(paper)* feuille *f.;* ~ *iron* tôle *f.*

shelf, *s.* rayon *m.*

shell, *s. (egg, nut)* coque *f.;* *(peas)* cosse *f.*

shelter, *s.* abri *m.; take* ~ s'abriter; — *v.a.* abriter (de); *v. n.* se mettre à l'abri (de).

shepherd, *s.* berger.

shield, *s.* bouclier *m.;* écu *m.*

shift, *s.* changement *m.;* *(work)* équipe *f.;* *make* ~ *to* s'arranger (de); — *v. n. & a.* changer de place.

shine, *v. n.* briller; rayonner (de); *the sun is shining* il fait du soleil.

ship, *s.* vaisseau *m.*, navire *m.;* — *v. a.* embarquer.

shipping, s. embarquement m.; navires m. pl.; ~ *company* compagnie f. de navigation.

shipping-agent, s. agent maritime, m.; *(goods)* expéditeur m.

shipwreck, s. naufrage m.; — v.a. be ~ed faire naufrage.

shipyard, s. chantier m. de construction.

shirt, s. chemise f.

shiver, v.n. frissonner; *(cold)* grelotter;

shock, s. choc m.; coup m.; — v.a. choquer; frapper d'horreur.

shocking, adj. affreux; choquant.

shoe, s. soulier m.

shoeblack, s. décrotteur m., cireur m.

shoe-lace, s. lacet m.

shoemaker, s. cordonnier m.

shoot, v.a. tirer, fusiller; lancer; décharger; *(game)* chasser; *(plant)* pousser; *(rays)* darder; *(film)* tourner; v.n. tirer; se précipiter, se lancer; *(plant)* pousser; *(pain)* élancer.

shooting, s. tir m., fusillade f.; *(game)* chasse f.; — adj. *(pain)* lancinant.

shop, s. boutique f., magasin m.; — v.n. go ~ping faire des achats or emplettes.

shop-assistant, s. commis m.; demoiselle f., vendeur, -euse m. f.

shopkeeper, s. marchand, -e m. f.; commerçant, -e m. f.

shore, s. rivage m.; rive f.

short, adj. court; petit; bref, brève; *(lacking)* de manque; — adv. be ~ of manquer de.

shorten, v. a. & n. raccourcir; abréger.

shorthand, s. sténographie f.

shortly, adv. sous peu; bientôt; brièvement.

shot, s. coup m.; trait m.; *(bullet)* balle f., *(cannon)* boulet m.

shoulder, s. épaule f.

shout, s. cri m.; — v. a. & n. crier.

shove, v.a. pousser.

shovel, s. pelle f.

show, v.a. montrer; indiquer; manifester; exposer; expliquer; v.n. se montrer; ~ *in* faire entrer; ~ *off* étaler; faire ressortir; se donner des airs; ~ *out* reconduire; ~ *up* ressortir; — s. blant m.; spectacle m.; parade f.; exposition f.

shower, s. averse f.; — v.a. faire pleuvoir.

shower-bath, s. douche f.

shrill, adj. aigre; aigu, -ë.

shrine, s. châsse f.; lieu saint m.

shrink, v. a. & n. rétrécir; reculer.

shroud, s. linceul m.

shrub, s. arbrisseau m., arbuste m.

shrug, s. haussement m. d'épaules; — v.a. hausser.

shudder, s. frisson m.; — v. n. frissonner (de).

shut, v.a. fermer; *(also* ~ *in)* enfermer; ~ *off* couper; ~ *up* fermer; se taire.

shutter, s. volet m.

shy, adj. timide.

sick, adj. malade; be ~ vomir; be ~ of être dégoûté de; fall ~

tomber malade.

sickle, s. faucille f.

sickly, adj. maladif; malsain.

sickness, s. maladie f.

side, s. côte m.; bord m.; (team) équipe f.

siege, s. siège m.

sieve, s. crible m.

sift, v.a. cribler.

sigh, s. soupir m.; — v. n. soupirer.

sight, s. vue f.; spectacle m.; ~s curiosités f. pl.

sightseeing: go ~ visiter les curiosités.

sign, s. signe m.; enseigne f.; — v. a. & n. signer; ~ on engager.

signal, s signal m.; — v.a. signaler; v.n.faire des signaux.

signature, s. signature f.

significant, adj. significatif.

signify, v.a. signifier; v.n. importer.

signpost, s. poteau m. indicateur.

silence, s. silence m.

silent, adj. silencieux; muet.

silk, s. soie f.

silly, adj. sot.

silver, s. argent m.; — adj. d'argent; argenté.

similar, adj. semblable.

simple, adj. simple.

simultaneous, adj. simultané.

sin, s. péché m.; — v.n. pécher.

since, adv. & prep. depuis; — conj. depuis que; (because) puisque.

sincere, adj. sincère.

sinew, s. tendon m.

sinful, adj. pécheur.

sing, v. a. & n. chanter.

singer, s. chanteur, -euse m. f.; cantatrice f.

single, adj. simple; seul; célibataire; particulier; ~ ticket billet m. d'aller.

singular, s. singulier m.; — adj. remarquable; singulier.

sink, v. n. tomber au fond, sombrer; s'enfoncer; baisser; v. a. enfoncer; faire baisser; foncer; couler; — s. évier m.

sinner, s. pécheur, -eresse m. f.

sir, s. monsieur m.; Sir m.

sister, s. sœur f.; (nurse) infirmière f.

sister-in-law, s. belle-sœur f.

sit, v.n. s'asseoir; être assis; rester; ~ down s'asseoir; se mettre (à); ~ for (exam) se présenter à; ~ up se dresser; (at night) veiller.

site, s. emplacement m.; terrain m.; site m.

sitting-room, s. petit salon m.

situation, s. situation f.; (employment) position f.; emploi m.

six, adj. & s. six (m.).

sixteen, adj. & s. seize (m.).

sixth, adj. sixième; six.

sixty, adj. & s. soixante.

size, s. grandeur f., mesure f.; (shoes etc.) pointure f.; numéro m., taille f.; (pers.) taille f.

skate, v.n. patiner.

skating, s. patinage m.

sketch, s. croquis m.; esquisse f.; — v.a. esquisser.

ski, s. ski m.

skid, v.n. déraper.

skier, s. skieur m.

skiff, s. esquif m.

skilful, adj. adroit.

skill, *s.* adresse *f.*

skim, *v.a.* écrémer.

skin, *s.* peau *f.;* — *v.a.* écorcher; peler.

skip, *v. a. & n.* sauter.

skirt, *s.* jupe *f.*

skull, *s.* crâne *m.*

sky, *s.* ciel *m. (pl.* cieux).

slack, *adj.* lâche; négligent.

slacken, *v.a.* ralentir; relâcher; *v.n.* se relâcher; diminuer.

slacks, *s. pl.* pantalon *m.*

slander, *s.* calomnie *f.;* — *v.a.* calomnier.

slant, *s.* biais *m.;* — *v. a.* faire pencher; *v. n.* être en pente.

slap, *s.* claque *f.;* soufflet *m.;* — *v. a.* claquer; souffleter.

slate, *s.* ardoise *f.*

slaughter, *s.* massacre *m.*

slave, *s.* esclave *m. f.*

sledge, *s.* traineau.

sleep, *s.* sommeil *m.;* go to ~ s'endormir; — *v. a. & n.* dormir.

sleeping-car, *s.* wagon-lit *m.*

sleepy, *adj.* somnolent; be ~ avoir sommeil.

sleeve, *s.* manche *f.*

slender, *adj.* mince, faible.

slice, *s.* tranche *f.*

slide, *s.* glissade *f.; (photo)* diapositive *f.*

slight, *adj.* mince; léger.

slim, *adj.* mince, svelte.

sling, *s.* fronde *f.*

slip, *v.n.* glisser; se glisser (dans); *v.a.* filer; pousser, glisser; ~ off ôter; ~ on mettre; ~ out s'esquiver; — *s.* glissade *f.; (mistake)* faux pas *m.; (paper)* fiche *f.; (underwear)* combinaison *f.*

slipper, *s.* pantoufle *f.*

slope, *s.* biais *m.;* pente *f.;* — *v. n.* incliner.

slot, *s.* fente *f.*

slow, *adj.* lent; *(clock)* en retard; *(dull)* peu intelligent; ~ to lent à; — *v.n. & a.* ~ down ralentir.

slumber, *s.* sommeil *m.;* — *v.n.* sommeiller.

slump, *s.* débâcle *f.; (in trade)* mévente *f.;* dépression *f.*

sly, *adj.* rusé.

small, *adj.* petit; faible; peu important; menu.

smart, *adj. (clever)* habile, débrouillard; *(witty)* spirituel; *(dress, pers.)* élégant, chic; pimpant; *(society)* élégant.

smash, *v. a.* briser; *fig.* écraser; — *s.* fracas *m.;* collision *f.*

smear, *v.a.* enduire; — *s.* tache *f.*

smell, *s.* odorat *m.;* odeur *f.;* — *v. a. & n.* sentir; ~ out flairer.

smile, *s.* sourire *m.;* — *v.n.* sourire (at à).

smoke, *s.* fumée *f.;* — *v.a. & n.* fumer.

smooth, *adj.* lisse; uni; doux, -ce; *(sea)* calme; — *v.a.* aplanir; lisser.

smuggle, *v.a.* ~ in faire passer en contrebande; *v.n.* faire la contrebande.

smuggler, *s.* contrebandier *m.*

snack, *s.* morceau (sur le pouce) *m.; have a* ~ casser la croûte.

snail, *s.* colimaçon *m.*

snake, *s.* serpent *m.*

snap, *s.* fermoir *m.;* coup *m.* de dents; claquement *m.; (photo)* instantané *m.;* — *v. a.* faire claquer; fermer;

~ *at* happer; ~ *off* casser.

snapshot, *s.* instantané *m.*

snatch, *s.* action de saisir, *f.;* accès *m.;* fragment *m.;* — *v. a.* saisir; ~ *at* saisir au vol.

sneeze, *v. n.* éternuer; — *s.* éternuement *m.*

sniff, *v.a.&n.* renifler.

snore, *v. n.* ronfler.

snow, *s.* neige *f.;* — *v.n.* neiger.

snug, *adj.* commode.

so, *adv.* ainsi; si; donc; ~ *that* de sorte que; afin que.

soak, *v.n.* tremper.

soap, *s.* savon *m.*

soar, *v.n.* prendre son essor; *fig.* s'élancer.

sob, *v.n.* sangloter; — *s.* sanglot.

sober, *adj.* sobre; sensé;

social, *adj.* social.

socialism, *s.* socialisme *m.*

society, *s.* société *f.*

sock, *s.* chaussette *f.*

socket, *s.* cavité *f.;* *(electric)* prise *f.* de contact.

soda-water, *s.* eau *f.* de Seltz.

sofa, *s.* canapé *m.*

soft, *adj.* mou, mol molle; doux, -ce.

soil, *s.* terroir; *(stain)* tache; — *v. a.* souiller.

soldier, *s.* soldat *m.*

sole[1], *s.* plante *f.;* semelle *f.;* *(fish)* sole *f.*

sole[2], *adj.* seul.

solicit, *v. a.* solliciter.

solicitor, *s.* avoué *m.* solicitor *m.*

solidarity, *s.* solidarité *f.*

solitude, *s.* solitude *f.*

solution, *s.* solution *f.*

solve, *v.a.* résoudre.

some, *adj.* quelque; de; — *pron.* quelques-uns; les uns; en *(+ verb)*

— *adv.* environ.

somebody, -one, *pron.* quelqu'un.

somehow, *adv.* d'une façon quelconque; ~ *or other* d'une façon ou d'une autre.

something, *s.* & *pron.* quelque chose *m.*

sometime, *adv.* quelque jour, autrefois.

sometimes, *adv.* quelquefois, parfois.

somewhere, *adv.* quelque part.

son, *s.* fils *m.*

song, *s.* chanson *f.*

son-in-law, *s.* gendre *m.*

soon, *adv.* bientôt.

sore, *adj.* douloureux; *have a* ~ ... avoir mal à ...; — *s.* plaie *f.*

sorrow, *s.* douleur *f.*

sorry, *adj. be* ~ *for* regretter; ~*!* pardon!

sort, *s.* sorte *f.;* genre *m.;* type *m.;* ~ *of* une espèce de.

soul, *s.* âme *f.*

sound[1], *s.* son *m.;* bruit *m.;* — *v. n.* sonner; — *v.a.* sonner; sonder; *(physician)* ausculter.

sound[2], *adj.* sain; solide; droit; profond; en bon état.

soup, *s.* potage *m.;(clear)* consommé *m.;* *(thick)* soupe *f.*

sour, *adj.* aigre; acide; *(milk)* tourné.

source, *s.* source *f.*

south, *s.* sud *m.*, midi *m.;* — *adj.* sud; du sud; — *adv.* vers le sud.

southeast, *adj.* & *s.* sud-est *(m.);* — *adv.* vers le sud-est.

southern, *adj.* du sud.

southwest, *adj.* & *s.* sud-ouest *(m.);* — *adv.* vers

le sud-ouest.

sovereign, *s.* souverain, -e *m. f.*

sow¹, *v. a. & n.* semer (de).

sow², *s.* truie *f.*

space, *s.* espace *m.*

space-craft, -ship, -vehicle, *s.* astronef *m.*

space-flight, *s.* navigation *f.* astronautique.

spaceman, *s.* cosmonaute *m.*, astronaute *m.*

spade, *s.* bêche *f.; (cards)* pique *m.*

span, *s.* empan *m.;* ouverture; — *v.a.* traverser; couvrir.

Spaniard, *s.* Espagnol, -e.

Spanish, *adj. & s.* espagnol *(m.).*

spanner, *s.* clef *f.*

spare, *adj.* maigre; disponible; de réserve; ∼ *parts* pièces de rechange *f. pl.;* ∼ *time* loisir *m.;* — *v.a.* épargner; économiser; *(evade)* éviter.

spark, *s.* étincelle *f.*

sparrow, *s.* moineau *m.*

speak, *v.n.* parler; *v.a.* dire; ∼ *out* parler hardiment; ∼ *up* parler plus haut; ... ∼*ing* ici ...

spear, *s.* lance *f.*

special, *adj.* spécial.

specialist, *s.* spécialiste *m. f.*

specific, *adj.* spécifique.

specify, *v.a.* spécifier.

speck, *s.* grain *m.;* tache *f.*

spectacles, *s. pl.* lunettes *f.*

spectacular, *adj.* impressionnant.

spectator, *s.* spectateur, -trice *m. f.*

speech, *s.* parole *f.;* langage *m.; (address)* discours *m.*

speed, *s.* vitesse *f.*

speedy, *adj.* rapide;

prompt.

spell¹, *v.a. & n.* épeler; orthographier, écrire; *how is it spelt?* comment cela s'écrit-il?

spell², *s.* période *f.;* tour *m.*

spelling, *s.* ortographe *f.*

spend, *v.a.* dépenser; *(time)* passer; *v.n.* dépenser.

sphere, *s.* sphère *f.*

spice, *s.* épice *f.*

spider, *s.* araignée *f.*

spill, *v.a.* repandre; renverser.

spin, *v.a. & n.* filer; faire tourner.

spinach, *s.* épinards *m. pl.*

spine, *s.* épine (dorsale) *f.*

spinster, *s.* vieille fille *f.;* célibataire *f.*

spiral, *adj.* en spirale.

spire, *s.* flèche *f.*

spirit, *s.* esprit *m.;* âme *f.;* spectre *m.;* caractère *m.,* cœur *m.;* ∼*s* spiritueux *m. pl.*

spiritual, *adj.* spirituel.

spit, *s.* crachat *m.;* — *v. a. & n.* cracher.

spite, *s.* dépit *m.; in* ∼ *of* malgré.

splash, *s.* éclaboussement *m.;* — *v. a. & n.* éclabousser (de).

spleen, *s.* rate *f.*

splendid, *adj.* splendide.

splinter, *s.* éclat *m.; (bone)* esquille *f.*

split, *v. a.* fendre; (also ∼ *up)* partager; *v.n.* se fendre; se diviser.

spoil, *v.a.* gâter; dépouiller (de); endommager; *v.n.* se gâter.

sponge, *s.* éponge *f.*

spontaneous, *adj.* spontané.

spoon, *s.* cuiller *f.*

spoonful, *s.* cuillerée *f.*

sport, *s.* sport *m.;* amuse-
ments *m. pl.*

sportsman, *s.* sportsman
m.

spot, *s.* tache *f.; (place)*
endroit *m.; — v.a.*
tacher; reconnaître.

spout, *s.* gouttière *f.;* bec
m.; — v.a. lancer.

sprain, *v.a.* donner une
entorse (à).

spray, *s.* embrun *m.,*
vaporisateur *m.;* ato-
miseur *m.; — v.a.* vapo-
riser, atomiser; arroser.

spread, *v.a.* étendre; répandre; *(cloth)* mettre;
(cover) couvrir; *(news)*
faire circuler; *v.n.*
s'étendre; — *s.* propa-
gation *f.;* étendue *f.*

spring[1], *s.* printemps *m.*

spring[2], *v.n.* sauter;
pousser; jaillir; prove-
nir (de), descendre (de),
naître (de); ~ up se
lever vite; jaillir; — *s.*
saut *m.; (watch etc.)*
ressort *m.*

sprinkle, *v.a.* répandre;
asperger (de), arroser.

sprout, *v. a. & n.* germer;
pousser; — *s.* pousse
f.; Brussels ~s choux
m. pl. de Bruxelles

spur, *s.* éperon *m.,* aiguillon *m.; — v. a.* éperon-
ner; ~ on pousser à.

spy, *s.* espion, -onne
m. f.; — v.n. espionner.

squander, *v. a.* gaspiller.

square, *s.* carré *m.; (town)*
place *f.; — adj.* carré;
honnête.

squeeze, *v.a.* serrer; presser.

squint, *v.n.* loucher; —
s. strabisme *m.*

squire, *s.* écuyer *m.;*
châtelain *m.*

squirrel, *s.* écureuil *m.*

stability, *s.* stabilité *f.*

stable, *s.* écurie *f.; — adj.*
stable.

stack, *s.* pile *f.;* meule *f.*

stadium, *s.* stade *m.*

staff, *s.* état-major *m.;*
bâton *m.;* hampe *f.;*
(institution) personnel
m.; ~ officer officier
d'état-major *m.*

stag, *s.* cerf *m.*

stage, *s.* scène *f.; (drama)* théâtre *m.; (pe-
riod)* période *f.; (platform)* estrade *f.; —
v.a.* mettre en scène.

stagger, *v.n.* chanceler;
v.a. bouleverser.

stain, *s.* tache *f.; — v.a.*
tacher; salir.

stair, *s.* marche; ~s
escalier *m.*

staircase, *s.* escalier *m.*

stake, *s.* pieu *m.; at* ~
en jeu; — *v.a.* garnir
de pieux; mettre au
jeu; jouer.

stale, *adj.* rassis.

stall, *s.* stalle *f.;* fauteuil
m.; (books) kiosque *m.*
à journaux.

stammer, *v. n.* bégayer.

stamp, *s.* timbre-poste *m.;*
estampe *f.;* contrôle
m.; empreinte *f.; —
v.a.* timbrer; estamper;
contrôler.

stand, *v.n.* être debout,
se tenir debout, se
soutenir; *(be situated)*
se trouver; *(remain)*
rester; ~ out ressortir;
~ up se lever; — *s.*
position *f.; (vehicles)*
station *f.; (stall)* étalage *m.;* stand *m.*

standard, *s.* étendard *m.;*
étalon *m.;* niveau *m.;*
— *adj.* régulateur; au
titre; *(authors)* clas-
sique.

star, *s.* étoile *f.*

stare, *v.n.* *(also ~ at)* regarder fixement.

start, *v.n.* partir; commencer; *v. a.* faire partir; faire lever; commencer; lancer; — *s.* commencement *m.;* départ *m.*

starve, *v.n.* mourir de faim; *v. a.* faire mourir de faim.

state, *s.* état *m.;* — *v. a.* affirmer; porter; déclarer.

statement, *s.* déclaration *f.*

statesman, *s.* homme *m.* d'état.

station, *s.* poste *m.;* endroit *m.; (railway)* gare *f.; (police)* poste *m.* de police.

stationer, *s.* papetier *m.; ~'s shop* papeterie *f.*

statistic(al), *adj.* statistique.

statistics, *s.* statistique *f.*

statue, *s.* statue *f.*

statute, *s.* statut *m.;* ordonnance *f.*

stay, *v.n.* rester; être installé; *~ away* rester absent; *~ up* veiller.

steady, *adj.* ferme; soutenu; *(pers.)* rangé; — *int.* attention!

steak, *s.* tranche *f.;* bifteck *m.*

steal, *v.a.* voler.

steam, *s.* vapeur *f.*

steamboat, *s.* bateau *m.* à vapeur

steam-engine, *s.* locomotive *f.*

steel, *s.* acier *m.*

steep, *adj.* raide, escarpé.

steeple, *s.* clocher *m.*

steer, *v.a.* gouverner; diriger.

steering-gear, *s.* appareil *m.* de direction.

steering-wheel, *s.* volant *m.*

stem, *s.* tige *f.;* queue *f.*

step, *s.* pas *m.; (stair)* marche *f.; (ladder)* échelon *m.; take ~s* faire des démarches; — *v.n.* faire un pas; marcher; aller, venir; *~ in* entrer.

stepmother, *s.* belle-mère *f.*

stereotype, *s.* cliché *m.*

sterile, *adj.* stérile.

stern, *s.* arrière *m.* — *adj.* sévère.

stew, *s.* ragoût *m.; (fruit)* compote *f.;* — *v.a. (meat)* faire un ragout de; *(fruit)* faire une compote de.

steward, *s.* régisseur *m.;* steward *m.*

stewardess, *s.* hôtesse *f.* de l'air.

stick, *s.* bâton *m.*, canne *f.*, petite branche *f.;* — *v.a.* coller; *v.n.* se coller; *~ on* attacher; *~ to* rester fidèle à.

sticky, *adj.* gluant.

stiff, *adj.* raide; dur.

still, *adj.* calme — *adv.* toujours; encore; cependant.

sting, *s.* aiguillon *m.;* — *v.a. & n.* piquer.

stink, *v.n.* puer; — *s.* puanteur *f.*

stipulate, *v.a.* stipuler.

stir, *v.a.* remuer; exciter; *v. n.* remuer; bouger; — *s.* remuement *m.*

stirrup, *s.* étrier *m.*

stitch, *s.* point *m.;* — *v.a. & n.* coudre.

stock, *s.* marchandises *f.* pl.; provision *f.; (tree)* tronc *m.; (cattle)* bes-

tiaux *m. pl.; (finance)*
valeurs *f. pl.; Stock
Exchange* Bourse *f.*
stockholder, *s.* actionnaire
m. f.
stocking, *s.* bas *m.*
stomach, *s.* estomac *m.*
stone, *s.* pierre; *(fruit)*
noyau *m.;* — *v.a.*
lapider.
stony, *adj.* pierreux.
stool, *s.* tabouret *m.;*
escabeau *m.*
stop, *v.a.* arrêter; empêcher (de); *(teeth)* plom-
ber; retenir suspendre,
v.n. s'arrêter; cesser;
— *s.* halte *f.;* arrêt
m.; (organ) jeu *m.;*
(sign) signe de ponc-
tuation, *m.*
store, *s.* provision *f.;*
~*s* grand magasin *m.;*
— *v.a.* emmagasiner.
stork, *s.* cigogne *f.*
storm, *s.* orage *m.*
story[1], *s.* histoire *f.*
story[2], *s.* étage *m.*
stout, *adj.* fort; intrépide.
stove, *s.* poêle *m.;* fourneau *m.*

straight, *adj.* droit; honnête; d'aplomb; — *adv.*
juste; droit.
straighten, *v.a.* (re)dres-
ser; *v.n.* se redresser.
strain, *s.* effort *m.;* tension *f.;* — *v. a.* tendre;
(filter) passer; *(mus-
cle)* forcer.
strange, *adj.* étrange(r).
stranger, *s.* étranger -ère
m. f.
strap, *s.* courroie *f.*
straw, *s.* paille *f.*
strawberry, *s.* fraise *f.*
stray, *adj.* égaré; — *v. n.*
errer.
streak, *s.* raie *f.;* bande *f.*
stream, *s.* courant *m.;* —
v.n. couler, ruisseler.

street, *s.* rue *f.*
strength, *s.* force *f.*
strengthen, *v.a.* forti-
fier.
stress, *s.* force *f.; (grammar)* accent *m.*
stretch, *s.* effort *m.;*
étendue *f.;* — *v.a.*
étendre; élargir.
stretcher, *s.* brancard *m.*
strew, *v.a.* semer.
strict, *adj.* strict.
stride, *s.* enjambée *f.;*
grand pas *m.;* —
v. n. enjamber.
strike, *v.a.* frapper;
(blow) asséner; *(work)*
cesser; *v.n.* frapper;
(clock) sonner; *(work-
ers)* se mettre en
grève — *s.* grève *f.;*
be on ~ être en grève.
striking, *adj.* frappant.
string, *s.* ficelle *f.;* corde *f.*
strip, *s.* bande *f.;* bout
m.; — *v. a.* déshabiller;
v.n. se déshabiller.
stripe, *s.* bande *f.*
strip-lighting, *s.* éclairage
m. par luminescent.
strive, *v. n.* s'efforcer (de).
stroke, *s.* coup *m.; (swimming)* brasse *f.; (pen)*
trait *m.*
strong, *adj.* fort; vigoureux; puissant; solide.
structure, *s.* structure *f.*
struggle, *v.n.* lutter
(avec); faire de grands
efforts (pour); — *s.*
lutte *f.;* mêlée *f.*
stub, *s.* souche *f.;* bout
m.
stubborn, *adj.* obstiné.
stud, *s.* bouton *m.*
student, *s.* étudiant, -e
m. f.
studio, *s.* atelier *m.*
study, *s.* étude *f.;* cabinet *m.* de travail —

v. a. & *n.* étudier.

stuff, *s.* étoffe *f.;* materiaux *m.pl.;* — *v.a.* remplir; fourrer.

stumble, *v.n.* trébucher; ~ *(up)on* tomber sur; — *s.* faux pas *m.*

stump, *s.* souche *f.;* — *v.a.* estomper.

stupid, *adj.* stupide.

style, *s.* style *m.*

subject, *s.* sujet, -te *m. f.;* — *adj.* ~ *to* sujet à; — *v.a.* assujettir (à).

submarine, *s.* sous-marin *m.*

submission, *s.* soumission *f.*

submit, *v.a.* soumettre.

subordinate, *adj.* & *s.* subordonné; — *v.a.* subordonner.

subscribe, *v.a.* & *n.* (~ *to)* souscrire (à); s'abonner (à).

subscriber, *s.* souscripteur *m.;* abonné; -e souscripteur *m.;* abonné, -e *m. f.*

subscription, *s.* souscription *f.;* abonnement *m.*

subsequent, *adj.* subséquent.

subsequently, *adv.* par la suite.

subsidy, *s.* subside *m.*

subsist, *v. n.* exister; subsister (de).

subsistence, *s.* subsistance *f.*

substance, *s.* substance *f.*

substantial, *adj.* substantiel.

substantive, *s.* substantif *m.*

substitute, *v.a.* substituer *(for* à).

substitution, *s.* substitution *f.*

subtle, *adj.* subtil.

subtract, *v.a.* soustraire.

subtraction, *s.* soustraction *f.*

suburb, *s.* faubourg *m.;* ~*s* banlieue *f.*

subway, *s.* souterrain *m.;* métro *m.*

succeed, *v.a.* succéder (à); *v.n.* *(be successful)* réussir (à); faire ses affaires; ~ *to* succéder à.

success, *s.* succès *m.*

successful, *adj.* heureux, *(exam)* reçu.

succession, *s.* succession *f.*

successive, *adj.* successif.

such, *adj.* tel, -le; ~ *and* ~ tel(le) ou tel(le); — *pron.* ~ *as* ceux, celles.

suck, *v.a.* & *n.* sucer; — *s. give* ~ *to* allaiter.

sudden, *adj.* soudain.

suddenly, *adv.* soudain.

suet, *s.* graisse *f.* de rognon.

suffer, *v. n.* & *n.* souffrir.

sufficient, *adj.* suffisant.

sufficiently, *adv.* suffisamment.

sugar, *s.* sucre *m.*

suggest, *v.a.* suggérer; proposer.

suggestion, *s.* suggestion *f.*

suicide, *s.* suicide *m.*

suit, *s. (clothes)* complet *m.; (cards)* couleur *f.; (law)* procès *m.; (request)* requête *f.;* — *v.a.* convenir (à); adapter (à); *v.n.* convenir (à); aller (avec).

suitable, *adj.* convenable; ~ *for* adapté à.

suitcase, *s.* mallette *f.,* valise *f.*

sum, *s.* somme *f.;* ~ *total* somme totale, *f.;*

— v.a. ~ up résumer
summary, s. résumé m.
summer, s. été m.
summon, v.a. convoquer; appeler.
sun, s. soleil m.
Sunday, s. dimanche m.
sunny, adj. ensoleillé; exposé au soleil.
sunrise, s. lever m. du soleil.
sunset, s. coucher m. du soleil.
sunshine, s. soleil m.
sunstroke, s. coup m. de soleil.
superannuate, v. a. mettre à la retraite.
superficial, adj. superficiel.
superfluous, adj. superflu.
superior, s. & adj. supérieur (m.).
supermarket, s. supermarché m.
supersonic, adj. supersonique.
superstition, s. superstition f.
superstitious, adj. superstitieux.
supervise, v.a. surveiller.
supervision, s. superveillance f.
supper, s. souper m.
supplement, s. supplément m.; — v.a. suppléer (à).
supplementary, adj. supplémentaire.
supply, s. provision f.; approvisionnement m.; ~ and demand l'offre et la demande; — v.a. fourner (de); suppléer.
support, s. appui m.; support m.; — v.a. supporter; soutenir; appuyer.
suppose, v.a. supposer.

supposition, s. supposition f.
suppress, v.a. supprimer.
suppression, s. suppression f.; répression f.
supreme, adj. suprême.
sure, adj. sûr; be ~ to ne pas manquer de; make ~ that s'assurer que.
surely, adv. sûrement.
surface, s. surface f.
surgeon, s. chirurgien m.
surgery, s. chirurgie f.
surname, s. nom m. de famille.
surpass, v.a. surpasser.
surprise, s. surprise f.; — v.a. surprendre.
surprising, adj. surprenant.
surrender, s. abandon m.; reddition f.; — v.a. rendre; renoncer; v.n. se rendre.
surround, v.a. entourer (de).
surroundings, s. pl. environs m. pl.; entourage m.
survey, s. vue f.; examen m.; — v.a. contempler, regarder; examiner; expertiser.
survive, v. n. & a. survivre (à).
suspect, adj. & s. suspect, -e (m. f.); — v. a. & n. soupçonner.
suspenders, s. pl. jarretelles f. pl.
suspicion, s. soupçon m.
suspicious, adj. soupçonneux; suspect.
swallow[1], s. hirondelle f.
swallow[2], v. a. avaler; gober.
swan, s. cygne m.
swarm, s. essaim m.; foule f.; — v.n. essaimer; s'assembler en

foule.

swear, *v.a.* jurer; prêter;
v.n. jurer.

sweat, *s.* sueur *f.;* — *v.a.*
exploiter; *v.n.* suer.

Swede, *s.* Suédois, -e *m. f.*

Swedish, *adj. & s.* suédois *(m.).*

sweep, *v.a.* balayer;
(chimney) ramoner; —
s. coup *m.* de balai;
courbe *f.;* grand geste
m.; (pers.) ramoneur
m.

sweet, *adj.* doux; *(pers.)*
gentil; — *s.* bonbon *m.;*
entremets *m.*

sweetheart, *s.* bien-aimé,
-ée *m. f.;* ~! mon
amour!, ma chérie!

swell, *v.n.* (s')enfler;
se gonfler; grossir;
v.a. gonfler; bouffir; —
s. houle *f.;* élévation *f.*

swim, *v. n.* nager; aller
à la nage; flotter; *v.a*
nager; — *s. have a* ~
aller nager.

swimmer, *s.* nageur, -eu-
se *m. f.*

swimming-pool, *s.* piscine
f.

swine, *s.* cochon *m.*

swing, *s.* va-et-vient *m.;*
rythme *m.; (for child-
ren)* escarpolette *f.*
balançoire *f.;* — *v.a.*
balancer; *v. n.* osciller;
se balancer.

Swiss, *adj.* suisse; — *s.*
Suisse *m. f.*

switch, *s.* badine *f.;*
aiguille *f.;* interrup-
teur *m.,* commutateur
m.; — *v.a.* cingler;
aiguiller; couper; ~ *off*
couper (le courant);

~ *on* donner (le cou-
rant), tourner (le bou-
ton).

sword, *s.* épée *f.;* sa-

bre *m.*

syllable, *s.* syllabe *f.*

symbol, *s.* symbole *m.*

symmetrical, *adj* symétrique.

symmetry, *s.* symétrie *f.*

sympathy, *s.* sympathie
f.

symphony, *s.* symphonie *f.*

synagogue, *s.* synagogue
f.

synthetic, *adj.* synthétique.

syringe, *s.* seringue *f.*

syrup, *s.* sirop *m.*

system, *s.* système *m.*

systematic(al), *adj.* systématique.

T

table, *s.* table *f.;* clear
the ~ desservir; *lay
the* ~ mettre le cou-
vert.

table-cloth, *s.* nappe *f.*

table-spoon, *s.* cuiller *f.* à
soupe.

tablet, *s.* tablette *f.*

tack, *s.* broquette *f.,*
petit clou *m.*

tackle, *s.* attirail *m.;*
apparaux *m. pl.;* —
v.a. saisir à bras le
corps; *(problem)* es-
sayer de résoudre.

tact, *s.* tact *m.*

tag, *s.* ferret *m.;* étiquette
(volante) *f.;* bout *m.*

tail, *s.* queue *f.*

tailor, *s.* tailleur *m.*

take, *v.a.* prendre; *(carry)* porter; *(walk)* faire; ~ *after* ressembler
à; ~ *away* enlever;
~ *down* descendre,
(write) prendre (par
écrit); ~ *in (paper)*
s'abonner à; ~ *off* ôter;
(v.n.) prendre son
élan; ~ *on* se charger

de; ~ *to* se mettre à; ~ *up* ramasser, relever.

tale, *s.* conte *m.*, histoire *f*

talent, *s.* talent *m.*

talk, *v.a. & n.* parler *(about, of* de); ~*ing of* à propos de; — *s.* conversation *f.*; causerie *f.*

tall, *adj.* grand; *how ~ is he?* quelle est sa taille?

tame, *adj.* apprivoisé.

tan, *s.* tan *m.*

tank, *s.* réservoir *m.*; char *m.* d'assaut.

t ankard, *s.* chope *f.*

tap, *s.* robinet *m.*; *(blow)* tape *f.*; petit coup *m.*; — *v.a.* mettre en perce; *(strike)* frapper légèrement, taper.

tape, *s.* ruban *m.* (de coton).

tape-recorder, *s.* magnétophone *m.*

tapestry, *s.* tapisserie *f.*

target, *s.* cible *f.*

tariff, *s.* tarif *m.*

tart, *s.* tart *f.*

task, *s.* tâche *f.*; *(school)* devoir *m.*

taste, *s.* goût *m.*

tasteless, *adj.* sans saveur.

tasty, *adj.* savoureux, de bon goût.

tatter, *s.* lambeau *m.*

tavèrn, *s.* taverne *f.*

tax, *s.* impôt *m.*; ~ *free* exempt d'impôts.

taxi, *s.* taxi *m.*

tea, *s.* thé *m.*

teach, *v.a.* enseigner, instruire; *(how to)* apprendre (à).

teacher, *s.* instituteur, -trice *m. f.*; professeur *m. f.*

teaching, *s.* enseignement *m.*

team, *s.* équipe *f.*

tea-pot, *s.* théière *f.*

tear[1], *s. (eye)* larme *f.*

tear[2], *v.a.* déchirer; ~ *away, down, out* arracher; ~ *up* déchirer; — *s.* déchirure *f.*

tease, *v.a.* taquiner.

tea-spoon, *s.* cuiller *f.* à thé.

technical, *adj.* technique.

technique, *s.* technique *f.*

technology, *s.* technologie *f.*

tedious, *adj.* ennuyeux.

teenager, *s.* adolescent, -e *m. f.*

telecast, *v.a.* téléviser.

telegram, *s.* télégramme *m.*

telegraph, *s.* télégraphe *m.*

telephone, *s.* téléphone *m.*; — *v.a. & n.* téléphoner *(to* à).

telescope, *s.* télescope *m.*; réfracteur *m.*; — *v.a.* télescoper.

televise, *v.a.* téléviser.

television, *s.* télévision *f.*

television-set, *s.* appareil *m.* de TV, téléviseur *m.*

telex, *s.* télex *m.*

tell, *v.a.* dire; raconter; distinguer; ~ *s.o.*

to do *sth.* enjoindre, dire à qn de faire qch.

temper, *s.* colère *f.*; tempérament *m.*

temperature, *s.* température *f.*

temporary, *adj.* temporaire.

tempt, *v.a.* tenter.

ten, *adj. & s.* dix *(m.)*.

tenant, *s.* locataire *m. f.*

tend, *v.n.* tendre (à).

tendency, *s.* tendance *f.*

tender[1], *v.a.* offrir; ~

for soumissionner; — *s.* soumission *f.*

tender², *adj.* tendre.

tennis, *s.* tennis *m.*

tension, *s.* tension *f.*

tent, *s.* tente *f.*

tenth, *adj.* dixième; dix.

term, *s.* terme *m.; (school)* trimestre *m.; be on good* ~s être bien (avec); — *v.a.* appeler.

terminate, *v.a.* terminer; *vn.* se terminer.

terminus, *s.* (gare *f.*) terminus *m.*

terrace, *s.* terrasse *f.*

terrible, *adj.* terrible.

territory, *s.* territoire *m.*

test, *s.* épreuve *f.;* examen *m.; (school)* composition *f., (oral)* épreuve *f.;* orale — *v.a.* mettre à l'épreuve.

testify, *v.a.* affirmer.

testimony, *s.* témoignage *m.*

text, *s.* texte *m.*

text-book, *s.* manuel *m.*

textile, *s.* textile *m.*

than, *conj.* que; *(with numbers)* de.

thank, *v.a.* remercier; ~ *you* merci; — *s.* ~s remerciements *m. pl.;* merci.

thankful, *adj.* reconnaissant.

that¹, *adj.* ce, cet, cette' ces; — *pron.* celui, celle, ceux; cela; ~'s *it* c'est cela.

that², *conj.* que.

the, *art.* le, la, les; ce, cet, cette; ces.

theatre, *s.* théâtre *m.*

their, *pron.* leur, leurs.

theirs, *pron.* le leur, la leur, les leurs; à eux, à elles.

them, *pron.* les; leur; eux, elles.

theme, *s.* thème *m.;* sujet *m.*

themselves, *pron.* se; eux-mêmes, elles-mêmes.

then, *adv.* alors; *(after that)* puis; *(consequently)* donc.

theology, *s.* théologie *f.*

theoretical, *adj.* théorique.

theory, *s.* théorie *f.*

there, *adv.* là; *(with verb)* y; ~ *is, are* il y a.

therefore *adv.* donc.

thermometer, *s.* thermomètre *m.*

thermos, *s.* thermos *f.*

they, *pron.* ils, elles; ~ *say* on dit

thick, *adj.* épais.

thief, *s.* voleur, -euse *m. f.*

thigh, *s.* cuisse *f.*

thimble, *s.* dé *m.*

thin, *adj.* mince; maigre; *fig.* pauvre.

thing, *s.* chose *f.;* ~s effets *m. pl.*

think, *v.a.* croire; concevoir; *v.n.* croire; penser *(about, of* à); ~ *out* élaborer; ~ *over* réfléchir à, penser.

third, *adj.* troisième; trois; — *s.* tiers *m.*

thirsty, *adj.* altéré; *be* ~ avoir soif.

thirteen, *adj. & s.* treize *(m.).*

thirty, *adj. & s.* trente *(m.).*

this, *pl.* these, *pron.* cela, — *adj.* ceci; ce, cet, cette; ces.

thorn, *s.* épine *f.*

thorough, *adj.* profond, complet; consommé.

thoroughfare, *s.* artère *f.* principal, grande rue *f.; no* ~ rue barrée, passage interdit.

thoroughly, *adv.* tout à fait, à fond.

though, *conj.* quoique, bien que; — *adv.* tout de même.

thought, *s.* pensée *f.;* idée *f.; (care)* souci *m.*

thoughtful, *adj.* pensif; attentif.

thoughtless, *adj.* étourdi; insouciant.

thousand, *s. & adj.* mille *(m.)*

thrash, *v.a.* battre.

thread, *s.* fil *m.;* — *v. a.* enfiler.

threat, *s.* menace *f.*

threaten, *v. a. & n.* menacer (de).

three, *adj. & s.* trois *(m.).*

threshold, *s.* seuil *m.*

thrifty, *adj.* économe.

thrill, *s.* tressaillement *m.;* — *v. a.be ~ed with* frissonner de.

thrive, *v. n.* prospérer.

throat, *s.* gorge *f.*

throne, *s.* tône *m.*

through, *prep.* à travers; au travers de; par; par suite de; pendant; — *adv.* d'un bout à l'autre; *be ~ with* avoir fini qch.; — *adj.* direct.

throughout, *prep. & adv.* d'un bout à l'autre.

throw, *v.a.* ·jeter; *~ away* jeter, dissiper; *~ down* renverser; jeter à terre; *~ off* se débarrasser de; ôter; *~ out* rejecter; *~ over* abandonner; — *s.* jet *m.*

thrust, *v.a.* fourrer, pousser; enforcer; — *s.* poussée *f.;* botte *f.*

thumb, *s.* pouce *m.*

thunder, *s.* tonnerre *m.;* — *v.n.* tonner.

Thursday, *s.* jeudi *m.*

thus, *adv.* ainsi.

ticket, *s.* billet *m.;* étiquette *f.*

ticket-collector, *s.* contrôleur *m.*

tide, *s.* marée *f.;* courant *m.*

tidy, *adj.* propre; bien rangé; *(pers.)* ordonné; — *v.a. (also ~ up)* mettre en ordre.

tie, *v.a.* attacher; lier; nouer; *~ down* lier; *~ up* attacher; — *s.* lien *m.;* cravate *f.; (sport)* partie *f.* égale.

tiger, *s.* tigre, -esse *m. f.*

tight, *adj.* serré; tendu.

tighten, *v.a.* serrer.

tile, *s.* tuile *f.*

till, *prep.* jusqu'à; — *conj.* jusqu'à ce que.

tilt, *s.* inclinaison *f.;* — *v. n.* s'incliner, pencher; *v.a.* pencher.

time, *s.* temps *m.;* moment *m.; (clock)* heure *f.; (occasions)* fois; *at ~s* de temps en temps; *by the ~ that* avant que; *for the ~ being* actuellement; *what ~ is it?* quelle heure est-il?; *have a good ~* s'amuser bien; *keep good ~* marcher bien.

timely, *adj.* opportun.

timetable, *s.* horaire *m.;* indicateur *m.; (school)* emploi *m.* du temps.

tin, *s.* étain *m.; (conserve)* boîte *f.* (en fer blanc).

tinned, *adj.* en boîte; conservé.

tint, *s.* teinte *f.*

tinv. *adi.* tout petit.

tip¹, *s.* bout *m.;* — *v.a.*

renverser; *v.n.* (also ~ *over*) se renverser.

tip², *s. (money)* pourboire *m.;* — *v.a.* donner un pourboire (à).

tire¹, tyre, *s.* pneu(matique) *m.*

tire², *v.a.* fatiguer; *v.n.* se fatiguer.

tired, *adj. be* ~ *of* être las de.

tissue, *s.* tissu *m.*

tissue-paper, *s.* papier *m.* de soie.

title, *s.* titre *m.*

to, *prep.* à; vers; en,

toast, *s.* rôtie *f.; (bread, drink)* toast *m.;* — *v.a.* rôtir.

tobacco, *s.* tabac *m.*

tobacconist, *s.* marchand *m.* de tabac; ~'s débit *m.* de tabac.

today, *adv.* aujourd'hui.

toe, *s.* orteil *m.,* doigt *m.* du pied.

together, *adv.* ensemble; en même temps.

toil, *s.* travail *m.;* — *v.n.* travailler.

toilet, *s.* toilette *f.*

toilet-paper, *s.* papier *m.* hygiénique.

tomato, *s.* tomate *f.*

tomb, *s.* tombeau *m.*

tomorrow, *adv.* demain.

ton, *s.* tonne *f.*

tone, *s.* ton *m.*

tongs, *s. pl.* pincettes *f. pl.;* pince *f.*

tongue, *s.* langue *f.*

tonight, *adv.* cette nuit; ce soir.

tonsil, *s.* amygdale *f.*

too, *adv.* trop; *(also)* aussi.

tool, *s.* outil *m.;* instrument *m.*

tooth, *s.* dent *f.*

toothache, *s.* mal *m.* de dents.

toothbrush, *s.* brosse *f.* à dents.

toothpaste, *s.* pâte *f.* dentrifrice.

top, *s.* sommet *m.,* faîte *m.;* dessus *m.;* couvercle *m.;* tête *f.;* premier, -ère *m. f.;* — *v.a.* couronner; dépasser.

topic, *s.* sujet *m.;* ~s *of the day* actualités *f. pl.*

torch, *s.* torche *f.*

tortoise, *s.* tortue *f.*

toss, *s.* mouvement *m.;* — *v.a.* jeter; lancer en l'air; ballotter; ~ *up* lancer en l'air.

total, *adj. & s.* total *(m.).*

totter, *v.n.* chanceler.

touch, *s.* toucher *m.;* attouchement *m.;* touche *f.;* légère *f.* attaque,; — *v.a.* toucher.

tough, *adj.* dur; robuste; rude.

tour, *s.* voyage *m.;* tour *m.;* tournée *f.;* — *v.n.* voyager.

tourism, *s.* tourisme *m.*

tourist, *s.* touriste *m.*

tournament, *s.* tournoi *m.*

tow, *s.* étoupe *f.;* remorque *f.;* — *v.a.* remorquer.

toward(s), *prep.* vers; envers; pour.

towel, *s.* essuie-main(s) *m.,* serviette *f.*

tower, *s.* tour *f.*

town, *s.* ville *f.*

town-hall, *s.* hôtel *m.* de ville.

toy, *s.* jouet *m.;* — *v.n.* jouer (avec).

trace, *s.* trace *f.;* trait *m.;* — *v.a.* tracer; ~ *back* remonter à.

track, *s.* traces *f. pl.;* sentier *m.; (railw.)* voie *f.; (running)* piste

f.

tractor, *s.* tracteur *m.*

trade, *s.* commerce *m.;* *(occupation)* métier *m.;* *v.n.* commercer; ~ *in* faire le commerce de.

trade-mark, *s.* marque *f.* de fabrique.

tradesman, *s.* commerçant *m.*

trade(s)-union, *s.* syndicat *m.*

tradition, *s.* tradition *f.*

traditional, *adj.* traditionnel.

traffic, *s.* trafic *m.;* circulation *f.;* ~ *lights* feux *m.pl.* de signalisation.

tragedy, *s.* tragédie

tragic(al), *adj.* tragique.

trail, *s.* trace *f.;* — *v.a.* & *n.* traîner.

train, *s.* train *m.; (series)* suite *f.;* — *v.a.* entraîner; former.

trainer, *s.* entraîneur *m.*

traitor, *s.* traître *m.*

tram, *s.* tramway *m.*

tramp, *v.n.* aller à pied; — *s.* bruit *m.* de pas; *(pers.)* chemineau *m.*

transaction, *s.* transaction *f.*

transfer, *s.* transport *m.;* — *v.a.* transférer.

transform, *v.a.* transformer (en).

transfusion, *s.* transfusion *f.*

transgress, *v.a.* transgresser; *v.n.* pécher.

transistor, *s.* transistor *m.*

transit, *s.* transit *m; in* ~ en cours de route.

translate, *v.a.* traduire.

translation, *s.* traduction *f.*

translator, *s.* traducteur,

-trice *m. f.*

transmission, *s.* transmission *f.*

transmit, *v.a.* transmettre, émettre.

transmitter, *s.* (poste) émetteur *m.*

transparency, *s.* diapositive *f.*

transport, *s.* transport *m.;* — *v.a.* transporter.

trap, *s.* piège *m.*

trash, *s.* rebut *m.;* niaiseries *f. pl.*

travel, *v.n.* voyager; — *s.* voyage *m.*

traveller, *s.* voyageur, -euse *m. f.*

tray, *s.* plateau *m.*

treachery, *s.* trahison *f.*

tread, *s.* pas *m.;* — *v.n.* & *a.* marcher (sur).

treasure, *s.* trésor *m.*

treasury, *s.* trésor *m.;* trésorerie *f.*

treat, *v.a.* traiter.

treatment, *s.* traitement *m.*

treaty, *s.* traité *m.*

tree, *s.* arbre *m.*

tremble, *v.n.* trembler.

tremendous, *adj.* terrible; immense.

trench, *s.* tranchée *f.*

trend, *s.* tendance *f.*

trespass, *v.n.* envahir sans autorisation; ~ *against* offenser; ~ *on* abuser de; — *s.* offense *f.*

trial, *s.* essai *m.;* épreuve *f.; (law)* procès *m.*

tribe, *s.* tribu *f.*

tribute, *s.* tribut *m.*

trick, *s.* ruse *f.;* tour *m.;* truc *m.;* — *v.a.* duper.

trifle, *s.* bagatelle *f.; a* ~ un peu; — *v.n.* ~ *with* traiter légèrement.

trim, *s.* état *m.;* tenue *f.;*
— *adj.* bien tenu; —
v.a. arranger; garnir,
orner; dresser.

trip, *s.* excursion *f.;*
voyage *m.; — v.a.* ~ *up*
faire trébucher.

triumph, *s.* triomphe *m.;*
— *v.n.* triompher.

triumphant, *adj.* triomphant.

trolley, *s.* fardier *m.,*
diable *m.;* trolley *m.*

trolley-bus, *s.* trolleybus
m.

troop, *s.* troupe *f.*

trophy, *s.* trophée *m.*

tropic(al), *adj.* tropique.

tropics, *s. pl.* tropiques
m. pl.

trot, *s.* trot *m.; — v.n.*
trotter.

trouble, *s.* affliction *f.;*
malheur *m.;* dérange-
ment *m.;* difficulté *f.;*
— *v.a.* inquiéter; dé-
ranger; affliger.

troublesome, *adj.* ennuyeux.

trousers, *s. pl.* pantalon *m.*

trout, *s* truite *f.*

truck, *s.* wagon *m.*

true, *aaj.* vrai; exact;
fidèle; *come* ~ se réaliser.

truly, *adv.* vraiment.

trumpet, *s.* trompette
f.; — v. a. proclamer.

trunk, *s.* melle *f. (tree)*
tronc *m.*

trunk-call, *s.* appel *m.* in-
terurbain.

trust, *s.* confiance *f.;*
espoir *m.;* dépôt *m.;*
trust *m.; — v.a.*
se confier (à); faire
crédit (à); *v.n.* espérer;
compter sur.

truth, *s.* vérité *f.*

try, *v.a.* essayer, éprouver; *(law)* mettre en
jugement; ~ *on* essa-
yer; — *s.* essai *m.*

tub, *s.* bac *m.; (bath)*
tub *m.*

tube, *s.* tube *m.;* tuyau
m.; métro *m.*

Tuesday, *s.* mardi *m.*

tug, *s.* effort *m.; — v.a.*
tirer; remorquer.

tug-boat, *s.* (bateau) remorqueur *m.*

tuition, *s.* enseignenient
m.

tumble, *v. n.* tomber.

tumour, *s.* tumeur *f.*

tune, *s.* air *m.;* accord *m.;*
harmonie *f.; in* ~ d'ac-
cord; *out of* ~ faux; —
v.a.&n. accorder; ~
in to mettre sur; ~
up régler; s'accorder.

tunnel, *s.* tunnel *m.*

turbine, *s.* turbine *f.*

turbo-jet: ~ *engine* turboréacteur *m.*

turbo-prop, *s.* turbopropulseur *m.*

turkey, *s.* dindon, din-
de *m. f.*

Turkish, *adj.* turc, -que:
— *s.* Turc, -que *m. f.;*
(lang.) turc *m.*

turn, *v.a.* tourner, détourner; diriger; *v.n.*
tourner; se diriger; de-
venir; avoir recours (à);
~ *about* (se) tourner;
~ *back* retourner; ~
down plier, baisser;
repousser; ~ *upside
down* renverser; ~ *in*
se coucher; ~ *off* fer-
mer, serrer; éteindre;
~ *on* ouvrir; allumer;
~ *over* (se) renverser;
~ *up* arriver, appa-
raître — *s.* tour *m.;* détour *m.; (mind, style)*
tournure *f.; (tide)*
changement *m.*

turning, s. tournant m.
turnip, s. navet m.
turnover, s. chiffre m. d'affaires.
turret, s. tourelle f.
turtle, s. tortue f.
tutor, s. précepteur m.; — v.a. instruire.
twelfth, adj. douzième; douze.
twelve, adj. & s. douze (m.).
twentieth, adj. vingtième.
twenty, adj. & s. vingt (m.).
twice, adv. deux fois.
twig, s. brindille f.
twin, adj. & s. jumeau (m.), jumelle (f.).
twist, s. (road) coude f.; torsion f.; — v. a. tordre; dénaturer; v. n. s'entortiller.
twitter, v.n. gazouiller.
two, adj. & s. deux (m.).
type, s. type m.; caractère m.; — v.a. taper (à la machine).
type-script, s. manuscrit m. dactylographié.
typewriter, s. machine à écrire, f.
typical, adj. typique.
typist, s. dactilo(graphe) m. f.
tyre see tire.

U

udder, s. mamelle f.
ugly, adj. laid.
ulcer, s. ulcère m.
ultimate, adj. final, dernier.
umbrella, s. parapluie m.
umpire, s. arbitre m. f.
unable, adj. incapable; ~ to impuissant à faire qch.; dans l'impossibilité de.

unaccustomed, adj. inaccoutumé, peu habitué (à).
unaided, adj. sans aide.
unanimous, adj. unanime.
unassisted, adj. sans aide.
unaware: be ~ of ignorer.
unbearable, adj. insupportable.
uncertain, adj. incertain,
uncertainty, s. incertitude f.
unchangeable, adj. immuable.
uncle, s. oncle m.
uncomfortable, adj. peu confortable.
uncommon, adj. rare; extraordinaire.
unconditional, adj. sans conditions.
unconscious, adj. sans connaissance; ~ of sans conscience de.
uncover, v. a. découvrir.
undamaged, adj. non endommagé.
undefined, adj. non défini.
undeniable, adj. incontestable.
under, prep sous; au-dessous de; dans.
undercarriage, s. châssis m., train (d'atterrissage) m.
underclothes, s. pl. vêtements m. pl. de dessous.
underdeveloped, adj. sous-développe.
underdone, adj. pas assez cuit, saignant.
undergo, v.a. subir.
undergraduate, s. étudiant, -e (non diplomé) m. f.
underground, s. métro(politain) m.
underline, v.a. souligner.

undermine, *v.a.* miner.
underneath, *prep. & adv.* au-dessous (de).
undersigned, *adj. & s.* soussigné, -e *(m. f.)*.
understand, *v.a.&n.* comprendre; *it is understood that* il est convenu que.
understanding, *s.* entendement *m.; intelligence f.*
undertake, *v.a.* entreprendre; ~ *to* se charger de, s'engager à.
undertaking, *s.* entreprise *f.*
underwear, *s.* vêtements *m.pl.* de dessous.
undesirable, *adj.* peu désirable.
undo, *v.a.* défaire.
undress, *v. n.* se déshabiller.
undue, *adj.* indu.
uneasy, *adj.* inquiet; mal à l'aise; incommode.
uneducated, *adj.* sans instruction.
unemployed, *adj. & s.* sans travail; *the* ~ les chômeurs *m.*
unemployment, *s.* chômage *m.*
unequal, *adj.* inégal.
uneven, *adj.* inégal; impair.
unexpected, *adj.* inattendu; soudain.
unfair, *adj.* injuste; déloyal.
unfavorable, *adj.* défavorable.
unfortunate, *adj.* malheureux.
unfortunately, *adv.* malheureusement.
unhappy, *adj.* malheureux.
unhealthy, *adj.* maladif;

(place) insalubre.
uninhabited, *adj.* inhabité.
uninteresting, *adj.* peu intéressant,sans intérêt.
union, *s.* union *f.*
unique, *adj.* unique.
unit, *s.* unité *f.; (motor)* bloc *m.*
unite, *v.a.* unir; *v.n.* s'unir.
unity, *s.* unité *f.;* harmonie *f.*
universal, *adj.* universel.
university, *s.* université *f.*
unjust, *adj.* injuste.
unkind, *adj.* dur; peu aimable.
unknown, *adj.* inconnu.
unless, *conj.* à moins que... ne; à moins de.
unlike, *adj.* dissemblable.
unload, *v.a.* décharger.
unlock, *v.a.* ouvrir.
unmarried, *adj.* célibataire.
unnatural, *adj.* non naturel, dénaturé.
unnecessary, *adj.* inutile.
unnoticed, *adj.* inaperçu.
unoccupied, *adj.* inoccupé; libre; non occupé.
unpack, *v.a.* déballer.
unpaid, *adj.* impayé.
unparalleled, *adj.* incomparable.
unpleasant, *adj.* désagréable.
unprecedented, *adj.* sans exemple. *or.* précédent.
unprejudiced, *adj.* sans préjugés, impartial.
unprepared, *adj.* non préparé; *be* ~ *for* ne pas s'attendre à qch.
unprofitable, *adj.* peu profitable.
unpromising, *adj.* qui s'annonce mal; peu prometteur.
unqualified, *adj.* non qua-

lifié; sans restriction.

unreal, *adj.* irréel.

unreasonable, *adj.* déraisonnable.

unsatisfactory, *adj.* peu satisfaisant.

unseen, *adj.* invisible; inaperçu.

unsettled, *adj.* non réglé; *(in mind)* indécis; incertain.

unskilled, *adj.* non spécialisé.

unsolved, *adj.* non résolu.

unspeakable, *adj.* inexprimable.

unsteady, *adj.* tremblant; peu fixe; chancelant; inconstant.

unsuccessful, *adj.* malheureux; infructueux.

unsuitable, *adj.* inconvenant; peu propre (à).

untidy, *adj.* sans ordre, malpropre; en désordre.

until, *prep.* jusqu'à; — *conj.* jusqu'à ce que; avant que.

unto, *prep.* jusqu'à.

unusual, *adj.* rare, peu commun.

unwell, *adj.* indisposé; souffrant.

unwilling, *adj.* peu disposé (à).

unworthy, *adj.* indigne.

unyielding, *adj.* inflexible.

up, *adv.* en montant, vers le haut; (en) haut; *go* ~ monter; *be* ~ *in* être fort en; *what's* ~? qu'est-ce qu'il y a?; — *prep.* vers le haut de; en haut; — *adj.* montant.

uphill, *adj.* montant; — *adv. go* ~ monter.

uphold, *v.a.* soutenir; appuyer.

upholsterer, *s.* tapissier *m.*

upon, *prep* sur.

upper, *adj.* supérieur; *(deck)* deuxième; *the* ~ *classes* les hautes classes.

upright, *adj.* droit; honnête.

upset, *v.a.* renverser; *fig.* troubler, bouleverser; — *adj.* renversé; *fig.* dérangé; *be* ~ être indisposé.

upside do ~n, *adv.* sens dessus dessous.

upstairs, *adv.* en haut; *go* ~ monter (l'escalier).

up-to-date, *adj* moderne, à la mode.

upwards, *adv.* en haut, vers le haut, en montant.

urge, *v.a.* prier instamment (de); recommander instamment; pousser en avant.

urgent, *adj.* urgent; pressant.

us, *pron.* nous.

usage, *s.* usage *m.*

use, *v.a.* se servir de; traiter; faire usage (de); consommer; ~ *up* user; consommer; ~*d to* habitué à; *get* ~*d to* s'habituer à; — *s.* usage *m.;* emploi *m.;* utilité *f.; be of* ~ être utile (à); *(of) no* ~ inutile; *out of* ~ hors d'usage *or* de service.

useful, *adj.* utile (à).

useless, *adj.* inutile.

usher, *s. (court)* (huissier) audiencier *m.*

usherette, *s. (theatre)* ouvreuse *f.*

usual, *adj.* usuel.

usually, *adv.* ordinairement.

utensil, *s.* ustensile *m.*

utility, *s.* utilité *f.*

utilize, *v.a.* utiliser.

utmost, *adj.* extrême; le plus grand; — *s.* le plus; tout son possible.

utter[1], *adj.* le plus grand; absolu.

utter[2], *v.a.* dire, prononcer; pousser.

utterance, *s.* prononciation. *f.*; expression *f.*; parole *f.*

V

vacancy, *s.* vacance *f.*

vacant, *adj.* vacant; vide; sans expression.

vacation, *s.* vacances *f. pl.*

vaccinate, *v.a.* vacciner.

vaccination, *s.* vaccination.

vacuum-cleaner, *s.* aspirateur *m.*

vague, *adj.* vague.

vain, *adj.* vain; vaniteux; *in ~* en vain.

valid, *adj.* valide.

validity, *s.* validité *f.*

valley, *s.* vallée *f.*

valuable, *adj.* de valeur.

value, *s.* valeur *f.*; *v.a.* évaluer; priser.

valve, *s.* soupape *f.*; lampe *f.*, tube *m.*

van, *s.* fourgon *m.*; camion *m.* de livraison; wagon *m.*

vanish, *v.n.* disparaître; *(also ~ away)* s'évanouir.

vanity, *s.* vanité *f.*

variety, *s.* variété *f.*

various, *adj.* divers.

varnish, *s.* vernis *m.*

vary, *v.a. & n.* varier.

vase, *s.* vase *m.*

vast, *adj.* vaste.

vault, *s.* voûte *f.*; cave *f.*, caveau *m.*

veal, *s.* veau *m.*

vegetable, *s.* légume *m.*

vehicle, *s.* véhicule *m.*

veil, *s.* voile *m.*

vein, *s.* veine *f.*

velvet, *s.* velours *m.*

venison, *s.* venaison *f.*

vent, *s.* ouverture *f.*; *give ~ to* donner libre cours à.

ventilation, *s.* ventilation *f.*

ventilator, *s.* ventilateur *m.*

venture, *s.* risque *m.*; hasard *m.*; — *v.a.* risquer; hasarder; *v.n. ~ (up-)on* se hasarder à, se risquer à.

verb, *s.* verbe *m.*

verdict, *s.* décision *f.*, verdict *m.*

verge, *s.* bord *m.*

verify, *v.a.* vérifier.

verse, *s.* vers *m.*; strophe *f.*

version, *s.* version *f.*

vertical, *adj.* vertical.

very, *adv.* très; *~ good* très bien; — *adj.* vrai; même.

vessel, *s.* vaisseau *m.*

vest, *s.* gilet *m.*; chemise *f.* américaine.

vestry, *s.* sacristie *f.*; assemblée *f.*

veterinary, *adj. ~ surgeon* vétérinaire *m.*

veto, *s.* véto *m.*; — *v.a.* mettre son véto (à).

vex, *v.a.* vexer.

vibrate, *v.n.* vibrer, osciller.

vibration, *s.* vibration *f.*

vicar, *s.* curé *m.*

vice-, *prefix* vice-.

vicinity, s. voisinage m.
victim, s. victime f.
victorious, adj. victorieux.
victory, s. victoire f.
victuals, s. pl. victuailles f. pl.
view, s. vue f.; avis m.; on ~ exposé; *have in* ~ se proposer (de); *with a* ~ *to* en vue de; *point of* ~ ~ point m. de vue; — v.a. voir; regarder; envisager.
viewer, s. spectateur, -trice m. f.
vigorous, adj. vigoureux.
vigour, s. vigueur f.
village, s. village m.
villain, s. scélérat m.
vine, s. vigne f.
vinegar, s. vinaigre m.
vineyard, s. vignoble m.
vintage, s. vendange f.
violate, v.a. violer.
violation, s. violation f.
violence, s. violence f.
violent, adj. violent.
violet, s. violette f.; *(colour)* violet m.; — adj. violet.
violin, s. violon m.
violinist, s. violoniste m. f.
violoncellist, s. violoncelliste m.
violoncello, s. violoncelle m.
virgin, s. vierge f.
virtue, s. vertu f.
visa, visé, s. visa m.
visibility, s. visibilité f.
visible, adj. visible.
vision, s. vision f., vue f.
visit, s. visite f.; séjour m.; *be on a* ~ *to* être en visite chez; — v.a. visiter.
visitor, s. visiteur, -euse m. f.
vital, adj. vital.
vitamin, s. vitamine f.
vocabulary, s. vocabulaire m.
vocation, s. vocation f.
voice, s. voix f.; — v.a. exprimer.
voltage, s. voltage m.
volume, s. volume m.
voluntary, adj. volontaire.
volunteer, s. volontaire m.; — v.n. s'engager (pour).
vomit, v.a. & n. vomir.
vote, s. voix; — v.a. & n. voter (sur).
voucher, s. pièce f. de dépense ; pièce f. de recette; bon m.
vow, s. vœu m.; — v. a. vouer; jurer; v. n. faire un vœu; jurer.
vowel, s. voyelle f.
voyage, s. voyage m.; — v. n. voyager (par mer).

vulgar, adj. vulgaire.

W

wade, v.a. passer à gué.
wafer, s. gaufrette f.; hostie f.
wag, v.a. hocher; *(tail)* agiter; v.n. s'agiter.
wage(s), s. *(pl.)* salaire m., gages m. pl.; — v.a. ~ *war* faire la guerre.
wag(g)on, s. wagon m.
waist, s. taille f.
waistcoat, s. gilet m.
wait, v. a. & n. attendre *(for* qn, qch).
waiter, s. garçon m. (de restaurant); *head*~ premier garçon m., maitre m. d'hôtel.
waiting-room, s. salle f. d'attente.
wake, v.a. (also ~ *up)* réveiller; v.n. (also ~

up) s'éveiller.

waken, *v.a.* éveiller; *v.n.* s'éveiller .

walk, *s.* marche *f.;* promenade *f.; (path)* allée *f.; go for a ~* faire une promenade; — *v.n.* aller à pied; marcher; *(pleasure)* se promener; *~ off* s'en aller; *~ out* sortir.

wall, *s.* mur *m.*

wallet, *s.* portefeuille *m.*

walnut, *s.* noyer *m.; (fruit)* noix *f.*

waltz, *s.* valse *f.*

wander, *v.n.* errer; s'égarer (de); divaguer.

want, *s.* besoin *m.;* manque *m.; for ~ of* faute de; — *v.a.* avoir besoin (de); manquer (de); vouloir; demander; *v.n.* faire défaut; *be ~ing in* manquer de.

war, *s.* guerre *f.*

ward, *s.* pupille *m. f.; (hospital)* salle *f.*

warden, *s.* gouverneur *m.;* directeur *m.*

warder, *s.* gardien, -enne *m. f.*

wardrobe, *s.* armoire *f.*

ware, *s.* marchandise(s) *f. (pl.);* article *m.*

warehouse, *s.* magasin *m.;* dépôt *m.*

warm, *adj.* chaud; *be ~* avoir chaud; — *v.a.* chauffer; *~ up* réchauffer; *v.n.* se chauffer.

warmth, *s.* chaleur *f.*

warn, *v.a.* avertir; prévenir; mettre sur ses gardes (contre).

warning, *s.* avertissement *m.;* avis *m.*

warrant, *s.* autorisation *f.;* mandat *m.;*

— *v. a.* garantir; justifier.

wash, *v.a.* laver; *v.n.* se laver; *~ away* effacer; *~ up the dishes* faire la vaisselle; — *s.* lavage *m.;* lotion *f.;* toilette *f.;* lessive *f.*

wash-basin, *s.* cuvette *f.* (de lavabo).

washing-machine, *s.* machine *f.* à laver.

wasp, *s.* guêpe *f.*

waste, *s.* désert *m.,* *(money)* gaspillage *m.; (energy)* déperdition *f.; (loss)* perte *f.;* déchets *m. pl.; ~ of time* perte de temps *f.;* — *adj.* inculte; de rebut; *~ paper* papier *m.* de rebut; — *v.a.* gaspiller; perdre; ravager.

watch, *s.* garde *f.;* gardien *m.,* garde *m.; (to indicate time)* montre *f.;* — *v. a.* veiller, garder; observer; regarder; *v.n.* veiller; *~ out!* ouvrez l'œil!

watch-maker, *s.* horloger *m.*

water, *s.* eau *f.*

water-closet , *s.* cabinet *m.*

waterfall, *s.* chute *f.* d'eau

watering-place, *s.* station *f.* balnéaire; ville *f.* d'eaux.

waterproof, *adj.* imperméable; — *s.* caoutchouc *m.*

wave, *s.* vague *f.;* onde *f.;* — *v.a.* agiter; *(hair)* onduler; *v. n.* flotter; onduler.

wave-length, *s.* longueur *f.* d'onde.

waver, *v.n.* vaciller.

wax, *s.* cire *f.*

way, *s.* chemin *m.,* route

f.; distance f.; côte
m.; (means) moyen
m.; façon f., manière
f.; which ~? de quel
côté?; it's a long ~
to il y a loin pour
aller (à); on the ~ che-
min faisant; ~ in en-
trée f.; ~ out sortie

f.; out of the ~ retiré;
extraordinaire; this ~
de ce côté-ci, par ici;
by ~ of par; by the ~
à propos; in a ~ à
certains égards; give ~
to céder à.
we, pron. nous.
weak, adj. faible.
weakness,. s. faiblesse f.
wealth, s. richesse f.;
profusion f.
wealthy, adj. riche.
weapon, s. arme f.
wear, v.a. porter; ~ away,
down, out (s')user; ~ off
(s')effacer; — s. usage
m.; usure f.
weary, adj. las, fatigué.
weather, s. temps m.
weather-forecast, s. pré-
visions f. pl. du temps;
bulletin m. météorolo-
gique.
weave, v. a. tisser.
web, s. tissu m.; (spider)
toile f.
wedding, s. mariage m.
wedding-ring, s. alliance
f., anneau m. de ma-
riage.
wedge, s. coin m.; —
v.a. coincer; caler.
Wednesday, s. mercredi
m.
weed, s. mauvaise herbe
f.; — v.a. sarcler.
week, s. semaine f.
week-day, s. jour m.
de semaine; on ~s en
semaine.
week-end, s. fin f. de

semaine, week-end m.
weekly, adj. de la semai-
ne; hebdomadaire; —
s. (journal) hebdoma-
daire m.
weep, v.n. pleurer.
weigh, v.a. & n. peser;
~ down faire pencher,
surcharger, accabler.
weight, s. poids m.;
put on ~ prendre du
corps.
welcome, adj. bienvenu;
~! soyez le bienvenu!;
— s. accueil m.: — v.a.
souhaiter la bien-
venue (à); accueillir
(avec plaisir).
well¹, adv. bien; ~, ~!
allons, allons!; — adj.
bien (portant).
well², s. puits m.
well-being, bien-être m.
well-informed, adj. bien
informé, renseigné.
well-to-do, adj. aisé; be ~
être dans l'aisance
west, s. ouest m.
western, adj. de l'ouest.
westward, adv. vers l'ou-
est.
wet, adj. mouillé, hu-
mide; pluvieux; ~
through trempé jus-
qu'aux os; — v.a.
mouiller; tremper.
whale, s. baleine f.
what, rel. pron. ce qui,
ce que; — interrog.
pron. qu'est-ce qui,
que; — int. quoi!
wheat, s. blé m., froment
m.
wheel, s. roue f.; (steer-
ing) volant m.
when, adv. & conj. quand.
whenever, adv. toutes les
fois que.
where, adv. où.
whereas, conj. tandis que;

vu que.
wherever, *adv.* partout où.
whether, *conj.* soit que; *(if)* si; ~ *or not* . . . qu'il en soit ainsi ou non . . .
which, *(interrogative) adj.* quel, quelle; *pron.* lequel; *(relative) adj.* lequel, laquelle; *pron.* qui, que, lequel.
while, *conj.* pendant que; *(whereas)* tandis que; *(as long as)* tant que; — *s.* temps *m.; be worth* ~ *to* cela vaut la peine de; — *v.a.* ~ *away* faire passer.
whip, *s.* fouet.
whisk, *v.a.* fouetter; — *s.* époussette *f.; (eggs)* fouet à œufs, *m.*
whisper, *s.* chuchotement *m.;* murmure *m.; v.a.* dire à l'oreille; *v.n.* chuchoter; murmurer.
whistle, *s.* sifflet *m.;* — *v.a. & n.* siffler.
white, *adj.* blanc, blanche; pâle.
Whit Sunday, dimanche *m.* de la Pentecôte.
who, *pron.* qui.
whole, *s.* tout *m.;* totalité *f.; on the* ~ à tout prendre; — *adj.* tout le, toute la; entier, -ère.
wholesale, *adj. & adv.* en gros.
wholesome, *adj.* sain.
wholly, *adv.* entièrement.
whom, *pron.* que; lequel; *interrog.* qui?, qui est-ce que?
whose, *pron.* dont; *interrog.* de qui?
why, *adv.* pourquoi.
wicked, *adj.* méchant.
wide, *adj.* large; étendue; *6 feet* ~ 6 pieds de largeur.

widow, *s.* veuve *f.*
widower, *s.* veuf *m.*
width, *s.* largeur *f.*
wife, *s.* femme *f.*
wild, *adj.* sauvage; déréglé; impétueux; frénétique.
wilful, *adj.* volontaire.
will, *s.* volonté *f.;* intention *f.;* testament *m.; at* ~ à volonté; *of one's own free* ~ de plein gré; — *v.n. & aux.* vouloir; *(future tense unexpressed,* see *grammar).*
willing *adj.* bien disposé; *be* ~ vouloir bien.
willingly, *adv.* volontiers.
win, *v. a. & n.* gagner.
winch, *s.* manivelle *f.*
wind¹, *s.* vent *m.;* souffle *m.*
wind², *v. a.* enrouler; dévider; ~ *up (clock)* remonter; *fig.* liquider; *v.n.* tourner, serpenter; s'enrouler.
window, *s.* fenêtre *f.; (car)* glace *f.*
windscreen, *s.* pare-brise *m.*
windy, *adj.* venteux.
wine, *s.* vin *m.*
wing, *s.* aile *f.;* vol *m.; take* ~ s'envoler.
wink, *s.* clin d'œil, *m.;* — *v.a.* clignoter.
winner, *s.* gagnant *m.*
winter, *s.* hiver *m.*
wipe, *v.a.* essuyer; ~ *out* effacer; — *s.* coup *m.* de torchon.
wire, *s.* fil *m.* (de fer); télégramme *m.; live* ~ fil *m.* en charge; — *v.a. & n.* télégraphier.
wireless, *s.* T.S.F.; télégraphie sans fil; ~ *set* poste *m.* (de T.S.F.).

wise, *adj.* sage; prudent.

wish, *s.* désir *m.;* ∼*es* vœux *m. pl.;* — *v.a.* désirer (de); souhaiter; *(should like)* vouloir *(in conditional).*

wit, *s.* esprit *m.; (pers.)* bel esprit *m.*

witch, *s.* sorcière *f.*

with, *prep.* avec; *(at)* chez.

withdraw, *v.n.* se retirer; *v.a.* retirer.

within, *adv.* dedans; — *prep.* *(time)* en; *(place)* dans; à.

without, *prep.* sans; *(place)* en dehors de.

witness, *s.* témoignage *m.; (pers.)* témoin *m.;* — *v.a.* être témoin de; *(attest)* témoigner; *(document)* signer (à).

witty, *adj.* spirituel.

wizard, *s.* sorcier *m.*

wolf, *s.* loup, louve *m. f.*

woman, *s.* femme *f.*

womb, *s.* matrice *f.; fig.* sein *m.*

wonder, *s.* étonnement *m.; (a thing)* merveille *f.;* — *v.n.* ∼ at être étonné de; *(curious)* se demander; *I* ∼ je me le demande.

wonderful, *adj.* étonnant.

wood, *s.* bois *m.*

wooden, *adj.* de bois.

woodman, *s.* bûcheron *m.*

wool, *s.* laine *f.*

woollen, *adj.* de laine.

word, *s.* mot *m.; (utterance)* parole *f.; (term)* terme *m.; (information)* avis *m.; upon my* ∼*!* ma parole!; *have a* ∼ *with* avoir deux mots avec.

work, *s.* travail *m.; (achievement)* ouvrage *m.;* ∼ *(of art)* œuvre *f.* d'art; ∼*s (of s.o.)* œuvres *f.pl., (factory)* usine *f.; set to* ∼ se mettre à l'œuvre; — *v.a.* faire travailler; *(wood)* ouvrager; *v.n.* travailler; *(operate)* fonctionner, marcher.

worker, *s.* travailleur, -euse *m. f.,* ouvrier, -ère *m. f.*

workman, *s.* ouvrier *m.*

workshop, *s.* atelier *m.*

world, *s.* monde *m.*

world-war, *s.* guerre *f.* mondiale.

world-wide, *adj.* universel; mondial.

worm, *s.* ver *m.*

worry, *s.* ennui *m.,* tracas *m.;* — *v.a.* tracasser; importuner; *v. n.* se tracasser (de), se tourmenter; *don't* ∼*!* soyez tranquille!

worse, *adj.* pire, plus mauvais; *grow* ∼ empirer; — *adv.* pis.

worship, *s.* culte *m.;* — *v.a. & n.* adorer.

worst, *adj.* le, la pire; le, la plus malade; — *adv.* le plus mal; — *s.* pis *m.*

worth, *s.* valeur *f.;* — *adj.* be ∼ valoir; *is it* ∼ *while?* cela (en) vaut-il la peine?; *it is not* ∼ *the trouble* cela ne vaut pas la peine.

worthless, *adj.* sans valeur, indigne.

worthy, *adj.* digne.

wound, *s.* blessure *f.*

wounded, *adj.* blessé; *the* ∼ les blessés.

wrap, *s. (garment)* peignoir *m.; v.a.* ∼ *up* envelopper; *fig.* être absorbé *(in* dans).

wrapper, *s.* toile d'emballage *f.; (book)* bande *f.*

wreck, *s.* naufrage *m.;* navire *m.* naufragé; *fig.* ruine *f.; v.a.* ruiner: *be ~ed* faire naufrage; être naufragé.

wrench, *s.* torsion *f.; (tool)* clef (à écrous) *f.; — v.a.* tordre; *(ankle)* fouler.

wrestle, *v.n.* lutter (avec).

wrestler, *s.* lutteur *m.*

wrestling, *s.* lutte *f.*

wring, *v.a.* tordre.

wrinkle, *s.* ride *f.; (crease)* faux pli *m.; — v.a.* rider.

wrist, *s.* poignet *m.*

writ, *s.* exploit *m.*

write, *v.a. & n.* écrire; *~ down* noter; *~ off* amortir; *~ out* transcrire.

writer, *s.* écrivain *m.*

writing, *s.* écriture *f.;* écrit *m.; in ~* par écrit.

writing-desk, *s.* bureau *m.*

wrong, *adj.* incorrect, faux; *be ~* avoir tort; se tromper (de); *take the ~ train* se tromper de train; *it is the ~ book* ce n'est pas le livre qu'il faut.

X

Xmas, *s.* Noël *m.*

x-ray, *adj. ~ treatment* radiothérapie *f.;~ photograph* radiograph e *f.*

Y

yacht, *s.* yacht *m.*

yard, *s.* yard *m.; cour f.*

yarn, *s.* fil *m;* histoire *f.*

yawn, *s.* baîllement *m.; — v.n.* bailler.

year, *s.* an *m.;* année *f.*

yearly, *adv.* annuellement.

yearn, *v.n. ~ for* soupirer après.

yeast, *s.* levure *f.*

yell, *v. n.* hurler.

yellow, *adj.* jaune.

yes, *adv.* oui; *(after negation)* si.

yesterday, *adv.* hier.

yet, *adv.* encore; *not ~* pas encore; *as ~* jusqu'à présent; *— conj.* néanmoins.

yield, *v.a.* produire; accorder; rendre; *v.n.* céder (à); fléchir.

yoke, *s.* joug *m.*

yolk, *s.* jaune *m.*

you, *pron.* tu; vous.

young, *adj.* jeune; *(animal)* petit; *~er* plus jeune. cadet.

your, *adj.* votre, *(pl.)* vos.

yours, *pron.* à vous; le, la vôtre, les vôtres.

yourself, *pron.* vous-même, *-s.*

youth, *s.* jeunesse *f.; (pers.)* jeune homme *m.*

youth-hostel, *s.* auberge *f.* de la jeunesse.

Z

zeal, *s.* zèle *m.*

zealous, *adj.* zélé.

zero, *s.* zéro *m.*

zest, *s.* enthousiasme *m.;* goût *m.*

zigzag, *s.* zigzag *m.; — adv.* en zigzag.

zinc, *s.* zinc *m.*

zipper, *s.* fermeture éclair. *f.*

zone, *s.* zone *f.*

zoo, *s.* zoo *m.*

zoology, *s.* zoologie *f.*

FRENCH-ENGLISH

DICTIONARY

A

à, au, *prep.* to; at.

abaisser, *v. a.* lower, let down; s'~ stoop.

abandonner, *v. a.* forsake, abandon.

abat-jour, *s. m.* lampshade.

abbaye, *s. m.* abbey.

abbé, *s. m.* abbot.

abdication, *s. f.* abdication.

abdiquer, *v. n.* abdicate; *v. a.* renounce.

abeille, *s. f.* bee.

abject, *adj.* abject, low.

abjurer, *v.a.* abjure; give up.

abolir, *v. a.* abolish.

abondance, *s. f.* plenty, abundance.

abondant, *adj.* abundant.

abonder, *v. n.* abound.

abonner: s'~ subscribe to, take in.

abord, *adv.* d'~ (at) first.

aboutir, *v. n.* end in, come to.

aboyer, *v. n.* bark.

abricot, *s. m.* apricot.

abrupt, *adj.* steep.

absence, *s. f.* absence; ~ d'esprit absence of mind.

absent, *adj.* absent.

absenter: s'~ leave, depart.

absolu, *adj.* absolute.

absorber, *v. a.* absorb;

absoudre*, *v. a.* absolve.

abstraction, *s. f.* abstraction.

abstrait, *adj.* abstract.

absurde, *adj.* absurd.

abus, *s. m.* abuse.

académie, *s. f.* academy.

accélérer, *v. a.* accelerate, hasten.

accent, *s.m.* accent, stress.

accentuer, *v.a.* accent.

accepter, *v. a.* accept; admit.

accès, *s. m.* access; fit.

accessible, *adj.* accessible.

accident, *s. m.* accident; *par* ~ accidentally.

accidentel, -elle, *adj.* accidental.

acclamer, *v.a.* acclaim.

acclimater, *v.a.* acclimatize; 's'~ become acclimatized.

accommoder, *v. a.* accommodate; fit up; s'~ put up with, come to terms.

accompagner, *v. a.* accompany.

accomplir, *v. a.* accomplish, carry out.

accord, *s. m.* agreement, accord, harmony.

accorder, *v.a.* grant, confer; agree.

accoutumer, *v. a.* accustom; s'~ get accustomed (to).

accréditer, *v. a.* accredit.

accrocher, *v. a.* hang up, hook; run against.

accroître, *v. a.* increase; s'~ increase.

accueil, *s. m.* reception.

accueillir, *v. a.* receive, welcome.

accumuler, *v. a.* accumulate, heap up.

accusation, *s. f.* accusation, charge.

accuser, *v.a.* accuse.

achat, *s. m.* purchase; *faire des* ~s go shopping.

acheter, *v.a.* purchase, buy.

achèvement, *s. m.* completion.

achever, *v.a.* complete finish; achieve.

acide, *adj.* acid, sour; — *s. m.* acid.

acier, *s. m.* steel.

acoustique, *s. f.* acoustics.

acquérir*, *v.a.* acquire, purchase; get.

âcre, *adj.* acrid, sour.

acte, *s. m.* action, deed, act; transaction, document, certificate; *(theatre)* act.

acteur, *s. m.* actor.

actif, -ive, *adj.* active; — *s.m.* assets *(pl.);*

action, *s. f.* action; act, deed; effect; lawsuit; plot; story.

activité, *s. f.* activity.

actrice, *s. f.* actress.

actualité, *s. f.* topic of the hour; ~s current events; news-reel.

actuel, -elle, present, of present interest; actual.

adapter, *v.a.* adapt; s'~ adapt oneself.

addition, *s. f.* addition; bill.

additionner, *v. a.* add up.

adhérer, *v. a.* adhere, stick.

adieu, *s. m. (pl. -x)* goodbye; *faire ses* ~x take one's leave.

adjoint, *adj.* & *s. m.* assistant; deputy.

adjuger, *v. a.* adjuge.

administrateur, -trice,

s. m. f. manager, director.

administratif, -ive- *adj.* administrative.

administration, *s. f.* management, direction; administration.

administrer, *v.a.* administer; manage.

admirable, *adj.* admirable.

admiration, *s. f.* admiration.

admirer, *v. a.* admire, wonder at.

admission, *s. f.* admission, admittance.

adolescent, *s. m.* adolescent, youth.

adopter, *v.a.* adopt, pass.

adoption, *s.f.* adoption.

adorer, *v.a.* adore.

adresse, *s. f.* address; skill, dexterity.

adresser, *v. a.* address, direct; s'~ apply (to).

adroit, *adj.* clever, skilful.

adulte, *adj.* & *s.* adult.

adversaire, *s. m.* adversary.

aérien, -enne, *adj.* aerial.

aérodrome, *s. m.* airport.

aéroport, *s. m.* airport.

affaiblir, *v. a.* weaken.

affaire, *s. f.* business, affair, matter; lawsuit.

affamé, *adj.* hungry.

affecter, *v. a.* affect, feign; move; assume.

affection, *s. f.* affection; disease.

affectueux, -euse, *adj.* affectionate.

affermir, *v. a.* strengthen; s'~ become stronger.

affiche, *s. f.* poster, bill.

afficher, *v. a.* post up, stick up, placard.

affiler, *v.a.* sharpen.

affirmatif, -ive, *adj.* affirmative.

affirmer, *v. a.* affirm.

affliger, *v. a.* afflict.

affluer, *v. n.* flow into.

affranchir, *v. a.* (set) free; stamp.

affreux, -euse, *adj.* dreadful, terrible.

affronter, *v.a.* face.

afin, *conj.* ~ *de* in order to; ~ *que* in order

that, so that.

africain (A.), *adj. & s. m. f.* African.

âge, *s. m.* age; period; *quel ~ avez-vous?* how old are you?

agence, *s. f.* agency.

agent, *s. m.* agent; policeman.

aggraver, *v. a.* aggravate.

agile, *adj.* agile, active.

agilité, *s. f.* agility.

agir, *v. n.* act; take effect; behave; *s'~* be in question.

agitation, *s. f.* agitation.

agiter, *v. a.* agitate.

agneau, *s. m.* lamb.

agonie, *s. f.* agony.

agréable, *adj.* agreeable.

agréer, *v. a.* accept, receive favourably.

agrément, *s. m.* consent, approval; pleasure.

agressif, -ive, *adj.* aggressive.

agression, *s. f.* aggression, attack.

agriculture, *s. f.* agriculture.

aide, *s. f.* help.

aider, *v. a.* help.

aïeux, *s. m. pl.* ancestors.

aigle, *s. m.* eagle.

aigre, *adj.* sour, acid.

aigrir: *s'~* turn sour.

aigu, *adj.* pointed, sharp; keen; *accent ~* acute accent.

aiguille, *s. f.* needle; hand, index; point, switch; *grande ~* minute hand.

aiguiser, *v. a.* sharpen.

ail, *s. m.* garlic.

aile, *s. f.* wing; flank; aisle; mudguard.

ailleurs, *adv.* somewhere else, elsewhere; *d'~* in addition, besides.

aimable, *adj.* amiable, pleasant, kindly.

aimer, *v. a. & n.* like, love,

be fond of, care to.

aîné, *adj. & s. m. f.* elder, eldest; senior.

ainsi, *adv. & conj.* so, thus; likewise; *~ de suite* and so on; *~ que* as well as.

air, *s. m.* air; look(s), appearance, manner; *(music)* air.

aisance, *s. f.* ease; comfort; facility; *être dans l'~* be well off.

aise, *s. f.* ease, comfort.

aisé, *adj.* easy; well-off.

ajourner, *v.a.* adjourn.

alcool, *s. m.* alcohol.

alcoolique, *adj.* alcoholic.

algèbre, *s. f.* algebra.

aliment, *s. m.* aliment, food.

alimentation, *s. f.* alimentation; feeding.

alimenter, *v. a.* feed.

aliter, *v. a. être alité* be confined to bed, be laid up.

allaiter, *v. a.* give suck to; nurse.

allée, *s. f.* (garden) path, lane, walk, alley.

alléger, *v.a.* lighten; alleviate, soothe.

allégresse, *s. f.* gaiety, delight.

allemand (A.), *adj. & s. m. f.* German.

aller*, *v. n.* go, proceed; get on; grow, get; *~ à pied* walk; *~ en auto* drive; *~ en avion* fly; *~ bien* be well; *comment allez-vous?* how are you?; *allons!* come on!; *allez!* indeed; *s'en ~* go away, be off.

alliance, *s. f.* alliance, union; wedding-ring.

allié, -e, *s. m. f.* ally; — *adj.* allied.

allier, *v.a.* alloy; match;

unite; s'~ join with, unite.

allonger, *v.a.* lengthen, stretch out, prolong; ~ *le pas* step out; s'~ get longer.

allumer, *v. a.* light (up), set on fire; excite.

allumette, *s. f.* match.

allure, *s.f.* gait, pace; manner, behaviour; direction.

allusion, *s. f.* allusion, hint; reference.

alors, *adv.* then.

alpinisme, *s.m.* mountaineering.

altérer, *v. a.* alter, change; s'~ alter, degenerate.

alternance, *s.f.* alternation.

alternatif, **-ive**, *adj.* alternate, alternative.

alterner, *v. n. & a.* alternate.

altitude, *s. f.* altitude.

aluminium, *s. f.* aluminium.

amaigrir, *v.a.* make thin; s'~ grow thin.

amant, **-e**, *s. m. f.* lover.

amas, *s.m.* heap, mass, pile.

amateur, *s. m.* amateur, lover, fancier.

ambassade, *s. f.* embassy.

ambassadeur, *s. m.* ambassador.

ambassadrice, *s.f.* ambassadress.

ambitieux, **-euse**, *adj.* ambitious.

ambition, *s. f.* ambition.

ambulance, *s. f.* ambulance; ~ *(automobile)* ambulance(-car).

âme, *s.f.* soul; mind.

améliorer, *v. a.* ameliorate, improve; s'~ improve.

aménager, *v.a.* fit up, out.

amender, *v.a.* amend, improve.

amener, *v. a.* bring, draw; bring before, in, out; introduce; induce.

amer, **-ère**, *adj.* bitter.

américain, **-e (A.)**, *adj.* & *s. m. f.* American.

ami, **-e**, *s. m. f.* friend; sweetheart; *bon* ~, *bonne* ~*e* sweetheart.

amical, *adj.* friendly, kind.

amiral, *s.m.* admiral.

amitié, *s. f.* friendship; affection; *meilleures* ~*s* kindest regards.

amortir, *v.a.* lessen, soften; pay (off), write off.

amortisseur, *s. m.* shock-absorber.

amour, *s. m.* love; *faire l'*~ court, make love to; *mon* ~ my darling.

amoureux, **-euse**, *adj.* in love *(de* with), enamoured *(de* of).

amplificateur, *s.m.* amplifier.

amplifier, *v. a.* amplify.

ampoule, *s. f.* blister; bulb.

amulette, *s. f.* amulet.

amusant, *adj.* amusing.

amusement, *s. m.* amusement, pastime, fun.

amuser, *v.a.* amuse, entertain; s'~ enjoy oneself.

an, *s. m.* year; *il y a un* ~ a year ago.

analogie, *s. f.* analogy.

analogue, *adj.* analogous.

analyse, *s. f.* analysis.

analyser, *v. a.* analyse.

ananas, *s. m.* pineapple.

anatomie, *s. f.* anatomy.

ancêtre, *s. m. f.* ancestor.

ancien, **-enne**, *adj.* ancient, old, antique.

ancre, *s. f.* anchor; *lever l'*~ weigh anchor.

âne, *s. m.* ass.

anéantir, *v. a.* annihilate.

anecdote, *s. f.* anecdote.

ange, *s. m.* angel.

anglais, -e (A.), *adj.* English; — *s. m. f.* Englishman, Englishwoman.

angle, *s. m.* angle, corner; bend.

angoisse, *s.f.* anguish.

animal, *s.m.* animal; beast.

anneau, *s. m.* circle, ring.

année, *s. f.* year; ~ *scolaire* school-year; *bonne* ~ a happy New Year!

annexer, *v. a.* annex.

anniversaire, *s. m.* anniversary, b rthday.

annonce, *s. f.* announcement, advertisement.

annoncer, *v. a.* announce, give notice of; advertise.

annuaire, *s. m.* year-book, annual, directory.

annuel, -elle, *adj.* annual.

annuler, *v. a.* annul.

anonyme, *adj.* anonymous; *société* ~ joint-stock company.

anormal, *adj.* abnormal.

anse, *s. f.* handle; creek.

antécédent, -e, *adj. & s. m.* antecedent.

antenne, *s. f.* aerial.

antérieur, *adj.* anterior, previous.

antibiotique, *s. m.* antibiotic.

antichambre, *s. f.* entrance hall.

anticiper, *v. a. & n.* anticipate; encroach.

antipathie, *s.f.* antipathy.

antiquaire, *s. m.* antiquarian.

antique, *adj.* antique, ancient.

antiquité, *s. f.* antiquity.

antiseptique, *adj. & s. m.* antiseptic.

anxiété, *s. f.* anxiety.

anxieux, -euse, *adj.* anxious.

août, *s.m.* August.

apaiser, *v. a.* appease, pacify, quiet.

apercevoir, *v. a.* perceive, catch sight of; remark, notice.

aplanir, *v.a.* smooth, level, even off; s'~ become level.

aplatir, *v.a.* fl atten.

apologie, *s. m.* apology, defence.

apoplexie, *s. f.* apoplexy.

apostolique, *adj.* apostolic(al).

apostrophe, *s. f.* apostrophe.

apôtre, *s. m.* apostle.

apparaître, *v. n.* appear.

appareil, *s. m.* apparatus, device, appliance, gear; camera; ~ *de TV* TV-set; ~ *de direction* steering-gear.

apparence, *s. f.* appearance, look(s); likelihood; *en* ~ apparently.

apparent, *adj.* apparent.

apparition, *s. f.* appearance; apparition.

appartement, *s.m.* flat; apartment.

appartenir, *v.n.* belong, appertain *(à* to).

appel, *s. m.* call; appeal; *faire l'*~ call the roll.

appeler, *v. a.* call in, out, up, down; ring up; name, term; *en* ~ appeal; *faire* ~ send for; s'~ be called, call oneself.

appendice, *s. m.* appendix.

appendicite, *s.f.* appedicitis.

appesantir, *v.a.* make heavy, weigh down.

appétit, *s. m.* appetite.

applaudir, *v. n.* applaud, clap.

application, *s. f.* application; diligence.

appliquer, *v. a.* apply; lay on.

apporter, *v.a.* bring.

appréciation, *s.f.* appreciation; estimation.

apprécier, *v. a.* value.

appréhension, *s. f.* apprehension, fear.

apprendre, *v. a.* learn, acquire: hear of; teach.

apprentissage, *s. m.* apprenticeship.

apprêter, *v. a.* prepare; season; dress; s'~ prepare oneself, get ready.

approbation, *s. f.* approbation, approval.

approche, *s. f.* approach, advance.

approcher, *v.a.* bring toward, forward.

approprié, *adj.* appropriate.

approprier: s'~ appropriate, take; accommodate, adapt oneself.

approuver, *v. a.* sanction; approve.

approximatif, -ive, *adj.* approximate.

approximation, *s.f.* approximation.

appui, *s. m.* support.

appuyer, *v. a.* support; lean; *v. n.* ~ *sur* lay stress (up)on; s'~ lean, rest, rely (upon).

après, *adv.* after; behind; next (to); ~ *coup* too late; ~ *tout* after all; d'~ after, according to; by.

après-demain, *adv.* & *s. m.* (the) day after tomorrow.

après-midi, *s. m.* afternoon.

à-propos, *adv.* in good time; — *s. m.* timely word; fitness.

apte, *adj.* apt, suitable.

aptitude, *s. f.* aptitude, ability, talent.

aquarelle, *s.f.* water-color.

arabe (A.), *adj.* & *s. m. f.* Arab, Arabian; Arabic.

araignée, *s. f.* spider.

arbitre, *s. f.* arbiter, judge; umpire, referee.

arbre, *s. m.* tree; shaft; ~ *fruitier* fruit-tree; ~ *coudé* crank shaft.

arc, *s. m.* bow; arc(h).

arcade, *s. f.* arcade.

arche, *s. f.* arch, vault.

archet, *s.m.* bow.

archevêque, *s.m.* archbishop.

architecture, *s. f.* architecture.

archives *s. f. pl.* archives.

ardemment, *adv.* ardently.

ardent, *adj.* burning, fiery, ardent, eager.

ardeur, *s. f.* keenness; ardour, zeal.

arête, *s. f.* fish-bone; edge; ridge.

argent, *s. m.* silver; money; ~ *en caisse* cash in hand ~ *comptant* ready money; ~ *de la poche* pocket-money; *à-court* d'~ pressed for money.

argenterie, *s. f.* plate.

argentin[1], *adj.* silvery.

argentin[2], -e (A.), *adj.* & *s. m. f.* Argentine.

argile, *s.f.* clay.

argot, *s. m.* slang.

argument, *s.m.* argument, proof, evidence.

aristocratie, *s.f.* aristocracy.

aristocratique, *adj.* aristocratic.

arme, *s.f.* arm, weapon; ~s *à feu* fire-arms; *faire des* ~s fence.

armée, *s. f.* army.

armer, *v.a.* arm; fortify; s'~ arm oneself.

armoire, *s. f.* cupboard;

wardrobe.

armure, s. f. armour; armature.

arracher, v.a. pull (out), tear up; extract, draw; remove from.

arrangement, s. m. arrangement; agreement, settlement; ~s terms.

arranger, v. a. arrange, settle, fix (up); s'~ come to an agreement, make arrangements (for); make shift (to).

arrestation, s. f. arrest.

arrêt, s. m. stop (of bus, tram etc.); pause; standstill; sentence; arrest; ~facultatif request stop; sans ~ non-stop.

arrêter, v.a. check, stop; arrest; engage, book; decide, decree; settle; s'~ stop; draw up; leave off.

arrière. adv. behind, backward; en ~ back(ward); ~ s. m. back part, rear.

arriéré, adj. overdue; backward; under-developed; — s.m. arrears (pl.).

arrivée, s. f. arrival; à l'~ on arrival.

arriver, v. n. arrive, come; turn up; happen; occur; ~ à attain, arrive at, reach; le train arrive à the train is due at.

arrogance, s. f. arrogance.

arroser, v. a. water, sprinkle; baste.

art, s. m. art; les beaux ~s the fine arts.

artère, s.f. artery; thoroughfare.

article, s. m. article; ~s de grande consommation consumer(s') goods.

articulation, s. f. joint.

articuler, v.a. articulate.

artificiel, -elle, adj. artifi-

cial.

artillerie, s. f. artillery.

artisan, s. m. craftsman.

artiste, s. m. & f. artist; player

ascenseur, s. m. lift.

asile, s. m. refuge, asylum.

aspect, s.m. aspect.

asperge, s. f. asparagus.

aspirateur, s.m. vacuum-cleaner.

aspiration, s. f. aspiration.

aspirer, v.a. inspire; v. n. aspire (à to).

assaillir*, v. a. assault.

assaisonner, v.a. season; dress.

assassin, s. m. assassin.

assassiner, v. a. assassinate, murder.

assaut, s.m. assault.

assemblage, s. m. assemblage, gathering, collection.

assemblée, s.f. assembly, meeting.

assembler, v. a. assemble; put together; gather; s'~ assemble.

asseoir*, v. a. seat; place; s'~ take a seat.

assez, adv. enough; pretty, fairly.

assiduité, s.f. assiduity.

assiéger, v.a. attack, besiege.

assiette, s. f. posture; seat; position; plate.

assimiler, v. a. assimilate (à to).

assistance, s.f. presence, attendance; audience; assistance, help.

assister, v. n. attend, be present (à at); v. a. assist, help.

association, s. f. association; partnership, company.

associer, v.a. associate, link up; share interests with; s'~ associate oneself *(avec* with).

assommant, *adj.* boring, dull.

assortir, *v.a.* match, assort; **s'~** be suitable, go well together.

assoupir, *v. a.* make drowsy, sleepy; **s'~** grow sleepy.

assujettir, *v.a.* subject, subjugate.

assumer, *v. a.* assume.

assurance, *s. f.* assurance; insurance; **~** *sur la vie* life-insurance.

assuré, *adj.* assured, confident, sure; insured.

assurer, *v. a.* assure, secure; insure; **s'~** make sure (of).

astre, *s. m.* star.

astronaute, *s. m.* astronaut, space man.

astronautique, *s. f.* astronautics, space travel.

astronef, *s. m.* spacecraft, space-ship.

atelier, *s.m.* workshop; studio.

athée, *s.m.f.* atheist.

athlète, *s.m.* athlete.

athlétique, *adj.* athletic.

atome, *s.m.* atom.

atomique, *adj.* atomic; *bombe* **~** atom(ic) bomb *énergie* **~** atomic energy.

attache, *s. f.* tie, fastener; bond, strap; *fig.* attachment.

attaché, *s. m.* attaché.

attacher, *v.a.* fasten, tie (up), attach; associate; engage; **s'~** attach (to), become attached (to).

attaque, *s. f.* attack.

attaquer, *v.a.* attack.

attarder, *v.a.* delay; *être attardé* be delayed.

atteindre*, *v. a.* attain, reach; hit, stirke.

atteinte, *s. f.* blow, stroke; fit; injury; *hors d'~* out of reach.

attendre, *v. a. & n.* await, wait for, expect; **s'~** hope for, expect.

attendrir, *v. a.* soften; *fig.* move, touch; **s'~** be moved.

attendrissement, *s.m.* compassino; tenderness.

attente, *s. f.* waiting; hope

attentif, **-ive,** *adj.* attentive, considerate.

attention, *s.f.* attention, notice, heed, care; *(pl.)* attentions; *faire* **~** be careful, mind, take notice of, take heed (to); **~!** look out!

atténuer, *v. a.* extenuate, attenuate.

atterrir, *v. n.* land.

atterrissage, *s. m.* landing; *piste d'~* landing-strip.

attester, *v.a.* attest.

attirail, *s. m.* implements *(pl.),* utensils *(pl.),* gear; tackle.

attirer, *v.a.* attract.

attitude, *s. f.* attitude.

attraction, *s. f.* attraction.

attrape, *s. f.* trap; catch.

attribuer, *v. a.* assign, allot; attribute, ascribe.

attribut, *s. m.* attribute.

au *(pl.* aux), to the, at the.

auberge, *s. f.* inn, tavern; **~** *de la jeunesse* youth hostel.

aucun, *adj. & pron.* no, none, no one, not any.

au-dessous, *adv.* below; **~** *de* under.

au-dessus, *adv.* (**~** *de*) above, over.

audience, *s. f.* audience; public; sitting, session.

audiovisuel, **-elle,** *adj.* audio-visual.

auditeur, **-trice,** *s. m. f.* listener; auditor.

auditoire, *s. m.* audience;

congregation.

auge, *s.m.* trough; bucket.

augmentation, *s.f.* augmentation, increase; rise.

augmenter, *v. a.* augment, increase; s'~ increase.

aujourd'hui, *adv.* today.

auparavant, *adv.* previously, earlier; before.

auprès, *adv.* near, by, close by; ~ *de* near.

auquel, *rel.pron.* to whom, to which.

aurore, *s.f.* dawn.

aussi, *adv.* also, too; ~ ... *que* as ... as; — *conj.* and so, therefore; ~ *bien que* as well as; ~ *bien* in fact.

austère, *adj.* austere, severe.

autant, *adv. & conj.* as much, as many, as far; ~ *que* as far as, as much as.

autel, *s. m.* altar.

auteur, *s. m.* author.

authentique, *adj.* authentic, genuine.

auto, *s. f.* car.

autobus, *s.m.* (motor-)bus.

autocar, *s. m.* (motor-) coach.

automatique, *adj.* automatic; — *s.m.* dial-telephone.

automne, *s. m. f.* autumn.

automobile, *s. m. f.* motor-car.

autonomie, *s.f.* autonomy.

autorisation, *s. f.* authorization, permission; licence.

autoriser, *v.a.* authorize.

autorité, *s.f.* authority; rule.

autoroute, *s. f.* motorway.

auto-stop, *s. m.* hitch-hiking.

auto-stoppeur, -euse, *s. m. f.* hitch-hiker.

autour, *adv. & prep.* ~ *de* about, (a)round; *tout* ~ all round.

autre, *adj.* different, other, another, else; *un* ~ another; *d'*~ *part* on the other hand; ~ *part* elsewhere; *de temps* ~ now and then, at times; *l'*~ *jour* the other day; *l'un et l'*~ both; *l'un l'*~ each other.

autrefois, *adv.* formerly, long ago.

autrichien, -enne (A.), *adj. & s.m.f.* Austrian.

autrui, *pron.* others, other people.

avalanche, *s.f.* avalanche.

avaler, *v.a.* swallow; *fig.* endure, pocket.

avance, *s.f.* advance.

avancé, *adj.* advanced.

avancement, *s.m.* advance, progress; promotion.

avancer, *v.a.* advance, bring, put forward; pay in advance; — *v. n.* advance, proceed, move on; s'~ come, move, go forward.

avant, *prep. & adv.* before, in front (of), in advance; ~ *tout* above all, before everything; *en* ~ forward, to the front; *mettre en* ~ bring forward; *en* ~ *de* in front of; — *s.m.* front (part); bow (of ship); forward.

avantage, *s. m.* advantage, benefit, profit; *(tennis)* vantage.

avantageux, -euse, *adj.* advantageous.

avant-hier, *adv.* day before yesterday.

avant-propos, *s. m.* foreword, preface.

avare, s. m. f. miser; —
adj. avaricious, mi-
serly.

avarice, s.f. avarice.

avec, prep. with.

avenir, s. m. future; à l'~
in the future.

aventure, s. f. adventure;
chance, luck.

aventurer, v:a. risk; (s'~)
venture.

aventurier, -ère, s. m. f.
adventurer.

avenue, s. f. boulevard;
avenue.

averse, s.f. shower (of
rain).

aversion, v. f. aversion,
dislike.

avertir, v.a. inform, let
know; warn; faire ~ de
give notice of.

avertissement, s. m. information, notification;
advice; warning.

aveu, s. m. admission,
confession; consent.

aveugle, adj. blind.

aveuglement, s. m. blindness.

avide, adj. greedy, eager.

avidité, s.f. avidity.

avilir, v.a. debase, disgrace, degrade.

avion, s.m. (aero)plane;
~ de ligne air-liner;
~ à réaction jet plane;
par ~ by air-mail.

avis, s. m. opinion; advice,
counsel; information,
notice; hint; mind;
changer d'~ change
one's mind.

aviser, v.a. perceive; inform; let know; advise;
s'~ de think, find.

avocat, s. m. barrister,
advocate, counsel.

avoine, s.f. oat(s).

avoir*, v. a. have, possess; have on, wear;

feel; ~ raison be right;
~ faim be hungry;
~ de take after; ~ à
have to; il y a there is,
there are; ago.

avorter, v. n. miscarry,
have a miscarriage.

avorton, s. m. abortion.

avoué, s. m. attorney,
solicitor; lawyer.

avouer, v. a. & n. admit,
confess; acknowledge;
approve.

avril, s.m. April.

axe, s.m. axis; axle.

azote, s.m. nitrogen.

B

baccalauréat, s. m. bacca-
laureate, bachelor's
degree.

bachelier, s. m. bachelor
(of arts etc.).

bacille, s.m. bacillus.

bagage, s. m. luggage;
plier ~ pack up one's
kit.

bague, s.f. ring.

bai, adj. bay.

baie¹, s. f. bay.

baie², s. f. berry.

baigner: se ~ bathe.

baignoire, s.m. bath,
bathtub; pit-box.

bâiller, v. n. yawn, gape.

bain, s. m. bath; salle de ~
bath-room.

baïonette, s.f. bayonet.

baiser, v.a. kiss.

baisse, s.f. fall; decline.

baisser, v.a. lower, let
down; bring down;
turn down; cast down;
v.n. decline, fall;
sink; se ~ stoop.

bal, s. m. ball; ~ costumé
fancy-dress ball.

balai, s.m. broom, mop;
(house-)brush; donner
un coup de ~ sweep.

balance, *s. f.* balance, scales *(pl.).*

balancer, *v.a.&n.* balance; weigh; swing, rock; give the sack; **se ~** swing, wave; balance.

balayer, *v.a.* sweep (out), clear away.

balcon, *s. m.* balcony; dress-circle.

baleine, *s.f.* whale.

ballade, *s.f.* ballad.

balle, *s.f.* ball; bullet; bale.

ballon, *s.m.* balloon; (foot-)ball.

balnéaire, *adj.* pertaining to baths; *station ~* watering place.

bambou, *s.m.* bamboo.

ban, *s. m.* ban; *~s de mariage* banns.

banal *adj.* banal, common, ordinary.

banane, *s. f.* banana.

banc, *s. m.* bench, form; bank; pew; stand.

bande, *s.f.* band, strip; bandage; troop, gang, set; *~ de papier* slip of paper; *~ transporteuse* conveyer belt.

bander, *v. a.* bind up.

bandit, *s. m.* bandit.

banlieu, *s. f.* outskirts, suburbs *(pl.).*

bannir, *v. a.* banish, exile.

banque, *s. f.* bank; *billet de ~* banknote; *compte en ~* bank-account.

banquet, *s. m.* banquet, feast.

banquier, *-ère,* *s.m.f.* banker.

baptême, *s. m.* baptism.

baptiser, *v.a.* baptize.

barbare, *adj. & s.m.* barbarian.

barbarie, *s. f.* barbarousness, cruelty.

barbe, *s. f.* beard; *faire la ~ à* shave.

barbet, *s. m.* poodle.

barbier, *s. m.* barber.

baron, *s. m.* baron.

baronne, *s.f.* baroness.

barque, *s.f.* boat, barge.

barrage, *s.m.* barrier, barrage, dam.

barre, *s.f.* bar.

barreau, *s. m.* (small) bar; the Bar.

barrer, *v.a.* fasten, bar; cut off, shut out; steer.

barrière, *s.f.* barrier, town-gate, gate; bar; obstacle.

barrique, *s.f.* barrel, cask.

bas¹, *adj.* low; *à ~ prix* cheap; *terre ~se* lowland; *en ~* (down) below, down(-wards), — *s. m.* bottom, lower part

bas², *s. m.* stocking; *~ nylons* nylon stockings.

base, *s. f.* base; basis.

basique, *adj.* basic.

basse, *s.f.* bass; bass-viol.

bassesse, *s.f.* lowness, meanness.

basset, *s. m.* basset (dog).

bassin, *s. m.* basin, pool.

bataille, *s.f.* battle.

bataillon, *s. m.* battalion.

bateau, *s. m.* boat.

batelier, *s.m.* boatman.

bâtiment, *s. m.* building; building trade; ship.

bâtir, *v.a.* build, erect.

bâtisseur, -euse *s. m. f.* builder.

bâton, *s. m.* stick, staff.

batte, *s.f.* bat; beater.

battement, *s.m.* clap-(ping); flapping.

batterie, *s.f.* battery; fight, row; percussive instruments *(pl.);* *~ de cuisine* kitchen utensils *(pl.)*.

battre*, *v. a. & n.* beat, strike, thrash; se ~ fight.

battu, *adj.* beaten.

bavard, -e *s.m.f.* gossip.

bavarder, *v.n.* chat(ter), gossip.

bazar, *s.m.* bazaar.

beau, bel; belle; beaux, belles, *adj.* beautiful, handsome, good-looking, fair; considerable; *il y a ~ temps que* it seems an age since; *un ~ jour* one fine day; — *s.m.* beauty.

beaucoup, *adv.* (*~ de*) a good deal, many, much; plenty (of); *a ~ près, de ~* by far.

beau-frère, *s. m.* brother-in-law.

beau-père, *s. m.* father-in-law.

beauté, *s. f.* beauty

beaux-arts, *s. m. pl.* (the) fine arts.

bébé, *s. m.* baby.

bec, *s. m.* beak, bill nib; mouth-piece; jet; *~ de gaz* gas-burner, gas-jet.

bêche, *s. f.* spade.

bégayer, *v. n. &a.* stammer, stutter.

belge (B.), *adj. & s. m. f.* Belgian.

belle-fille, *s. f.* daughter-in-law; step-daughter.

belle-mère, *s. f.* mother-in-law; stepmother.

belle-sœur, *s. f.* sister-in-law.

bémol, *s. m. & adj.* flat *(music)*.

bénédiction, *s.f.* benediction, blessing.

bénéfice, *s. m.* benefit, advantage, profit.

bénir, *v. a.* bless; praise.

berceau, *s. m.* cradle; *fig.* origin.

bercer, *v. a.* rock, lull (to sleep); *fig.* lull (with promises).

béret, *s.m.* beret.

berger, *s. m.* shepherd.

bergère, *s. f.* shepherdess; deep easy chair.

bésicles, *s. f. pl.* spectacles; goggles.

besogne, *s. f.* (piece of) work, job, task.

besoin, *s. m.* need, want; requirement; *avoir ~ de* want, need; *être dans le ~* be poor.

bétail, *s. m.* cattle.

bête, *s. f.* beast; animal; — *adj.* foolish, silly, stupid, dull.

bêtise, *s. f.* foolishness, stupidity; nonsense; trifle.

beurre, *s. m.* butter.

biais, *s. m.* bias, slant, slope.

biaiser, *v. n.* slant, slope.

bibelot, *s. m.* trinket, gew-gaw.

biberon, *s. m.* feeding-bottle.

bible, *s. f.* Bible.

bibliothécaire, *s. m. f.* librarian.

bibliothèque, *s. f.* library; bookcase; book-stall.

bicyclette, *s. f.* bicycle, bike.

bicycliste, *s. m. f.* cyclist.

bien, *adv.* well, right, properly, fully; *assez ~* fairly; *faire du ~* benefit; *ou ~* or else; *très ~* very well, all right; *~ avant* long before; very bad indeed; *~ que* (al)though; — *s. m.* good, welfare, benefit; property, goods;

aller *à* ~ prosper, be successful.

bien-être, *s. m.* welfare, well-being.

bienfaisance, *s. f.* beneficence.

bienfaisant, *adj.* charitable, kind; humane.

bienfait, *s.m.* kindness; benefaction.

bientôt, *adv.* soon, shortly; *à* ~! so long!

bienveillance, *s.f.* benevolence, kindness.

bienveillant, *adj.* kind(ly), benevolent, charitable.

bienvenu, *adj.* welcome; *soyez le* ~ welcome!

bière, *s.f.* beer.

bifteck, *s. m.* beef-steak.

bijou, *s. m.* *(pl.* -x) jewel.

bijouterie, *s.f.* jewellery; jeweller's shop.

bijoutier, -ière *s. m. f.* jeweller.

bile, *s. f.* bile; *se faire de la* ~ worry, fret.

bille, *s.f.* billiard-ball.

billet, *s. m.* note; ticket; certificate; ~ *d'aller et retour* return ticket; ~ *d'entrée* admission ticket; ~ *de banque* banknote.

billot, *s. m.* block; yoke.

biographe, *s. m. f.* biographer.

biographie, *s. f.* biography.

biologie, *s. f.* biology.

biologiste, biologue, *s. m. f.* biologist.

bis, *int.* encore!

biscuit, *s. m.* biscuit.

bison, *s. m.* bison.

bistro, *s. m.* pub; wine-shop.

bizarre, *adj.* strange, odd.

blague, *s.f.* pouch.

blaireau, *s. m.* badger; shaving-brush.

blâme, *s. m.* blame, reprimand.

blâmer, *v. a.* blame; find fault with.

blanc, blanche, *adj.* white; hoary; blank.

blanchir, *v.a.* whiten, bleach; whitewash; *v.n.* turn white, whiten.

blasphème, *s. m.* blasphemy.

blasphémer, *v.a. & n.* blaspheme.

blé, *s. m.* wheat.

blême, *adj.* pale.

blesser, *v. a.* wound, injure, hurt; offend; *se* ~ wound oneself; be offended.

blessure, *s. f.* wound, injury; offence.

bleu, *adj. & s. m.* blue; ~ *marine* navy blue.

bloc, *s. m.* block; *en* ~ in the lump.

blond, *adj.* fair, blond.

bloquer, *v.a.* blockade; block (up); tighten.

blouse, *s.f.* blouse, smock.

bobine, *s. f.* bobbin, spool.

bœuf, *s. m.* ox, beef.

bohème, *adj.* bohemian.

boire*, *v. a. & n.* drink; swallow; ~ *à la santé de* X drink X's health; — *s. m.* drink(ing).

bois, *s. m.* wood; timber; *de, en* ~ wood(en).

boisson, *s. f.* drink, beverage.

boîte, *s. f.* box, case; can, tin; ~ *aux lettres* letter-box; ~ *de vitesse* gear-box; *en* ~ tinned.

boiteux, -euse *adj.* lame.

bombardement, *s. m.* bombardment.

bombarder, *v. a.* bombard, shell.

bombe, *s. f.* bomb, shell; ~ H H-bomb.

bon, bonne, *adj.* good;
kind, nice; right; valid;
c'est ~! (all) right!;
~ *à rien* good for
nothing; *~ne année!*
happy new year!; *de*
~ne heure early; —
s. m. good(ness); bond,
order.

bonbon, *s. m.* bonbon,
sweet.

bond, *s. m.* bound, leap.

bondé, *adj.* crowded.

bonder, *v. a.* load, cram.

bondir, *v. n.* bound, leap,
spring.

bonheur, *s. m.* happiness; good fortune; suc-
cess.

bonhomme, *s. m.* good-
natured man; simple
man; fellow.

bonjour, *s.m.* good
morning; salutation.

bonne, *s. f.* maid-serv-
ant; ~ (*d'enfants*)
nursery-maid.

bonnet, *s. m.* cap, hood.

bonsoir, *s. m.* good evening.

bonté, *s. f.* goodness,
kindness, benevolence.

bord, *s. m.* edge, border,
brink, (b)rim, verge;
side, board, bank; *à*
~ on board; *monter*
à ~ go on board.

border, *v.a.* border, adjoin.

bordure, *s. f.* border,
edging; verge; kerb.

borne, *s. f.* milestone;
bound(ary), limit.

borner, *v. a.* bound, limit,
restrict.

bosse, *s. f.* bump, protu-
berance; knob.

botanique, *adj.* botanical; — *s. f.* botany.

botte[1]**,** *s. f.* (high) boot.

botte[2]**,** *s. f.* bottle; truss.

bottine, *s. f.* boot.

bouche, *s. f.* mouth;
orifice, muzzle.

boucher, *s. m.* butcher.

boucherie, *s. f.* butcher's
(shop).

bouchon, *s. m.* plug, cork,
stopper.

boue, *s. f.* mud, dirt.

bouger, *v. n.* stir, budge.

bougie, *s.f.* candle.
(sparking-)plug.

bouillir*, *v. n. & a.*
(also *faire ~*) boil.

bouillon, *s. m.* bubble;
stock; ~ *de bœuf* beef-
tea.

bouillotte, *s. f.* kettle.

boulanger, -ère, *s. m. f.*
baker; baker's wife.

boulangerie, *s. f.* bakery,
baker's (shop).

boule, *s. f.* ball, bowl.

boulevard, *s. m.* boulevard.

bouleverser, *v. a.* overthrow, upset; turn up-
side down; distract.

boulon, *s. m.* bolt, pin.

bouquet, *s. m.* cluster,
bunch; bouquet.

bourdonnement, *s.m.*
buzz(ing), humming.

bourdonner, *v.n.* buzz,
hum, drone.

bourg, *s. m.* (small)
town; village.

bourgeois, e, *s. m. f.* citizen; townsman.

bourgeoisie, *s. f.* citizens
(*pl.*); middle class.

bourse, *s. f.* purse; exchange; Stock Ex-
change; scholarship,
bursary.

bousculade, *s. f.* hustling.

bousculer, *v. a.* upset, hustle, jostle; *se ~* hustle
each other.

bout, *s. m.* end, extremity, tip, top, button;
un ~ de chemin a
short distance.

bouteille, *s. f.* bottle.

boutique, *s. f.* shop; booth, stall.

bouton, *s. m.* button; stud; bud; nipple; knob; ~*s de manchette* cuff-links.

boutonnière, *s. f.* button-hole.

boxer, *v. n.* box, fight.

boxeur, *s. m.* boxer.

bracelet, *s. m.* bracelet.

braconner, *v. n.* poach.

braconnier, *s. m.* poacher.

brancard, *s. m.* stretcher; shaft.

branche, *s. f.* branch.

branler, *v. a.* shake, totter, waver.

bras, *s. m.* arm; hand; branch.

braser, *v. a.* braze, solder

brasserie, *s. f.* brewery; beershop.

brave, *adj.* brave; honest. worthy, good.

braver, *v. a.* face, brave.

bravoure, *s. f.* bravery, courage.

brebis, *s. f.* ewe, sheep.

brèche, *s. f.* breach, gap.

bref, brève, *adj.* brief, short.

bretelles, *s. f. pl.* braces.

brevet, *s. m.* patent; certificate.

bride, *s. f.* bridle, reins.

brièveté, *s. f.* brevity.

brigade, *s. f.* brigade.

brigadier, *s. m.* corporal, overseer.

brigand, *s. m.* brigand, armed robber.

brillant, *adj.* brilliant, shiny, glittering.

briller, *v. n.* shine, glitter, sparkle.

brin, *s. m.* shoot, sprig, blade (of grass).

brioche, *s. f.* brioche.

brique, *s. f.* brick; bar (of soap).

briquet *s. m.* lighter.

briquette, *s. f.* briquette.

brise, *s. f.* breeze.

briser, *v. a.* break (to pieces), smash; *v. n.* break; se ~ break to pieces.

britannique, *adj.* British.

broche, *s. f.* brooch; knitting-needle; spindle spit.

brochure, *s. f.* pamphlet.

broder, *v. a.* embroider.

broderie, *s. f.* embroidery, braid.

bronchite, *s. f.* bronchitis.

bronze, *s. m.* bronze.

brosse, *s. f.* brush; ~ *à barbe* shaving-brush; ~ *à dents* tooth-brush; ~ *à cheveux* hairbrush; *donner un coup de* ~ *a* brush up.

brosser, *v. a.* brush; se ~ brush oneself.

brouillard, *s. m.* mist, fog.

brouille, *s. f.* quarrel.

brouiller, *v. a.* mingle, mix; confuse, embroil; shuffle (cards).

broyer, *v. a.* crush, pound.

bruire, *v. n.* rustle.

bruit, *s. m.* noise, din; fuss; rumour.

brûlant, *adj.* burning, hot, scorching; fiery.

brûler, *v. a. & n.* burn, schorch, roast; ~ *de* long for.

brume, *s. f.* mist, fog.

brumeux,-euse *adj.* foggy.

brun, *adj.* brown.

brusque, *adj.* sudden, curt, gruff.

brutal, *adj.* brutal, rude savage.

brute, *s. f.* brute.

bruyant, *adj.* noisy, loud.

budget, *s. m.* budget.

buffet, *s. m.* sideboard; buffet; refreshment room.

buisson, *s. m.* bush, shrub.

bulbe, *s. m.* bulb.

bulle, *s. f.* bubble; bull.

bulletin, *s.m.* bulletin.

bureau, *s. m.* (writing-) desk; bureau, office; department; board, committee; ~ *de location* box-office; ~ *de poste* post-office; ~ *de tabac* tobacconist's (shop); ~ *central* exchange.

burlesque, *adj.* burlesque, ridiculous; — *s.m.* burlesque.

but, *s. m.* butt, target; goal; aim, object, purpose; scope.

buter, *v.n.* stumble *(contre* against); se ~ grow obstinate.

butin, *s. m.* booty.

butte, *s. f.* hill, mound, knoll.

C

ça, *pron.* that; *comme* ~ in that way; — *adv.* here; — *int.* now then!

cabaret, *s. m.* tavern; wine-shop; night-club, music-hall.

cabine, *s. f.* cabin, berth; cage, car; ~ *téléphonique* call-box.

cabinet, *s. m.* small room; study; water-closet; office; business; cabinet (council); cabinet; ~ *de consultation* consulting room; surgery.

câble, *s. m.* rope, cable.

cabriolet, *s. m.* cabriolet,

cacao, *s. m.* cocoa.

cacher, *v.a.* hide, conceal; se ~ hide oneself.

cadeau, *s. m.* present, gift.

cadet, *adj. & s.m.* younger, junior; cadet.

café, *s. m.* coffee; café, coffee-house; ~ *au lait* white coffee; ~ *concert* music-hall.

cafetière, *s. f.* coffee-pot.

cage, *s.f.* cage; coop; case, crate.

cahier, *s. m.* exercise book.

caillou, *s.m.* pebble, stone.

caisse, *s.f.* box, case; cash(-box), till; cashier's office; drum; *en* ~ in hand.

caissier, **-ère,** *s.m.f.* cashier.

calcul, *s. m.* calculation, reckoning; arithmetic.

calculateur, *s. m.* calculator, computer.

calculer, *v.a. & n.* calculate, reckon, compute.

caleçon, *s. m.* pants *(pl.);* ~ *de bain* bathing-drawers *(pl.).*

calendrier, *s. m.* calendar.

calme, *adj.* quiet, calm; *fig.* cool; — *s. m.* calm.

calmer, *v. a.* quiet, calm.

calomnier, *v. a.* calumniate, slander.

calorie, *s. f.* calorie.

calorifère, *s. m.* heating apparatus.

calvaire, *s. m.* Calvary.

camarade, *s. m.* comrade, fellow; ~ *d'école* school-friend.

cambrioler, *v. a.* burgle, break into.

cambrioleur, *s.m.* burglar.

caméra, *s. f.* (cine-)camera.

camion, *s. m.* lorry.

camp, *s. m.* camp; side.

campagnard, *s. m.* countryman, peasant.

campagne, *s. f.* country-(side), fields *(pl.);* campaign, expedition.

camper, *v. n.* camp.

camping, *s. m.* camping;
(terrain de) ~ camping site; *matériel de* ~ camping equipment; *faire du* ~ camp.

canal, *s. m.* canal; channel.

canapé, *s. m.* sofa, couch.

canard, *s. m.* duck, drake.

candidature, *s. f.* candidature, candidacy.

canif, *s. m.* penknife.

canne, *s. f.* stick, cane; ~ *á pêche* fishing-rod.

canon, *s. m.* gun, cannon

canot, *s. m.* boat.

cantine, *s. f.* canteen.

canton, *s.m.* canton, district.

cantonade, *s.f.* wings *(pl.); à la* ~ behind the scenes.

caoutchouc, *s.m.* rubber; waterproof, mackintosh.

capable, *adj.* capable, able; efficient; fit.

capacité, *s. f.* capacity, (cap)ability.

capitaine, *s. m.* captain, leader.

capital, *adj.* capital, chief; —*s.m.* main point; capital, fund.

capitale, *s.f.* capital; capital letter.

capitalisme, *s. m.* capitalism.

capituler, *v. n.* capitulate.

caprice, *s. m.* caprice.

capricieux, *adj.* capricious, fickle.

capsule, *s. f.* capsule.

captif, -ive, *adj. & s. m. f.* captive.

captiver, *v. a.* captivate.

capturer, *v. a.* capture.

car, *conj.* for, because.

caractère, *s. m.* character, temper; nature; type, print, letter.

caractériser, *v.a.* characterize, distinguish.

caractéristique, *adj. &. s.f.* characteristic.

cardinal, *s.m.* cardinal; — *adj.* chief, cardinal; *points card naux* cardinal points.

caresser, *v.a.* caress, fondle; foster.

caricature, *s. f.* caricature.

carnaval, *s. m.* carnival.

carnet, *s. m.* note-book, pocket-book; book of tickets; ~ *de chèques* cheque-book.

carotte, *s. f.* carrot.

carreau, *s. m.* square; (paving-)tile; tile flooring; pane; diamond.

carrière, *s.f.* career; race-course; race; quarry.

carrosserie, *s.f.* body.

carte, *s.f.* card; map; ticket; bill (of fare); *partie de* ~s game of cards; ~ *postale* postcard; ~ *routière* roadmap; ~ *de visite* visiting-card; ~ *marine* chart; ~ *d'entrée* admission ticket; ~ *grise* driving licence; *à la* ~ à la carte.

carton, *s. m.* pasteboard, cardboard; (paper)box.

cas, *s.m.* case, event; instance, fact; *dans le* ~ *où, en* ~ *de* in case; *en tout* ~ in any case.

caserne, *s.f.* barracks *(pl.).*

casquette, *s. f.* cap.

casser, *v. a. & n.* break; crack, snap; annul; dismiss; *se* ~ break, get broken.

casserole, *s. v.* saucepan

casuel, -elle, *adj.* casual,

accidental.

catalogue, *s. m.* catalogue.

catastrophe, *s. f.* catastrophe, disaster.

catégorie, *s. f.* category, class.

cathédrale, *s. f.* cathedral.

catholicisme, *s. m.* catholicism.

catholique, *adj.* catholic.

cause, *s. f.* cause, reason, ground; case; *à ∼ de* on account of, owing to.

causer[1], *v. a.* cause.

causer[2], *v.n.* talk, converse, chat.

cavalerie, *s. f.* cavalry.

cavalier, *s. m.* horseman, cavalier.

cave, *s. f.* cave; cellar.

caverne, *s. f.* cave(rn).

ce[1], c', *pron.* this, it.

ce[2], cet; cette; *dem. adj. (pl.* ces) this *(pl.* these); that *(pl.* those).

ceci, *pron.* this.

céder, *v. a.* give up, yield, cede, make over; *v. n.* yield, give in, up.

ceinture, *s. f.* belt, girdle.

cela, *pron.* that, it; *c'est ∼* that's right.

célébration, *s. f.* celebration.

célèbre, *adj.* celebrated.

célébrer, *v. a.* celebrate.

célibataire, *adj.* unmarried, single.

cellule, *s. f.* cell.

celtique, *adj.* Celtic.

celui, celle, *dem. pron. (pl.* ceux, celles) he, she, they, those.

celui-ci, celui-là, celle-ci, celle-là, *dem. pron. (pl.* ceux-ci, -là, celles-ci, -là) this one, this person, the latter, these ones.

cément, *s. m* cement.

cendre, *s. f.* ash(es).

cendrier, *s. m.* ash-tray.

cent, *adj. & s. m.* hundred; *pour ∼* per cent.

centime, *s. m.* centime.

centimètre, *s. m.* centimetre.

central, *adj.* central.

centrale, *s. f.* *∼ électrique* power-plant, -station.

centre, *s. m.* centre.

cependant, *conj.* however, yet, still, nevertheless; in the meantime; *∼ que* while.

céramique, *s. f.* ceramics; — *adj.* ceramic.

cercle, *s. m.* circle, ring; party, club.

cercueil, *s. m.* coffin.

cérémonie, *s. f.* ceremony.

cerf, *s. m.* stag, hart,

cerise, *s. f.* cherry.

certain, *adj.* certain, sure.

certainement, *adv.* certainly, surely.

certificat, *s. m.* certificate, testimonial.

certifier, *v. a.* certify.

certitude, *s. f.* certainty.

cerveau, *s. m.* brain(s).

ces *see* ce[2]

cesse, *s. f.* ceasing, pause; *sans ∼* unceasingly.

cesser, *v. a. & n.* cease, stop; give up; *faire ∼* put an end to.

c'est-à-dire, *conj.* that is to say, viz., i.e.

cet *see* ce[2].

ceux *see* celui.

chacun, *pron.* each, each one, every one; everybody.

chagrin, *s. m.* grief, sorrow, vexation; — *adj.* sad, sorrowful; sorry; gloomy.

chaîne, *s. f.* chain; range (of mountains); *∼ de*

montage assembly line.
chair, *s. f.* flesh; pulp (of fruit).
chaire, *s. f.* chair; pulpit; seat, see.
chaise, *s. f.* chair.
châle, *s. m.* shawl.
chaleur, *s. f.* heat; fire.
chambre, *s.f.* room: bedroom; chamber; apartment; hall; ~ *à coucher* bedroom; ~ Haute Upper House; ~ *de commerce* chamber of commerce.
chameau, *s.m.* camel.
champ, *s.m.* field, country; *fig.* space, opportunity, theme.
champagne, *s. m.* champagne.
champignon, *s. m.* mushroom.
champion, -onne, *s.m. f.* champion.
championnat, *s. m.* championship.
chance, *s. f.* chance, fortune, risk; luck.
chancelier, *s. m.* chancellor.
chancellerie, *s.f.* chancery.
chandail, *s. m.* sweater, pullover.
chandelle, *s. f.* candle.
change, *s. m.* change, changing; succession; (foreign) exchange, barter; *agent de* ~ stockbroker; *bureau de* ~ exchange office; *lettre de* ~ bill of exchange.
changer, *v. a.* change, alter; exchange; se ~ betransformed; change one's clothes.
chanson, *s. f.* song.
chant, *s. m.* singing; song, tune; chant(ing).
chanter, *v. a. & n.* warble; chant; praise.

chanteur, -euse, *s.m.f.* singer
chantier, *s.m.* yard, timber-yard, work-yard.
chapeau. *s.m.* hat; bonnet; cap.
chapelain, *s. m.* chaplain.
chapelle, *s. f.* chapel.
chapitre, *s.m.* chapter; subject, head.
chaque, *adj.* each, every.
charbon, *s. m.* coal; embers *(pl.)*; ~ *de bois* charcoal.
charcuterie, *s. f.* pork-butchery.
charcutier, -ière, *s. m. f.* pork-butcher.
charge, *s. f.* load, burden; post, function, charge, office; attack; accusation.
charger, *v. a. & n.* load; burden; charge; entrust.
charité, *s. f.* charity.
charmant, *adj.* charming.
charme, *s. m.* charm.
charpente, *s.f.* timber-work.
charpentier, *s.m.* carpenter.
charrette, *s:f.* cart, wagon.
charrue, *s. f.* plough.
charte, *s. f.* charter.
chasse, *s. f.* chase, hunt(ing), shooting.
chasser, *v. a. & n.* chase, pursue, hunt, shoot, go shooting; drive out.
chasseur, *s.m.* hunter; page-boy.
chaste, *adj.* chaste, pure.
chat, *s. m.* (he-)cat.
châtaigne, *s. f.* chestnut.
château, *s.m.* castle; palace.
chatte, *s. f.* (she-)cat.
chaud, *adj. & adv.* hot, warm; ardent.
chauffage, *s. m.* heating,

warming; ~ *central* central heating.

chauffe-bain, *s. m.* geyser.

chauffer, *v. a. & n.* heat, warm; urge on; coach.

chauffeur, *s. m.* driver.

chausse, *s.f.* hose

chausser, *v. a. & n.* put on (shoes etc.), wear; **se ~** put on one's stockings etc.

chaussette, *s. f.* sock.

chaussure, *s. f.* footwear, shoes *(pl.).*

chauve, *adj.* bald.

chef, *s. f.* chief; ~ *de train* guard; ~ *d'orchestre* conductor.

chemin, *s. m.* road, way; lane; *se mettre en ~* start; ~ *de fer* railway.

cheminée, *s. f.* chimney, fireplace, funnel.

chemise, *s. f.* shirt.

chêne, *s. m.* oak(-tree).

chèque, *s. m.* cheque; ~ *en blanc* blank cheque; ~ *de voyage* traveller's cheque.

cher, chère, *adj.* dear.

chercher, *v. a.* seek, look for, search for.

chéri, -e, *adj.* dear; — *s. m. f.* darling.

cheval, *s. m.* horse; *à* ~ on horseback; *monter à* ~ ride.

chevalerie, *s. f.* chivalry.

chevalier, *s. m.* knight.

chevelure, *s. f.* hair.

cheveu, *s. m.* hair; *en* ~ bareheaded.

cheville, *s.f.* wooden pin, peg; ankle.

chèvre, *s.f.* (she-)goat.

chevreau, *s.m.* kid-(leather).

chez, *prep.* at, in, at the house of; ~ *X* at X's.

chic, *adj.* smart, spruce, fashionable; — *s. m.* chic; trick; elegance.

chien, -enne, *s. m. f.* dog.

chiffon, *s. m.* rag, scrap; chiffon.

chiffre, *s. m.* figure, digit; number.

chignon, *s.m.* knot (of hair), bun.

chimie, *s.f.* chemistry.

chimique, *adj.* chemical.

chimiste, *s. m. f.* chemist.

chinois, -e (Ch.), *adj &* *s.m.f.* Chinese.

chirurgie, *s. f.* surgery.

chirurgien, -enne, *s.m.f.* surgeon.

choc, *s.m.* shock, clash, collision.

chocolat, *s. m.* chocolate.

chœur, *s. m.* chorus; choir.

choisir, *v.a.* choose, pick out, select.

choix, *s. m.* choice.

chômage, *s. m.* stoppage, cessation of work; unemployment.

choquer, *v. a.* run into, strike against, collide with; shock, offend; **se ~** come into collision; be shocked.

chose, *s. f.* thing, object, matter; goods; event; *quelque* ~ something, anything.

chou, *s. m.* cabbage, cole.

chou-fleur, *s. m.* cauliflower.

chrétien, -enne, *adj. & s. m. f.* Christian.

christianisme, *s.m.* Christianity.

chronique, *adj.* chronic; — *s. f.* chronicle.

chuchoter, *v.n.&a.* whisper.

chute, *s. f.* fall, downfall, descent; slope.

ci, *adv.* here.

ci-dessous, *adv.* below, underneath.

ci-dessus, *adv.* above; aforesaid.

cidre, *s. m.* cider.
ciel, *s. m. (pl.* **cieux)**
heaven; sky; weather;
climate.
cierge, *s. m.* wax candle.
cigare, *s. m.* cigar.
cigarette, *s. f.* cigarette.
cigogne, *s. f.* stork.
cil, *s. m.* eyelash.
cime, *s. f.* top, summit.

ciment, *s. m.* cement.
cimetière, *s. m.* cemetery;
churchyard.
cinéma, *s. m.* cinema.
cinérama, *s. m.* cinerama.
cinq, *adj. & s. m.* five;
fifth.
cinquante, *adj. & s. m.*
fifty; fiftieth.
circonstance, *s.f.* circumstance; occurrence,
occasion, event.
circuit, *s. m.* circuit.
circulation, *s. f.* circulation; currency; traffic.
circuler, *v. n.* circulate;
circulez! move on!
cire, *s. f.* wax.
cirer, *v. a.* wax; polish.
ciseau, *s.m.* chisel.
ciseaux, *s. m. pl.* scissors.
citation, *s.f.* citation.
cité, *s. f.* city, town.
citer, *v.a.* cite; quote.
citoyen, **-enne,** *s.m.f.*
citizen.
citron, *s. m.* lemon.
citronnade, *s.f.* lemon
squash.
civil, *adj.* civil; — *s. m.*
civilian.
civilisation, *s. f.* civilization, culture.
clair, *adj.* light, clear.
clapet, *s. m.* valve.
claquement, *s. m.* clap-
(ping); snap.
claquer, *v. n. a.* crack,
clap; chatter; bang,
clarté, *s. f.* light, brightness; clearness.

classe, *s. f.* class; order,
rank; form, class-room.
classer, *v.a.* class, rank.
classifier, *v.a.* classify.
classique, *adj.* classic(al).

clause, *s. f.* clause.
clé, clef, *s. f.* key; spanner, wrench; *fig.* clue;
~ *de contact* ignition
key.
clerc, *s. m.* clerk; scholar.
clergé, *s. m.* clergy.
clérical, *adj.* clerical.
client, *s. m.* client, customer, patron.
clientèle, *s. f.* clients *(pl.).*
cligner, *v. a. & n.* wink.
clignotant, *s. m.* indicator.
clignoter, *v.a.&n.* blink,
wink.
climat, *s. m.* climate.
clinique, *adj. & s.f.*
clinic, clinical.
cloche, *s. f.* bell.
cloître, *s. m.* cloister.
clore*, *v. a.* shut, close.
clos, *adj.* closed.
clôture, *s. f.* enclosure,
fence; close.
clou, *s. m.* nail, stud;
boil, furuncle.
clouer, *v. a.* nail (down).
club, *s. m.* club.
cocher, *s. m.* coachman,
driver.
cochon, *s. m.* pig, swine.
code, *s. m.* code; law,
rule.
cœur, *s. m.* heart; *fig.*
mind, soul, courage;
par ~ by heart.
coffre, *s. m.* chest.
coffre-fort, *s. m.* safe.
cognac, *s. m.* cognac.
cogner, *v. n. & a.* beat,
knock, strike; *se* ~
knock against.
coiffer, *v. a.* put on (hat);
dress, do s.o.'s hair.
coiffeur, **-euse,** *s.m.f.*
hairdresser.

coiffure, *s. f.* head-dress, cap; hair-do; *salon de* ~ hairdresser.

coin, *s. m.* corner; angle.

coïncider, *v.n.* coincide.

coke, *s.m.* coke.

col, *s.m.* collar; neck.

colère, *s.f.* anger.

colis, *s.m.* parcel; item (of luggage).

collaborateur, -trice, *s. m. f.* fellow worker; collaborator.

collaborer, *v.n.* work jointly, collaborate.

collectif, -ive, *adj.* collective.

collection, *s. f.* collection.

collège, *s.m.* college; grammar school.

collègue, *s.m.f.* colleague, fellow worker.

coller, *v.a.* stick, paste.

collet, *s.m.* collar; neck.

collier, *s.m.* necklace; collar.

colline, *s.f.* hill.

collision, *s.f.* collision; *entrer en* ~ collide.

colombe, *s. f.* dove.

colonel, *s.m.* colonel.

colonie, *s. f.* colony; dominion.

colonne, *s.f.* column.

coloré, *adj.* coloured; colourful.

colossal, *adj.* colossal.

combat, *s.m.* fight, combat.

combattre, *v.a.&n.* fight (against), combat (with).

combien, *adv.* (~ *de*) how much, how many, how far; ~ *de temps?* how long?

combinaison, *s.f.* combination.

combiner, *v.a.* combine, unite; contrive, devise.

comédie, *s.f.* comedy.

comédien, *s.m.* comedian, actor.

comestible, *adj.* edible.

comique, *adj.* comic; — *s. m.* comic actor.

comité, *s. m.* committee.

commandant, *s. m.* commander.

commande, *s.f.* order.

commandement, *s. m.* command, order; commandment.

commander, *v. a.* command, order; control.

comme, *adv. & conj.* as, like; as...as; while; ~ *il faut* decent, proper; *tout* ~ just like; ~ *si* as if, as though.

commémorer, *v.a.* commemorate.

commençant, -e, *s. m. f.* beginner; — *adj.* beginning.

commencement, *s.m.* beginning.

commencer, *v. a. & n.* begin, commence.

comment, *adv.* how, in what manner; why; ~ *allez-vous?* how are you?; ~ *(dites-vous)?* (I beg your) pardon?

commentaire, *s. m.* comment; commentary.

commenter, *v. a.* comment (on); criticize.

commerçant, -e, *s. m. f.* merchant, dealer.

commerce, *s. m.* commerce, trade; *voyageur de* ~ commercial traveller; ~ *de gros* wholesale trade; *faire le* ~ trade.

commercer, *v. n.* trade, deal with, in.

commercial, *adj.* commercial.

commettre, *v. a.* commit; *se* ~ commit oneself.

commis, *s.m.* clerk, employee.

commissaire, *s.m.* commisary; commissioner.

commissariat, *s.m.* police-station.

commission, *s. f.* commission; charge; committee; errand.

commode, *adj.* convenient, handy, comfortable; — *s. f.* chest of drawers.

commun, *adj.* common; joint; usual; vulgar; *peu ~* unusual; — *s.m.* common people.

communauté, *s. f.* community.

commune, *s. f.* district.

communication, *s. f.* communication, message; call.

communier, *v. n.* communicate.

communion, *s.f.* communion.

communiqué, *s. m.* communiquè.

communiquer, *v. a. & n.* communicate.

compact, *adj.* compact.

compagnie, *s.f.* company.

compagnon, *s. m.* companion, fellow.

comparaison, *s.f.* comparison.

comparer, *v. a.* compare.

compartiment, *s. m.* compartment; *~ de fumeurs* smoking compartment; *~ pour non-fumeurs* non-smoker.

compas, *s.m.* compass-(es).

compatriote, *s. m. f.* compartiot, (fellow) countryman.

compensation, *s. f.* compensation.

compenser, *v.a.&n.* com-

pensate.

cŏmpétent, *adj.* competent.

compétiteur, -trice, *s. m. f.* competitor.

compétition, *s. f.* competition.

compilation, *s. f.* compilation.

compiler, *v. a.* compile.

complainte, *s.f.* complaint.

complaisance, *s. f.* complaisance, kindness.

complaisant, *adj.* complaisant, obliging, kind.

complément, *s. m.* complement; object.

complémentaire, *adj.* complementary.

complet, -ète, *adj.* complete, full.

compléter, *v.a.* complete.

complexe, *adj.* complex, compound.

complication, *s. f.* complication.

compliment, *s. m.* compliment; congratulation.

compliquer, *v.a.* complicate.

comploter, *v.a.* plot.

composant, -e, *adj. & s. f.* component.

composer, *v. a.* compose, *se ~ de* be composed of, consist of.

compositeur, -trice ,*s. m. f.* composer.

composition, *s. f.* composition; paper.

comprendre, *v. a.* comprehend; understand.

comprimé, -e, *adj.* pressed; — *s. m.* tablet.

compromettre, *v. a.* compromise, commit; *se ~* commit oneself.

compromis, *s. m.* compromise.

comptabilité, *s. f.* book-keeping, accounts *(pl.)*

compte, *s.m.* account; amount, sum; ~ *courant* current account; *faire le ~ de* count; *régler un* ~ settle an account; ~ *rendu* report, account, statement; review; *tenir ~ de* take into account.

compter, *v. a. & n.* count, reckon, calculate.

comptoir, *s. m.* counter.

computer, *v. a.* compute.

comte, *s. m.* count.

comtesse, *s. f.* countess.

concéder, *v. a.* grant.

concentration, *s. f.* concentration; reduction.

concentrer, *v. a.* condense, concentrate.

concept, -tion, *s. m. f.* concept(ion), idea.

concernant, *prep.* concerning.

concerner, *v. a.* concern, relate to.

concert, *s. m.* concert.

concevoir*, *v. a. & n.* conceive; think; imagine; apprehend.

concierge, *s. f. m.* porter.

concile, *s. m.* council.

concis, *adj.* concise.

conclure*, *v.a.&n.* conclude, end.

conclusion, *s.f.* conclusion, end.

concombre, *s. m.* cucumber.

concorder, *v.n.* agree.

concourir, *v. n.* contribute, concur; compte.

concours, *s. m.* concourse; help; assistance; competition.

concret, -ète, *adj.* concrete.

concurrence, *s. f.* competition: rivalry.

concurrent, *s. m.* competitor; rival.

condamnation, *s. f.* condemnation; sentence.

condamner, *v.a.* condemn, sentence.

condenser, *v. a.* condense.

condition, *s. f.* condition, state; service; stipulation, condition; *à* ~ *que* on condition that, provided that.

conditionnel, *adj.* conditional.

conditionnement, *s.m.* ~ *de l'air* air-conditioning.

conducteur, -trice, *s. m. f.* conductor; driver.

conduire*, *v. a. & n.* conduct, lead; drive; show (to), take (to); manage; *permis de* ~ driving licence.

conduit, *s. m.* pipe, tube.

conduite, *s. f.* conducting, leading; driving; behaviour, conduct.

cône, *s. m.* cone.

confection, *s. f.* ready-made clothes *(pl.).*

confédération, *s. f.* confederation, confederacy.

conférence, *s. f.* comparison; conference; lecture; *maître de* ~s lecturer; *faire une* ~ deliver a lecture.

conférencier, -ère, *s. m. f.* lecturer.

conférer, *v.a.* grant, confer, bestow; compare.

confesser, *v.a.* confess.

confession, *s. f.* confession.

confiance, *s. f.* confidence, trust, reliance; *avoir* ~ count on, trust.

confiant, *adj.* confident.

confidence, *s. f.* confidence.

confidentiel, -elle *adj.*

confidential.

confier, v.a. trust; entrust, give in charge.

confinement, s. m. imprisonment.

confiner, v. n. & a. confine.

confirmation, s.f. confirmation.

confirmer, v.a. confirm.

confiserie, s.f. confectionery, sweet-shop.

confiture, s.f. jam, preserve.

conflit, s. m. conflict.

confondre, v. a. confound.

conformer, v. a. conform, adapt; se ~ à conform oneself (to).

confort, s.m. comfort, ease.

confortable, adj. comfortable.

confrère, s.m. fellow-worker, colleague.

confronter, v. a. confront, compare.

confus, adj. confused.

confusion, s. f. confusion.

congé, s. m. leave, holiday; permission; discharge; warning, notice; donner ~ give notice (to); dismiss; prendre ~ de take leave of; être en ~ be on holiday.

congédier, v. a. dismiss.

congratulation, s. f. congratulation.

congrès, s.m. congress, assembly.

conjecture, s.f. conjecture.

conjecturer, v.a.&n. conjecture, guess.

conjonction, s.f. conjunction, union.

connaissance, s. f. knowledge; acquaintance; faire ~ avec get acquainted with.

connaître*, v.a. know, understand; be acquainted with.

connexion, s.f. connection.

conquérir*, v. a. & n. conquer; win (over).

conscience, s.f. consciousness; conscience; avoir la ~ de be conscious of, be aware of.

conscient, adj. conscious.

conscrit, s. m. conscript.

conseil, s. m. counsel, advice; adviser; council, board, staff.

conseiller[1], -ère, s. m. f. counsellor, councillor.

conseiller[2], v. a.&n. advise, counsel.

consentir, v. n. consent, agree (à to).

conséquence, s. f. consequence, result.

conséquent, adj. consistent; par ~ consequently.

conservatoire, s. m. conservatory.

conserver, v.a. keep, preserve; tin.

considérable, adj. considerable.

considération, s. f. consideration; esteem.

considérer, v. a. consider; esteem.

consigne, s. f. cloak-room, left-luggage office.

consigner, v.a. deposit.

consister, v.n. consist (of), be made (of).

consoler, v.a. console.

consommateur, -trice, s. m. f. consumer, customer.

consommer, v.a. consummate; consume.

consomption, s.f. consumption.

consonne, s. f. consonant.

conspiration, s.f. conspiracy.

conspirer, *v. a. & n.* conspire, plot.

constant, *adj.* constant, firm.

constipation, *s.f.* constipation.

constituer, *v. a.* constitute, compose.

constitution, *s. f.* constitution.

constitutionnel, -elle, *adj.* constitutional.

constructeur, *s. m.* builder.

construction, *s.f.* construction, building.

construire*, *v.a.* build, construct.

consul, *s. m.* consul.

consulat, *s. m.* consulate.

consulter, *v.a.* consult.

consumer, *v. a.* consume.

contact, *s.m.* contact, touch, switch.

contaminer, *v. a.* contaminate.

conte, *s.m.* story, tale.

contemplation, *s.f.* contemplation.

contempler, *v.a. & n.* contemplate.

contemporain, -e, *adj. & s. m. f.* contemporary.

contenance, *s. f.* capacity, contents *(pl.)*.

contenir, *v.a.* contain, hold; restrain; se ~ restrain oneself.

content, *adj.* content.

contentement, *s. m.* content, satisfaction.

contenter, *v.a.* content, satisfy; se ~ be contented, do with.

contenu, *s.m.* contents *(pl.)*.

conter, *v.a. & n.* tell, relate.

continent, *s. m.* continent.

continental, *adj.* continental:

continuation, *s.f.* continuation, continuance.

continuel, -elle, *adj.* continual.

continuer, *v.a. & n.* go on (with), keep on; se ~ be continued.

contour, *s.m.* contour, outline.

contracter, *v. a.* contract, bargain for.

contradiction, *s. f.* contradiction.

contraindre*, *v. a.* compel, force; se ~ restrain oneself.

contrainte, *s.f.* constraint.

contraire, *adj. & s. m.* contrary; au ~ on the contrary.

contrairement, *adv.* ~ à contrary to.

contraste, *s. m.* contrast.

contraster, *v. n.* contrast *(avec* with).

contrat, *s.m.* contract.

contre, *prep.* against.

contrée, *s.f.* country.

contrefaçon, *s. f.* counterfeit(ing); forgery.

contrefaire, *v. a.* counterfeit; pirate; forge.

contre-partie, *s. f.* counterpart.

contresigner, *v. a.* countersign.

contribuant, *s. m.* contributor.

contribuer, *v. n.* contribute *(à* to).

contribution, *s.f.* contribution, tax.

contrôle, *s.m.* control, check; hall-mark.

contrôler, *v.a.* control, check.

contrôleur, *s. m.* ticket-collector.

contusion, *s. f.* bruise.

convaincre*, *v.a.* convince.

convenable, *adj.* suitable, appropriate.

convenance, *s.f.* suitability, convenience.

convenir, *v.n.* suit, be convenient (to), fit.

conventionnel, -elle, *adj.* conventional.

conversation, *s.f.* conversation, talk.

converser, *v. n.* converse.

convertir, *v.a.* convert.

conviction, *s. f.* conviction.

convier, *v.a.* invite.

convive, *s.m.* guest.

convoi, *s.m.* convoy; funeral procession.

convoquer *v.a.* convoke.

coopération, *s. f.* co-operation.

coopérer, *v. n.* co-operate.

copie, *s. f.* (fair) copy.

copier, *v.a.* copy.

coq, *s. m.* cock.

coquille, *s. f.* shell.

coquin, *s.m.* rogue.

corail, *s.m.* coral.

corbeau, *s. m.* raven.

corbeille, *s. f.* basket.

corde, *s.f.* cord, rope.

cordial, *adj.* cordial.

cordonnier, *s.m.* shoemaker.

corne, *s. f.* horn; hooter.

corneille, *s. f.* crow, rook.

cornet, *s. m.* horn; cornet.

cornichon, *s. m.* gherkin.

corporation, *s. f.* corporation.

corps, *s. m.* body, corpse; corporation, corps.

correct, *adj.* correct.

correction, *s. f.* correction.

correspondance, *s. f.* correspondence; relation; communication; connection.

correspondant, *adj.* corresponding.

correspondre, *v. n.* correspond; communicate.

corriger, *v.a.* correct.

corrompre, *v.a.* corrupt, spoil; se ~ become corrupted.

corruption, *s. f.* corruption.

corset, *s. m.* stays *(pl.)*.

cortège, *s. m.* escort.

cosmétique, *adj.* cosmetic; — *s. m.* ~s cosmetics.

cosmonaute, *s. m.* cosmonaut, spacemen.

costume, *s. m.* dress, costume; ~ de bain(s) bathing-costume.

côte, *s. f.* rib; slope; shore.

côté, *s. m.* side, part; à ~ by the side; de ~ on one side; d'un ~ on the one hand; de l'autre ~ on the other hand; passer à ~ pass by; à ~ de next (door) to; beside.

côtelette, *s. f.* chop.

coton, *s. m.* cotton.

cottage, *s. m.* cottage.

cou, *s. m.* neck.

couche, *s. f.* bed; napkin, diaper; coat; layer; *(pl.)* confinement.

coucher, *v. a.* put to bed; lay; *v.n.* lie down; sleep; être couché lie; se ~ go to bed, lie down; — *s. m.* bedtime; setting.

couchette, *s.f.* berth, bunk; napkin.

coude, *s. m.* elbow; angle, bend.

coudre*, *v. a. & n.* sew.

couler, *v.n.* flow, run, stream; leak; sink.

couleur, *s. f.* colour.

coulisse, *s. f.* groove; slip, wings *(pl.)*; dans les ~s behind the scenes.

couloir, *s.m.* passage; corridor; lobby.

coup, *s. m.* blow, stroke, knock; smack; pull;

kick; shot; draught; cast, move; *d'un seul* ~ at once; ~ *de feu* rush hours *(pl.); de froid* chill; ~ *de main* sudden attack; ~ *d'œil* glance, look; ~ *de soleil* sunstroke.

coupe, *s.f.* wine-cup.

couper, *v.a.* cut; cut down, off, up; divide; cross; mix; se ~ cut oneself, cut one's (finger etc.).

couple, *s. f.* pair, brace; *m.* couple.

cour, *s. f.* (court)yard; court; courting, courtship; *faire la* ~ *à* court, make love to.

courage, *s. m.* courage.

courageux, -euse, *adj.* courageous, brave.

courant, *adj.* current; running; — *s.m.* current; stream; course run; ~ *d'air* draught.

courbe, *s. f.* curve, bend.

courbé, *adj.* curved; bent.

courber, *v. a. & n.* bend, bow; se ~ bend, be bent; bow.

courir*, *v. n.* run; hurry; flow; be curent.

couronne, *s.f.* crown.

couronner, *v.a.* crown.

courrier, *s. m.* messenger, courier, post, mail.

cours, *s. m.* course; current, flow; currency.

course, *s. f.* race, run; course; drive.

court, *adj.* short, brief; — *adv.* short; suddenly; — *s. m.* tennis-court.

courtiser, *v. a.* pay court to, court.

courtois, *adj.* courteous, polite.

courtoisie, *s. f.* courtesy.

cousin, -e *s. m. f.* cousin.

coussin, *s.m.* cushion.

coût, *s.m.* cost, price.

couteau, *s.m.* knife.

coûter, *v. n. & a.* cost.

coûteux, -euse, *adj.* costly, expensive, dear; *peu* ~ inexpensive.

coutume, *s.f.* custom, habit; *de* ~ customary.

couture, *s.f.* sewing, seam; needlework; scar.

couturière, *s.m.* dressmaker.

couvent, *s.m.* convent.

couver, *v.a.* brood (on), sit; hatch, breed.

couvercle, *s. m.* cover, lid, cap.

couvert, *adj.* covered; covert, sheltered; cloudy; secret; — *s.m.* set (of fork and spoon); cover; protection; *mettre le* ~ lay the table.

couverture, *s. f.* cover(ing); blanket; ~s bedclothes.

couvrir*, *v.a.* cover; load; protect; be sufficent for.

crabe, *s. m.* crab.

cracher, *v.n. & a.* spit.

craie, *s. f.* chalk.

craindre, *v.a.* fear, be afraid of.

crainte, *s. f.* fear; *de* ~ *de* for fear of; *de* ~ *que* lest.

crampe, *s.f.* cramp.

crampon, *s.m.* cramp.

crâne, *s. m.* skull; — *adj.* bold.

craquer, *v.n.* crack.

cravate, *s. f.* (neck)tie.

crayon, *s. m.* pencil; crayon.

créance, *s. f.* credence, belief, trust.

créancier, -ère, *s. m. f.* creditor.

création, *s. f.* creation.

créature, *s. f.* creature.

crèche, s. f. crèche.

crédit, s. m. credit; *à ~* on credit.

créditer, v.a. credit.

crediteur, s.m. creditor.

créer, v.a. create, make.

crème, s. f. cream, custard; *~ à raser* shaving cream.

crémerie, s.f. dairy.

crêpe, s. m. crape, crêpe.

creuser, v. a. dig; deepen.

creux, -euse, adj. hollow, empty; — s. m. hollow.

crevaison, s. f. puncture.

crever, v. a. & n. burst; puncture; die.

cri, s. m. cry, scream; call, shout.

crible, s.m. sieve, screen.

cric, s. m. jack.

crier, v.a. & n. cry (out).

crime, s. m. crime, guilt.

criminel, -elle, adj. & s. m. f. criminal.

crise, s. f. crisis.

crisper, v.a. contract, shrivel.

cristal, s. m. crystal.

critique, adj. critical; — s.f. criticism, critique; s.m.f. critic, reviewer.

crochet, s. m. hook; crochet(-work); hanger.

croire*, v. a. & n. believe, credit, trust; think.

croiser, v.a. cross; v.n. cruise.

croître*, v.n. grow, increase; grow up; v.a. increase.

croix, s. f. cross.

croquis, s.m. sketch.

crouler, v. n. fall (to pieces), fall in.

croûte, s. f. crust; *casser la ~* have a snack.

croyance, s.f. belief, faith; creed.

croyant, -e, s. m. f. believer; — adj. faithful.

cru, adj. raw; crude.

cruauté, s. f. cruelty.

crue, s. f. rise, growth.

cruel, -elle, adj. cruel.

crypte, s. f. crypte.

cube, s. m. cube.

cueillir*, v.a. gather, pick, glean.

cuiller, -ère, s. f. spoon; *~ à pot* ladle; *~ a café* teaspoon.

cuir, s. m. skin; leather.

cuire*, v. a. & n. cook; boil; roast; burn; *faire trop ~* overdo.

cuisine, s. f. kitchen; cooking, cookery; *batterie de ~* kitchen utensils; *de ~* culinary; *livre de ~* cookery-book.

cuisinière, s.f. cook; kitchen range, cooker.

cuisse, s. f. thigh; leg.

cuit, adj. cooked, baked.

cuivre, s. m. copper.

cul, s. m. bottom.

culinaire, adj. culinary.

culotte, s. f. panties; breeches *(pl.)*.

culte, s. m. cult, worship.

cultivateur, -trice, s. m. f. farmer.

cultiver, v.a. cultivate, till; *fig.* improve.

culture, s.f. culture.

culturel, -elle, adj. cultural.

cure, s. f. care; cure.

curé, s. m. priest; vicar.

cure-dent, s. m. toothpick.

curieux, -euse, adj. curious, strange, inquisitive.

curiosité, s. f. curiosity; *~s* sights.

cuve, s. f. tub, vat.

cuvette, s. f. *~ (de lavabo)* wash-basin.

cycle, s. m. cycle.

cygne, s. m. swan.

cylindre, *s. m.* cylinder.

D

dactylo(graphe), *s. m. f.* typist.

dame, *s.f.* lady; queen.

danger, *s. m.* danger.

dangereux, -euse, *adj.* dangerous.

danois, -e (D.), *adj. &* *s. m. f.* Dane, Danish.

dans, *prep.* in, into; inside; during; ~ *le temps* formerly.

danse, *s. f.* dance.

danser, *v. n.* dance.

danseur, *s. m.* dancer.

danseuse: *s. f.* ballet-girl, dancer.

date, *s. f.* date; *prendre* ~ fix a day.

dater, *v. a. & n.* date.

datte, *s. f.* date.

davantage, *adv.* more, further; *bien* ~ much more; *pas* ~ no more; *en* ~ some more.

de, *prep.* of, from, out of, on account of.

dé, *s. m.* thimble.

déballer, *v. a.* unpack.

débarquer, *v. a. & n.* land, disembark, arrive.

débarrasser, *v. a.* clear (up), rid, free; se ~ get rid (of).

débat, *s. m.* debate.

débattre, *v. a. & n.* debate.

débit, *s. m.* sale; debit; output; utterance; ~ *de tabac* tobbaconist's shop.

déborder, *v. n. & a.* overflow, run over.

débouché, *s. m.* outlet, issue.

déboucher, *v. a.* uncork, open; *v. n.* run into.

débourser, *v. a.* disburse.

debout, *adv.* upright, standing; *être* ~ stand.

début, *s.m.* start, outset; first appearance.

débuter, *v. n.* begin, start; make one's first appearance.

décadence, *s.f.* decadence.

décagramme, *s.m.* decagramme.

décéder, *v.n.* die, decease.

décembre, *s. m.* December.

déception, *s. f.* deception, deceit; disappointment.

décharge, *s. f.* discharge; outlet.

décharger, *v.a.* unload, unburden; release; discharge; se ~ unburden oneself.

déchausser, *v.a.* take off (shoes).

déchéance, *s.f.* decadence, decay; decline.

déchiffrer, *v.a.* decipher; make out.

déchirer, *v.a.* tear, rend.

dechoir*, *v.n.* fall off, decay.

décider, *v. a. & n.* decide, settle; se ~ make up one's mind; be settled.

décilitre, *s. m.* decilitre.

décimal, -e, *adj. & s. f.* decimal.

décimètre, *s.m.* decimetre.

décisif, -ive, *adj.* decisive, final.

décision, *s.f.* decision.

déclaration, *s.f.* declaration, statement.

déclarer, *v.a.* declare, state; se ~ declare itself.

décliner, *v.n.* decline.

décolletage, *s.m.* low neck.

décolleter, *v.a.* cut low

turn; *tour* a ~ turning lathe.

décomposer, *v. a.* decompose; spoil; se ~ decompose.

décomposition, *s. f.* decomposition.

décompte, *s. m.* discount; particulars *(pl.).*

décor, *s. m.* decoration; scene, environment; scenery.

décoratif, -ive, *adj.* decorative.

décorer, *v.a.* decorate; trim.

découper, *v.a.* cut out, carve.

décourager, *v.a.* discourage

découverte, *s. f.* discovery.

découvrir*, *v. a.* discover, find out; uncover; se ~ uncover oneself, disclose oneself.

décret, *s. m.* decree, order.

décrier, *v.a.* cry down.

décrire, *v.a.* describe.

décrocher, *v.a.* unhook, take down.

décroissance, *s. m.* decrease.

décroître, *v. n.* decrease.

déçu, *adj.* disappointed.

dédain, *s.m.* disdain, scorn.

dedans, *adv.* within, inside; indoors, at home.

dédicace, *s. f.* dedication.

dédier, *v.a.* dedicate.

déduire*, *v.a.* deduct.

défaire, *v. a.* undo; break; unfasten; take off; defeat; se ~ come undone.

défaite, *s. f.* defeat

défaut, *s. m.* defect, deficiency, want; fault; flaw; à ~ de for want

of; *sans* ~ faultless.

défavorable, *adj.* unfavourable.

défendre, *v.a.* defend; forbid; se ~ defend oneself.

défense, *s.f.* defence, protection; prohibition; tusk; *se mettre en* ~ stand on one's guard.

défiance, *s.f.* distrust, mistrust.

défier, *v. a.* defy.

défigurer, *v. a.* disfigure, deface, spoil.

défiler, *v. n.* defile.

défini, *adj.* definite.

définir, *v. a.* define.

définitif, -ive, *adj.* definitive, final.

définition, *s. f.* definition.

défunt, -e, *adj. & s. m. f.* deceased, defunct.

dégager, *v. a.* redeem, release, disengage; emit.

dégorger, *v.a.* disgorge, discharge; *v.n.* discharge, overflow.

dégoût, *s. m.* disgust.

dégoûtant, *adj.* disgusting.

dégoûter, *v.a.* disgust; se ~ get tired of.

dégradation, *s. f.* degradation.

dégrader, *v.a.* degrade; damage.

degré, *s. m.* degree.

déguisement, *s.m.* disguise.

déguiser, *v.a.* disguise, hide.

dehors, *adv.* out, outside, out of doors; *au* ~ outside, abroad; *en* ~ *de* outside of, apart from.

déjà, *adv.* already; previously.

déjeuner, *s. m.* lunch(eon); *petit* ~ breakfast; — *v.n.* have breakfast; take lunch.

delà, *prep.* beyond; *au ~ de* beyond.

délai, *s. m.* delay; *à bref ~* at short notice.

délégation, *s. f.* delegation.

déléguer, *v. a.* delegate.

délibération, *s. f.* deliberation, resolution; *en ~* under consideration.

délibérer, *v. n.* deliberate, ponder; *v.a.* bring under discussion.

délicat, *adj.* delicate; feeble; fastidious, dainty.

délicatesse, *s. f.* delicacy; delicateness; daintiness.

délice, *s. m.* delight.

délicieux, -euse, *adj.* delicious, delightful.

délier, *v. a.* untie; loosen.

délivrance, *s. f.* deliverance.

délivrer, *v.a.* deliver, (set) free.

déloyal, *adj.* disloyal, unfair.

demain, *adv.* tomorrow.

demande, *s.f.* request, application, inquiry, call, request, demand.

demander, *v.a.* ask, inquire (after); beg, demand; request, require; *se ~* wonder.

démanger, *v.n.* itch.

démarche, *s. f.* walk, gait; proceeding.

démasquer, *v. a.* unmask.

déménagement, *s. m.* removal, moving.

déménager, *v.n.&a.* move (house); remove.

démesuré, *adj.* immoderate, excessive.

demeure, *s.f.* delay; home, dwelling.

demeurer, *v.n.* live; stay.

demi, -e, *adj.* half; *à ~* by half; *une heure et ~e*

half past one; an hour and a half; — *s. f.* half-hour.

demi-cercle, *s. m.* semicircle.

demi-heure, *s. f.* half an hour.

demi-jour, *s. m.* twilight.

démobiliser, *v.a.* demobilize.

démocratie, *s. f.* democracy.

démocratique, *adj.* democratic.

démodé, *adj.* old-fashioned.

demoiselle, *s.f.* young lady, miss.

démolir, *v. a.* demolish, pull down.

démon, *s. m.* demon.

démonstratif, -ive, *adj.* demonstrative.

démonstration, *s.f.* demonstration.

démontrer, *v. a.* demonstrate.

dénaturé, *adj.* unnatural.

dénombrer, *v. a.* number.

dénomination, *s. f.* denomination.

dénoncer, *v. a.* denounce.

dénoter, *v. a.* denote; indicate.

dense, *adj.* dense, compact.

densité, *s. f.* density.

dent, *s. f.* tooth; *mal de ~s* toothache.

dental, *adj.* dental.

dentelle, *s. f.* lace.

dentier, *s. m.* set of (false) teeth, denture.

dentifrice, *s. m. pâte ~* tooth-paste.

dentiste, *s. m. f.* dentist.

dénué, *adj.* destitute.

dénuement, *s. m.* destitution.

départ, *s. m.* departure.

département, *s. m.* department; territory.

départir, *v. a.* grant, allot;
se ~ give up

dépasser, *v. a. & n.* pass,
exceed, go beyond.

dépêche, *s. f.* despatch,
wire, telegram.

dépêcher, *v. a.* dispatch;
v. n. & se ~ hurry.

dépendance, *s. f.* depen-
dance.

dépendant, -e, *adj.* dependent; — *s. m. f.* de-
pendant.

dépendre, *v. n.* depend.

dépense, *s. f.* expense;
larder.

dépenser, *v. a. & n.* spend;
waste.

dépit, *s. m.* spite; *en ~ de*
in spite of.

déplacement, *s. m.* displacement; shift.

déplacer, *v.a.* displace,
move, shift; se ~ move.

déplaire, *v.n.* displease.

déplier, *v.a.* unfold, lay
out.

déplorer, *v. a.* deplore.

déportation, *s. f.* transpor-
tation, deportation.

déposer, *v. a.* put down,
set down; deposit; —
se ~ settle.

dépôt, *s.m.* deposit;
store-room, warehouse;
lock-up.

dépourvu, *adj.* needy.

dépraver, *v. a.* deprave.

déprécier, *v. a.* depreciate.

dépression, *s. f.* depression.

déprimer, *v. a.* depress.

depuis, *prep.* since, from;
~ *longtemps* long since.

députation, *s. f.* deputa-
tion.

député, *s.m.* deputy;
member of the French
parliament.

dérangé, *adj.* deranged;
upset.

déranger, *v. a.* upset, put
out of order.

déraper, *v. n.* skid.

dérèglement, *s. m.* irregu-
larity; disorder.

dérivation, *s. f.* deriva-
tion.

dériver, *v.n.* drift; be
derived.

dernier, -ère, *adj. & s. m.
f.* latter, last, latest; *le*
~ the latter.

dernièrement, *adv.* lately.

dérober, *v. a.* rob, steal.
se ~ steal away.

déroger, *v.n.* derogate
(from).

dérouler, *v.a.* unroll,
unfold.

déroute, *s.f.* defeat.

derrière, *adv. & prep.*
behind, back; — *s. m.*
back (part); bottom.

dès, *prep.* from, as early
as, since; ~ *que* as
soon as.

désagréable, *adj.* disagreeable, unpleasant.

désarmer, *v.a.* disarm.

désastre, *s.m.* disaster.

désavantage, *s. m.* disadvantage.

descendance, *s.f.* descent.

descendant, *adj.* de-
scending; *en ~* down-
ward, downhill.

descendre, *v. n.* descend,
come down, go down;
alight; ~ *terre* land;
— *v.a.* take down.

descente, *s.f.* descent;
landing.

description, *s. f.* description.

désert¹, *s. m.* desert.

désert², *adj.* deserted,
desolate.

déserter, *v. n. & a.* leave,
desert.

désespérer, *v.n.* despair,

give up.

désespoir, *s. m.* despair.

déshabiller, *v. a.* undress; take off clothes.

déshonneur, *s.m.* dishonour, disgrace.

déshonorer, *v.a.* dishonour, disgrace.

désigner, *v. a.* designate; denote; appoint.

desinfecter, *v. a.* disinfect.

désir, *s. m.* desire.

désirable: *adj.* desirable.

désirer, *v. a. & n.* desire, long for.

désireux, -euse, *adj.* desirous, anxious.

désobéir, *v.n.* disobey.

désobéissance, *s.f.* disobedience.

désobéissant, *adj.* disobedient.

désœuvré, *adj.* idle, unoccupied.

désolation, *s. f.* devastation; desolation.

désoler, *v.a.* desolate; afflict, distress; se ~ grieve, be sorry.

désordre, *s.m.* disorder.

dessert, *s. m.* dessert.

dessin, *s.m.* drawing, sketch; design; ~ *animé* cartoon.

dessiner, *v.a.* draw; sketch; design.

dessous, *adv. & prep.* under, underneath, below, beneath; — *s. m.* under-part; undies *pl.*

dessus, *adv. & prep.* on, upon, over, above, on top; — *s. m.* upper part, top.

destin, *s. m.* destiny, fate.

destinataire, *s. m. f.* receiver, addressee.

destination, *s. f.* destination.

destinée, *s.f.* destiny.

destiner, *v.a.* destine;

mean (for); se ~ be destined (á for).

détachement, *s. m.* disengagement; detachment.

détacher, *v.a.* loose(n), unfasten; detach; se ~ get loose, come undone.

détail, *s.m.* detail, particular; retail; *en* ~ in detail.

détention, *s. f.* detention.

détermination, *s.f.* determination.

déterminé, *adj.* definite, determinate; resolute; limited.

déterminer, *v.a.* determine, fix; limit; settle.

détestable, *adj.* hateful.

détester, *v.a.* detest.

détonation, *s.f.* detonation.

détour, *s.m.* turning, winding, turn; roundabout way; evasion.

détourner, *v.a.* turn aside; lead astray.

détroit, *s. m.* strait, pass.

détruire*, *v.a.* destroy, ruin; do away with.

dette, *s. f.* debt.

deuil, *s.m.* mourning.

deux, *adj. & s. m.* two; both.

deuxième, *adj.* second.

devancer, *v. a.* precede; anticipate.

devant, *prep. adv.* before; in front of; opposite to; ~ *que* before; *au-*~ *de* ~ in front of; — *s. m.* front; foreground.

dévaster, *v. a.* devastate, destroy.

développement, *s. m.* development, growth.

développer, *v.a. (also se ~)* develop.

devenir, *v.n.* become, get, turn, grow.

dévier, *v. a. & n.* deviate, turn away.

devise, *s. f.* device.

dévoiler, *v. a.* unveil, reveal.

devoir*, *v.a.* owe, be in debt for; have to, must, be bound to, ought to; — *s. m.* duty; task; work., prep.

dévorer, *v. a.* devour, eat up.

dévouement, *s. m.* devotion.

dévouer, *v. a.* devote, dedicate; se ~ devote oneself.

diable, *s. m.* devil; trolley, truck.

diacre, *s. m.* deacon.

diadème, *s. m.* diadem.

diagnostic, *s. m.* diagnosis.

dialecte, *s. m.* dialect.

dialogue, *s. m.* dialogue.

diamant, *s. m.* diamond.

diapositive, *s. f.* transparency, slide.

diarrhée, *s. f.* diarrhoea.

dictée, *s. f.* dictation.

dicter, *v. a.* dictate.

dictionnaire, *s. m.* dictionary.

diesel, *s. m.* diesel engine.

dieu, *s. m. (pl. -x)* God.

différence, *s. f.* difference.

différent, *adj.* different.

différer, *v.a.* defer, put off; *v.n.* differ, be different, vary.

difficile, *adj.* difficult, hard.

difficulté, *s. f.* difficulty, trouble.

diffusion, *s. f.* diffusion.

digne, *adj.* worthy; ~ *de* ... worthy of ...

dignité, *s.f.* dignity.

diligence, *s.f.* diligence.

diligent, *adj.* diligent.

dimanche, *s. m.* Sunday.

dimension, *s.f.* dimension.

diminuer, *v.a. & n.* diminish, lessen, reduce.

dindon, *s.m.* turkey.

dîner, *s. m.* dinner; — *v. n.* dine.

diplomate, *s. m.* diplomat.

diplomatie, *s. f.* diplomacy.

diplomatique, *adj.* diplomatic.

diplôme, *s.m.* diploma.

dire*, *v.a.* say, tell; speak; ~ *à qn de faire qch.* tell s.o. to do sth.; *c'est à* ~ that is to say; *pour ainsi* ~ as it were; *vouloir* ~ mean; *dites donc!* look here!

direct, *adj.* direct.

directeur, *s.m.* director, manager; head master.

direction, *s.f.* direction; management; guidance; streering-gear.

directrice, *s. f.* directress; head mistress.

diriger, *v.a.* direct; lead, guide; manage; turn; steer.

disciple, *s.m.* disciple, follower.

discipline, *s. f.* discipline.

discorde, *s.f.* discord.

discours, *s.m.* discourse, speech.

discrédit, *s.m.* discredit.

discréditer, *v. a.* discredit.

discret, -ète *adj.* discreet; discrete.

discrètement, *adv.* discreetly.

discrétion, *s.f.* discretion.

discussion, *s. f.* discussion.

discuter, *v.a.* discuss, debate.

disparaître, *v.n.* disappear.

dispenser, *v. a.* dispense; se ~ *de* dispense with.

disposer, *v. a. & n.* dispose, lay out; se ~ prepare (to), be about (to); *bien disposé* willing.

disposition, *s. f.* disposition, arrangement; *la ~ de qn.* at s.o.'s disposal.

dispute, *s. f.* dispute.

disputer, *v. a. & n.* dispute, contest, argue; se ~ quarrel, dispute.

disqualifier, *v.a.* disqualify.

disque, *s. m.* disc, record; discus; *~ microsillon* or *longue durée* long playing record.

dissimulation, *s. f.* dissimulation, dissembling.

dissimuler, *v.a. & n.* dissemble, conceal; se ~ conceal oneself.

dissolution, *s. f.* dissolution; undoing, breaking up.

dissoudre*, *v. a.* dissolve, disperse.

distance, *s. f.* distance; *à quelle ~ est-ce?* how far is it?

distant, *adj.* distant, far.

distiller, *v.a. & n.* distil.

distinct, *adj.* distinct, clear.

distinction, *s.f.* distinction.

distinguer, *v.a.* distinguish, discriminate; make out, tell.

distraction, *s. f.* abstraction; recreation; entertainment; distraction.

distraire, *v.a.* subtract; divert, distract; amuse, entertain.

distrait, *adj.* inattentive, absent-minded.

distribuer, *v. a.* distribute; deal out.

district, *s.m.* district.

divan, *s.m.* sofa, divan.

divergence, *s.f.* divergence; difference.

divers, *adj.* diverse, different, miscellaneous.

diversion, *s. f.* diversion.

divertir, *v. a.* divert, entertain; se ~ enjoy oneself.

divertissement, *s. m.* diversion; entertainment.

divin, *adj.* divine.

diviser, *v.a.* divide, separate.

division, *s.f.* division, department.

divorce, *s. m.* divorce.

divorcer, *v n. & n.* divorce, be divorced.

dix, *adj. s. m.* ten.

dix-huit, *adj. & s.m.* eighteen.

dixième, *adj. & s.f.* tenth.

dix-neuf, *adj. & s.m.* nineteen.

dix-sept, *adj. & s.m.* seventeen.

dizaine, *s. f.* ten.

docteur, *s. m.* doctor.

document, *s.m.* document.

documentaire, *s. m.* documentary (film).

dogme, *s. m.* dogma.

doigt, *s.m.* finger; toe.

dollar, *s.m.* dollar.

domaine, *s.m.* domain; landed property.

dôme, *s. m.* dome.

domestique, *adj. & s. m. f.* domestic, servant.

domicile, *s. m.* domicile, dwelling.

domination, *s. f.* domination, rule.

dominer, *v. a. & n.* dominate, rule.

dommage, *s. m.* damage; pity.

dompter, *v. a.* subdue, master, tame.

don, *s. m.* present, gift.
donateur, *s.m.* giver.
donc, *conj.* therefore, then, so; of course.
donne, *s. f.* deal.
donner, *v. a.* give, grant, present with, afford, hand over; ~ *congé* give notice to; se ~ *pour* claim to be.
dont, *pron.* whose, of whom; of which.
dormir*, *v.n.* sleep.

dortoir, *s. m.* dormitory.
dos, *s. m.* back.
dose, *s. f.* dose.
dossier, *s. m.* back-piece; record, file.
dot, *s. f.* dowry.
doter, *v. a.* endow.
douane, *s.f.* customs; custom-house; duty; *déclaration de* ~ customs declaration; *droits de* ~ customs duties; *la visite de la* ~ customs formalities.
douanier, *s.m.* custom-house officer.
double, *s.m.* double; *en* ~ duplicate; — *adj.* double, dual.
doubler, *v. a.* double (up); line; dub.
doublure, *s.f.* lining; understudy.
douce *see* doux.
douceur, *s. f.* sweetness; gentleness.
douche, *s. f.* shower-bath.
douer, *v. a.* endow, gift.
douleur, *s. f.* pain, ache.
douloureux, -euse, *adj.* painful.
doute, *s. m.* doubt; *sans* ~ no doubt, undoubtedly.
douter, *v. n.* doubt; se ~ suspect.
douteux, -euse, *adj.*

doubtful, dubious.
doux, douce, *adj.* sweet; mild, soft.
douzaine, *s.f.* dozen.
douze, *adj. & s. m.* twelve; twelfth.
douzième, *adj.* twelfth.
dramatique, *adj.* dramatic; *l'art* ~ drama.
drame, *s.m.* drama.
drap, *s.m.* cloth, sheet.
drapeau, *s.m.* flag.
dresser, *v. a.* set up, erect; prepare; se ~ stand up, get up.
drogue, *s. f.* drug.
droguerie, *s. f.* drugs *pl.*
droit, *s. m.* right; law; duty, due; *avoir* ~ *à* be entitled to; ~ *de cité* citizenship; ~ *d'auteur,* copyright; *exempt de* ~s duty-free; ~(s) *de sortie,* export duty; — *adj.* right, direct, straight.
droite, *s. f.* right hand.
drôle, *adj.* droll, funny, strange; — *s. m.* rogue.
du, *art.* of the, some, any.
dû, *adj. & s. m.* due.
duc, *s. m.* duke.
duchesse, *s.f.* duchess.
duel, *s. m.* duel.
duplicata, *s. m.* duplicate, copy.
dur, *adj.* hard, tough.
durable, *adj.* lasting.
durant, *prep.* during, for.
durcir, *v. a. & n.* harden.
durée, *s.f.* duration, term.
durer, *v.n. & a.* last, endure, hold out.
dureté, *s. f.* hardness.
dynastie, *s.f.* dynasty.

E

eau, *s. f. (pl. -x)* water;

~ *de mer* salt water;
~ *de Seltz* soda-water.

ébaucher, *v.a.* sketch; outline.

ébouriffer, *v.a.* ruffle.

ébullition, *s.f.* boiling.

écaille, *s.f.* scale.

écailler, *v.a.* scale.

écart, *s.m.* deviation; *à l'*~ aside, apart.

écarter, *v.a.* set aside; dispel, take away; s'~ turn aside.

ecclésiastique, *adj. & s.m.* ecclesiastic.

échafaud, *s.m.* scaffold-(ing).

échange, *s. m.* exchange.

échanger, *v. a.* exchange.

échapper, *v. n.* escape, get away.

échauder, *v.a.* scald.

échauffer, *v. a.* heat; s'~ get hot.

échéance, *s. f.* expiration.

échéant, *adj.* due.

échec, *s. m.* check.

échecs, *s. m. pl.* chess.

échelle, *s.f.* ladder; scale.

échine, *s.f.* backbone.

écho, *s.m.* echo.

échoir*, *v.n.* expire, fall due; happen.

éclabousser, *v. a.* splash, spatter with mud.

éclair, *s.m.* lightning; flash.

éclairage, *s. m.* lighting; ~ *au néon* strip-lighting.

éclaircir, *v. a.* make clear, clear up; clarify; throw light on; s'~ become clear, clear up.

éclairer, *v. a.* light, illuminate; enlighten.

éclaireur, *s. m.* boy scout.

éclat, *s.m.* splinter; burst; brightness.

éclatant, *adj.* bright.

éclater, *v. n.* split; burst; break out; flash.

éclipser, *v. a.* eclipse; s'~ be eclipsed; take French leave.

école, *s.f.* school; *maître d'*~ schoolmaster; ~ *normale* teachers' training college; ~ *secondaire* grammar-school.

écolier, *s. m.* schoolboy.

écolière, *s. f.* schoolgirl.

économe, *adj.* economical; — *s. m.* bursar.

économie, *s. f.* economy; thrift; ~ *politique* political economy; ~s savings; *faire des* ~s save up.

économique, *adj.* economic; economical.

économiser, *v. a. & n.* economize, save, spare.

écorce, *s. f.* bark; rind.

écossais, *adj.* Scottish, Scotch.

Écossais, *s. m.* Scotsman.

écouler, *v.a.* sell.

écouter, *v.a.* listen to; hear.

écouteur, *s.m.* headphone; receiver.

écran, *s.m.* screen; *le petit* ~ television.

écrier: s'~ cry out.

écrire*, *v. a.* write (down); *machine à* ~ typewriter.

écrit, *adj.* written; — *s. m.* writing; *par* ~ in writing.

écriture, *s.f.* writing, handwriting; style.

écrivain, *s.m.* writer, author.

écuelle, *s. f.* bowl, basin, dish.

écume, *s.f.* foam.

écureuil, *s.m.* squirrel.

écurie, *s.f.* stable.

édifice, *s.m.* building.

édifier, v.a. build, erect;
  edify.
édit, s.m. edict, decree.
éditer, v. a. publish; edit.
éditeur, s. m. publisher.
édition, s. f. publication;
  edition.
éducation, s. f. education;
  training.
effacer, v. a. efface, rub
  out; wipe out.
effectif, -ive adj. actual,
  real.
effectuer, v.a. effect,
  carry out.
effet, s. m. effect, result;
  impression; bill (of exchange); (pl.) clothes,
  belongings.
efficacité, s. f. efficacy.
effondrer: s'~ fall in,
  collapse.
effort, s. m. effort, exertion, endeavour.
effrayant, adj. frightful.
effrayé, adj. afraid.
cffrayer, v.a. frighten;
  s'~ be frightened.
effroi, s.m. fright.
effroyable, adj. frightful.
effusion, s.f. effusion,
  gush.
égal, adj. equal, like,
  alike; (all the) same;
  even.
également, adv. equally.
égaler, v.a. equal.
égalité, s.f. equality.
égard, s. m. regard; à cet
  ~ on that account;
  à l'~ de with regard to;
  en ~ à considering.
égarer, v. a. mislead, mis-
  guide; s'~ lose one's
  way.
égayer, v. a. cheer (up);
  s'~ cheer up.
église (É), s. f. church.
égoïste, adj. egoistic, selfish.
egyptien, -enne (E.), adj.
  & s.m.f. Egyptian.

eh, int. ah!;~ bien! well!
élaborer, v. a. work out,
  think out, elaborate.
élan, s.m. dash; run;
  élan, zest.
élancé, adj. slim.
élancer, v. n. shoot; s'~
  bound, dash, rush; soar.
élargir, v. a. make wider,
  enlarge; set at liberty.
élastique, adj. & s. m.
  elastic.
électeur, -trice, s. m. f.
  voter.
élection, s.f. election.
électricien, -enne, s. m. f.
  electrician.
électricité, s.f. electricity; usine d'~ power-
  plant, -station.
électrique, adj. elec-
  tric(al).
électron, s.m. electron.
électronique, adj. elec-
  tronic.
élégance, s.f. elegance.
élégant, adj. elegant.
élément, s. m. element.
élémentaire, adj. ele-
  mentary.
éléphant, s. m. elephant.
élévation, s.f. eleva-
  tion.
élève, s.m.f. pupil.
élevé, adj. educated.
élever, v. a. raise, lift
  up; increase; bring up,
  educate; rear; s'~ rise;
  exalt oneself.
éliminer, v. a. eliminate.
élire, v. a. choose; elect.
elle, pron. (pl. elles) she,
  it, her; they.
elle-même, pron. herself.
éloigné, adj. far, distant.
éloigner, v.a. remove;
  take away; set aside.
émail, s. m. enamel.
émaner, v.n. emanate.
emballer, v.a. pack up;
  pack off.
embarquement, s. m. em-

barking; shipment.

embarquer, *v.a.* ship, embark; *v.n.* go on board.

embarrasser, *v. a.* embarrass.

embellir, *v. a.* embellish.

embêter, *v.a.* bore; annoy.

emblème, *s. m.* emblem.

embouchure, *s. f.* mouthpiece; mouth (of river).

embranchement, *s.m.* branchline; junction.

embrasser, *v. a.* embrace; kiss; s'~ kiss.

embrayage, *s. m.* clutch, coupling.

embrouillement, *s.m.* tangle; muddle.

embrouiller, *v. a.* embroil, entangle; muddle; s'~ become confused.

émetteur, *s. m.* transmitter.

émettre *v. a.* emit; transmit, broadcast.

émigration, *s. f.* emigration.

émigré, -e, *s.m.f.* emigrant.

émigrer, *v.n.* emigrate.

éminent, *adj.* eminent.

emmener, *v.a.* take away.

émotion, *s.f.* emotion; feeling.

émouvoir, *v.a.* move, touch; s'~ be moved.

emparer: s'~ *de* get hold of, seize.

empêchement, *s. m.* hindrance.

empêcher, *v.a.* keep from; prevent; hinder.

empire, *s.m.* empire.

emplette, *s. f.* purchase.

emplir, *v.a.* fill (up).

emploi, *s.m.* employment, job; use.

employé, -e, *s.m.f.* employee; clerk; attendant.

employer, *v.a.* employ; use.

empoigner, *v.a.* grasp, grip; lay hands on.

empoisonner, *v. a.* poison.

emporter, *v.a.* carry, take away, carry off, remove; s'~ get angry, lose one's temper.

empreinte, *s. f.* stamp, print, impression.

empresser: s'~ hurry, hasten.

emprisonnement, *s.m.* imprisonment.

emprisonner, *v.a.* imprison.

emprunter, *v. a.* borrow.

en, *prep.* in; to; into; at; like, as; by, through;

— *pron.* of him, of her, of it, of them, their; any, some.

encan, *s.m.* auction.

enceinte, *adj.* pregnant.

enchaîner, *v.a.* chain; link up; detain.

enchantement, *s. m.* spell; delight.

enchanter, *v.a.* charm, delight.

enclore, *v.a.* enclose.

enclose, *s. m.* enclosure; close.

enclume, *s.f.* anvil.

encombrement, *s. m.* stoppage; (traffic) jam.

encombrer, *v. a.* block up, jam.

encore, *adv.* yet, still; again; *pas* ~ not yet; ~ *une fois* once again; ~ *que* although; ~ *du* some more; ~ *quelque chose, Madame?* anything else, madam?

encouragement, *s. m.* encouragement.

encourager, *v. a.* encourage; cheer.

encre, *s.f.* ink.

encyclopédie, s. f. ency-
clopaedia.

endommager, v.a. dam-
age; injure.

endormir, v.a. put to
sleep; s'~ go to sleep,
fall asleep.

endosser, v.a. endorse.

énergie, s. f. energy; ~ a-
tomique atomic energy.

énergique, adj. energe-
tic.

enfance, s.f. infancy,
childhood.

enfant, s. m. f. infant,
child; chambre d'~s
nursery; d'~s juvenile.

enfermer, v.a. shut in,
up, lock up.

enfin, adv. at last; fi-
nally; in short.

enflammer, v. a. set on
fire; s'~ take fire.

enfler, v. a. swell (up);
s'~ swell.

enflure, s. f. swelling.

engagement, s. m. obli-
gation; commitment;
engagement.

engager, v. a. & n. pledge;
pawn; engage, sign on.

engloutir, v. a. swallow
up, devour.

engraisser, v.a. fatten;
v.n. grow fat.

enlèvement, s.m. removal.

enlever, v.a. remove,
clear away, take away.

ennemi, s.m. enemy.

ennui, s. m. bore(dom);
vexation; nuisance.

ennuyer, v. a. bore, wea-
ry; s'~ be bored.

ennuyeux, -euse, adj.
boring, tedious.

énoncer, v.a. state.

énorme, adj. enormous.

enquérir: s'~ de inquire
about.

enrager, v. n. be enraged.

enregistrer, v. a. register,
enter, record.

enrhumer, v.a. être
enrhumé have a cold;
s'~ catch a cold.

enrôler, v. a. enrol, draft.

enroué, adj. hoarse.

enrouler, v. a. roll (up).

enseignement, s. m. in-
struction, tuition.

enseigner, v.a. & n.
teach, instruct (in).

ensemble, adv. together;
— s. m. whole, mass;
unity; two-piece suit;
set of furniture, suite.

ensuite, adv. then; next.

ensuivre: s'~ follow, en-
sue.

entasser, v.a. heap up.

entendement, s. m. under-
standing.

entendre, v. a. & n. hear;
understand; ~ parler
de hear of; ne pas ~
miss; qu'entendez-vous
par là? what do you
mean by that?; bien
entendu of course;
c'est entendu! that's
settled!; agreed!

entente, s.f. meaning;
understanding; agree-
ment.

enterrement, s. m. burial.

enterrer, v.a. bury.

enthousiasme, s. m. en-
thusiasm.

enthousiaste, adj. enthusiastic; keen.

entier, -ère, adj. entire.

entièrement, adv. entirely,
wholly.

entorse, s.f. sprain;
donner une ~ à sprain
one's (foot, ankle).

entourage, s. m. circle of
friends; surroundings
(pl.); attendants (pl.).

entourer, v.a. surround;
encircle.

entracte, s. m. interval.

entrailles, s. f. pl. entrails.

entraîner, v.a. draw

along; carry away; involve, entail; coach.

entraîneur, *s. m.* trainer, coach.

entre, *prep,* between, among; into, in.

entrée, *s. f.* entry, entrance, beginning; free access; duty.

entremets, *s. m.* second course.

entreprendre, *v.a.* attempt, undertake, contract for; worry.

entrepreneur, *s.m.* contractor.

entreprise, *s. f.* undertaking, enterprise.

entrer, *v. n.* enter; come in, go in; get in; get into; faire ~ show in.

enveloppe, *s. f.* envelope; wrapper, cover.

envelopper, *v. a.* wrap up, do up; envelop.

envers, *prep.* towards, to.

enviable, *adj.* enviable.

envie, *s. f.* envy; desire.

envier, *v. a.* envy; desire.

environ, *adv.* & *prep.* about.

environner, *v.a.* surround.

environs, *s. m. pl.* surroundings.

envoi, *s. m.* sending; consignment, shipment.

envoler: s'~ fly away, take wing.

envoyer*, *v.a.* send, dispatch, forward.

envoyeur, *s.m.* sender.

épais, -aisse, *adj.* thick.

épaisseur, *s. f.* thickness.

épargne, *s.f.* savings *(pl.).*

épargner, *v. a.* save (up).

épaule, *s.f.* shoulder.

épée, *s.f.* sword.

éperon, *s.m.* spur.

épice, *s. f.* spice.

épicerie, *s.f.* grocery, grocer's (shop).

épicier, -ère, *s. m. f.* grocer.

épidémie, *s. f.* epidemic.

épinard, *s.m.* spinach.

épine, *s. f.* thorn; spine, backbone; obstacle.

épingle, *s. f.* pin; ~ *de sûreté* safety-pin.

épisode, *s.m.* episode.

éplucher, *v. a.* peel; pick; sift, preen, thin out.

éponge, *s.f.* sponge.

éponger, *v. a.* sponge; mop (up).

époque, *s. f.* period, age, epoch, time.

épouse, *s.f.* wife.

épouser, *v.a.* marry.

épouvante, *s.f.* fright.

époux, *s. m.* husband.

épreuve, *s. f.* test, trial; proof; print.

éprouver, *v. a.* test, prove; feel; experience.

épuisé, *adj.* exhausted; out of print.

épuiser, *v. a.* exhaust; use up; wear out.

équation, *s.f.* equation.

équilibre, *s.m.* balance, equilibrium.

équipage, *s. m.* suite, retinue; carriage; crew.

équipe, *s. f.* gang, shift; crew, team, side; train.

équipement, *s. m.* equipment.

équiper, *v.a.* equip.

équivalent, *adj.* equivalent.

ère, *s.f.* era.

errant, *adj.* wandering.

errer, *v. n.* stray; err.

erreur, *s. f.* error, mistake.

érudit, *adj.* learned.

érudition, *s.f.* learning.

escalateur, *s. m.* escalator.

escale, *s.f.* port; landing; *sans* ~ non-stop.

escalier, *s. m.* stairs *(pl.),* staircase; ~ *de sauve-*

tage fire-escape; ~ *de service* backstairs *(pl.)*; ~ *roulant* escalator.

escargot, *s.m.* snail.

escarpins, *s. m. pl.* pumps.

esclavage, *s.m.* slavery.

esclave, *s. m. f.* slave; — *adj.* slavish.

escrime, *s.f.* fencing; *faire de l'*~ fence.

escrimer, *v.n.* fence.

espace, *s. m.* space; room.

espagnol, -e (E.), *adj.* Spanish; — *s. m. f.* Spaniard; Spanish.

espèce, *s. f.* species, kind.

espérance, *s. f.* hope, expectation.

espérer, *v. a.* hope (for).

espion, -onne, *s.m.f.* spy.

espionnage, *s. m.* espionage, spying.

espoir, *s.m.* hope.

esprit, *s. m.* spirit; mind; character; wit; sense.

esquille, *s.f.* splinter.

esquiver, *v.a.* evade.

essai, *s.m.* trial, test; essay; attempt.

essayer, *v. a.* try, attempt; essay; assay.

essence, *s.f.* essence; petrol.

essentiel, -elle, *adj.* essential.

essieu, *s.m.* axle.

essor, *s.m.* flight.

essoreuse, *s. f.* spin-drier.

essuie-glace, *s. m.* windscreen wiper.

essuie-main(s), *s. m. (pl.)* towel; ~ *à rouleau* roller-towel.

essuyer, *v.a.* dust; wipe; dry; mop up.

est, *s.m.* east.

esthétique, *adj.* aesthetic.

estime, *s.f.* esteem.

estimer, *v.a. & n.* estimate, value; esteem, regard; consider.

estomac, *s.m.* stomach.

estrade, *s.f.* platform.

estuaire, *s.m.* estuary.

et, *conj.* and; ~ ...~ both ... and.

étable, *s.f.* cow-shed; ~ *à porcs* pigsty.

établi, *s.m.* (joiner's) bench.

établir, *v.a.* establish, found, settle, set up; build; prove; s'~ settle (down).

établissement, *s. m.* establishment.

étage, *s. m.* floor, stor(e)y.

étagère, *s. f.* shelf.

étaler, *v.a.* display; spread (out); show off; s'~ stretch oneself out.

étang, *s.m.* pond.

étape, *s.f.* stage.

état, *s.m.* state; condition; profession, station office; statement; *homme d'*~ statesman; *coup d'*~ revolt.

été, *s.m.* summer.

éteindre*, *v. a.* put out, extinguish; turn off; s'~ be extinguished.

étendre, *v. a.* spread out; stretch out; extend; s'~ lie down; stretch one-self out.

étendu, *adj.* wide, vast, extensive.

étendue, *s.f.* expanse, reach, range; extent.

éternel, -elle, *adj.* eternal.

éternuement, *s. m.* sneeze.

éternuer, *v.n.* sneeze.

étincelle, *s.f.* spark.

étiquette, *s.f.* ticket, label; etiquette.

étoffe, *s.f.* cloth, material.

étoile, *s.f.* star.

étonnant, *adj.* astonishing, amazing.

étonnement, *s. m.* astonishment, wonder.

étonner, *v.a.* astonish,

amaze; s'~ be astonished.

étouffer, *v.a.* choke.

étrange, *adj.* strange.

étranger, -ère, *adj.* foreign, strange; — *-s.m.f.* foreigner; *à l'~* abroad.

être*, *v.n.* be, exist; *il est...* it is...; ~ *bien* be good-looking; be well; *c'est que* the fact is; ~ *à* belong to; — *s.m.* being.

étreindre*, *v.a.* clasp; press; embrace.

étreinte, *s.f.* embrace.

étrier, *s. m.* stirrup.

étroit, *adj.* narrow, strait; close.

étude, *s. f.* study; chambers *(pl.).*

étudiant, -e, *s.m.f.* student, undergraduate.

étudier, *v. a.* study, read; practise.

étui, *s.m.* case, box.

étuver, *v.a.* stew, steam.

eucharistie, *s.f.* eucharist.

européen, -enne, *adj.* European.

eux, *pron. m.* they, them.

évader: s'~ escape; get away.

évaluer, *v. a.* value, estimate.

évangélique, *adj.* evangelical.

évangile, *s.m.* gospel.

évaporer, *v. a.* evaporate; s'~ evaporate.

éveil, *s. m. en ~* on the lookout.

éveiller, *v. a.* awaken; s'~ wake up.

événement, *s.m.* event.

éventail, *s.m.* fan.

éventuel, -elle, *adj.* eventual.

évêque, *s.m.* bishop.

évidemment, *adv.* evi-

dently, obviously.

évidence, *s.f.* evidence.

évident, *adj.* evident, obvious.

éviter, *v. a.* avoid, evade.

évoluer, *v.n.* evolve.

évolution, *s. f.* evolution.

exact, *adj.* exact, accurate.

exactement, *adv.* exactly.

exactitude, *s.f.* exactitude, precision.

exagérer, *v. a.* exaggerate.

examen, *s. m.* exam(ination); test.

examiner, *v. a.* examine; investigate, look into.

excédent, *s.m.* surplus; ~*s de bagages* excess luggage.

excéder, *v. a.* exceed, surpass; tire out.

excellence, *s. f.* excellence; excellency.

excellent, *adj.* excellent.

excepté, *adj.* excepted; — *prep.* except(ing), but.

excepter, *v.a.* except.

exception, *s. f.* exception.

exceptionnel, -elle, *adj.* exceptional.

excès, *s. m.* excess.

excessif, -ive, *adj.* excessive.

excitation, *s.f.* excitement.

exciter, *v.a.* excite, stir up; urge on.

exclamation, *s.f.* exclamation.

exclure*, *v.a.* exclude.

exclusif, -ive, *adj.* exclusive.

excursion, *s. f.* excursion.

excursionniste, *s.m.f.* holiday-maker, tourist.

excuse, *s. f.* excuse; apology; *faire des ~s* apologize.

excuser, *v.a.* excuse; pardon; apologize for; s'~ apologize; ask to be

excused; *excusez-moi*
I beg your pardon;
excuse me.

exécuter, *v.a.* execute,
carry out, perform.

exécutif, -ive, *adj.* executive.

exécution, *s. f.* execution.

exemplaire, *s.m.* copy.

exemple, *s. m.* example;
par ~ for example;
sans ~ unprecedented.

exempt, *adj.* exempt, free
(de from).

exemption, *s.f.* exemp-
tion.

exercer, *v.a.* exercise;
practise; carry on; s'~
practise.

exercice, *s.m.* exercise.

exhibition, *s.f.* exhibition; display.

exigence, *s.f.* demand;
exigency.

exil, *s.m.* exile.

existence, *s. f.* existence.

exister, *v. n.* exist.

expansif, -ive, *adj.* expan-
sive.

expansion, *s.f.* expansion.

expédient, *s.m.* expedi-
ent, device.

expédier, *v.a.* forward,
send off.

expéditeur, -trice, *s. m. f.*
sender, shipping-agent.

expédition, *s. f.* consignment; expedition, for-
warding, dispatch.

expérience, *s. f.* experience; experiment; *faire
des ~s* to experiment.

expérimental, *adj.* experimental.

expert, *adj.* expert.

expirer, *v.n.* expire; die.

explication, *s. f.* explanation.

expliquer, *v.n.* explain,
account for, show.

exploration, *s. f.* exploration.

explorer, *v.a.* explore.

explosion, *s. f.* explosion.

exportateur, *s.m.* exporter.

exportation, *s. f.* export,
exportation.

exporter, *v. a.* export.

exposé, *s.m.* statement.

exposer, *v.a.* expose,
show; state; set forth.

exposition, *s. f.* exhibition, display; state-
ment, exposure; exposi-
tion.

exprès, *adv.* on purpose.

express, *adj.* express; —
s.m. express (train).

expression, *s.f.* expression

exprimer, *v.a.* express.

expulser, *v.a.* expel.

expulsion, *s.f.* expulsion.

extension, *s. f.* extension;
extent.

exténuer, *v.a.* tire out,
exhaust.

extérieur, *s. m.* exterior;
outside; *à l'~* outwards
— *adj.* outward.

extinction, *s.f.* extinction; quenching.

extraire, *v. a.* extract;
draw, pull out.

extraordinaire, *adj.* extraordinary, unusual.

extravagant, *adj.* extravagant.

extrême, *adj.* extreme.

extrêmement, *adv.* ex-
tremely, very.

extrémité *s. f.* extremity;
last moment.

F

fabricant, *s.m.* manu-
facturer, maker.

fabrication, *s.f.* manu-
facture; fabrication.

fabrique, *s.f.* factory,
works.

fabriquer, *v.a.* manufacture, make.

façade, *s.f.* front.

face, *s.f.* face; look; *en ~ de* opposite, in front of.

facétieux, -euse, *adj.* facetious; humorous.

fâché, *adj.* offended.

fâcher, *v. a.* offend; make angry; se ~ get angry.

facile, *adj.* easy; fluent.

facilité, *s.f.* ease; facility; convenience.

faciliter, *v.a.* facilitate; make easy.

façon, *s. f.* making; fashion, shape; way, manner; *de ~ à* so as to; *de ~ que* so that; *en aucune ~* by no means; *d'une ~ quelconque* somehow.

facteur, *s.m.* factor; postman; porter, carrier; *fig.* circumstance.

faction, *s.f.* faction; sentry, watch.

facture, *s.f.* bill, invoice.

facultatif, -ive, *adj.* optional.

faculté, *s.f.* faculty.

fade, *adj.* flat, insipid.

faible, *adj.* weak; feeble.

faiblesse, *s. f.* weakness.

faiblir, *v. n.* become weak.

faillir, *v. n.* fail, fall short; err; ~ + *inf.* nearly; *j'ai failli manquer le train* I nearly missed the train.

faim, *s. f.* hunger; *avoir ~* be hungry.

faire*, *v.a.* make; do; build; cause; ~ *allusion* refer to; ~ *attention* (*à*) pay attention (to); ~ *une chambre* do a room; ~ *le commerce* trade; ~ *la cuisine* do the cooking; ~ *ses études* study; be at school; ~ *la guerre* make war; ~ *un lit* make a bed; ~ *mal à* hurt; ~ *part à* let know; ~ *des progrès* make progress; ~ *une promenade* take a walk; ~ *queue* queue; ~ *savoir* let know, inform (of); ~ *usage (de)* make use (of); ~ *voir* show; *que ~?* what's to be done?; *qu'est-ce que cela fait?* what does it matter?; *n'avoir rien à ~* have nothing to do; *deux et deux font quatre* two and two make four; ~ *70 km. à l'heure* do 70 km. an hour; *il fait du vent* it is windy; *il fait chaud* it is warm; *il fait jour* it is daylight; — *se ~* be made, be done; get used (to).

faisan, *s. m.* pheasant.

fait, *s. m.* fact; *en ~* in fact, after all, as a matter of fact.

falloir*, *v. impers.* be necessary, be required; must, have to, should, ought to; *comme il faut* proper, decent; *s'en ~* be wanting.

fameux, -euse, *adj.* famous.

familier, -ière, *adj.* familiar.

famille, *s. f.* family.

faner, *v.n.* fade.

fantaisie, *s.f.* fancy.

fantastique, *adj.* fantastic.

fardeau, *s.m.* burden.

farine, *s.f.* flour, meal.

fatal, *adj.* mortal, fatal.

fatigant, *adj.* fatiguing.

fatigue, *s.f.* fatigue.

fatigué, *adj.* tired, weary.

fatiguer, *v. a.* tire, weary,

fatigue.

faubourg, *s.m.* suburb.

faucher, *v.a.* mow, cut.

faucheuse, *s.f.* ~ *(a moteur)* (lawn-)mower.

faucille, *s. f.* sickle.

faucon, *s.m.* falcon.

faute, *s. f.* mistake, error, fault; lapse; want; *faire* ~ fail.

fauteuil, *s. m.* arm-chair, easy chair; stall, dress-circle seat.

fauve, *s.m.* wild beast.

faux¹, fausse, *adj.* false.

faux², *s. f.* scythe.

faveur, *s. f.* favour; *en* ~ *de* in favour of, on behalf of.

favorable, *adj.* favourable.

favori, -ite, *adj.* favorite.

fécond, *adj.* fertile.

féconder, *v.a.* fertilize.

fédéral, *adj.* federal.

fédération, *s.f.* federation.

fédéré, -e, *adj. & s. m. f.* federate.

feindre*, *v. a. & n.* feign.

félicitation, *s.f.* congratulation.

félicité, *s.f.* happiness.

féliciter, *v.a.* congratulate.

féminin, *adj.* feminine.

femme, *s.f.* woman; wife.

fendre, *v. a.* split; rend.

fenêtre, *s. f.* window.

fente, *s. f.* crack, split.

fer, *s. m.* iron; ~ *à cheval* horseshoe.

férié, *adj. jour* ~ holiday.

ferme¹, *adj.* firm; — *adv.* fast; firmly.

ferme², *s. f.* farm.

fermé, *adj.* closed.

fermer, *v. a.* close, shut; *se* ~ close, be shut.

fermeté, *s. f.* firmness.

fermeture, *s. f.* shutting;
shutter; ~ *éclair* zip fastener; zipper.

fermier, *s. m.* farmer.

féroce, *adj.* wild, cruel.

férocité, *s. f.* ferocity.

ferronnerie, *s.f.* ironworks.

fertile, *adj.* fertile.

fervent, *adj.* fervent.

ferveur, *s. f.* fervour.

fesse, *s.f.* buttock.

festin, *s.m.* feast.

fête, *s. f.* feast, holiday; birthday.

fêter, *v. a.* observe; celebrate.

fêteur, -euse, *s. m. f.* holiday-maker.

feu, *s. m.* fire, flame; light; *mettre le* ~ *à* set on fire; *prendre* ~ take fire; ~ *d'artifice* fireworks *(pl.);* ~*x de circulation* traffic lights; ~*x d'arrière* tail lights.

feuillage, *s.m.* foliage.

feuille, *s.f.* leaf; sheet.

février, *s.m.* February.

fiancé, -e, *s. m. f.* fiancè, -e.

fiancer, *v.a.* engage; *se* ~ be engaged.

fibre, *s. f.* fibre.

ficelle, *s. f.* string.

fiche, *s. f.* pin, peg; slip (of paper).

ficher, *v. a.* drive in, fix; do, work; deal (a blow).

fidèle, *adj.* faithful.

fidélité, *s. f.* fidelity.

fier: se ~ trust, count on.

fierté, *s. f.* pride.

fièvre, *s. f.* fever.

figue, *s. f.* fig.

figure, *s. f.* form, shape; face; figure.

figurer, *v.a.* figure, represent; *se* ~ imagine.

fil, *s.m.* thread, yarn; edge; clue; ~ *(de fer)* wire.

file, *s. f.* row, file, line.

filer, *v.a. & n.* spin.

filet, *s.m.* net; fillet; rack.

fille, *s. f.* daughter; girl; maid; *jeune ~* young lady.

fillette, *s.f.* little girl.

filleul, -e, *s. m. f.* godson, god-daughter.

film, *s. m.* film; *le grand ~* feature film; *~ avec* film featuring ...; *~ annonce* trailer.

fils, *s. m.* son.

fin[1], *s.f.* end; close; *à la ~* in the end, finally; *mettre ~ à* put an end to; *tirer à sa ~* come to an end; *~ de semaine* week-end.

fin[2], *adj.* fine; nice.

final, *adj.* final.

finance, *s. f.* finance.

financier, *adj.* financial.

fini, *adj.* finished; ended; over.

finir, *v. a. & n.* end, finish, put an end to; eat up.

finlandais, -e (F.), *adj.* Finnish; — *s. m. f.* Finn; Finnish.

fixe, *adj.* fixed, firm.

fixer, *v.a.* fix, fasten; stare at; settle.

flacon, *s. m.* flagon, bottle.

flagrant, *adj.* flagrant.

flairer, *v. a.* smell, scent.

flambeau, *s. m.* torch.

flamboyer, *v.n.* flame, flare.

flamme, *s.f.* flame.

flanelle, *s. f* flannel.

flanquer, *v.a.* fling.

flatter, *v. a.* caress; flatter.

flatterie, *s.f.* flattery.

flèche, *s. f.* arrow.

fléchir, *v. a.* bend, bow; *fig.* move.

fleur, *s. f.* flower, blossom.

fleurir, *v.n.* flower, blossom.

fleuve, *s. m.* river.

flirter, *v. n.* flirt.

flocon, *s. m.* flake (snow etc.).

flot, *s. m.* wave; flood; *être à ~* be floating.

flottant, *adj.* floating.

flotte, *s.f.* fleet; navy.

flotter, *v.n. & a.* float.

fluide, *s. m. & adj.* fluid.

flute, *s. f.* flute.

foi, *s.f.* faith, belief; credit.

foie, *s. m.* liver.

foin, *s.m.* hay; grass.

foire, *s.f.* fair, market.

fois, *s.f.* time; *une ~* once; *encore une ~* again; *deux ~* twice; *à la ~* at same time; *chaque ~* every time.

folie, *s. f.* folly, madness.

folle *see* fou.

foncer, *v. a.* sink; darken, deepen.

fonction, *s.f.* function, duty.

fonctionnaire, *s.m.f.* functionary, official.

fonctionner, *v.n.* function, operate, work.

fond, *s. m.* bottom, ground, foundation; *à ~* thoroughly.

fondamental, *adj.* fundamental, basic.

forcer, *v. a.* force; break open; compel, impel.

forêt, *s. f.* forest.

forger, *v. a.* forge.

formalité, *s. f.* formality.

forme, *s. f.* form, shape.

formel, -elle, *adj.* formal, express; flat.

former, *v. a.* form, shape.

formidable, *adj.* formidable, terrible.

formule, *s.f.* formula.

formuler, *v. a.* formulate, draw up.

fort, *adj.* strong, robust; fat; stout, stiff; skil-

ful; heavy; *être ~ en*
be well up in; — *adv.*
very (much), highly,
hard; *~ bien* very well;
— *s. m.* strong man;
stronghold.

forteresse, *s.f.* fortress.

fortification, *s. f.* fortification.

fortifier, *v. a.* strengthen,
fortify.

fortune, *s.f.* fortune;
chance; luck; wealth,
property.

fou, fol, folle, *adj.* mad,
foolish; crazy.

foudre, *s.f.* lightning,
thunderbolt.

fouille, *s. f.* excavation.

fouiller, *v. a. & n.* dig,
excavate.

fouillis, *s.m.* muddle, mess.

foule, *s. f.* crowd, mass.

four, *s. m.* oven, furnace.

fourchette, *s.f.* fork
(table).

fourgon, *s. m.* (delivery)
van; wagon; *~ (aux
bagages)* luggage-van.

fourmi, *s.f.* ant.

fourneau, *s.m.* stove,
range; *~ à gaz* gas-
ring, -stove; *~ électrique*
electric cooker.

fourniment, *s.m.* outfit,
kit.

fournir, *v.a.* furnish
(with), supply; provide
(with).

fourreau, *s.m.* sheath,
case, scabbard.

fourreur, *s.m.* furrier.

fourrure, *s.f.* fur.

foyer, *s.m.* fireside,
home; foyer, lounge.

fracas, *s.m.* crash; uproar; fuss; noise.

fracasser, *v.a.* shatter,
smash.

fraction, *s.f.* fraction;
portion; instalment.

fracture, *s.f.* fracture.

fragile, *adj.* fragile.

frais¹, fraîche, *adj.* fresh,
cool; chilly.

frais², *s. m. pl.* expenses,
charges, fees.

fraise, *s.f.* strawberry.

framboise, *s. f.* raspberry.

franc, franche, *adj.* frank,
free, open.

français (F.), *adj.* French;
— *s. m.* Frenchman;
French (language).

Française, *s.f.* Frenchwoman.

franchir, *v.a.* clear, jump
over, cross.

franchise, *s. f.* exemption;
frankness.

frapper, *v.a.* strike, hit,
knock; impress; sur-
prise.

frein, *s. m.* bit (of bridle);
brake; *fig.* check.

frêle, *adj.* weak, frail.

fréquent, *adj.* frequent.

frère, *s.m.* brother.

fricassée, *s.f.* fricassee.

friction, *s.f.* friction.

frigidaire, *s.m.* refrigerator.

frigo, *s.m.* fridge.

frileux, -euse, *adj.* chilly.

frire*, *v.n. & a.* fry.

friser, *v.a. & n.* curl.

frissonner, *v. n.* shiver,
tremble.

frivole, *adj.* frivolous,
flimsy.

froid, *s. m.* cold; *avoir ~*
feel cold; — *adj.* cold,
cool; *il fait froid* it
is cold.

froisser, *v.a.* rumple,
crumple; bruise; *fig.*
offend, hurt; **se ~** take
offence.

frôler, *v.a.* graze.

fromage, *s.m.* cheese.

front, *s.m.* forehead;
face; front (part).

frontière, *s.f.* frontier,
border.

frotter, *v. a.* rub.

fruit, *s.m.* fruit; produce.

fruitier, *s.m.* fruiterer, greengrocer.

fuir*, *v. n. & a.* run away, flee.

fuite, *s. f.* flight; leakage, leak.

fumée, *s.f.* smoke.

fumer, *v. a. & n.* smoke.

fumeur, -euse *s.m.f.* smoker.

fumier, *s.m.* dung.

funèbre, *adj.* funereal.

funérailles, *s.f.pl.* funeral.

funiculaire, *s.m.* rope railway.

fureur, *s.f.* fury, rage.

furie, *s. f.* fury.

furieux, -euse, *adj.* furious.

furoncle, *s.m.* boil, furuncle.

fusée, *s.f.* fuse; rocket.

fusil, *s.m.* gun.

fusillade, *s.f.* firing, shooting.

futur, *adj. & s. m.* future.

fuyant, *adj.* flying, fleeing; passing.

G

gâchis, *s.m.* mortar; mire; *fig.* muddle, mess.

gaffe, *s. f.* blunder.

gage, *s. m.* pledge; security; ~s wages.

gagner, *v. a.* gain; win.

gai, *adj.* gay, cheerful.

gaieté, *s.f.* gaiety.

gain, *s.m.* gain, profit.

galant, *adj.* courteous.

galerie, *s. f.* gallery.

galop, *s. m.* gallop.

gamin, *s.m.* urchin.

gamme, *s. f.* scale; range.

gant, *s. m.* glove.

garage, *s.m.* garage; siding.

garantie, *s. f.* guarantee.

garantir, *v. a.* guarantee.

garçon, *s. m.* boy; young man; fellow; bachelor; waiter.

garde[1], *s. f.* guard; watch; police; nurse.

garde[2], *s.m.* warden, guardian; watch.

garde-bébé, *s. m.* babysitter, sitter-in.

garde-boue, *s.f.* mudguard.

garde-chasse, *s. m.* gamekeeper.

garder, *v.a.* keep, take care of; attend (to).

garde-robe, *s.f.* wardrobe.

gardien, -enne, *s.m. f.* guardian, keeper; warden; watch(man); ~ *de la paix* constable; ~ *(de but)* goalkeeper.

gare, *s. f.* station; depot; ~ *des marchandises* goods station; *aller recevoir qn à la* ~ meet sy at the station.

garni, *s.m.* furnished lodgings *(pl.)*, digs.

garnir, *v. a.* furnish; fit up, trim.

garnison, *s. f.* garrison.

garniture, *s.f.* fittings *(pl.)*; set; garnishing.

gâteau, *s. m.* cake.

gâter, *v. a.* waste, impair; spoil.

gauche, *adj.* left.

gaz, *s. m.* gas; *usine à* ~ gas-works.

gazon, *s. m.* grass; lawn.

géant, *s. m.* giant.

gelée, *s. f.* jelly.

gémir, *v. n.* groan.

gênant, *adj.* inconvenient, annoying.

gendre, *s. m.* son-in-law.

gêne, *s. f.* inconvenience;

trouble; *être dans la* ~ be hard-up.

gêné, *adj.* uneasy; stiff; embarrassed.

gêner, *v.n.* inconvenience; be in the way of; interfere with.

général, *adj. & s. m.* general; *en* ~ in general, generally.

généraliser, *v.a. & n.* generalize.

générateur, *s.m.* generator.

génération, *s.f.* generation.

généreux, -euse, *adj.* generous.

générosité, *s.f.* generosity.

génie, *s. m.* genius; corps of engineers.

genou, *s.m.* *(pl.* -x) knee; *(pl.)* lap; *se mettre à* ~s kneel down.

genre, *s. m.* genus, kind.

gens, *s.m. f.* people; attendants.

gentil, -ille, *adj.* gentle.

géographie, *s.f.* geography.

géographique, *adj.* geographic(al).

géologie, *s. f.* geology.

géométrie, *s. f.* geometry.

géométrique, *adj.* geometric(al).

gérant, -e, *s. m. f.* manager; manageress.

gérer, *v. a.* manage.

germanique, *adj.* Germanic.

germe, *s.m.* germ.

gésir*, *v.n.* lie.

geste, *s.m.* gesture.

gesticuler, *v. n.* gesticulate.

gibier, *s. m.* game.

gifle, *s. f.* slap, box on the ear.

gifler, *v. a.* give s.o. a slap (in the face).

gilet, *s.m.* waistcoat, vest.

girafe, *s. f.* giraffe.

glace, *s. f.* ice; ice-cream; mirror; *mer de* ~ glacier.

glacer, *v. a.* freeze, chill.

glacial, *adj.* icy, glacial.

glacier, *s. m.* glacier.

glissade, *s. f.* slide; slip.

glissant, *adj.* slippery.

glisser, *v.n.* slide; slip; glide over; *se* ~ slip, creep (into).

globe, *s. m.* globe; earth.

gloire, *s. f.* glory, fame.

glorieux, -euse, *adj.* glorious; proud.

gober, *v.a.* swallow.

golfe, *s. m.* gulf.

gomme, *s. f.* gum; india-rubber.

gommer, *v. a.* gum.

gonfler, *v.a.* inflate.

gorge, *s.f.* throat, gullet.

gorgée, *s. f.* gulp.

gosse, *s.m.* kid, brat.

gothique, *adj.* Gothic.

goudron, *s. m.* tar.

gourmand, *adj.* greedy.

goût, *s. m.* taste; savour.

goûter, *v. a.* taste; relish, enjoy; — *s.m.* tea *(meal).*

goutte, *s. f.* drop.

gouvernail, *s. m.* rudder, helm.

gouvernante *s. f.* governess.

gouvernement, *s.m.* government.

gouverner, *v. a.* govern, control, rule; manage; steer.

gouverneur, *s. m.* governor; tutor, preceptor.

grâce, *s. f.* grace; pardon; thanks *(pl.);* favour.

gracieux, -euse, *adj.* graceful; gracious.

grade, *s. m.* rank, grade.

grain, s. m. grain, berry, corn; a touch (of).

graine, s. f. seed, berry.

graissage, s. m. lubrication.

graisse, s. f. fat, grease, lard.

graisser, v.a. grease, lubricate.

grammaire, s.f. grammar.

grammatical, adj. grammatical.

gramme, s. m. gramme.

gramophone, s. m. gramophone.

grand, adj. great; large; big; tall; grand.

grandeur, s.f. size; length; breadth; greatness.

grandir, v.n. grow (up); grow big, tall.

grand'mère, s. f. grandmother.

grand-père, s. m. grandfather.

granit, s. m. granite.

grappe, s. f. bunch; ~ de raisin bunch of grapes.

gras, grasse, adj. fat; thick.

gratitude, s.f. gratitude.

gratter, v. a. & n. scratch, overtake; brush.

gratuit, adj. free (of charge).

grave, adj. grave; heavy.

graver, v.a. engrave.

gravure, s.f. engraving.

grec, grecque (G.), adj. & s. m. f. Greek.

grêle, adj. slender, delicate, slim.

grelotter, v.n. shiver.

grenier, s. m. loft; granary.

grenouille, s. f. frog.

grève, s. f. strike; beach.

grief, s. m. grievance.

griffe, s. f. claw; clutch.

grill, s. m. grill, gridiron.

grille, s. f. iron railing, grating.

griller, v.a. grill, toast.

grimace, s.f. grimace.

grimacer, v.n. grimace.

grimper, v. n. & n. climb.

grincer, v. n. & a. grind, grate; creak.

grippe, s.f. influenza.

gris, adj. gray.

grogner, v.n. groan; grunt, grumble.

gronder, v. n. roar; rumble; v.a. scold.

gros, grosse, adj. large, big; stout; great; thick: — s. m. bulk; wholesale; en ~ roughly; wholesale.

grossier, adj. coarse, gross.

grossir, v. a. make bigger; increase; v. n. grow bigger.

grotesque, adj. grotesque.

groupe, s.m. group.

grouper, v.a. group.

grue, s.f. crane.

gué, s. m. ford (across river).

guêpe, s. f. wasp.

guérir, v.a. cure, heal; v. n. & se ~ be cured, get well again.

guerre, s. f. war.

gueule, s. f. mouth, jaws (pl.); opening.

guichet, s.m. ticket window; counter; booking-office.

guide, s. m. guide; conductor; guide-book.

guider, v. a. guide, lead.

guillemets, s. m. pl. inverted commas.

guise, s. f. way, manner; à votre ~ as you like.

guitare, s. f. guitar.

gymnastique, s. f. gymnastics.

H

habile, *adj.* able, clever.

habileté, *s. f.* skill, cleverness; ability.

habiller, *v. a.* clothe; dress (up); **s'~** dress, put on one's clothes.

habit, *s. m.* (dress-)suit; coat; **~s** clothes.

habitant, **-e**, *s.m.f.* inhabitant.

habitation, *s. f.* habitation, dwelling.

habiter, *v. a. & n.* inhabit, live in, dwell in.

habitude, *s. f.* habit, use.

habituel, **-elle**, *adj.* habitual, usual.

habituer, *v. a.* accustom; **s'~** *à* get accustomed to, get used to.

hache, *s. f.* axe.

hacher, *v.a.* chop, cut up, hack, mince.

hachis, *s. m.* hash.

haine, *s. f.* hate, hatred.

haïr*, *v.a.* hate.

haleine, *s. f.* breath.

hall, *s. m.* lounge; **~** *de montage* erecting shop.

halle, *s.f.* market-hall.

hanche, *s.f.* haunch, hip.

hangar, *s. m.* shed, hangar.

happer, *v.a.* snap up.

harasser, *v.a.* harass.

hardi, *adj.* bold, daring.

hareng, *s.m.* herring.

haricot, *s.m.* bean; **~s** *verts* French-beans.

harmonie, *s. f.* harmony.

harmonieux, **-euse**, *adj.* harmonious.

harnais, *s.m.* harness.

harpe, *s.f.* harp.

hasard, *s. m.* hazard, risk; *par* **~** by chance.

hasarder, *v.a.* hazard, risk, stake.

hasardeux, **-euse**, *adj.* risky; unsafe.

hâte, *s. f.* haste, hurry, rush; *à la* **~** in a hurry.

hâter, *v. a.* hasten, urge on; **se ~** hurry (up).

hausse, *s. f.* rise.

hausser, *v. a. & n.* raise, lift; **se ~** rise.

haut, *adj.* high; elevated; upright; loud; upper; *terre* **~e** highland; *à voix* **~e** aloud: — *adv.* high, highly, up; aloud; *en* **~** at the top; upstairs; — *s. m.* top, height, summit.

hauteur, *s.f.* height, altitude.

haut-parleur, *s. m.* loudspeaker.

havresac, *s.m.* haversack, knapsack.

hebdomadaire, *adj. & s. m.* weekly.

hébreu (H.), *adj. & s. m.* Hebrew.

hectare, *s.m.* hectare.

hélice, *s.f.* air-screw, propeller.

hélicoptère, *s.m.* helicopter.

herbe, *s.f.* herb, grass; pot-herb.

herbeux, **-euse**, *adj.* grassy.

hérédité, *s.f.* heredity.

hérisser, *v.a.* bristle; ruffle; **se ~** bristle up, stand on end.

hérisson, *s. m.* hedgehog.

héritage, *s. m.* inheritance, heritage.

hériter, *v.a. & n.* inherit.

héritier, *s.m.* heir.

héritière, *s.f.* heiress.

héroïne, *s.f.* heroine.

héros, *s. m.* hero.

hésitation, *s.f.* hesitation.

hésiter, *v.n.* hesitate.

heure, *s. f.* hour, time; *quelle ~ est-il?* what time is it?; *il est dix ~s moins le quart* it's a quarter to ten; *dix ~s* ten o'clock; *dix ~s et quart* a quarter past ten; *dix ~s et demie* half past ten; *de bonne ~* early; *~s de pointe* rush hours; *~s d'ouverture* business hours; *~s supplémentaires* overtime.

heureux, -euse, *adj.* happy, fortunate, successful.

heurter, *v. a. & n.* knock against, hit, run into, against; *se ~* run, hit, dash against, collide.

hibou, *s. m. (pl. -x)* owl.

hideux, -euse, *adj.* hideous, terrible.

hier, *adv.* yesterday; *~ soir* last night.

hirondelle, *s. f.* swallow.

histoire, *s. f.* (hi)story.

historique, *adj.* historic.

hiver, *s.m.* winter.

hollandais, -e (H.), *adj. & s. m. f.* Dutch(man), Dutch-woman.

homard, *s.m.* lobster.

homme, *s.m.* man; *~ d'affaires* business man; *~ d'état* statesman.

hongrois, -e, (H.), *adj. & s.m.f.* Hungarian.

honnête, *adj.* honest.

honnêteté, *s. f.* honesty.

honneur, *s.m.* honour; credit.

honorable, *adj.* honourable.

honoraires, *s. m. pl.* fee(s).

honorer, *v.a.* honour.

honte, *s.f.* shame; *avoir ~ de* be ashamed of.

honteux, -euse, *adj.* shameful, disgraceful.

hôpital, *s. m. (pl. -aux)* hospital.

hoquet, *s.m.* hiccup.

horaire, *s.m.* time-table.

horizon, *s.m.* horizon.

horizontal, *adj.* horizontal.

horloge, *s.f.* clock.

horloger, *s.m.* watch-maker.

horreur, *s.f.* horror.

horrible, *adj.* horrible.

hors, *adv.* out, outside; *— prep.* out of, outside.

hospitalité, *s. f.* hospitality.

hostie, *s.f.* wafer *(Church).*

hostile, *adj.* hostile.

hostilité, *s.f.* hostility.

hôte, *s.m.* host; guest.

hôtel, *s.m.* hotel; large house; *~ de ville* town-hall.

hôtesse, *s. f.* hostess; *~ de l'air* air-hostess.

houe, *s. f.* hoe.

houillère, *s.f.* colliery.

hublot, *s.m.* window.

huile, *s. f.* oil.

huissier, *s. m.* usher.

huit, *adj. & s. m.* eight.

huitième, *adj.* eighth.

huître, *s. f.* oyster.

humain, *adj.* human.

humanité, *s. f.* humanity.

humble, *adj.* humble.

humecter, *v.a.* wet.

humer, *v. a.* inhale, suck in.

humide, *adj.* humid, wet.

humidité, *s. f.* humidity.

humiliation, *s. f.* humiliation.

humilier, *v. a.* humiliate.

humilité, *s. f.* humility.

humoristique, *adj.* humorous.

humour, *s. m.* humour.

hurlement, *s. m.* howl(ing), roar(ing).

hurler, *v.n.* howl, roar.

hutte, *s.f.* hut, cabin.

hydrogène, *s. m.* hydrogen.

hygiène, *s. f.* hygiene.
hymne, *s. m.* hymn.
hypocrite, *s. m. f.* hypocrite; — *adj.* hypocritical.
hypothèse, *s. f.* supposition; hypothesis.
hystérique, *adj.* hysterical.

I

ici, *adv.* here; d'∼ from here; *par* ∼ this way.
idéal, -e, *adj.* ideal.
idéalisme, *s. m.* idealism.
idéaliste, *s. m. f.* idealist.
idée, *s. f.* idea, notion; *il m'est venu à l'*∼ it occurred to me.
identique, *adj.* identical.
identité, *s.f.* identity.
idiome, *s. m.* language, dialect.
idiot, *adj.* idiotic; — *s. m.* idiot.
idiotisme, *s. m.* idiom.
ignition, *s. f.* ignition.
ignorance, *s. f.* ignorance.
ignorant, *adj.* ignorant.
ignorer, *v.a.* not know, be ignorant of, be unaware of.
il, elle, *pron.* *(pl.* ils, elles)* he, she, it; they; there.
île, *s. f.* island.
illégal, *adj.* illegal.
illicite, *adj.* illicit, unlawful.
illumination, *s.f.* illumination; ∼ *par projecteurs* flood-lighting.
illuminer, *v. a.* illuminate, light up; ∼ *par projecteurs* flood-light.
illusion, *s.f.* illusion, delusion.
illustration, *s. f.* illustration.
illustrer, *v.a.* illustrate, explain.

image, *s. f.* image, picture, likeness.
imagé, *adj.* vivid.
imaginaire, *adj.* imaginary, fantastic.
imaginatif, -ive, *adj.* imaginative.
imagination, *s. f.* imagination, fancy.
imaginer, *v.a.* s'∼ imagine.
imbécile, *s.m. f.* fool, idiot; — *adj.* foolish.
imitation, *s.f.* imitation, copy.
imiter, *v. a.* imitate, copy.
immédiat, *adj.* immediate.
immense, *adj.* immense.
immeuble, *s. m.* real estate, landed property.
immigrant, -e, *adj.* & *s. m. f.* immigrant.
immigration, *s.f.* immigration.
immigrer, *v. a.* immigrate.
immobile, *adj.* immobile.
immoral, *adj.* immoral.
immortel, -elle, *adj.* immortal.
imparfait, *adj.* & *s. m.* imperfect.
impartial, *adj.* impartial.
impatience, *s. f.* impatience.
impatient, *adj.* impatient.
impayé, *adj.* unpaid.
impératif, -ive, *adj.* & *s. m.* imperative.
impératrice, *s. f.* empress.
imperfection, *s.f.* imperfection.
impérial, *adj.* imperial.
impérialisme, *s.m.* imperialism.
imperméable, *adj.* impermeable; waterproof.
impertinent, *adj.* impertinent.
impétueux, -euse, *adj.* impetuous, headlong.
impliquer, *v. a.* implicate,

involve, imply.

implorer, *v.a.* implore, beg.

impoli, *adj.* impolite.

impopulaire, *adj.* unpopular.

importance, *s.f.* importance.

important, *adj.* important.

importateur, -trice, *s.m.f.* importer.

importation, *s.f.* importation; ~s imports.

importer, *v.n.* matter, be of moment; *n'importe* it does not matter.

importun, *adj.* troublesome, importunate.

importuner, *v.a.* annoy, molest, worry.

imposer, *v.a.* impose, inflict, lay (on); levy.

impossible, *adj.* impossible.

impôt, *s. m.* tax, duty.

impression, *s. f.* impression; print, edition; *faute d'~* misprint.

impressionner, *v. a.* impress, affect.

imprimé, *s.m.* printed matter.

imprimer, *v. a.* (im)print, impress; publish.

imprimerie, *s. f.* printing; printing office.

impropre, *adj.* unfit, improper.

imprudent, *adj.* imprudent.

impuissant, *adj.* powerless, ineffectual, helpless.

impulsion, *s. f.* spur, impulse.

inaccoutumé, *adj.* unaccustomed.

inachevé, *adj.* unfinished.

inanimé, *adj.* inanimate.

inapplicable, *adj.* inapplicable, irrelevant.

inattendu, *adj.* unexpected.

inattentif, -ive, *adj.* inattentive, heedless.

incapable, *adj.* incapable, unable, inefficient.

incendie, *s. m.* fire.

incendier, *v. a.* set fire to.

incertain, *adj.* uncertain.

incessant, *adj.* incessant.

incident, *s. m.* incident; — *adj.* incidental.

inciter, *v.a.* incite, urge.

inclinaison, *s. f.* inclination, gradient.

inclination, *s. f.* inclination; bent; love.

incliner, *v. a. & n.* incline, bend; slope; slant; s'~ bow down, bend.

inclusif, -ive *adj.* inclusive.

incommode, *adj.* inconvenient, uncomfortable.

incommoder, *v.a.* inconvenience, annoy.

incomparable, *adj.* incomparable.

incompatible, *adj.* incompatible.

incompétent, *adj.* incompetent.

incomplet, *adj.* incomplete, imperfect.

inconscient, *adj.* unconscious.

inconséquent, *adj.* inconsistent.

inconvenant, *adj.* improper, unsuitable.

inconvénient, *s.m.* inconvenience.

incorrect, *adj.* incorrect.

incroyable, *adj.* incredible.

incurable, *adj.* incurable.

indécis, *adj.* uncertain.

indécision, *s. f.* indecision.

indéfini, *adj.* indefinite,

underlined.

indépendance, *s.f.* independence.

index, *s.m.* forefinger, index.

indicateur, *s. m.* indicator, gauge; time-table.

indication, *s. f.* indication; direction; sign.

indice, *s. m.* sign, token, mark; index.

indien, -enne (I.), *adj. & s.m.f.* Indian.

indifférent, *adj.* indifferent.

indigestion, *s. f.* indigestion.

indignation, *s. f.* indignation.

indiquer, *v.a.* indicate, point out, show.

indirect, *adj.* indirect.

indiscret, -ète, *adj.* indiscreet.

indiscrétion, *s. f.* indiscretion.

indispensable, *adj.* indispensable, essential.

indisposé, *adj.* unwell; upset.

individu, *s. m.* individual, person.

individuel, -elle, *adj.* individual.

indulgence, *s. f.* indulgence.

indulgent, *adj.* indulgent.

industrie, *s. f.* industry.

industriel, -elle, *adj.* industrial; — *s. m.* manufacturer.

inefficace, *adj.* inefficient.

inégal, *adj.* unequal.

inégalité, *s. f.* inequality.

inerte, *adj.* inert; dull.

inévitable, *adj.* inevitable.

inexpérimenté, *adj.* inexperienced.

inexplicable, *adj.* inexplicable.

infâme, *adj.* infamous.

infanterie. *s. f.* infantry.

infection, *s. f.* infection.

inférieur, *adj.* inferior.

infinitif, *s. m.* infinitive.

infirmerie, *s. f.* infirmary.

infirmier, -ère, *s. m. f.* nurse.

influence, *s. f.* influence.

influencer, *v. a.* influence.

information, *s. f.* information.

informer, *v. a.* inform, let know; s'~ *de* inquire about.

infructueux, -euse, *adj.* unsuccessful.

ingénieur, *s. m.* engineer.

ingénieux, -euse, *adj.* ingenious.

ingéniosité, *s. f.* ingenuity.

ingrat, *adj.* ungrateful.

ingrédient , *s. m.* ingredient.

inhabité, *adj.* uninhabited.

inintéressant, *adj.* uninteresting.

initial, -e, *adj. & s. f.* initial.

initiative, *s. f.* initiative; *syndicat d'~* tourist office.

injection, *s. f.* injection.

injure, *s.f.* injury.

injurier, *v.a.* insult.

injurieux, -euse, *adj.* injurious.

injuste, *adj.* unjust.

injustice, *s. f.* injustice.

innocence, *s. f.* innocence.

innocent, *adj.* innocent.

innombrable, *adj.* innumerable, countless.

inoccupé, *adj.* unoccupied.

inoculer, *v.a.* inoculate.

inondation, *s. f.* flood.

inonder, *v. a.* flood.

inquiet, -ète, *adj.* anxious, restless, uneasy.

inquiéter, *v.a.* worry.

insecte, *s.m.* insect.

insensé, *adj.* insane, mad.

insensible, *adj.* insensible.

inséparable, *ad.j* inseparable.

insigne, *s. m.* badge.

insignifiant, *adj.* insignificant.

insipide, *adj.* dull, flat.

insister, *v. a.* insist, lay stress on.

insolence, *s. f.* insolence.

insolent, *adj.* insolent.

insouciant, *adj.* careless.

inspecter, *v.a.* inspect, survey.

inspiration, *s. f.* inspiration.

inspirer, *v.a.* inspire, suggest; inhale.

installation, *s. f.* installation; fitting up.

installer, *v.a.* install; fit up; *v.n.* **s'~** to settle down.

instant, *adj.* instant, pressing; — *s.m.* instant, moment; *à l'~* instantly, at once.

instantané, *s.m.* snap-(shot).

instinct, *s. m.* instinct.

instituer, *v.a.* institute.

institut, *s.m.* institute.

institution, *s. f.* institution; boarding-school.

instruction, *s. f.* instruction, tuition; knowledge, learning; direction; inquiry.

instruire*, *v.a.* instruct, teach.

instrument, *s. m.* instrument, implement, tool.

instrumental, *adj.* instrumental.

insuffisance, *s. f.* insufficiency.

insuffisant, *adj.* insufficient, deficient.

insulte, *s. f.* insult.

insulter, *v. a. & n.* insult.

insupportable, *adj.* intolerable, unbearable.

intact, *adj.* intact, entire.

intégral, *adj.* integral.

intégrité, *s.f.* integrity.

intellectuel, -elle, *adj. & s.m.* intellectual.

intelligence, *s. f.* intelligence, understanding.

intelligent, *adj.* intelligent, clever.

intendant, *s. m.* manager.

intense, *adj.* intense.

intensité, *s. f.* intensity.

intention, *s. f.* intention, purpose; *avoir l'~* intend, mean.

interdire, *v. a.* forbid.

intéressant, *adj.* interesting; *peu* ~ uninteresting.

intéressé, *adj.* interested, concerned.

intéresser, *v. a. & n.* interest; concern; **s'~** take an interest (*à* in); be concerned.

intérêt, *s.m.* interest; concern; share; *avoir* ~ *à* have an interest in.

intérieur, *s.m.* inside, interior; *à l'~* inside, indoors; *Ministre de l'Intérieur* Home Secretary.

intermédiaire, *adj.* intermediate; — *s. m. f.* intermediary.

international, *adj.* international.

interne, *adj.* internal, inward.

interpellation, *s. f.* interpellation.

interpeller, *v. a.* interpellate, question.

interposer, *v. a.* interpose.

interprétation, *s. f.* interpretation.

interprète, *s. m. f.* interpreter.

interpréter, *v.a.* interpret; render.

interrogation, s. f. interrogation; inquiry.

interrogatoire, s.m. (cross-)examination.

interroger, v.a. interrogate, cross-examine, question.

interrompre, v.a. interrupt.

interrupteur, s. m. interrupter; switch.

interruption, s. f. interruption.

intervalle, s.m. interval; dans l'~ in the meantime.

intervenir, v.n. intervene, interfere, go between.

intervention, s. f. intervention.

interview, s. f. m. interview.

intime, adj. intimate.

intimité, s.f. intimacy.

intolérable, adj. intolerable.

intrigue, s.f. intrigue.

intriguer, v.n. & n. intrigue.

introduction, s. f. introduction.

introduire, v.a. introduce; show in.

inutile, adj. useless.

invalide, adj. invalid, disabled.

invasion, s. f. invasion.

inventer, v.a. make up.

inventeur, s. m. inventor.

invention, s. f. invention.

investigation, s. f. investigation, inquiry.

invisible, adj. invisible.

invitation, s.f. invitation.

invité, -e, s. m. f. guest.

inviter, v. a. invite.

iris, s. m. iris.

irlandais (I.), adj. Irish;
— s. m. Irishman.

ironie, s. f. irony.

ironique, adj. ironical.

irradier, v. a. (ir)radiate.

irréel, adj. unreal.

irrésistible, adj. irresistible.

irritation, s. f. irritation.

irriter, v.a. irritate.

isolement, s. m. isolation.

isoler, v.a. isolate.

isotope, s.m. isotope.

issue, s. f. issue, outlet, way out.

italien, -enne (I.), adj. & s. m. f. Italian.

itinéraire, adj. itinerary;
— s.m. guide-book.

ivre, adj. drunk.

J

j' see **je.**

jadis, adv. once, long ago, formerly.

jalousie, s.f. jealousy; blind.

jaloux, -se, adj. jealous.

jamais, adv. never, ever.

jambe, s. f. leg, shank.

jambon, s. m. ham.

janvier, s. m. January.

japonais, -e (J.), adj. & s. m. f. Japanese.

jardin, s. m. garden.

jardinier, -ère, s. m. f. gardener.

jarre, s. f. jar.

jarretière, s. f. garter.

jauge, s. f. gauge.

jauger, v. a. gauge.

jaune, adj. yellow; — s. m. yolk.

je, j', pron. I.

jersey, s. m. jersey.

jet, s.m. throw(ing).

jeter, v.a. throw, throw away, down; cast,

fling; shoot; discharge; se ~ rush.

jeton, s. m. counter.

jeu, s.m. game, play, set.

jeudi, s. m. Thursday.

jeune, adj. young.

jeûne, s.m. fast(ing).

jeûner, v.n. fast.

jeunesse, s. f. youth.

joie, s. f. joy, delight

joindre*, v. a. & n. join, unite; se ~ join.

joint, s. m. joint, articulation.

jointure, s. f. joint.

joli, adj. pretty, nice.

jonction, s. f. junction.

jongleur, s. m. juggler.

joue, s. f. cheek (face).

jouer, v. a. & n. play; gambol; gamble.

jouet, s. m. toy.

joueur, -euse, s. m. f. player; gambler.

joug, s. m. yoke.

jouir, v.n. (~ de) enjoy.

jouissance, s.f. enjoyment, pleasure, joy.

jour, s. m. day; daylight, light; life; ~ de fête holiday; ~ de semaine week-day; un ~ some day; tous les ~s every day; à ~ up to date.

journal, s. m. (news)paper; journal; diary.

journalier, -ère, adj. daily; — s.m. day-labourer.

journaliste, s. m. f. journalist.

journée, s. f. day; day's wages (pl.); day's work.

joyau, s. m. jewel.

joyeux, -euse, adj. joyful, merry.

judiciaire, adj. judicial, legal.

judicieux, -euse, adj. judicious, sensible, reasonable.

juge, s. m. judge.

jugement, s. m. judg(e)ment; sentence.

juger, v. a. & n. judge.

juif, -ive (J.), adj. Jewish; — s. m. f. Jew.

juillet, s. m. July.

juin, s. m. June.

jumeau, -elle adj. s. m. f. twin; f. pl. binoculars.

jungle, s. f. jungle.

jupe, s. f. skirt.

juré, s. m. juryman.

jurer, v. a. & n. swear.

jurisprudence, s..f jurisprudence.

juron, s. m. oath.

jury, s. m. jury.

jus, s.m. juice.

jusque, jusqu'à, prep. till; as far as.

juste, adj. just, right; fair.

justice, s.f. justice.

justification, s.f. justification.

justifier, v.a. justify.

juvénile, adj. juvenile.

K

kangourou, s. m. kangaroo.

kayak, s. m. kayak.

képi, s. m. cap.

kilogramme, s.m. kilogram(me).

kilomètre, s.m. kilometre.

kiosque, s. n. kiosk.

L

l' = le or la.

la, *art.* the; —*pron.* her,
it.

là, *adv.* there; here.

labeur, *s.m.* labour,
work.

laboratoire, *s.m.* labo-
ratory.

laborieux, -euse, *adj.* la-
borious, hard-working.

labourer, *v.a.* plough.

lac, *s. m.* lake.

lacer, *v. a.* lace.

lacet, *s. m.* lace; braid;
bowstring; shoe-lace.

lâche, *adj.* loose; coward-
ly; — *s. m.* coward.

lâcher, *v.a.* loosen, slack-
en; let go.

lactation, *s. f.* lactation.

laid, *adj.* ugly; plain.

laideur, *s. f.* ugliness.

lainage, *s.m.* woollen
goods *(pl.);* wool.

laine, *s. f.* wool; *pure* ~
all wool.

laïque, *adj.* lay.

laisser, *v.a.* leave, quit;
give up; let alone;
leave behind, off; ~
aller let go, neglect.

lait, *s. m.* milk.

laiterie, *s. f.* dairy.

laitier, *s. m.* milkman,
dairyman.

laitière, *s. f.* dairymaid.

laitue, *s. f.* lettuce.

lambeau, *s. m.* rag, strip.

lame, *s. f.* blade; plate;
sheet; ~ *de rasoir*
razor-blade.

lamentation, *s. f.* lamentation.

lampe, *s. f.* lamp.

lançement, *s. m.* throw-
ing; launching.

lancer, *v. a.* throw, fling;

se ~ dart, rush.

langage, *s. m.* language,
tongue; speech, way
of speaking.

lange *s. m.* baby's nappy.

langue, *s. f.* tongue; language; ~ *maternelle*
mother-tongue.

laper, *v. a.* lap (up).

lapin, *s. m.* rabbit.

laps, *s. m.* lapse, space
(of time).

lapsus, *s. m.* lapse, slip.

laque, *s. f.* lacquer.

lard, *s. m.* bacon.

large, *adj.* broad, wise;
generous; liberal; —
s.m. room, breadth.

largeur, *s. f.* width.

larme, *s. f.* tear.

las, lasse, *adj.* weary.

lasser, *v.a.* tire, wear
out; se ~ *de* get tired
of.

latéral, *adj.* lateral, side.

latin, -e, *adj. & s. m. f.*
Latin.

latitude, *s.f.* latitude;
scope, freedom.

lavable, *adj.* washable.

lavabo, *s. m.* wash-ba-
sin; lavatory.

lavage, *s.m.* washing;
~ *de vaisselle* washing-
up.

lavande, *s. f.* lavender.

laver, *v. a.* wash; se ~
wash (oneself); *machine*
à ~ washing-machine.

layette, *s. f.* baby-lin-
en.

le, la, l', *art.* the; —*pron.*
(pl. les) him, her, it;
them.

lécher, *v. a.* lick, lap.

leçon, *s. f.* lesson; lecture.

lecteur, -trice, *s. m. f.*
reader; lector.

lecture, *s. f.* reading.

légal, *adj.* legal, lawful.

légende, s. f. legend.

léger, -ère, adj. light, slight; loose.

légèreté, s. f. lightness; ease.

légion, s. f. legion.

législation, s.f. legislation.

législature, s. f. legislature.

légitime, adj. legitimate, lawful.

légume, s.m. vegetable.

lendemain, s.m. next day, day after.

lent, adj. slow; tardy.

lenteur, s.f. slowness.

lentille, s.f. lentil; lens.

léopard, s.m. leopard

lequel, laquelle, rel. pron. (pl. lesquels, lesquelles) who, whom; which, that.

lettre, s.f. letter; type character; ~s literature; arts; à la ~ literally, word for word; ~ de change bill of exchange; ~ de crédit letter of credit; ~ recommandée registered letter; boîte aux ~s letter-box.

lettré, adj. learned; literary.

leur, poss. adj. (pl. -s) their; — pron. to them, them; le or la ~, les ~s theirs, their own.

levée, s. f. raising; removal; levy.

lever, v. a. lift (up), raise; hoist; v. n. rise; se ~ rise get up.

levier, s. m. lever; ~ des vitesses gear-lever.

lèvre, s. f. lip.

lexique, s.m. lexicon.

liaison, s.f. joining, junction; union; connection; tie; liaison.

libéral, adj. liberal.

libérer, v.a. liberate.

liberté, s.f. liberty.

libraire, s.m. f. bookseller.

librairie, s. f. bookshop.

libre, adj. free; unoccupied.

licence, s.f. licence, degree.

licencié, -e, s. m. f. licenciate; licensee.

licencieux, -euse, adj. licentious.

lie, s. f. dregs, grounds (pl.).

liège, s.m. cork.

lien, s.m. tie, bond; band, strap, cord; link.

lier, v. a. bind, tie (up); fasten; link up.

lieu, s. m. place; au ~ de instead of; avoir ~ take place.

lieutenant, s. m. lieutenant.

lièvre, s. m. hare.

ligne, s. f. line; ~ aérienne air-line.

lilas, s. m. lilac.

limace, s. f. slug.

limaçon, s. m. snail.

lime, s. f. file.

limer, v. a. file.

limite, s.f. bound(s), border, limit.

limiter, v.a. limit, restrict.

limon, s.m. mud, silt.

limonade, s. f. lemonade.

lin, s. m. flax.

linge, s. m. linen.

linger, -ère, s.m.f. linendraper.

lingerie, s. f. ladies' underclothing, lingerie.

lion, s. m. lion.

liqueur, s. f. liqueur.

liquide, adj. liquid.

liquider, v.a. liquidate.

lire*, v.a. read.

liste, *s. f.* list, roll; panel.
lit, *s. m.* bed.
litre, *s. m.* litre.
littéraire, *adj.* literary.
littérature, *s.f.* literature.
livraison, *s.f.* delivery; part (of book).
livre¹, *s. m.* book; work; *teneur de* ~s bookkeeper.
livre², *s. f.* pound.
livrer, *v.a.* deliver; give up.
local, *s.m.* spot, premises; — *adj.* local.
localité, *s. f.* place, spot.
locataire, *s. m. f.* tenant, lodger.
location, *s. f.* letting out; hiring, renting; *prendre en* ~ hire; *bureau de* ~ box-office; ~ *des places* seat reservation.
locomotive, *s.f.* (railway) engine.
loge, *s.f.* hut. cabin; box.
logement, *s. m.* lodging.
loger, *v.a.* accommodate, lodge; house; *v. n.* reside, live (in).
logeur, *s. m.* landlord.
logeuse, *s. f.* landlady.
logique, *s. f.* logic; — *adj.* logical.
loi, *s.f.* law, statute; *projet de* ~ bill, draft.
loin, *adv.* far, far off, away; *au* ~ far off.
lointain, *adj.* far, remote.
loisif, *s. m.* spare time, leisure.
long, longue, *adj. & s. m. f.* long; *être* ~ *à* be long in.
longitude, *s.f.* longitude.
longtemps, *adv.* long, a long time; *depuis* ~ for a long time, long since.
longueur, *s. f.* length.

loquet, *s. m.* latch.
lors, *adv.* then; *dès* ~ from that time.
lorsque, *conj.* when.
lot, *s. m.* lot, fate; prize.
loterie, *s. f.* lottery.
lotion, *s. f.* lotion.
louage, *s.m.* hiring; hire.
louche, *s.f.* ladle.
louer¹, *v.a.* hire (out); let; *à* ~ for hire; to let.
louer², *v. a.* praise.
loup, *s. m.* wolf.
lourd, *adj.* heavy; clumsy.
louve, *s. f.* she-wolf.
loyal, *adj.* loyal, true.
loyauté, *s.f.* honesty.
loyer, *s. m.* rent; hire.
lubrifier, *v.a.* lubricate.
lucratif, -ive, *adj.* lucrative.
luge, *s. f.* sledge.
lugubre, *adj.* dismal.
lui, *pron.* (to) him, (to) her, (to) it.
lui-même, *pron.* himself.
luire*, *v. n.* shine, gleam.
lumière, *s. f.* light, daylight.
lumineux, -euse, *adj.* luminous, bright.
lundi, *s. m.* Monday.
lune, *s.f.* moon; ~ *de miel* honeymoon.
lunette, *s. f* telescope; *(pl.)* spectacles, specs; ~s *de soleil* sun-glasses.
luthérien, -enne, *adj. & s. m. f.* Lutheran.
lutte, *s.f.* wrestling; fight, struggle.
lutter, *v.n.* wrestle, fight.
lutteur, *s. m.* wrestler.
luxe, *s. m.* luxury.
luxeux, -euse, *adj.* luxurious.
lycée, *s.m.* secondary

school,grammar-school.

M

m' *see* me.

ma *see* mon.

mâcher, *v. a.* chew.

machine, *s. f.* machine, engine, apparatus; ~ *à coudre*, sewing-machine.

mâchoire, *s. f.* jaw.

maçon, *s m.* mason.

madame, *s. f. (pl.* mesdames) madam.

mademoiselle, *s. f. (pl.* mesdemoiselles) miss.

magasin, *s.m.* shop; store; warehouse; *grand* ~ department store.

magique, *adj.* magic.

magnétique, *adj.* magnetic.

magnétophone, *s.m.* tape-recorder.

magnifique, *adj.* magnificent.

mai, *s. m.* May.

maigre, *adj.* lean, thin.

maigrir, *v.n.* grow lean, get thin.

maille, *s. f.* stitch; knot.

maillot, *s.m.* tights (pl.); ~ *(de bain)* bathing-costume.

main, *s. f.* hand; lead; *en* ~ in hand; *se donner la* ~ shake hands; *tenir la* ~ *à* see to, see that; *de seconde* ~ second-hand.

maintenant, *adv.* now, at present

maintenir, *v. a.* (up)hold, support, keep (up), maintain.

maintien, *s. m.* maintenance.

maire, *s. m.* mayor.

mais, *conj.* but.

maïs, *s. m.* maize.

maison, *s. f.* house, resi-dence; home; firm; *à la* ~ at home, in-doors; *tenir* ~ keep house.

maître, *s.m.* master; proprietor; teacher; ~ *d'école* schoolmaster; ~ *de maison* host.

maîtresse, *s. f.* mistress; (land)lady; sweetheart; ~ *d'école* schoolmistress.

maîtrise, *s.f.* mastery, control.

maîtriser, *v.a.* master.

majesté, *s. f.* majesty.

majeur, *adj.* major; main; chief; — *s. m.* major.

majorité, *s. f.* majority.

majuscule, *s. f.* capital letter.

mal, *s. m.* ill, evil, wrong; pain, harm; trouble, hardship; *avoir* ~ *à* have a pain in; — *adv.* wrong, badly, ill.

malade, *adj.* sick, ill; *tomber* ~ fall ill, be taken ill; — *s. m. f.* invalid, patient.

maladie, *s.f.* illness; sickness; disease.

maladroit, *adj.* awkward, clumsy.

malaise, *s. m.* uneasiness.

malchance, *s.f.* bad luck.

mâle, *s. m.* male.

malentendu, *s. m.* misun-derstandig.

malgré, *prep.* in spite of; ~ *tout* for all that.

malheur, *s.m.* misfortune, ill luck; mischance; accident.

malheureux, -euse, *adj.* unfortunate, unlucky.

malice, *s. f.* malice.

malin, maligne, *adj.* mali-cious, malignant; evil.

malle, *s. f.* trunk; mail;

faire la ~ pack.

mallette, *s.f.* suit-case.

malpropre, *adj.* dirty, filthy; untidy.

malsain, *adj.* unhealthy.

malveillant, *adj.* malevolent, evil-minded.

maman, *s.f.* mamma.

manche¹, *s.m,* handle. holder.

manche², *s. f.* sleeve.

Manche, *s.f.* English Channel.

manchette, *s. f.* cuff.

mandat, *s. m.* mandate; money-order.

manger, *v.a.* eat; *donner à* ~ feed; *salle à* ~ dining-room; — *s. m.* eating; food.

manicure, *s. m. f.* manicure.

manier, *v.a.* handle.

manière, *s. f.* manner, way, fashion; *(pl.)* manners.

manifestation, *s. f.* manifestation.

manifester, *v.a.* manifest, show; **se** ~ man fest oneself.

manipuler, *v. a.* manipulate, operate.

manœuvre, *s.f.* action; proceeding; manœuvre; *s. m.* labourer.

manœuvrer, *v. a. & n.* handle, manœuvre, work.

manoir, *s. m.* manor.

manque, *s.m.* want; deficiency.

manquer, *v. a.* miss; *v. n.* fail; be missing, be wanting.

mansarde, *s.f.* garret.

manteau, *s. m.* coat.

manuel, -elle, *adj.* manual; — *s. m.* manual, handbook.

manufacture, *s. f.* manufacture; factory.

manufacturer, *v. a.* manufacture.

manuscrit, *s. m.* manuscript.

maquillage, *s.m.* make-up.

marbre, *s. m.* marble.

marchand, -e, *s. m. f.* merchant, tradesman; shopkeeper.

marchandise, *s. f.* merchandise, goods *(pl.).*

marche, *s. f.* walk; march; progress; move.

marché, *s. m.* market; bargain; agreement: *bon* ~ cheap.

marcher, *v.n.* walk; travel; march; work; run; proceed.

mardi, *s. m.* Tuesday; ~ *gras* Shrove Tuesday.

mare, *s.f.* pool, pond.

maréchal, *s. m.* marshal.

marée, *s.f.* tide, flood.

margarine, *s. f.* margarine.

marge, *s. f.* margin.

mari, *s.m.* husband.

mariage, *s. m.* marriage.

marié, -e, *adj.* married; — *s. m. f.* bridegroom, married man; bride, married woman.

marier, *v. a.* marry; match; — **se** ~ marry, get married.

marin, *adj.* marine; — *s.m.* seaman, sailor, mariner.

marmelade, *s. f.* marmalade.

marque, *s. f.* mark, imprint; trade-mark.

marquer, *v.a.* mark; stamp; brand.

marron, *s. m.* chestnut.

mars, *s. m.* March.

marteau, *s. m.* hammer.

martyr, -e, *s.m.f.* martyr.

masque, *s. m.* mask.
masquer, *v.a.* mask.
massacre, *s. m.* massacre.
massage, *s. m.* massage.
masse, *s. f.* mass; heap.
massif, -ive, *adj.* massive, bulky, clumsy.
mât, *s. m.* mast.
match, *s. m.* match.
matelas, *s. m.* mattress.
matelot, *s.m.* sailor, seaman.
matérialisme, *s. m.* materialism.
matériaux, *s.m.pl.* material(s).
matériel, -elle, *adj.* material; — *s. m.* matter; material; implements *(pl.)*.
maternel, -elle, *adj.* maternal; motherly; *école ~le* infant-school.
mathématicien, -enne, *s. m. f.* mathematician.
mathématique, *adj.* mathematical; — *s. f.* mathematics.
matière, *s.f.* matter; material; substance; *~ première* raw material.
matin, *s.m.* morning; *le ~* in the morning; *du ~* a.m.
matinal, *adj.* morning.
matinée, *s.f.* morning; matinée.
matrice, *s. f.* womb.
maturité, *s. f.* maturity.
maudire*, *v.a.* curse.
mauvais, *adj.* bad, ill, evil; — *s. m.* bad.
me, m' *pron.* (to) me; (to) myself.
mécanicien, *s. m.* mechanic; engine-driver.
mécanique, *adj.* mechanic(al); — *s.m.* mechanics; machine; mechanism.

mécaniser, *v. a.* mechanize.
mécanisme, *s. m.* mechanism; machinery.
méchant, *adj.* evil, bad.
mécontent, *adj.* displeased, dissatisfied, unhappy.
mécontenter, *v. a.* dissatisfy.
médaille, *s. f.* medal.
médecin, *s.m.* doctor, physician.
médecine, *s. f.* medicine.
médical, *adj.* medical.
médicament, *s. m.* medicament; medicine.
médiéval, *adj.* medieval.
méditation, *s. m.* meditation.
méditer, *v. a. & n.* meditate.
méfiance, *s. f.* mistrust.
méfier: se ~ be suspicious *(de* of); mistrust.
meilleur, -e, *adj.* better; — *s. m. f.* the best.
mélancolie, *s. f.* melancholy, gloom.
mélancolique, *adj.* melancholy, sad.
mélange, *s.m.* mixture, blend.
mélanger, *v.a.* mix, blend.
mêler, *v.a.* mix (up), mingle; se ~ mingle, be mixed; interfere with.
mélodie, *s. f.* melody.
melon, *s.m.* melon.
membre, *s.m.* member, limb.
même, *adj.* same; self; — *adv.* even, also, likewise; *de ~* in the same way; *de ~ que* as well as; *quand ~* even if.
mémoire, *s.f.* memory; *s.m.* memorandum; bill; *(pl.)* memoirs.

menace, *s.f.* menace.
menacer, *v.a.* threaten.
ménage, *s. m.* housekeeping; household.
ménager, *v. a.* be sparing of; take care of; manage.
ménagère, *s.f.* housewife, housekeeper.
mendiant, -e, *s.m.f.* beggar.
mendier, *v. a. & n.* beg.
mener, *v.a.* guide, conduct, lead.
mensonge, *s.m.* lie.
mensuel, *adj.* monthly.
mental, *adj.* mental.
mention, *s.f.* mention.
mentionner, *v. a.* mention.
mentir*, *v.n.* lie, tell a lie.
menton, *s.m.* chin.
menu, *adj.* slim; small; minute; — *s. m.* bill of fare, menu.
menuisier, *s. m.* joiner, carpenter.
méprendre: se ∼ make a mistake, be mistaken.
mépris, *s.m.* contempt.
mer, *s.f.* sea; *par* ∼ by sea; *bord de la* ∼ seaside.
mercerie, *s. f.* haberdashery.
merci, *s. f.* mercy; — *int.* thanks!, (no) thank you!
mercredi, *s. m.* Wednesday.
mercure, *s.m.* mercury.
mère, *s.f.* mother.
mérite, *s. m.* merit, worth.
mériter, *v.a.* merit, deserve.
merveille, *s.f.* wonder.
merveilleux, -euse, *adj.* wonderful.
message, *s.m.* message.
messe, *s.f.* mass.
mesure, *s.f.* measure,

gauge, measurement; size; metre.
mesurer, *v.a.* measure.
métal, *s.m.* metal.
métallique, *adj.* metallic.
météorologie *s. f.* meteorology.
méthode, *s.f.* method.
méthodique, *adj.* methodical, systematic.
métier, *s. m.* trade; business; employment, occupation.
mètre, *s. m.* metre.
métro, *s. m.* tube, underground.
métropolitain, *adj.* metropolitan; underground.
mets, *s.m.* dish, food.
mettre*, *v.a.* put, set, place; put in, on; bring; ∼ *de c té* set aside, save; ∼ *en ordre* set in order, tidy up; se ∼ sit down; *se* ∼ *à* set about, take to.
meuble, *s. m.* (piece of) furniture; — *adj.* movable; *biens* ∼s personal property.
meubler, *v.a.* furnish, fit up.
meunier, *s.m.* miller.
meurtre, *s.m.* murder.
meurtrier, *s. m.* murderer.
meurtrir, *v.a.* bruise, injure.
mi-, half, mid.
microbe, *s. m.* microbe.
microphone, *s. m.* microphone.
microscope, *s. m.* microscope.
midi, *s. m.* noon, midday; south.
miel, *s. m.* honey.
mien, *pron.* mine, my own.
miette, *s. f.* crumb.
mieux, *adv.* better.
mignon, -onne, *adj.* tiny; — *s.m.f.* darling.

migraine, s. f. headache.

milieu, s.m. middle, centre; environment.

militaire, adj. military; — s. m. soldier.

mille[1], adj. & s.m. thousand.

mille[2], s. m. mile (= 1609 metres).

millier, s.m. thousand.

million, s.m. million.

millionaire, s. m. f. millionaire.

mince, adj. thin, slim.

mine[1], s.f. mine.

mine[2], s.f. look(s); de bonne ~ good-looking.

miner, v. a. (under)mine.

minerai, s.m. ore.

minéral, adj. mineral.

mineur[1], s.m. miner.

mineur[2], -e, adj. & s. m. f. minor.

ministère, s. m. ministry.

ministre, s. m. minister; premier ~ prime minister, premier.

minorité, s. f. minority.

minuit, s.m. midnight.

minuscule, s.f. small letter.

minute, s.f. minute; instant.

miracle, s.m. miracle.

miraculeux, -euse, adj. miraculous, wonderful.

miroir, s.m. mirror.

misérable, adj. miserable.

misère, s. f. misery.

miséricorde, s. f. mercy.

mission, s.f. mission.

missionnaire, adj. & s. m. f. missionary.

mite, s. f. moth.

mobile, adj. movable, mobile.

mobilier, s. m. furniture, suite.

mobilisation, s. f. mobilization.

mobiliser, v.a.&n. mobilize.

mode[1], s.f. fashion, vogue; à la ~ in vogue, in fashion.

mode[2], s. m. mode, way; mood.

modèle, s.m. model.

modération, s. f. moderation.

modérer, v.a. moderate.

moderne, adj. modern.

modeste, adj. modest.

modestie, s.f. modesty.

modification, s. f. modification, change.

modifier, v.a. modify.

modiste, s.f. milliner.

moelleux, -euse, adj. soft, mellow.

mœurs, s. f. pl. manners, customs, ways.

moi, pron. me, to me.

moi-même, pron. myself.

moindre, adj. less, lesser, smaller; le ~ the least.

moineau, s. m. sparrow.

moins, adv. & s. m. less (que, de than); fewer (de than); minus; le ~ the least; à ~ que unless; au ~ at least.

mois, s. m. month; par ~ monthly; a month.

moisson, s.f. harvest, crop.

moissonner, v. a. harvest, reap.

moitié, s.f. half.

molécule, s. f. molecule.

mollet, s. m. calf (of leg).

moment, s. m. moment, instant.

mon, ma, pron. (pl. mes) my.

monarchie, s. f. monarchy

monastère, s. m. monastery, convent.

mondain, adj. worldly.

monde, s.m. world; people, company; mettre au ~ give birth to; tout le ~ everybody.

monnaie, *s.f.* money, coin, change; currency; ~ *légale* legal tender; ~ *étrangère* foreign currency.

monopole, *s.m.* monopoly.

monotone, *adj.* monotonous.

monseigneur, *s.m.* my lord, your lordship.

monsieur, *s. m.* gentleman; M. Mr.

monstrueux, -euse, *adj.* monstrous.

mont, *s. m.* mountain.

montage, *s. m.* carrying up; mounting, setting; wiring.

montagne, *s. f.* mountain.

montagneux, -euse, *adj.* mountainous.

montant, *adj.* ascending, uphill; en ~ upwards.

monte-charge, *s. m.* goods lift.

montée, *s. f.* rise, slope.

monter, *v.n.* go up, come up, ascend, climb; mount; ride; amount *(à* to); equip, fit up; ~ *à cheval* ride; *faire* ~ *qn. (dans sa voiture)* give s.o. a lift.

montre¹, *s.f.* watch.

montre², *s.f.* display, show; show-window.

montrer, *v.a.* show, display, point out; se ~ show oneself.

montueux, -euse, *adj.* hilly, steep.

monument, *s. m.* monument.

monumental, *adj.* monumental.

moquerie, *s. f.* mockery.

moral, *adj.* moral.

morale, *s. f.* ethics; morality.

moralité, *s. f.* morality, morals *(pl.).*

morceau, *s. m.* piece, morsel, bit; snack.

mordre, *v. a.* bite; gnaw.

mors, *s. m.* bit; *fig.* check.

mort, *s. f.* death; — *adj.* dead, lifeless.

mortel, -elle, *adj.* mortal; boring, tedious.

mot, *s. m.* word; short note; ~*s croisés* crossword (puzzle).

motel, *s. m.* motel.

moteur, *s. m.* motor, engine.

motif, *s. m.* motive; cause.

motion, *s.f.* motion, movement.

motocyclette, *s. f.* motor-(bi)cycle, motor-bike.

mou, mol, molle, *adj.* soft; loose.

mouche, *s. f.* fly.

moucher: se ~ blow one's nose.

mouchoir, *s. m.* handkerchief.

moudre*, *v.a.* grind.

mouette, *s.f.* gull.

mouiller, *v.a.* & *n.* soak, wet.

moule, *s. m.* mould, cast.

moulin, *s. m.* mill; ~ *à vent* windmill; ~ *à café* coffee-mill.

mourant, *adj.* dying, expiring.

mourir*, *v. n.* die, expire.

mousse, *s. f.* foam, froth, lather; moss.

moustache, *s. f.* moustache.

moustique, *s.m.* mosquito.

moutarde, *sf.* mustard.

mouton, *s.m.* sheep; mutton.

mouvement, *s. m.* movement, motion, move.

mouvoir*, *v.a.* move; start; se ~ move, stir.

moyen, -enne, *adj.* mean, middle, average; *le ~ âge* the Middle Ages; — *s. m.* means, way, manner; *au ~ de* by means of; *avoir les ~s de* can afford.

moyenne, *s. f.* average, mean; *en ~* on the average.

muet, -ette, *adj.* dumb, mute; speechless.

multiplication, *s. f.* multiplication.

multiplier, *v.a.&n.* multiply.

multitude, *s. f.* multitude, crowd.

municipal, *adj.* municipal, city.

munir, *v.a.* provide *(de* with).

munition, *s. f.* (am)munition.

mur, *s. m.* wall.
mûr, *adj.* ripe; mature.
mûrir, *v. a. & n.* ripen.
murmure, *s.m.* murmur.
murmurer, *v.n.* murmur.
muscle, *s.m.* muscle.
muse, *s. f.* muse.
museau, *s. m.* muzzle.
musician; — *adj.* musical.
musical, *adj.* musical.
musicien, -enne, *s. m. f.*
musique, *s.f.* music; *instrument de ~* musical instrument.
mutuel, -elle, *adj.* mutual.

myope, *adj.* short-sighted.
mystère, *s.m.* mystery.
mystérieux, -euse, *adj.* mysterious.
mystification, *s. f.* mystification.
mystique, *adj.* mystic.

N

nacre, *s.f.* mother-of-pearl.
nage, *s.f.* swimming; rowing, paddling.
nager, *v.n.* swim; float; row.
nageur, -euse, *s. m. f.* swimmer.
naïf, -ïve, *adj.* naïve.
nain, -e, *s. m. f.* dwarf.
naissance, *s. f.* birth; *lieu de ~* birth-place.
naître*, *v. n.* be born; arise (from).
nappe, *s.f.* table-cloth.
narine, *s.f.* nostril.
nasal, *adj.* nasal.
natal, *adj.* natal, native, birth.
natif, -ive, *adj. & s. m. f.* native.
nation, *s.f.* nation.
national, *adj.* national.
nationalité, *s.f.* nationality.
naturaliser, *v.a.* naturalize.
nature, *s.f.* nature.
naturel, -elle, *adj.* natural, native.
naturellement, *adv.* naturally, of course.
naufrage, *s. m.* shipwreck; *faire ~* be shipwrecked.
nausée, *s.f.* nausea.
nautique, *adj.* nautical.
naval, *adj.* naval.
navigateur, *s.m.* navigator.
navigation, *s.f.* navigation; sailing; *compagnie de ~* shipping company; *~ spatiale* space-flight.
naviguer, *v. a. & n.* navigate.
navire, *s.m.* ship; *~s*

shipping.

ne, n', *adv.* not; ~... *pas* not; ~ ... *que* only.

né, -e, *adj.* born; née.

nécessaire, *adj.* necessary.

nécessité, *s. f.* necessity.

nécessiter, *v.a.* necessitate, make necessary.

nef, *s. f.* ship, vessel; nave; ~ *latérale* aisle.

négatif, -ive, *adj. & s. m.* negative.

négative, *s. f.* negative.

négligence, *s. f.* neglect, negligence.

négligent, *adj.* negligent.

négliger, *v.a.* neglect.

négociant, -e, *s. m. f.* merchant, trader.

négociation, *s. f.* negotiation, transaction.

nègre, *s.m.* negro.

neige, *s.f.* snow.

neiger, *v.n.* snow.

neigeux, -euse, *adj.* snowy

néon, *s. m.* neon.

nerf, *s. m.* nerve; sinew.

nerveux, -euse, *adj.* nervous.

net, nette, *adj.* clean, neat, clear, tidy; net; — *adv.* flatly, point-blank.

nettoyage, *s. m.* cleaning, cleansing.

nettoyer, *v.a.* clean, cleanse, clear.

neuf¹, *adj. & s. m.* nine.

neuf², neuve, *adj.* new.

neutre, *adj.* neutral.

neuvième, *adj.* ninth.

neveu, *s.m.* nephew.

nez, *s.m.* nose.

ni, *conj.* ~ ... ~ (n)either ... (n)or; ~ *l'un* ~ *l'autre* neither (one).

nid, *s.m.* nest; berth.

nièce, *s.f.* niece.

nier, *v.a.* deny.

niveau, *s. m.* level.

noble, *adj.* noble.

noblesse, *s.f.* nobility.

noce, *s. f. (often pl.)* wedding; *(sing.)* revelry.

Noël, *s. m.* Christmas; *veillée de* ~ Christmas eve.

nœud, *s. m.* knot, bow, tie.

noir, *adj.* black.

noix, *s. f.* (wal)nut; ~ *de coco* coconut.

nom, *s. m.* name, surname; fame; noun; ~ *de famille* surname.

nombre, *s.m.* number.

nombreux, -euse, *adj.* numerous.

nomination, *s. f.* nomination, appointment.

nommer, *v. a.* name, give name to; appoint, nominate.

non, *adv.* no, not.

nonne, *s. f.* nun.

nord, *s. m.* north; *du* ~, *au* ~ northern.

nord-est, *s. m.* northeast.

nord-ouest, *s. m.* northwest.

normal, *adj.* normal.

norvégien, -enne (N.), *adj. & s. m. f.* Norwegian.

nos, *poss. adj.* our.

notable, *adj.* notable, remarkable.

notaire, *s. m.* notary (-public).

note, *s. f.* note, mark; bill; account; note *(music)*; ~ *(au bas de la page)* foot-note.

noter, *v.a.* note, jot down; notice.

notice, *s. f.* notice.

notion, *s. f.* notion, idea.

notre, *poss. adj.* our.

nôtre, *pron. poss.* ours, our own.

nourrir, *v.a.* nourish, feed.

nourriture, *s. f.* nourishment food.

nous, *pron.* we; us.

nous-mêmes, *pron.* our-selves.

nouveau, -el, -elle, *adj.* new; further; de ~ again.

nouvelle, *s.f.* news; short story.

novembre, *s. m.* November.

noyau *s.m.* stone, kernel; nucleus, core.

noyer¹, *v. a.* drown; se ~ be drowning; drown oneself.

noyer², *s. m.* walnut-tree.

nu, *adj.* naked, bare.

nuage, *s. m.* cloud.

nuageux, -euse, *adj.* cloudy, clouded.

nuance, *s. f.* shade, tint, nuance.

nucléaire, *adj.* nuclear.

nuire*, *v. n.* hurt, harm, be harmful.

nuit, *s. f.* night; *il (se) fait* ~ it is night, it is getting dark; de ~ by night; *la* ~ at night, *bonne* ~! good night!

nul, nulle, *adj.* not one, not any; null, nil; — *pron.* no one, nobody.

numéro, *s. m.* number, size; ticket; copy, issue.

nu-pied, *adv.* barefoot.

nylon, *s. m.* nylon.

O

obéir, *v.n.* obey.

obéissance, *s. f.* obedience.

objectif, -ive, *adj.* objective; — *s. m.* object, purpose; lens.

objection, *s. f.* objection.

objet, *s. m.* object, thing, article; purpose; ~

d'art work of art.

obligation, *s. f.* obligation.

obligatoire, *adj.* compulsory, obligatory.

obliger, *v.a.* oblige, compel.

obscur, *adj.* dark, dim.

obscurité, *s. f.* darkness, dimness; *dans l'*~ in the dark.

observation, *s. f.* observation; remark.

observer, *v. a. & n.* observe, watch; keep.

obstacle, *s. m.* obstacle; hindrance; bar.

obstine, *adj.* obstinate.

obtenir, *v. a.* obtain, get.

occasion, *s. f.* occasion, chance, event; *a l'*~ if need be, eventually; *d'*~ second-hand.

occidental, *adj.* western, occidental.

occupant, -e, *s. m. f.* occupier, occupant.

occupation, *s. f.* occupation; pursuit.

occupé, *adj.* occupied, busy, engaged; *non* ~ unoccupied.

occuper, *v.a.* occupy, employ; s'~ occupy oneself (de with), be engaged; think (de of).

occurrence, *s.f.* occurrence; *en l'*~ in this case.

océan, *s.m.* ocean.

octobre, *s.m.* October.

odieux, -euse, *adj.* odious.

œil, *s. m.* (*pl.* yeux) eye; sight; *coup d'*~ glance; *au premier coup d'*~ at first sight, at a glance; *ouvrez l'*~! look out!

œillet, *s.m.* carnation; eyelet.

œuf, *s.m.* egg; ~ *à la coque* boiled egg; ~s

brouillés scrambled eggs; ~s *durs* hard-boiled eggs; *blanc d'*~ white of egg; *jaune d'*~ egg-yolk.

œuvre, *s. f.* work; composition; ~ *d'art* work of art.

offense, *s. f.* offence, insult; trespass.

offenser, *v.a.* offend, shock, injure; s'~ take offence, be offended *(de* with), be angry.

office, *s.m.* office; service; post; agency; *exercer un* ~ hold an office.

officiel, **-elle**, *adj.* official.

officier, *s.m.* officer.

offre, *s. f.* offer, tender.

offrir*, *v. a.* offer, present, hold out; s'~ offer, propose oneself.

oh!, *int.* oh!, O!, indeed!

oie, *s.f.* goose.

oignon, *s. m.* onion; bulb.

oiseau, *s. m.* bird.

olympique, *adj.* Olympic; *les jeux* ~ the Olympic games.

ombre, *s.m.* shade; ghost; obscurity, darkness.

ombreux, **-euse**, *adj.* shady, shaded.

omelette, *s.f.* omelet.

omettre, *v. a.* omit.

omission, *s. f.* omission, oversight.

omnibus, *s. m.* bus; — *adj.* slow; *train* ~ slow train.

on, *pron.* one, we, people *(pl.);* you; they; somebody; some one; ~ *dit* they say, it is said, people say; *ferme!* closing time!

oncle, *s.m.* uncle.

onde, *s. f.* wave; undulation;

ondulation, *s. f.* undulation; waving.

onduler, *v. a. & n.* undulate, wave; ripple.

ongle, *s. m.* nail *(finger).*

onze, *adj. & s. m.* eleven; eleventh.

opéra, *s. m.* opera; opera-house; ~ *comique* comic opera.

opérateur, *s. m.* operator; cameraman.

opération, *s. f.* operation; *salle d'*~ operating-theatre.

opérer, *v. a. & n.* operate (on); *se faire* ~ undergo an operation.

opérette, *s.f.* operetta.

opinion, *s.f.* opinion.

opportun, *adj.* opportune, timely.

opposer, *v.a.* oppose.

opposition, *s. f.* opposition.

oppression, *s. f.* oppression.

opprimer, *v. a.* oppress.

optimiste, *adj.* optimistic; — *s. m. f.* optimist.

optique, *adj.* optic(al); — *s. f.* optics.

or, *s. m.* gold: *d'*~, *en* ~ golden.

orage, *s.m.* storm.

orange, *s.f.* orange.

orateur, *s.m.* speaker.

orbite, *s. f.* orbit.

orchestre, *s. m.* orchestra.

ordinaire, *adj.* ordinary, usual, common.

ordinairement, *adv.* usually, generally.

ordonnance, *s. f.* order; statute; prescription.

ordonner, *v.a.* order, command.

ordre, *s. m.* order, command; *mettre en* ~ arrange, clear up.

ordure, *s. f.* refuse, rubbish.

oreille, *s. f.* ear; hearing; *prêter l'~ à* listen to, lend an ear to.

oreiller, *s.m.* pillow.

organe, *s.m.* organ.

organique, *adj.* organic.

organisation, *s. f.* organization, arrangement.

organiser, *v. a.* organize.

organisme, *s. m.* organism, system.

orgue, *s.m.* organ.

orgueil, *s.m.* pride.

orient, *s. m.* the East; *de l'~* eastern.

oriental, *adj.* oriental, eastern.

original, *adj.* original.

origine, *s. f.* origin, source; *avoir ~* come from.

ornement, *s. m.* ornament, adornment.

orner, *v. a.* adorn, ornament, trim, decorate.

orphelin, -e, *s. m. f.* orphan.

orthographie, *s. f.* spelling.

os, *s. m.* bone.

osciller, *v.n.* oscillate.

oser, *v. a. & n.* dare, venture.

ôter, *v.a.* take away, take off, remove, pull off; *s'~* remove oneself.

ou, *conj.* or, either, else.

où, *adv.* where; whence; at which, in which; *n'importe ~* anywhere.

ouate, *s.f.* cotton-wool

oublier, *v. a. & n.* forget; overlook.

ouest, *s. m.* west; *à l'~* to, in the west, westward; *de l'~* western.

oui, *adv.* yes.

ouragan, *s. m.* hurricane.

ours, *s.m.* bear.

ourse, *s.f.* she-bear.

outil, *s.m.* tool.

outré, *adj.* exaggerated.

ouvert, *adj.* open; free; open-hearted; *à bras ~s* with open arms.

ouverture, *s. f.* opening; overtures *(pl.)*, proposal; overture.

ouvrage, *s. m.* (piece of) work.

ouvre-boîte, *s. m.* tin-opener.

ouvreuse, *s. f.* box-opener, attendant.

ouvrier, -ère, *s. m. f.* workman, worker; workwoman; hand; *premier ~* foreman.

ouvrir*, *v. a. & n.* open (up); break open; *s'~* be opened, open.

oxygène, *s. m.* oxygen.

P

pacifique, *adj.* pacific, peaceful; *l'Océan ~* the Pacific Ocean.

pacte, *s. m.* pact.

page¹, *s. f.* page; *être à la ~* be up to date.

page², *s. m.* page *(boy)*.

paiement *see* **payement.**

paille, *s. f.* straw, chaff.

pain, *s.m.* bread, loaf; cake, tablet.

pair¹, *adj.* equal, even; *au ~* at par; "au pair".

pair², *s. m.* peer.

paire, *s. f.* pair; couple.

paisible, *adj.* peaceful.

paître*, *v. a. & n.* graze, feed.

paix, *s. f.* peace; calm.

palais¹, *s. m.* palace.

palais², *s. m.* palate.

pâle, *adj.* pale.

paletot, *s. m.* overcoat.

pâleur, *s. f.* pallor.

pâlir, *v. n. & a.* (grow) pale.

palmier, *s.m.* palm-tree.

palpiter, *v.n.* palpitate.

pamphlet, *s.m.* pamphlet.

pamplemousse, *s. m.* grapefruit.

pan, *s. m.* flap; coat-tail.

panache, *s.m.* plume.

panier, *s. m.* basket.

panique, *s. f.* panic.

panne, *s.f.* break-down; power-cut.

panneau, *s. m.* panel.

panorama, *s. m.* panorama.

pansement, *s. m.* dressing, bandage.

pantalon, *s. m.* trousers *(pl.).*

pantoufle(s), *s. f. (pl.)* slipper(s).

papa, *s. m.* dad, daddy.

papauté, *s. f.* papacy.

pape, *s. m.* pope.

papeterie, *s. f.* paper-mill; stationery.

papetier, *s. m.* stationer.

papier, *s.m.* paper; ~ *hygiénique* toilet-paper; ~ *peint* wallpaper.

papillon, *s. m.* butterfly.

pâques, *s. m. pl.* Easter.

paquet, *s.m.* packet, parcel.

par, *prep.* by, by way of, by means of; across; through; per; for.

parade, *s. f.* parade, show.

paragraphe, *s. m.* paragraph.

paraître*, *v.n.* appear, come in sight; come out; *faire* ~ publish.

parallèle, *adj. & s. f.* parallel.

paralysie, *s. f.* paralysis.

paralytique, *s. m.f.* paralytic.

parapluie, *s. m.* unbrella.

paratonnerre, *s. m.* lightning-conductor.

parbleu, *int.* indeed!

parc, *s. m.* park; fold.

parce que, *conj.* because, on account of.

parcourir, *v.n.* travel through, go over; cover; run over, look over.

parcours, *s.m.* course, run; distance; mileage.

pardessus, *s. m.* overcoat.

par-dessus, *prep.* above.

pardon, *s. m.* pardon; *je vous demande* ~ *!* I beg your pardon!; pardon me!; excuse me!; ~? (I beg your) pardon?

pardonner, *v.a.* pardon.

pare-boue, *. s.m.* mudguard.

pare-brise, *s.m.* windscreen.

pare-choc, *s. m.* bumper.

pareil, -eille, *adj.* like, similar; such; same.

parent, *s. m. f.* relative, relation; ~s parents; relatives.

parer, *v. a.* adorn, trim; parry, ward off.

paresseux, -euse, *adj.* lazy, idle.

parfait, *adj. & s. m.* perfect.

parfaitement, *adv.* perfectly; ~ *!* quite so!

parfois, *adv.* sometimes.

parfum, *s. m.* perfume.

parfumer, *v. a.* perfume.

parfumerie, *s. f.* perfumery.

parier, *v. a.* bet, stake.

parisien, -enne, *adj. & s. m. f.* Parisian.

parlement, *s. m.* parliament.

parlementaire, *adj.* parliamentary.

parler, *v. n. & a.* speak, talk; — *s. m.* speech, utterance; parlance.

parmi, *prep.* among.

paroi, *s. f.* wall, partition.

paroisse, *s. f.* parish.

parole, *s. f.* speech, utterance; language; word.

parquet, *s. m.* parquet.

part, *s. f.* part, share; side; *prendre* ~ *à* take part in, participate; *faire* ~ *a* inform (of), let know; *à* ~ apart; *d'une* ~ ... *d'autre* ~ on the one hand ... on the other (hand).

partager, *v.a.* divide, share out; share.

partenaire, *s. m. f.* partner.

parterre, *s. m.* flower-bed; pit.

parti, *s. m.* party; side.

participant, -e, *s. m. f. & adj.* participant.

participation, *s. f.* participation, share.

participe, *s. m.* participle; ~ *passé* past participle.

participer, *v.n.* participate, take part (*à* in).

particulier, -ère, *adj.* particular, special, specific; peculiar; private; — *s. m. f.* private person; *en* ~ in particular.

partie, *s. f.* part; match, game; party; *en* ~ partly, in part.

partir*, *v. n.* start, leave, go (away), set out.

partisan, *s. m.* partisan, follower.

partition, *s. f.* score.

partout, *adv.* everywhere.

parure, *s. f.* ornament; set.

parvenir, *v. n.* attain (*à* to), reach.

pas[1], *s. m.* step, pace.

pas[2], *adv.* no, not, not any; ~ *du tout* not at all; ~ *nécessaire* unnecessary.

passage, *s. m.* passing; passage; corridor; crossing; thoroughfare. ~ *clouté* pedestrian crossing; ~ *à niveau* level-crossing; ~ *interdit* no thoroughfare.

passager, -ère, *adj.* passing, transient, fugitive; — *s. m. f.* passenger.

passant, -e, *adj. en* ~ by the way, cursorily; — *s. m. f.* passer-by.

passe, *s. f.* pass, passage; channel; permit.

passé, *adj.* past; — *prep.* after, beyond.

passeport, *s. m.* passport.

passer, *v. n. & a.* pass; pass along, by; cross; go on, pass on; hand; pass away; omit; forgive; strain; *en* ~ *par là* submit to it; ~ *un examen* take an examination; ~ *la nuit* spend the night; *se* ~ happen; disappear; do without.

passif, -ive, *adj.* passive — *s.m.* liabilities *(pl.)*.

passion, *s. f.* passion.

passionné *adj.* passionate.

pastel, *s. m.* pastel.

pastille, *s.f.* pastille.

pâte, *s. f.* paste; dough.

pâté, *s. m.* pie, pasty; block (of buildings); blot.

patente, *s.f.* patent, licence.

patience, *s. f.* patience.

patient, -e, *adj. & s. m. f.* patient.

patin, *s. m.* skate.

patinage, *s. m.* skating.

patiner, *v.n.* skate.

patinoire, *s.f.* skating-rink.

pâtisserie, *s.f.* pastry; pastry-shop, cake-shop.

pâtissier, -ère, s. m. f.
pastry-cook.
pâtre, s. m. shepherd.
patrie, s. f. country.
patriote, adj. patriotic; —
s. m. f. patriot.
patron[1], -onne, s. m. f.
patron; employer, boss.
patron[2], s. m. model, pattern.
patronage, s. m. patron-
age, support.
patronner, v. a. patronize,
protect.
patrouille, s. f. patrol.
patte, s. f. paw, foot.
pâture, s. f. fodder, pas-
ture.
paume, s. f. palm.
paupière, s. f. eyelid.
pause, s. f. pause, stop,
break; rest.
pauvre, adj. poor.
pauvreté, s. f. poverty.
pavé, s. m. paving-stone;
pavement; street.
paver, v. a. pave.
pavillon, s. m. pavilion,
summer-house; flag.
payable, adj. payable,
due.
paye, s.f. pay, wages pl.
payement, paiement, s. m.
payment.
payer, v.a. pay; pay
down, for, off; repay.
pays, s. m. country, land;
home; nation; district,
region.
paysage, s. m. landscape;
scenery.
paysan, -anne, s. m. f.
peasant, countryman;
countrywoman.
peau, s. f. skin; hide;
leather.
pêche[1], s. f. peach.
pêche[2], s. f. fishing; angling; ~ à la ligne
angling.
péché, s. m. sin, trespass.
pécher, v. n. sin, trespass.

pêcher, v. a. & n. fish,
angle.
pécheur, -eresse, s. m. f.
sinner.
pêcheur, s.m. angler,
fisher.
pécuniaire, adj. pecu-
niary.
pédagogie, s. f. pedagogy.
pédale, s. f. pedal.
pédant, adj. pedant.
pédicure, s. m. pedicure.
peigne, s. m. comb.
peigner, v. a. comb.
peignoir, s.m. wrapper,
dressing-gown.
peindre*, v.a. paint.
peine, s. f. punishment;
pain, grief; trouble.
peintre, s. m. painter.
peinture, s. f. painting.
pêle-mêle, adv. pell-mell,
in a muddle.
pelle, s. f. shovel, spade.
pellicule, s. f. film.
pelote, s. f. ball.
pelouse, s. f. lawn.
pelure, s. f. rind, peel.
pénalité, s. f. penalty.
penchant, s. m. slope,
slant; bent, liking.
pencher, v. a. & n. incline,
bend; stoop; lean (to-
wards).
pendant[1], adj. hanging,
pendent; — s. m. pend-
ant; match.
pendant[2], prep. during; ~
que while.
pendre, v. a. & n. hang
(up), suspend; hang
down; be hanging.
pendule, s. f. clock.
pénétrer, v. a. & n. pene-
trate, go through;
search; see through.
pénitence, s. f. penitence.
pensée, s.f. thought,
thinking; mind; pansy.
penser, v. n. & a. think.
pension, s.f. pension;
board (and lodging);

boarding-house; boarding-school; life annuity; ~ *et chambre(s)* board and lodging; ~ *pour étudiants* hostel.

pensionnaire, *s.m.f.* boarder; paying guest.

pensionnat, *s. m.* boarding-school.

pente, *s. f.* slope, descent; *en* ~ downhill.

Pentecôte, *s.f.* Whitsuntide; *dimanche de la* ~ Whit Sunday.

pépier, *v.n.* chirp.

pépin, *s. m.* pip, stone.

perçant, *adj.* piercing.

perception, *s.f.* perception.

percer, *v. a. & n.* pierce, bore; punch; tap.

percevoir, *v. a.* perceive, understand.

perdre, *v. a. & n.* lose; waste; be the ruin of; *se* ~ get lost, disappear; be ruined.

perdrix, *s. f.* partridge.

père, *s. m.* father.

perfection, *s.f.* perfection.

perforation, *s. f.* perforation.

perforer, *v.a.* perforate.

peril, *s.m.* peril, danger.

période, *s. f.* period, term.

périodique, *adj.* periodic, periodical.

périr, *v. n.* perish.

perle, *s. f.* pearl, bead.

permanent, *adj.* permanent.

permanente, *s. f.* perm.

permettre, *v.a.* allow, permit, let; *permettez-moi de* allow me to; *vous permettez?* may I?

permis, *s.m.* permit, licence.

permission *s. f.* permission, leave (of absence).

perron, *s. m.* stair, steps *(pl.)*.

perroquet, *s. m.* parrot.

persan, -e (P.), *adj. & s. m. f.* Persian.

persécuter, *v. a.* persecute.

persécution, *s. f.* persecution.

persil, *s. m.* parsley.

persister, *v.n.* persist.

personnage, *s. m.* personage, person.

personnalité, *s. f.* personality.

personne, *s.f.* person; *grande* ~ grown-up; — *pron.* any one; anybody; no one.

personnel, -elle, *adj.* personal; — *s. m.* personnel, staff.

perspective, *s. f.* perspective, prospect, outlook.

persuader, *v. a.* persuade, convince.

persuasion, *s. f.* persuasion, conviction.

perte, *s. f.* loss; ruin.

pertinent, *adj.* pertinent.

peser, *v. a.* weigh; ponder.

pessimiste, *s. m. f.* pessimist; — *adj.* pessimistic.

petit, *adj.* small, little.

petite-fille, *s.f.* granddaughter.

petit-fils, *s. m.* grandson.

pétition, *s.f.* petition, request.

petits-enfants, *pl.* grandchildren.

pétrole, *s.m.* petroleum.

peu, *adv. & s. m.* little, bit, few; ~ *à* ~ little by little, bit by bit; *un (petit)* ~ a (little) bit; *quelque* ~ somewhat; ~ *abondant* scanty; ~ *commun* unusual; ~ *confortable* uncomfortable; ~ *nécessaire* unnecessary.

peuple, s. m. people.

peur, s. f. fear; fright; avoir ~ (de) be afraid (of); de ~ que for fear that.

peut-être, adv. perhaps.

phare, s. m. lighthouse; headlight.

pharmacie, s.f. pharmacy, chemist's (shop).

pharmacien, -enne, s. m. f. chemist.

phase, s.f. phase.

phénomène, s. m. phenomenon.

philologie, s. f. philology.

philosophe, s. m. philosopher.

philosophie, s. f. philosophy.

philosophique, adj. philosophical.

phono(graphe), s.m. gramophone.

photo, s. f. photo, snap.

photographe, s.m. photographer.

photographie, s. f. photograph; photography.

photographier, v. a. photograph.

photographique, adj. photographic; appareil ~ camera.

phrase, s. f. phrase; sentence.

phtisie, s.f. consumption.

physicien, -enne, s. m. f. physicist.

physique, adj. physical; — s. f. physics; ~ nucléaire nuclear physics; — s. m. physique, constitution.

pianiste, s. m. f. pianist.

piano(forte), s. m. piano.

pièce, s. f. piece, part, bit, coin; play; room; joint.

pied, s. m. foot, leg; à ~ on foot; aller à ~ walk.

pierre, s. f. stone; rock.

piéton, s. m. pedestrian.

pieu, s. m. stake, post.

pieux, -euse, adj. pious.

pigeon, -onne, s. m. f. dove, pigeon.

pile, s. f. pile, heap; battery.

pilier, s. m. pillar, post, column.

piller, v. a. & n. pillage.

pilot, s. m. pile.

pilote, s. m. pilot.

piloter, v.a. pilot, guide.

pilule, s. f. pill.

pin, s. m. pine(-tree).

pince, s. f. pinch; pincers, pliers, tongs (pl.).

pincer, v. a. pinch.

pipe, s. f. pipe.

piquant, adj. pungent, sharp; piquant.

pique, s. f. pike; s. m. (cards) spade.

pique-nique, s. m. picnic.

piquer, v. a. & n. prick, sting; lard; goad, spur.

piqûre, s. f. prick, sting; puncture; injection.

pirate, s. m. pirate.

pire, adj. worse.

pis, adv. worse.

piscine, s. f. swimming-pool.

piste, s. f. track; trace; runway.

pistolet, s. m. pistol.

pitié, s.f. pity.

placard, s. m. placard, poster; cupboard.

place, s. f. place; room; seat; square.

placement, s. m. placing; investment; bureau de ~ labour-exchange.

placer, v. a. place, put, set; invest; sell.

plafond, s. m. ceiling.

plage, s. f. beach.

plaider, v. a. & n. plead.

plaindre, v. a. pity, feel compassion for; se ~ complain.

plaine, s. f. plain.

plainte, s. f. complaint.

plaire*, v. n. please; vous plaît-il de? would you like to?; s'il vous plaît (if you) please; se ~ take pleasure, enjoy.

plaisant, adj. pleasant, pleasing.

plaisanterie, s.f. joke,jest; par ~ as a joke.

plaisir, s. m. pleasure.

plan, s. m. plan; design; plane.

planche, s.f. board, plank.

plancher, s. m. floor.

planer, v. a. plane.

plante, s. f. plant; sole.

planter, v. a. plant; set.

planteur, s. m. planter.

plaque, s. f. plate; slab; plaque; ~ de police number-plate.

plaquer, v. a. plate; lay on.

plastique, adj. plastic; — s. f. plastic art; fig-ure; — s. m. plastics pl.

plastron, s. m. (shirt-)front; plastron; stiff shirt.

plat, adj. flat; plain; dull; — s. m. flat (part); blade.

plateau, s.m. tray; scale (of balance); plateau.

plate-bande, s. f. flower-bed.

plate-forme, s.f. plat-form.

plâtre, s. m. plaster.

plein, adj. full; filled; en ~ fully, entirely.

pleurer, v. n. cry, weep.

pleuvoir: il pleut it rains.

pli, s. m. fold, crease.

pliant, adj. flexible, pliant; folding.

plier, v. a. & n. fold (up), bend; se ~ submit (à to).

plisser, v. a. & n. plait, fold, tuck; wrinkle.

plomb, s.m. lead.

plombage, s. m. filling.

plombier, s. m. plumber.

plonger, v. a. & n. plunge, immerse, dip, dive.

pluie, s. f. rain.

plume, s. f. feather, plume, pen.

plupart, s. f. most, the greatest part, majority.

pluriel, s. m. plural.

plus, adv. more, most; further, longer; any more; de ~ en ~ more and more; en ~ de in addition to; ne . . .~ no more, no longer.

plusieurs, adj. several, many, some, a few; — pron. several people.

plutôt, adv. rather, pref-erably.

pluvieux, -euse, adj. rain-y, wet.

pneu(matique), s. m. tyre.

pneumonie, s. f. pneu-monia.

poche, s.f. pocket; pouch.

poêle[1], s. m. stove.

poêle[2], s. f. frying pan.

poème, s. m. poem.

poésie, s. f. poetry; poesy.

poète, s. m. poet.

poétique, adj. poetic(al).

poids, s. m. weight.

poignant, adj. poignant.

poigne, s. f. grip, grasp.

poignée, s. f. handle; hilt; handful.

poignet, s. m. wrist; cuff.

poil, s. m. hair; bristle; coat.

poinçon, s.m. punch, bodkin.

poinçonner, v. a. punch, clip; stamp.

poing, s.m. fist.

point, s. m. point, dot; full stop; deux ~s co-lon; ~ et virgule semi-colon; à ~ just in time; être sur le ~ de be about

to; ~ *de vue* point of view.
pointe, *s. f.* point, head, tip.
pointer, *v. a. & n.* point.
pointu, *adj.* sharp, pointed.
poire, *s. f.* pear.
pois, *s. m.* pea.
poison, *s. m.* poison.
poisson, *s. m.* fish.
poissonnier, -ère, *s. m. f.* fishmonger.
poitrine, *s. f.* chest, breast.
poivre, *s. m.* pepper.
pôle, *s. m.* pole.
poli, *adj.* polished; polite.
police, *s. f.* police; policy; *agent de* ~ policeman.
policier, *s. m.* policeman.
policlinique, *s.f.* out-patients' department.
polir, *v. a.* polish, refine.
politesse, *s. f.* politeness.
politicien, -enne, *s. m. f.* politician.
politique, *s. f.* politics.
polonais, -e (P.), *adj.* Polish; — *s. m.* Pole; *s. f.* Polish woman; polonaise.
pomme, *s. f.* apple; ~ *de terre* potato.
pommier, *s. m.* apple tree.
pompe¹, *s. f.* pomp, ceremony.
pompe², *s. f.* pump; ~ *à incendie* fire-engine; ~ *à essence* petrol pump.
pompier, *s. m.* fireman; *les* ~s fire-brigade.
ponctuel, -elle, *adj.* punctual.
pont, *s. m.* bridge; deck; ~ *suspendu* suspension-bridge; ~ *inférieur* lower deck.
populaire, *adj.* popular; vulgar, common.
popularité, *s. f.* popularity.
population, *s. f.* population.

populeux, -euse, *adj.* populous.
porc, *s. m.* pig, hog; pork.
porcelaine, *s. f.* porcelain, china(ware).
pore, *s. m.* pore.
poreux, -euse, *adj.* porous.
port¹, *s.m.* harbour (sea-)port; *arriver à bon* ~ arrive safely.
port², *s. m.* bearing, gait; carriage; postage; ~ *payé* postage paid.
portable, *adj.* portable.
porte, *s. f.* door(way), entrance; ~ *d'entrée* front-door.
porte-cigarettes, *s. m. pl.* cigarette-case.
portée, *s. f.* litter; range, scope; *à* ~ within reach.
portemanteau, *s.m.* coat-stand; suit-case.
porter, *v. a. & n.* bear; carry; convey; wear, have on; hold; ~ *intérêt* yield interest; show interest; ~ *la santé de B* drink B's health; *se* ~ be worn, be carried; *comment vous portez-vous?* how are you?
porteur, *s. m.* porter, carrier; bearer.
portier, -ère, *s. m. f.* porter, door-keeper.
portière, *s. f.* door (on vehicle); (door-)curtain.
portion, *s. f.* portion, part, share; helping.
portrait, *s. m.* portrait.
portugais, -e (P.), *adj. & s. m. f.* Portuguese.
posemètre, *s. m.* light-meter.
poser, *v. a. & n.* place, lay down, put; state.
positif, -ive, *adj. & s. m. f.* positive.
position, *s.f.* position, situation; attitude.

posséder, *v.a.* possess.

possession, *s.f.* possession; property.

possibilité, *s.f.* possibility.

possible, *adj.* possible; *faire tout son* ~ do one's best.

postal, *adj.* postal; post; *carte* ~e post-card.

poste[1], *s. f.* post(-office), mail; *mettre à la* ~ post (a letter); *bureau de* ~ post-office; *timbre* ~ stamp; ~ *aérienne* air-mail.

poste[2], *s. m.* post, station, office; police-station; receiver, set; ~ *de T. S. F.* wireless-set.

postulant, -e, *s. m. f.* applicant, candidate.

pot, *s. m.* pot, can, jug, vessel, pitcher.

potager, *s.m.* kitchen garden.

poteau, *s. m.* post.

poterie, *s. f.* pottery.

potin, *s. m.* noise; (piece of) gossip.

poubelle, *s. f.* dustbin.

pouce, *s.m.* thumb.

pouding, *s.m.* pudding.

poudre, *s. f.* powder, dust.

poudrier, *s. m.* compact.

poule, *s.f.* hen; fowl.

poulet, *s.m.* chicken, fowl.

pouls, *s. m.* pulse.

poumon, *s. m.* lung(s).

poupée, *s. f.* doll.

pour, *prep.* for; ~ *cent* per cent; ~ *que* in order that.

pourboire, *s. m.* tip.

pourquoi, *conj. & adv.* why; what for; for what reason.

poursuite, *s. f.* pursuit, chase; ~s suit, action.

poursuivre, *v. a.* pursue, chase, prosecute.

pourtant, *adv.* however, still.

pourvoir, *v. n. & a.* provide (*à* for), supply, cater (*à* for).

pousser, *v. a. & n.* push; shove; urge; impel; grow; utter.

poussière, *s. f.* dust

poussiéreux, -euse *adj.* dusty.

pouvoir*, *v. a. & n.* be able, may; *se* ~ be possible; *cela se peut* that may be; — *s. m.* power.

pratique, *s. f.* practice, execution; experience; customers (*pl.*); — *adj.* practical, convenient.

pratiquer, *v. a.* practise, carry out; exercise.

préalable, *adj.* previous, *au* ~ first of all.

précédent, *adj.* precedent, previous; — *s. m.* precedent.

précéder, *v. a. & n.* precede; come before.

prêcher, *v. a. & n.* preach.

prêcheur, *s. m.* preacher.

précieux, -euse, *adj.* precious, valuable, costly.

précipice, *s. m.* precipice.

précipitation, *s.f.* precipitation, haste, hurry.

précipité, *adj.* hasty.

précipiter, *v.a.* precipitate; hasten, hurry.

précis, *adj.* exact, precise; — *s. m.* summary.

préciser, *v.a.* specify.

prédécesseur, *s. m.* predecessor.

prédire, *v.a.* foretell.

préfabriqué, *adj.* prefabricated.

préface, *s.f.* preface.

préférable, *adj.* preferable, better.

préférer, *v.a.* prefer; like

better.

préfet, *s.m.* prefect.

préjugé, *s. m.* prejudice, presumtion.

prélat, *s.m.* prelate.

préliminaire, *adj.* preliminary.

premier, -ère, *adj.* first, former; ~ *plan* foreground; close-up; *de* ~ *ordre* first-rate; ~ — *s. m.* first floor.

première, *s. f.* first night; first class (in a carriage).

prendre*, *v. a.* take, take up, seize; receive, accept; put on, wear; charge; catch; ~ *place* take a seat: *à tout* ~ on the whole; ~ *pour* mistake for; ~ *du corps* put on weight; ~ *l'air* take a walk; se ~ be taken, be caught.

prénom, *s. m.* Christian name.

préoccuper, *v. a.* preoccupy, engross; worry; se ~ trouble oneself.

préparatifs, *s.m.pl.* preparations.

préparation, *s. f.* preparation.

préparer, *v. a.* prepare, make ready; read for; se ~ prepare oneself, get ready.

préposition, *s. f.* preposition.

prérogative, *s. f.* prerogative, privilege.

près, *adv. & prep.* near, close by, close to; nearly; *à peu* ~ nearly (so); *de* ~ closely.

prescription, *s. f.* prescription.

prescrire*, *v. ι.* prescribe.

présence, *s. f.* presence, attendance; *en* ~ *de*

in the presence of.

présent[1], *s. m.* present, gift; *faire* ~ *de* give as a present.

présent[2], *s. m.* present (time); present tense; — *adj.* present, current *à* ~ at present; *jusqu'à* ~ till now, as yet; *pour le* ~ for the time being.

présentation, *s. f.* presentation, introduction.

présenter, *v. a.* present, offer; introduce; se ~ appear.

préserver, *v. a.* preserve.

président, *s. m.* president.

présomption, *s. f.* presumption; concéit.

presque, *adv.* almost.

pressant, *adj.* pressing.

presse, *s. f.* press; printing-press; haste; crowd.

pressé, *adj.* pressing; *être* ~ be in a hurry.

pressentiment, *s. m.* presentiment; misgiving.

pressentir, *v.a.* have a presentiment of.

presser, *v. a.* press, crush; hurry; *pressez-vous!* hurry up!; se ~ hurry (up).

pression, *s.f.* pressure.

pressurer, *v.a.* press, squeeze; oppress.

prestige, *s.m.* marvel; influence, prestige.

présumer, *v. a.* suppose, expect; presume.

prétendre, *v. a. & n.* pretend, claim; intend.

prétention, *s.f.* pretension, claim.

prêter, *v.a.* lend, attribute; se ~ lend oneself (*à* to).

prétexte, *s. m.* pretext.

prêtre, *s. m.* priest.

preuve, *s. f.* proof; *faire*

~ *de* show.
prévaloir, *v .n.* prevail.
prévenir, *v. a.* anticipate, inform, let know.
préventif, -ive, *adj.* preventive.
prévention, *s.f.* bias, prejudice.
prévision, *s. f.* prevision, anticipation; forecast.
prévoir, *v.a.* foresee, anticipate, forecast.
prévoyance, *s. f.* foresight.
prier, *v. a.* pray, beg; ask.
prière, *s.f.* prayer; request.
primaire, *adj.* primary.
prime, *adj.* first, early.
primer, *v. a.* surpass, excel; award a prize to.
primeur, *s. f.* early vegetables *(pl.)*.
primitif, -ive, *adj.* primitive, original.
prince, *s. m.* prince.
princesse, *s. f.* princess.
principal, *adj.* principal.
principalement, *adv.* principally, mainly.
principe, *s. m.* principle.
printemps, *s. m.* spring-(time); *au* ~ in spring.
priorité, *s.f.* priority.
prise, *s.f.* taking; capture, catch; ~ *de courant* (electric) plug.
prisme, *s. m.* prism.
prison, *s. f.* prison.
prisonnier, -ère, *s. m. f.* prisoner.
privation, *s. f.* privation.
privé, *adj.* private.
priver, *v. a.* deprive.
privilège, *s. m.* privilege.
prix, *s. m.* price, cost, charge; prize; *au* ~ *de* at the cost of; ~ *de la course* fare; ~ *par mille* mileage; ~*courant* market-price; ~ *fixe* fixed price.

probabilité, *s. f.* probability.
probable, *adj.* probable.
probablement, *adv.* probably.
problématique, *adj.* problematic(al).
problème, *s. m.* problem.
procédé *s. m.* proceeding.
procéder, *v. n.* proceed.
procédure, *s. f.* procedure.
procès, *s.m.* (law-)suit, trial; *faire un* ~ *à* bring an action against.
procession, *s.f.* procession.
prochain, *adj.* near(est), next. — *s. m.* neighbour
prochainement, *adv.* shortly, soon.
proche, *adj.* near, neighbouring, close at hand.
proclamer, *v. a.* proclaim.
procurer, *v. a.* procure.
procureur, *s. m.* attorney.
prodigieux, -euse, *adj.* wonderful, prodigious.
producteur, -trice, *s. m. f.* producer; — *adj.* producing.
production, *s. f.* production.
produire*, *v. a.* produce, bring forth, yield.
produit, *s. m.* produce; product.
professer, *v. a. & n.* profess; teach.
professeur, *s. m.* teacher; professor; lecturer.
profession, *s.f.* profession.
professionnel, -elle, *adj. & s. m. f.* professional.
profil, *s. m.* profile.
profit, *s. m.* profit, gain.
profitable, *adj.* profitable.
profiter, *v. n.* profit (by).
profond, *adj.* deep, profound.

profondeur, *s. f.* depth; *dix pieds de* ~ ten feet deep.

programme, *s. m.* program(me); scheme.

progrès, *s. m.* progress, improvement; *faire des* ~ make progress.

prohiber, *v.a.* prohibit.

projecteur, *s. m.* headlight; searchlight; projector.

projectile, *s. m.* projectile, missile.

projection, *s. f.* projection.

projet, *s. m.* project, plan; scheme; ~ *de loi* bill.

projeter, *v.a.* project throw; scheme, plan.

prolonger, *v.a.* prolong.

promenade, *s.f.* walk; promenade.

promener: se ~ *go* for a walk; *se* ~ *en voiture* go for a drive.

promesse, *s. f.* promise.

promettre, *v. a.* promise.

promotion, *s. f.* promotion.

prompt, *adj.* prompt.

pronom, *s. m.* pronoun.

prononcer, *v.a.* &*n.* pronounce; utter; deliver.

prononciation, *s. f.* pronunciation; delivery.

propagande, *s. f.* propaganda.

propager, *v.a.* propagate.

prophète, *s.m.f.* prophet.

prophétie, *s. f.* prophecy.

proportion, *s. f.* proportion; ratio.

propos, *s. m.* talk, remark; *à* ~ in good time; by the way.

proposer, *v.a.* propose, offer.

proposition, *s. f.* proposal, proposition.

propre, *adj* own, peculiar; proper, fit.

propriétaire, *s.m.f.* owner, proprietor; landlord, landlady.

propriété, *s. f.* ownership; property.

propulsion, *s. f.* propulsion; ~ *à réaction* jet propulsion.

prosaïque, *adj.* prosaic.

proscrire*, *v. a.* proscribe.

prose, *s. f.* prose.

prospectus, *s.m.* prospectus.

prospère, *adj.* prosperous.

prospérer, *v. n.* prosper, get on (well).

prospérité, *s.f.* prosperity.

protecteur, *s. m.* protector, patron.

protection, *s.f.* protection, support.

protéger, *v.a.* protect; patronize.

protestant, -e, *s. m. f.* & *adj.* Protestant.

protestation, *s.f.* protest(ation).

protester, *v. n.* & *a.* protest.

prouver, *v.a.* prove.

provenir, *v.n.* come (from), issue, arise.

province, *s. f.* province, country, district.

provincial, *adj.* provincial, country.

provision, *s. f.* provision.

provisoire, *adj.* provisional, temporary.

provoquer, *v. a.* provoke; stir up.

proximité, *s.f.* proximity.

prudence, *s. f.* prudence, caution.

prudent, *adj.* prudent, cautious.

prune, *s. f.* plum.

pruneau, *s. m.* prune.

prunelle, *s. f.* pupil.

psaume, s. m. psalm.

psychologie, s. f. psychology.

psychologique, adj. psychological.

public, publique, adj. public, common; — s. m. public, audience.

publication, s.f. publication.

publicité, s. f. publicity.

publier, v. a. publish.

puce, s. f. flea.

puer, v. n. stink.

puéril, adj. childish.

puis, adv. then, after that.

puiser, v. a. draw up, fetch up.

puisque, conj. as, since.

puissance, s.f. power, might, force.

puissant, adj. powerful, strong; tout~ almighty.

puits, s. m. well; pit.

punaise, s. f. drawing-pin; bug.

punch, s.m. punch (drink).

punir, v. a. punish.

punition, s.f. punishment.

pupille, s.m.f. ward, pupil; — s. f. pupil (of the eye).

pupitre, s. m. desk.

pur, adj. pure, clean.

purée, s. f. mash, purée.

purement, adv. purely, merely.

pureté, s. f. purity.

purgatif, -ive, adj. & s. m. purgative.

purger, v. a. purge.

purifier, v.a. purify, cleanse.

puritain, -e, adj. & s. m. f. Puritan.

pyramide, s. f. pyramid.

Q

quai, s. m. quay; wharf; platform; billet de ~ platform ticket.

qualification, s. f. qualification.

qualifié, adj. qualified.

qualifier, v.a. qualify.

qualité, s.f. quality.

quand, adv. & conj. when; while; ~ même all the same.

quant à, prep. as for, with regard to.

quantité, s. f. quantity; amount; ~ de plenty of.

quarante, adj. & s. m. forty.

quart, s.m. quarter, fourth part; quart.

quartier, s. m. quarter; piece, slice; district; ~ général headquarters (pl.).

quatorze, adj. & s.m. fourteen.

quatre, adj. &s.m. four; fourth.

quatre-vingt-dix, adj. & s. m. ninety.

quatre-vingts, adj. & s. m. eighty.

quatrième, adj. & s. m. fourth; fourth floor; — s. f. third form.

quatuor, s. m. quartet(te).

que, qu', rel. pron. whom, which, that; of which, at which; — adv. how much, how many; — conj. that; than; as; if; as though.

quel, quelle, adj. what, which.

quelque, adj. some, any; a few; ~ chose something, anything; ~ part somewhere; ~ peu somewhat — adv. about, some.

quelquefois, adv. sometimes.

quelqu'un, -e, pron.

somebody; anybody.

querelle, *s. f.* quarrel·

quereller, *v. a. & n.* quarrel with.

question, *s.f.* question; point, matter, issue.

questionner, *v.a.* question, interrogate.

queue, *s.f.* tail; rear; queue; handle.

qui, *rel. pron.* who, whom; which; that; *à* ~ to whom.

quille, *s. f.* keel, skittle.

quincaillerie, *s. f.* hardware (shop).

quintal, *s. m.* hundredweight.

quinze, *adj. & s. m.* fifteen; fifteenth; ~ *jours* fortnight.

quittance, *s. f.* receipt.

quitte, *adj.* quit, free.

quitter, *v. a.* leave, give up, quit.

quoi, *rel. pron.* what, which; *à propos de* ~ what is it about?; ~ *qu'il en soit* at any rate.

quoique, *conj.* (al)though.

quotidien, -enne, *adj. & s. m.* daily.

R

rabais, *s. m.* reduction in price, rebate.

rabaisser, *v. a.* lower.

rabattre, *v.a.* beat down, pull down; reduce.

raccommoder, *v. a.* mend, repair.

raccourcir, *v.a. & n.* shorten, abridge.

raccrocher, *v.a.* hang up again.

race, *s. f.* race; stock; breed.

racine, *s. f.* root; *prendre* ~ take root.

raconter, *v.a.* tell, relate.

radar, *s. m.* radar.

radiateur, *s. m.* radiator.

radiation *s. f.* radiation.

radical, *adj.* radical.

radieux, -euse, *adj.* radiant, beaming.

radio, *s. f.* radio.

radio-actif, -ive, *adj.* radioactive.

radiodiffuser, *v.a.* broadcast.

radiodiffusion, *s. f.* broadcasting.

radiogramme, *s. m.* X-ray photograph; radiogram.

radiographie, *s. f.* X-ray photograph(y).

radioreportage, *s. m.* running commentary.

radioscopie, *s. f.* radioscopy.

radioscopique, *adj. examen* ~ X-ray examination.

radis, *s.m.* radish.

raffermir, *v.a.* strengthen, fortify.

raffinage, *s.m.* refining.

raffiné, *adj.* refined.

raffinement, *s. m.* refinement.

raffiner, *v. a.* refine.

rafraîchir, *v. a.* refresh, cool; *se* ~ cool down.

rafraîchissement, *s.m.* refreshment; ~s refreshments.

rage, *s.f.* rage, fury.

ragoût, *s. m.* ragout, stew.

raide, *adj.* stiff, rigid.

raidir, *v. a.* make stiff.

raifort, *s.m.* horse radish.

rail, *s. m.* rail.

railler, *v.a.* mock, rail at.

raillerie, *s.f.* raillery, mocking.

raisin, *s. m.* grape(s);

~ *sec* raisin.

raison, *s.f.* reason; judgement; *à* ~ *de* at the rate of; *avoir* ~ be right.

raisonnable, *adj.* reasonable.

raisonnement, *s. m.* reasoning.

raisonner, *v. n. & a.* reason, argue.

ralentir, *v. a. & n.* slow down.

ramasser, *v.a.* gather up, pick up; take up.

rame, *s. f.* oar; prop.

ramener, *v.a.* bring back, take back.

ramer, *v. n.* row.

rampe, *s.f.* banister; footlights *(pl.)*.

ramper, *v.n.* crawl, creep.

rance, *adj.* rancid.

rancune, *s.f.* spite, grudge.

randonneur, -euse, *s. m. f.* excursionist, hiker.

rang, *s.m.* row, line; rank.

rangé, *adj.* tidy.

rangée, *s.f.* row, line, range.

ranger, *v. a.* put in order; arrange; range; se ~ settle down; make room.

ranimer, *v.a.* revive, restore to life, refresh.

râpe, *s.f.* rasp, grater.

râpé, *adj.* shabby.

rapide, *adj.* rapid, fast; steep.

rapidité, *s.f.* rapidity, speed.

rappel, *s.m.* recall.

rappeler, *v. a.* recall, call back; bring back; se ~ remember.

rapport, *s.m.* product, yield; report, account; connection, relation; reference; *sous ce* ~ in this respect.

rapporter, *v.a.* bring back; produce, yield; report, state; se ~ relate to, refer to.

rapprochement, *s. m.* drawing closer.

rapprocher, *v. a.* bring closer; se ~ draw nearer.

raquette, *s. f.* racket.

rare, *adj.* rare.

raser, *v. a.* shave, graze; pull down; bore; *v.n.* se ~ shave.

rasoir, *s. m.* razor; ~ *électrique* electric razor; ~ *de sûreté* safety razor.

rassembler, *v. a.* gather, assemble, collect.

rassis, *adj.* settled; stale.

rassurer, *v.a.* reassure, comfort.

rat, *s. m.* rat.

râteau, *s. m.* rake.

ratelier, *s. m.* rack; set of false teeth.

rater, *v. n. & a.* miss fire; fail.

ratification, *s. f.* ratification.

ration, *s. f.* ration.

rattacher, *v.a.* tie up again, join.

rattraper, *v.a.* catch again; catch up; overtake.

rauque, *adj.* hoarse.

ravager, *v. a.* ravage, lay waste.

ravir, *v. a.* delight.

ravissant, *adj.* ravishing, charming.

rayer, *v. a.* scratch (out); cross out.

rayon, *s.m.* ray, beam; spoke; radius; shelf.

rayonnement, *s. m.* radiation; radiance.

rayonner, *v.n.* radiate, shine.

razzia, s. f. raid.
réacteur, s.m. reactor.
réactoin, s.f. reaction.
réagir, v.n. react.
réalisation, s.f. realization; carrying out.
réaliser, v.a. realize.
réaliste, adj. realistic.
réalité, s. f. reality; en ~ in fact.
rebelle, adj. rebellious; — s. m. f. rebel.
rébellion, s. f., rebellion.
rebord, s.m. edge, brim.
rébus, s.m. riddle.
récemment, adv. recently, lately.

récent, adj. recent.
récepteur, s. m. receiver.
réception, s. f. reception, receipt; at-home.
recette, s.f. receipt; recipe.
receveur, s.m. receiver; conductor (bus).
recevoir*, v.n. receive; admit, take in; accept; v. n. entertain; aller ~ qn. à la gare meet s.o. at the station.
rechange, s. m. pièces de ~ spare parts.
recharge, s. f. refill.
réchaud, s.m. dish-warmer.
réchauffer, v. a. warm up again.
recherche, s.f. research; inquiry.
rechercher, v. a. look for, search for; research into.
récipé, s.m. recipe.
réciproque, adj. reciprocal, mutual.
récit, s. m. recital, account.
récital, s. m. recital.
récitation, s. f. recitation.
réciter, v.a. recite.
réclamation, s. f. claim, complaint.
réclame, s. f. advertisement; faire de la ~ (pour) advertise.
réclamer, v.a. demand, claim.
recommandation, s. f. recommendation.
recommander, v. a. recommend; introduce; request; register.
recommencer, v. a. & n. begin again.
récompense, s. f. reward.
récompenser, v. a. reward, repay.
réconcilier, v. a. reconcile.
reconnaissance, s. f. recognition, gratitude.
reconnaître, v. a. recognize, know; acknowledge; explore.
reconstruction, s. f. reconstruction.
reconstruire*, v.a. rebuild.
record, s.m. record (sport etc.).
recourir, v. n. ~ à have recourse to.
recouvrir, v.a. cover again, hide.
récréation, s. f. recreation, amusement, pastime.
recrue, s. f. recruit.
recteur, s.m. rector, chancellor.
rectifier, v.a. rectify, correct.
reçu, s. m. receipt; au ~ de on receipt of.
recueil, s. m. collection.
recueillir, v.a. collect; se ~ collect oneself.
reculer, v.a. put back; v. n. draw back, recoil.
rédacteur, -trice, s. m. f. editor; writer.
rédaction, s. f. drawing up; composition; editorial staff.

rédemption, s. f. redemption.

rédiger, v.a. draw up; edit.

redingote, s.f. frock-coat.

redire, v. a. repeat, say again; trouver à ~ à find fault with.

redoubler, v.a. redouble.

redoutable, adj. formidable, dreaded.

redouter, v.a. dread, be afraid of.

redresser, v. a. & se ~ straighten (up).

réduction, s. a. reduction, cut.

réduire*, v. a. reduce, cut down.

réduit, adj. reduced.

réel, réelle, adj. real, actual.

réélection, s.f. re-election.

réélire, v. a. re-elect.

refaire, v.a. do (over) again.

réfectoire, s. m. refectory, dining-hall.

référence, s. f. reference.

référer, v. a. refer; se ~ à refer to; nous référant à referring to.

réfléchir, v.a. reflect; consider, think over.

réflecteur, s. m. reflector.

reflet, s. m. reflection.

refléter, v. a. reflect.

réflexe, adj. reflex.

réflexion, s. f. reflection, consideration.

reflux, s. m. ebb.

réformation, s.f. reformation.

réforme, s.f. reform, improvement.

Réforme, s. f. Reformation.

réformer, v. a. reform.

refrain, s. m. refrain.

refréner, v. a. bridle, curb.

réfrigérateur, s.m. refrigerator.

réfrigérer, v. a. refrigerate.

refroidir, v. a. chill, cool.

refuge, s. m. refuge; lay-by.

réfugié, -e, s. m. f. refugee.

réfugier: se ~ take shelter, take refuge.

refus, s. m. refusal, denial.

refuser, v. a. refuse, deny; ~ de connaître ignore; être refusé fail.

regagner, v.a. regain, recover; return to.

regard, s. m. look.

regarder, v. a. look at; concern; regard.

régime, s. m. (form of) government; diet.

régiment, s. m. regiment.

région, s. f. region, area.

régional, adj. local.

régir, v.a. rule, administer.

régisseur, s. m. steward; stage-manager.

registre, s.m. register; record.

règle, s. f. rule; ruler.

réglé, adj. regular; punctual; steady; ruled.

règlement, a.m. rule, regulation.

régler, v. a. rule; regulate; time; settle.

règne, s.m. reign.

régner, v.a. reign.

regret, s. m. regret.

regretter, v. a. regret, be sorry for.

régulariser, v. a. regularize.

régularité, s. f. regularity.

régulateur, s. m regulator.

régulier, -ière, adj. regular; correct.

rein, s.m. kidney.

reine, *s.f.* queen.
reine-claude, *s. f.* green-gage.
rejeter, *v. a.* reject, throw out.
rejoindre, *v.a.* rejoin; overtake, catch up; se ~ meet.
réjouir, *v. a.* give joy to, cheer up, delight; se ~ rejoice.
relâche, *s. f.* relaxation; respite.
relâcher, *v.a.* slacken, loosen; relax; se ~ relax.
relatif, -ive, *adj.* relative; ~ à relating to.
relation, *s.f.* relation, connection; report; *entrer en ~ avec* get in touch with.
relever, *v. a.* lift, take up, pick up; set off; *v. n.* recover.
relief, *s.m.* relief.
relier, *v. a.* bind (a book); hoop (casks).
religieux, -euse, *adj.* religious; — *s. m.* monk; *s. f.* nun.
religion, *s.f.* religion.
relique, *s.f.* relic.
relire, *v.a.* read (over) again.
remarquable, *adj.* remarkable, noticeable.
remarque, *s. f.* remark, observation, notice.
remarquer, *v. a.* remark, notice, observe; *faire ~* point out.
rembourser, *v.a.* repay, reimburse.
remède, *s.m.* remedy; medicine.
remerciement, *s.m.* thanks *(pl.)*.
remercier, *v.a.* thank *(de* for).
remettre, *v. a.* put back; put on again; post-

pone; se ~ recover (oneself).
remilitariser, *v. a.* rearm.
remise, *s. f.* remittance; delivery; allowance; revival, restoration.
remonter, *v. n. & a.* go up, remount; bring up again; set up again.
remords, *s. m.* remorse.
remorque, *s. f.* tow(ing), trailer.
remorqueur, *s. m. (bateau)* ~ tug-boat.
remous, *s. m.* eddy(-water), whirl.
remplacer, *v. a.* replace, substitute.
remplir, *v. a.* fill; fill up; fulfil; carry out.
remporter, *v.a.* take away, carry off; get, obtain.
remuer, *v. a. & n.* move, fidget about; se ~ be busy, move.
rémunération, *s. f.* remuneration.
renaissance, *s. f.* renascence; revival; *la Renaissance* the Renaissance.
renaître, *v.n.* be born again, revive.
renard, *s.m.* fox.
rencontre, *s. f.* meeting, encounter; collision.
rencontrer, *v.a.* meet, meet with; come across; run into; se ~ *avec* meet, be met with.
rendement, *s. m.* output.
rendez-vous, *s. m.* appointment, rendezvous.
rendormir: se ~ go to sleep again.
rendre, *v.a.* give back, return; yield; render; convey; ~ *un arrêt* issue a decree; ~ *compte* render an account, realize; ~ *visite*

pay a visit.

renfermer, *v. a.* lock up again, confine; contain, include.

renfler, *v.a.&n.* swell.

renforcer, *v. a.* strengthen, reinforce.

renfort, *s. m.* reinforcement; help.

renier, *v. a.* deny.

renom, *s.m.* reputation.

renommée, *s. f.* renown.

renoncer, *v.n.&a.* renounce, give up.

renouveler, *v.a.* renew, renovate.

renseignement, *s. m.* information; indication; *bureau des ~s* inquiry office.

renseigner, *v. a.* give information to; se ~ inquire, ask *(sur about).*

rente, *s. f.* income; rent.

rentrée, *s. f.* return; re-opening.

rentrer, *v. n.* reenter, go in; get back, return home.

renversé, *adj.* reversed, upset.

renverser, *v.a.* upset; overthrow; turn upside down; **se ~** be upset, tip over.

renvoi, *s.m.* return; (cross-)reference.

renvoyer, *v.a.* return; dismiss; refer.

réorganiser, *v.a.* reorganize.

répandre, *v.a.* pour; spread, scatter, diffuse.

réparation, *s.f.* repair, amends.

réparer, *v. a.* repair, mend; make up for.

repartir*, *v.a.* answer.

repas, *s. m.* meal.

repasser, *v. n.* pass again.

répéter, *v. a.* repeat; say again; rehearse.

répétition, *s. f.* repetition; rehearsal.

réplique, *s. f.* retort, reply, answer.

répliquer, *v. a. & n.* reply, answer.

répondre, *v. a. & n.* answer, reply; respond to.

réponse *s.m.* answer; response; ~ *payée* reply paid.

reporter, *v. a.* carry back, take back.

repos, *s. m.* rest; *sans* ~ restless.

reposer, *v. a.* lay again; *v. n.* rest, lie.

repoussant, *adj.* repulsive.

repousser, *v. a.* push back; repulse; drive back.

reprendre, *v.a. & n.* take back, get back; take up, go on; ~ *sa parole* go back on one's word.

représentant, -e, *s. m. f.* representative.

représentation, *s. f.* show, production; performance; display; representation.

représenter, *v. a.* represent; show, display.

reprise, *s.f.* renewal.

reproche, *s. m.* reproach, blame.

reprocher, *v. a.* reproach (with); blame for.

reproduction, *s.f.* reproduction.

reproduire*, *v. a.* reproduce.

républicain, -e, *adj. & s. m. f.* republican.

république, *s. f.* republic.

répulsion, *s.f.* repulsion.

réputation, *s. f.* reputation.

requête, *s.f.* request,

demand.

réserve, s.f. reserve; reservation; caution; de ~ spare; *mettre en* ~ lay by.

réserver, v. a. reserve, lay by; book (in advance).

réservoir, s.m. tank *(petrol etc.)*.

résidence, s. f. residence, dwelling.

résident, s. m. résident.

résignation, s. f. resignation; submission.

résigner, v. a. resign; se ~ *à* resign oneself, make up one's mind.

résistance, s. f. resistance.

résister, v. n. resist.

résolu, adj. resolute.

résolution, s. f. resolution.

résonance, s. f. resonance.

résonner, v. n. resound, ring.

résoudre*, v.a. resolve; solve; settle; se ~ resolve, make up one's mind (to).

respect, s. m. respect.

respectable, adj. respectable, decent.

respecter v. a. respect.

respectif, -ive, adj. respective.

respectueux, -euse, adj. respectful.

respiration, s. f. respiration, breath(ing).

respirer, v. n. & a. breathe.

responsabilité, s. f. responsibility.

responsable, adj. responsible.

ressaisir, v. a. seize again.

ressemblance, s. f. resemblance, likeness.

ressemblant, adj. like, similar.

ressembler, v emble.

ressentiment, s. m. resentment, grudge.

ressentir, v.a. feel; resent; se ~ be hurt; feel still.

resserrer, v.a. tighten; bind.

ressort, s.m. spring; energy.

ressortir, v. n. come out again; stand out.

ressource, s. f. resource.

restaurant, s. m. restaurant; ~ *à libre service* self-service restaurant.

restaurateur, -trice, s. m. f. restorer; restaurant keeper.

restauration, s.f. restoration.

restaurer, v. a. restore.

reste, s. m. rest, remainder.

rester, v. n. remain, be left, keep; ~ *en arrière,* lag behind.

restituer, v. a. restore.

restreindre*, v. a. restrict.

restriction, s. f. restriction.

résultat, s.m. result, issue; *avoir pour* ~ result in.

résulter, v. n. result *(de* from).

résumé, s.m. summing up.

résumer, v.a. sum up.

rétablir, v.a. restore.

retard, s. m. delay; *être en* ~ be late; be overdue.

retarder, v.a. delay, retard.

retenir, v.a. keep back, hold back; hinder.

retirer, v.a. draw back, pull back; extract, get, derive; se ~ retire.

retomber, v. n. fall again, fall back; relapse.

retour, s. m. return; *en* ~ homeward bound; *être*

de ~ be back.

retourner, *v. n.* turn back; return, go back; se ~ turn round.

retracer, *v.a.* retrace; relate, tell.

retraite, *s.f.* retreat; retirement; *mettre à la* ~ superannuate.

retrancher, *v. a.* retrench.

rétrécir, *v.a.* contract; make narrower; shrink.

retrousser, *v. a.* turn up.

retrouver, *v. a.* find again, recover.

rétroviseur, *s. m.* (rear-vision) mirror.

réunion, *s.f.* reunion.

réunir, *v.a.* reunite; join again.

réussi, *adj.* successful.

réussir, *v. n.* succeed.

réussite, *s. f.* success.

revanche, *s. f.* revenge; return match; *en* ~ in return.

rêve, *s. m.* dream.

réveil, *s. m.* waking.

réveille-matin *s. m.* alarm-clock.

réveiller, *v.a.* & se ~ wake (up).

révéler, *v.a.* reveal; se ~ come to light.

revenir, *v. n.* return, come back; recur; cost.

revenu, *s. m.* income.

rêver, *v. n.* dream.

révérence, *s. f.* reverence; curtsey.

révérend, *adj.* reverend.

rêverie, *s.f.* reverie, fancy.

revers, *s. m.* back, reverse, wrong side.

revêtir, *v.a.* put on; clothe; cover.

révision, *s. f.* revision.

revivre, *v. n.* live again; *faire* ~ revive.

revoir, *v. a.* see again, look over; *au* ~ good-bye (for the present).

révolte, *s. f.* revolt.

révolter, *v. a.* revolt; se ~ revolt, rebel.

révolution, *s. f.* revolution; turn.

révolutionnaire, *adj.* & *s. m. f.* revolutionary.

revolver, *s. m.* revolver.

revue, *s. f.* review; magazine.

rez-de-chaussé, *s. m.* ground floor.

rhétorique, *s. f.* rhetoric.

rhum, *s. m.* rum.

rhumatisme, *s. m.* rheumatism.

rhume, *s. m.* cold (in the head).

ricaner, *v. n.* sneer, grin.

riche, *adj.* rich, well off.

richesse, *s.f.* wealth, riches *(pl.).*

ride, *s. f.* wrinkle.

rideau, *s. m.* curtain.

rider, *v. a.* wrinkle.

ridicule, *adj.* ridiculous; — *s. m.* ridicule.

rien, *pron.* nothing; not ... anything; trifle.

rigoureux, -euse, *adj.* rigorous, severe.

rigueur, *s. f.* rigour.

rime, *s. f.* rhyme.

rincer, *v. a.* rinse.

rire*, *v. n.* laugh; *pour* ~ for fun; — *s.m.* laugh(ing), laughter.

risque, *s. m.* risk.

risquer, *v.a.* risk, run the risk of.

rivage, *s. m.* beach, shore.

rival, -e, *adj.* & *s. m. f.* rival.

rivalité, *s. f.* rivalry.

rive, *s. f.* bank, shore, beach.

rivière, *s. f.* river, stream.

riz, *s. m.* rice.

robe, *s. f.* gown, dress,

frock; robe; ~ *de chambre* dressing-gown.

robinet, *s. m.* tap, cock.

robuste, *adj.* robust; strong, sturdy.

roc, *s. m.* rock.

roche, *s.f.* rock, boulder.

rocher, *s. m.* rock, crag.

roder, *v. a.* run in.

rôder, *v.n.* rove.

rogner, *v. a.* clip, pare.

rognon, *s. m.* kidney.

roi, *s. m.* king.

rôle, *s. m.* roll; part, rôle.

romain, -e (R.), *adj. & s. m. f.* Roman.

roman, *s. m.* novel; ~s fiction.

romancier, -ère, *s. m. f.* novelist.

romanesque, *adj.* romantic.

romantique, *s. m.* romantic.

romantisme, *s. m.* romanticism.

rompre, *v. a. & n.* break.

rond, *adj.* round; — *s. m.* round, circle.

ronde, *s. f.* round; patrol; *à la* ~ round about, around.

rondelle, *s. f.* ring, collar, washer.

ronfler, *v. n.* snore; roar.

ronger, *v.a.* gnaw, eat.

rose, *s. f.* rose; — *adj.* rosy, pink.

roseau, *s. m.* reed.

rosée, *s. f.* dew.

rosier, *s.m.* rose-tree, rose-bush.

rossignol, *s. m.* nightingale.

rôti, *s. m.* roast (meat).

rôtir, *v.a.* roast; toast; *faire* ~ roast, bake.

roucouler, *v. n.* coo.

roue, *s.f.* wheel; ~ *de secours* spare wheel; ~ *dentée* cog-wheel.

rouge, *adj.* red; — *s. m.* red (colour); *bâton de* ~ lipstick.

rougeur, *s.f.* redness, blush.

rougir, *v.n. & a.* turn red, make red; blush.

rouille, *s. f.* rust.

rouiller, *v. n. & a.* rust, get rusty.

roulage, *s.m.* rolling; carriage (of goods); haulage.

rouleau, *s.m.* roll; roller; scroll.

roulement, *s. m.* roll(ing), rotation; ~ *a billes* ball-bearings.

rouler, *v. a. & n.* roll; roll up, wind up; turn, revolve.

roulotte, *s.f.* ~ *(de camping)* caravan.

roumain, -e (R.), *adj. & s. m. f.* Rumanian.

route, *s. f.* road; highway; course; way; *en* ~ on the way; *en* ~ *pour* bound for; *code de la* ~ highway code.

routine, *s. f.* routine.

roux, rousse, *adj.* red(dish).

royal, *adj.* royal.

royaliste, -e, *adj. & s. m. f.* royalist.

royaume, *s. m.* kingdom.

ruban, *s m.* ribbon; band.

rubis, *s m.* ruby.

ruche, *s. f.* hive.

rude, *adj.* rough, rude.

rue, *s. f.* street; ~ *barrée* no thoroughfare; ~ *de traverse* crossroad.

ruée, *s. f.* rush.

ruelle, *s. f.* lane.

ruer; se ~ rush, dash.

rugissement, *s. m.* roar.

ruine, *s. f.* ruin; wreck.

ruiner, *v.a.* ruin, destroy.

ruisseau, *s. m.* stream, brook; gutter.

ruisseler, *v.n.* stream, run, flow.

rumeur, *s. f.* noise; rumour.

ruminer, *v. a. & n.* ruminate, chew (the cud).

rupture, *s. f.* rupture.

ruse, *s. f.* craft, cunning.

rusé, *adj.* cunning, sly.

russe (R.), *adj. & s. m. f.* Russian.

russien, -enne (R.), *adj. & s. m. f.* Russian.

rustique, *adj.* rustic, rural.

rythme, *s. m.* rhythm.

rythmique, *adj.* rhytmical.

S

s' see se.

sa, *adj. poss.* his, her, its.

sable, *s. m.* sand.

sablonneux, -euse, *adj.* sandy.

sabre, *s. m.* sabre.

sac, *s. m.* bag, sack; ~ *a main* handbag; ~ *de couchage* sleeping-bag.

saccager, *v. a.* plunder.

sacré, *adj.* sacred, holy.

sacrement, *s. m.* sacrament.

sacrifice, *s.m.* sacrifice.

sacrifier, *v.a.* sacrifice.

sacristain, *s.m.* sexton.

sage, *adj.* wise, well-behaved.

sagesse, *s. f.* wisdom.

saignant, *adj.* bleeding; underdone.

saigner, *v. a. & n.* bleed.

saillant, *adj.* projecting.

saillir, *v. n.* stand out, project.

sain, *adj.* sound; ~ *et sauf* safe and sound.

saint, -e, *adj.* holy, sacred; — *s. m. f.* saint.

saisir, *v.a.* seize.

saison, *s. f.* season.

salade, *s. f.* salad.

salaire, *s. m.* wages *(pl.)*, pay, salary.

sale, *adj.* dirty, filthy.

saler, *v. a.* salt.

saleté, *s. f.* dirt.

salière, *s. f.* salt-cellar.

salir, *v. a.* soil, dirty.

salle, *s. f.* hall; assembly room; house; ~ *d'attente* waiting-room; ~ *de classe* schoolroom; ~ *(de cours)* auditorium; ~ *familiale, ~ de séjour* living-room.

salon, *s. m.* drawing-room; saloon; *petit* ~ sitting-room.

saluer, *v. a. & n.* bow to; greet.

salut, *s. m.* salvation; bow, greeting.

samedi, *s. m.* Saturday.

sanatorium, *s. m.* sanatorium.

sanction, *s. f.* sanction.

sanctuaire, *s. m.* sanctuary.

sandale, *s. f.* sandal.

sang, *s. m.* blood.

sanglier, *s. m.* wild boar.

sanitaire, *adj.* sanitary.

sans, *prep.* without.

santé, *s. f.* health.

sapin, *s. m.* fir(-tree).

sarcasme, *s. m.* sarcasm.

sarcastique, *adj.* sarcastic.

sardine, *s. f.* sardine.

satellite, *s. m.* satellite.

satire, *s. f.* satire.

satisfaction, *s. f.* satisfaction.

savoir*, *v. n.* know, be aware; be trained in; understand; be able to; — *s. m.* knowledge, learning.

savon, *s. m.* soap.

savourer, v. a. taste, relish.

savoureux, -euse, adj. savoury, tasty.

scandale, s. m. scandal.

scaphandre autonome, s. m. skin diver.

scaphandrier, s. m. diver.

scarabée, s. m. beetle.

sceau, s. m. seal.

sceller, v. a. seal; fix.

scénario, s. m. scenario.

scène, s. f. scène; scenery; fig. stage; mettre en ~ produce (a play).

sceptre, s. m. sceptre.

scie, s. f. saw.

satisfaire, v. a. & n. satisfy, please.

satisfaisant, adj. satisfactory.

satisfait, adj. satisfied.

sauce, s. f. sauce.

saucisse, s. f. sausage.

sauf, sauve, adj. safe; — prep. except, save.

saumon, s. m. salmon.

saut, s. m. jump, leap.

sauter, v. n. leap, jump; spring; faire ~ blow up.

sauvage, adj. savage, wild.

sauver, v. a. save, rescue; se ~ run away.

sauveur, s. m. Saviour.

savant, -e, adj. learned, clever; expert; — s. m. f. scholar.

saveur, s. f. savour, taste.

science, s. f. science, knowledge; homme de ~ scientist.

scientifique, adj. scientific.

scier, v. a. saw.

scolaire, adj. school; année ~ school year.

scooter, s. m. motorscooter.

scrupule, s. m. scruple.

sculpter, v. a. carve, sculpture.

sculpteur, s. m. sculptor.

sculpture, s. f. sculpture.

se, s' pron. himself, herself, itself; each other.

séance, s. f. sitting, meeting.

seau, s. m. pail.

sec, sèche, adj. dry, dried up.

sécher, v. a. & n. dry (up).

sécheresse, s. f. dryness.

second, adj. second.

secondaire, adj. secondary.

seconde, s. f. second.

seconder, v. a. back.

secouer, v. a. shake.

secourir, v. a. help.

secours, s. m. help, succour, aid; au ~ help!

secousse, s. f. shake, jolt, jerk.

secret, -ète, adj. & s. m. secret.

secrétaire, s. m. f. secretary; — s. m. writing-desk.

secrétariat, s. m. secretariate.

secteur, s. m. sector, section; ~ (de courant) mains.

section, s. f. section

sécurité, s. f. security.

sédatif, -ive, adj. & s. m. sedative.

sédiment, s. m. sediment.

séduire, v. a. seduce.

seigle, s. m. rye.

seigneur, s. m. lord, squire.

seize, adj. & s. m. sixteen; sixteenth.

seizième, adj. sixteenth.

séjour, s. m. stay, visit; (place of) residence.

séjourner, v. n. stay, sojourn.

sel, s. m. salt.

selle, s. f. saddle.

selon, *prep.* according to; after.

semaine, *s. f.* week.

semblable, *adj.* (a)like.

semblant, *s. m.* semblance; appearance.

sembler, *v. n.* appear, look, seem.

semelle, *s. f.* sole *(footwear)*.

semer, *v. a.* sow.

semestre, *s. m.* half year; semester.

séminaire, *s. m.* seminary.

sénat, *s. m.* senate.

sénateur, *s. m.* senator.

sens, *s. m.* sense; judgement, opinion; direction.

sensation, *s. f.* feeling; sensation.

sensé, *adj.* sensible, reasonable.

sensibilité, *s. f.* sensibility, feeling.

sensible, *adj.* sensible, perceptible; sensitive.

sentence, *s. f.* sentence.

senteur, *s. f.* scent, smell.

sentier, *s. m.* path.

sentiment, *s. m.* feeling, sense, sentiment.

sentimental, *adj.* sentimental.

sentinelle, *s. f.* sentry, sentinel.

sentir*, *v. a.* feel, perceive; experience; smell; se ~ feel.

séparation, *s. f.* separation.

séparer, *v. a.* separate, divide; se ~ part.

sept, *adj. & s. m.* seven; seventh.

septembre, *s. m.* September.

septième, *adj.* seventh.

sérénade, *s. f.* serenade.

sérénité, *s. f.* serenity.

sergent, *s. m.* sergeant.

série, *s. f.* series.

sérieux, -euse, *adj.* grave, serious.

serin, -e, *s. m. f.* canary.

seringue, *s. f.* syringe.

serment, *s. m.* oath.

sermon, *s. m.* sermon.

serpent, *s. m.* snake, serpent.

serpenter, *v. n.* wind, meander.

serre, *s. f.* claw; hothouse.

serré, *adj.* tight, close, serried.

serrer, *v. a.* press, crush, jam, tighten.

serre-tête, *s. m.* crash-helmet, headband.

serrure, *s. f.* lock.

serrurier, *s. m.* locksmith.

servante, *s. f.* servant.

service, *s. m.* service, duty; favour; set; *être de ~* be on duty; *à votre ~* at your disposal.

serviette, *s. f.* napkin; towel; briefcase.

servir*, *v. a. & n.* serve; be in the service of; *~ à* be used for; *ne se ~ à rien* be of no use; *Mme est servie* dinner is ready; se ~ use, make use of, help oneself.

serviteur, *s. m.* servent.

servitude, *s. f.* servitude.

ses, *adj. poss.* his, her, its; one's.

session, *s. f.* session.

seuil, *s. m.* threshold.

seul, *adj.* alone, single, sole, only.

sévère, *adj.* severe, hard.

sévir, *v. n.* punish; rage.

sexe, *s. m.* sex.

sexuel, -elle, *adj.* sexual.

shampooing, *s. m.* shampoo.

si, *conj,* if, whether; — *adv.* so, so much, such.

siècle, *s. m.* century.

siège, *s. m.* seat.

sien, -enne, *poss. adj.* his, hers; its; one's.

siffler, *v. n.* whistle, hiss.

sifflet, *s. m.* whistle.

signal, *s. m.* signal; ~ *d'alarme* communication-cord.

signaler, *v. a.* signal.

signalisation, *s. f.* signals *(pl.); feux de* ~ traffic-lights.

signature, *s. f.* signature.

signe, *s. m.* sign.

signer, *v. a. & n.* sign.

significatif, -ive, *adj.* significant.

signification, *s. f.* signification; meaning.

signifier, *v. a.* signify.

silence, *s. m.* silence.

silencieux, -euse, *adj.* silent.

silhouette, *s. f.* outline, silhouette.

sillon, *s. m.* furrow.

simple, *adj.* simple.

simplicité, *s. f.* simplicity.

simplifier, *v. a.* simplify.

simultané, *adj.* simultaneous.

sincère, *adj.* sincere.

sincérité, *s. f.* sincerity.

singe, *s. m.* monkey.

singulier, -ère, *adj.* singular, strange.

sinon, *conj.* (or) else, otherwise.

sire, *s. m.* sir, lord.

sirène, *s. f.* siren; hooter, fog-horn.

site, *s. m.* site, place.

sitôt, *adv.* as soon; ~ *que* as soon as; ~ . . . ~ no sooner. . . than.

situation, *s. f.* situation; state; office, position.

situer, *v. a.* place, locate.

six, *adj. & s. m.* six; sixth.

sixième, *adj.* sixth.

ski, *s. m.* ski; *faire du* ~ ski.

skieur, *s. m.* skier, ski-runner.

smoking, *s. m.* dinner-jacket.

sobre, *adj.* sober.

social, *adj.* social.

socialisme, *s. m.* socialism.

socialiste, *adj. & s. m. f.* socialist.

société, *s. f.* society; company; ~ *anonyme* limited liability company.

sœur, *s. f.* sister.

soi, *pron.* oneself; himself, herself; itself.

soi-disant, *adj.* so-called.

soie, *s. f.* silk.

soif, *s. f.* thirst; *avoir* ~ be thirsty.

soigner, *v. a.* take care of, look after.

soigneux, -euse, *adj.* careful.

soin, *s. m.* care; *prendre* ~ *de* take care of; *aux bons* ~s *de* c/o.

soir, *s. m.* evening.

soirée, *s. f.* evening (party).

soit, *conj.* say; suppose; either . . . or; ~ *que* whether.

soixante, *adj. & s. m.* sixty.

soixante-dix, *adj. & s. m.* seventy.

sol, *s. m.* soil; ground.

soldat, *s. m.* soldier.

soleil, *s. m.* sun; *il fait du* ~ the sun is shining.

solennel, -elle, *adj.* solemn.

solennité, *s. f.* solemnity.

solidarité, *s. f.* solidarity.

solide, *adj.* solid.
solidité, *s. f.* solidity.
solitaire, *adj.* solitary.
solitude, *s. f.* solitude.
solliciter, *v. a.* solicit, entreat.
sollicitude, *s. f.* care.
soluble, *adj.* soluble.
solution, *s. f.* solution.
sombre, *adj.* dark; dim.
sombrer, *v.n.* founder, sink.
sommaire, *adj. & s. m.* summary.
somme, *s. f.* sum, amount.
sommeil, *s. m.* sleep; *avoir ~* be sleepy.
sommeiller, *v. n.* slumber.
sommer, *v. a.* summon.
sommet, *s. m.* top, summit.
sommier, *s. m.* spring mattress.
somnifère, *s. m.* sleeping-pill.
somnolent, *adj.* sleepy.
son¹, sa, *adj. poss. (pl. ses)* his, her, its; one's.
son², *s. m.* sound.
songe, *s. m.* dream.
songer, *v. n.* dream.
sonner, *v. a. & n.* ring, sound; *on sonne (à la porte)* there is a ring at the door.
sonnette, *s. f.* bell.
sonore, *adj.* sonorous.
sorcier, *s. m.* sorcerer, wizard.
sorcière, *s. f.* witch, sorceress.
sornette, *s. f.* nonsense.
sort, *s. m.* fate, lot.
sorte, *s. f.* sort, kind.
sortie, *s. f.* going out; way out, exit; *~ secours* emergency exit.
sortir*, *v. n.* go out, walk out, leave; *ne pas ~* keep indoors; *v.a.* take out, bring out.
sot, sotte, *adj.* foolish, silly.
sottise, *s. f.* foolishness, nonsense.
sou, *s. m.* sou, copper, penny.
souci, *s. m.* care, concern.
soucier: se ~ de care for.
soucieux, -euse, *adj.* full of care, anxious.
soucoupe, *s. f.* saucer.
soudain, *adj.* sudden; — *adv.* suddenly.
soude, *s. f.* soda *(chemical)*.
souffle, *s. m.* breath.
souffler, *v.a. & n.* breathe; blow (out).
soufflet, *s. m.* box (on the ear); bellows *(pl.)*.
souffrance, *s. f.* pain, suffering.
souffrir*, *v. a. & n.* suffer, bear.
souhaiter, *v. a.* desire.
soulever, *v. a.* lift, raise; *se ~* rise (in rebellion).
soulier, *s. m.* shoe.
souligner, *v. a.* underline.
soumettre, *v. a.* submit, subdue; *se ~* submit.
soumission, *s. f.* submission.
soupçon, *s. m.* suspicion.
soupçonner, *v. a.* suspect.
soupe, *s. f.* soup.
souper, *s. m.* supper; — *v. n.* have supper.
soupir, *s. m.* sigh.
soupirer, *v. n.* sigh; *~ après* long for.
souple, *adj.* supple, flexible.
source, *s. f.* source, spring.
sourcil, *s. m.* eyebrow.
sourd, *adj.* deaf.
sourd-muet, sourde-muette, *adj. & s. m. f.* deaf and dumb (per-

son).

sourire, *v. n.* smile.

souris, *s. f.* mouse.

sous, *prep.* under; be-
neath; before.

souscripteur, *s. m.* subscriber.

souscription, *s. f.* subscription.

souscrire, *v. a. & n.*
sign, subscribe (to).

sousdéveloppé, *adj.* un-
der-developed.

sous-marin, *s. m.* sub-
marine.

soussigné, -e, *adj. & s.
m. f.* undersigned.

sous-sol, *s. m.* basement.

sous-titre, *s. m.* subtitle,
caption.

soustraction, *s. f.* subtraction.

soustraire, *v. a.* take
away; subtract.

soutenir, *v. a.* support,
sustain, maintain.

souterrain, *adj.* under-
ground; — *s. m.* sub-
way.

soutien, *s. m.* support.

soutien-gorge, *s. m.* bra.

souvenir*, *s. m.* remem-
brance; souvenir; mem-
ory; — *v. reflex.* se
~ remember.

souvent, *adv.* often.

souverain, -e, *s. m. f.*
sovereign.

spatial, *adj. vaisseau* ~,
véhicule ~ space-craft,
space-vehicle.

speaker, *s. m.* announcer.

speakerine, *s. f.* lady
announcer.

spécial, *adj.* special.

spécialement, *adv.* spe-
cially, particularly.

spécialiser, *v. a.* special-
ize.

spécialiste, *s. m. f.* specialist.

spécialité, *s. f.* special(i)-
ty.

spécifier, *v. a.* specify.

spécifique, *adj.* specific.

spectacle, *s. m.* spectacle,
sight.

spectateur, -trice, *s. m. f.*
spectator, spectatress,
onlooker; bystander.

spéculation, *s. f.* specu-
lation.

spéculer, *v. n.* speculate.

sphère, *s. f.* sphere.

spirale, *adj.* spiral.

spirituel, -elle, *adj.* spiritual; witty.

splendeur, *s. f.* splen-
dour.

splendide, *adj.* splendid.

spontané, *adj.* spontaneous.

sport, *s. m.* sport.

sportif, -ive, *adj.* sporting;
sportsmanlike.

squelette, *s. m.* skeleton.

stade, *s. m.* stadium;
fig. stage.

stalle, *s. f.* stall; box.

station, *s. f.* standing;
stay; station, stop; ~
balnéaire watering-
place, spa.

stationnement, *s. m.* sta-
tioning; parking; ~
interdit no parking.

stationner, *v. n.* stop;
park.

station-service, *s. f.* service-station.

statistique, *s. f.* statistics; — *adj.* statistical.

statue, *s. f.* statue.

statut, *s. m.* statute.

sténographie, *s. f.* shorthand.

stérile, *adj.* sterile.

stimuler, *v. a.* stimulate.

stipuler, *v.a.* stipulate.

store, *s. m.* (Venetian)
blind.

strabisme, *s. m.* squint-

(ing).

stratégie, s. f. strategy.

structure, s. f. structure.

studieux, -euse, adj. studious.

stupéfier, v. a. stupefy.

stupide, adj. stupid, dull.

stupidité, s. f. stupidity.

style, s. m. style.

stylo, s.m. ~ à bil'e ball(-point) pen.

stylo(graphe), s. m. fountain-pen.

suave, adj. soft, gentle.

subjonctif, s.m. subjunctive.

subjuguer, v.a. subjugate, overcome.

submerger, v. a. submerge, flood.

subordonné, adj. subordinate.

subordonner, v. a. subordinate.

subséquent, adj. subsequent.

subsistance, s. f. subsistence.

subsister, v. n. subsist.

substance, s. f. substance.

substantiel, -elle, adj. substantial.

substantif, s.m. substantive.

substituer, v.a. substitute.

substitution, s. f. substitution.

subtil, adj. subtle.

subvention, s. f. subvention, subsidy.

succéder, v. n. succeed (à to), follow; **se ~** follow one another.

succès, s. m. success; result.

success'', -ive, adj. successive.

succession, s. f. succession.

sucer, v. a. suck (in).

sucre, s. m. sugar.

sucré, adj. sweet(ened).

sud, adj. & s. m. south; du ~ southern; au ~ southward.

sud-est, adj. & s. m. south-east.

sud-ouest, adj. & s. m. south-west.

suédois, -e, (S.), adj. Swedish; — s. m. f. Swede; Swedish (language).

suer, v. n. & a. sweat.

sueur, s. f. sweat.

suffire*, v.n. be sufficient, be enough.

suffisamment, adv. sufficiently, enough.

suffisant, adj. sufficient, enough; conceited.

suffoquer, v.a. & n. suffocate, choke.

suggérer, v.a. suggest, propose.

suggestion, s. f. suggestion, hint.

suicide, s. m. suicide.

suisse (S.), adj. & s. m. (f. Suissesse) Swiss.

suite, s. f. retinue; suite, sequence, result; a la ~ after; tout de ~ at once, directly; par ~ consequently; par ~ de due to.

suivant, adj. following, next; — prep. according to.

suivre*, v.a. & n. follow; comme suit as follows; ce qui suit the following.

sujet, -ette, s. m. f. subject; s. m. subject.

superficie, s. f. surface, area.

superficiel, -elle, adj. superficial.

superflu, adj. superfluous.

supérieur, adj. superior, upper.

supériorité, *s. f.* superiority.

supermarché, *s. m.* supermarket.

supersonique, *adj.* supersonic.

superstitieux, -euse, *adj.* superstitious.

superstition, *s. f.* superstition.

suppléer, *v.a.* supply; substitute, do duty for; *v. n.* make up for.

supplément, *s. m.* supplement; extra charge; excess.

supplémentaire, *adj.* supplementary, extra.

suppliant, -e, *adj.* suppliant; — *s. m. f.* supplicant.

supplier, *v.a.* beseech.

support, *s.m.* prop; support.

supporter, *v.a.* bear, support.

supposer, *v. a.* suppose.

supposition, *s. f.* supposition, conjecture.

suppression, *s. f.* suppression.

supprimer, *v. a.* suppress, abolish, do away with.

suprême, *adj.* supreme.

sur, *prep.* on; over; concerning.

sûr, *adj.* certain, sure; secure, safe; *pour ~!* to be sure!

surcharger, *v.a. & n.* overload; weigh down.

sûrement, *adv.* surely, certainly.

sûreté, *s. f.* safety; security.

surface, *s.f.* surface.

surgir, *v. n.* arise, spring up, emerge.

surmonter, *v.a.* surmount, overcome.

surnaturel, -elle, *adj.* supernatural.

surpasser, *v. a.* surpass, outdo.

surpeuplé, *adj.* overcrowded.

surplus, *s.m.* surplus, excess.

surprendre, *v. a.* surprise.

surprise, *s.f.* surprise.

surseoir*, *v.n. & a.* postpone, delay, put off.

surtaxe, *s. f.* surtax.

surtout, *s. m.* overcoat.

surveillance, *s. f.* supervision.

surveiller, *v.a.* supervise.

survenir, *v. a.* arrive unexpectedly; happen, occur.

survivant, -e, *s.m.f.* survivor.

survivre, *v.n.* survive, outlive.

susceptible, *adj.* susceptible.

suspect, *adj.* suspicious, suspect.

suspendre, *v· a.* hang up; suspend.

suspension, *s. f.* suspension.

svelte, *adj.* slender, slim.

syllabe, *s. f.* syllable.

symbole, *s. m.* symbol.

symétrie, *s. f.* symmetry.

symétrique, *adj.* symmetrical.

sympathie, *s. f.* sympathy.

symphonie, *s.f.* symphony.

symptome, *s. m.* symptom.

synagogue, *s.f.* synagogue.

syndical, *adj.* trade.

syndicat, *s. m.* syndicate; trade-union; *~d'initiative* tourist information office.

synthétique, *adj.* synthetic(al).

systématique, *adj.* systematic.

système, *s. m.* system.

T

tabac, *s.m.* tobacco; *bureau de ~* tobacconist's (shop).

table, *s. f.* table; board; food; *~ des matières,* table of contents.

tableau, *s.m.* picture; scene; board, panel.

tablette, *s. f.* tablet.

tablier, *s.m.* apron; dash-board.

tabouret, *s. m.* stool.

tache, *s. f.* spot, stain; *sans ~* spotless.

tâche, *s. f.* task, job.

tacher, *v.a.* spot, stain.

tâcher, *v.n.* try.

tact, *s. m.* touch.

tactique, *s.f.* tactics.

taille, *s.f.* cut; height, stature, size; waist.

tailler, *v.a.* hew, trim; cut.

tailleur, *s. m.* tailor.

taire*, *v.a.* be silent about, conceal; *se ~* be quiet.

talent, *s. m.* talent, attainment(s).

talon, *s. m.* heel; counterfoil.

talus, *s. m.* slope, bank.

tambour, *s. m.* drum.

tamis, *s. m.* sieve.

tamiser, *v. a.* sift, sieve.

tampon, *s. m.* plug; tampon.

tamponner, *v. a.* plug.

tandis que, *conj.* whereas, while.

tangible, *adj.* tangible.

tant, *adv.* so much, so many, such, so.

tante, *s. f.* aunt.

tantôt, *adv.* shortly, by and by; *~ ... ~* now ... now.

tapage, *s. m.* noise, fuss.

taper, *v.a. & n.* tap, strike, knock; type.

tapis, *s. m.* carpet, rug.

tapisser, *v. a.* upholster.

tapisserie, *s. f.* tapestry.

tapissier, *s. m.* upholsterer.

tard, *adv.* late.

tarder, *v.n.* delay, put off; be long.

tardif, -ive, *adj.* late.

tarif, *s.m.* tariff, rate; price-list; fare.

tarte, *s. f.* tart.

tas, *s. m.* heap, pile; mass; crowd.

tasse, *s. f.* cup.

tâter, *v.a. & n.* feel, taste, handle.

tâtonner, *v.n.* grope.

taureau, *s.m.* bull.

taux, *s.m.* price, rate (of exchange); tax.

taverne, *s. f.* tavern.

taxe, *s. f.* tax.

taxer, *v. a.* tax, rate.

taxi, *s. m.* taxi; *station de ~s* taxi-rank.

tchèque (T.), *adj. & s. m. f.* Czech.

te, *pron.* you; to you.

technicien, -enne, *s. m. f.* technician.

technique, *adj.* technical; *s. f.* technique, technics.

technologie, *s. f.* technology.

teindre*, *v.a.* dye, stain.

teint, *s. m.* complexion; dye.

teinte, *s. f.* tint, shade.

teinter, *v. a.* tint.

teinture, *s. f.* dye; tincture.

teinturerie, *s.f.* dyeworks, dyer.

tel, telle, *adj.* such, like, similar.

télécommunication, *s.f.*
telecommunication.

téléférique, *s.m.* rope-
way.

télégramme, *s.m.* tele-
gram, wire.

télégraphe, *s.m.* telegraph.

télégraphie, *s.f.* tele-
graphy.

télégraphier, *v.a. & n.*
wire.

télégraphique, *adj.* tele-
graphic.

télémètre, *s.m.* range-
finder.

téléphone, *s.m.* tele-
phone.

télescope, *s. m.* telescope.

téléspectateur, -trice, *s.
m. f.* (tele)viewer.

téléviser, *v. a.* televise,
telecast.

téléviseur, *s.m.* tele-
vision-set.

télévison, *s. f.* television.

télex, *s. m.* telex.

tellement, *adv.* so (much).

témoigner, *v.a. & n.*
testify; give evidence.

témoin, *s.m.* witness;
testimony.

tempe, *s.f.* temple *(forehead)*.

tempérament, *s. m.* tem-
per(ament), constitu-
tion.

température, *s.f.* tem-
perature.

tempête, *s. f.* storm.

temple, *s. m.* temple,
church; chapel; lodge.

temporel, -elle, *adj.* tem-
poral, transient.

temps[1], *s. m.* time; opportunity; à ~ in time;
pendant ce ~ *l* in the
meantime; *en* ~ *voulu*
in due time; *combien
de* ~? how long?;
la plupart du ~ mostly;
de ~ *en* ~ at times.

temps[2], *s.m.* weather;
prévisions du ~
weather-forecast.

tenaille, *s.f.* pincers,
pliers, tongs *(pl.)*.

tendance, *s. f.* tendency,
trend.

tendon, *s.m.* tendon,
sinew.

tendre[1] [1]*adj.* tender, soft.

tendre[2], *v.a.* stretch;
strain; bend; hang.

tendresse, *s. f.* tenderness.

tendu, *adj.* tense, taut.

ténébreux, -euse, *adj.*
dark, gloomy, dismal.

tenir*, *v. a. & n.* hold; get
hold of; hold on; take,
contain; keep; se ~
stay, remain.

tennis, *s. m.* tennis.

tension, *s.f.* tension.

tentation, *s. f.* tempta-
tion.

tentative, *s. f.* attempt.

tente, *s. f.* tent.

tenter, *v.a.* attempt;
try; tempt.

ténu, *adj.* thin, slender.

tenue, *s. f.* holding; session; behaviour.

terme, *s. m.* term; expression; goal, aim.

terminer, *v. a.* terminate,
end, close; se ~ (come
to an) end.

terminus, *s. m.* terminus.

terne, *adj.* dull, dim.

terrain, *s. m.* soil, earth;
site; ground; ~ *de
jeux* sports-ground.

terrasse, *s.f.* terrace.

terre, *s.f.* earth, land.

terreur, *s.f.* fear.

terrible, *adj.* terrible.

terrifier, *v.a.* terrify,
frighten.

territoire, *s. m.* territory.

testament, *s.m.* will,
testament.

tête, *s. f.* head.

têtu, *adj.* stubborn.
texte, *s.m.* text; type.
textile, *s.m.* textile.
textuel, -elle, *adj.* textual.
texture, *s. f.* texture.
thé, *s. m.* tea.
théâtral, *adj.* theatrical.
théâtre, *s.m.* theatre, stage; drama; *pièce de* ~ play.
théière, *s. f.* tea-pot.
thème, *s. m.* theme, topic; prose.
théologie, *s. f.* theology.
théologique, *adj.* theological.
théorie, *s. f.* theory.
théorique, *adj.* theoretic, theoretical.
thermal, *adj.* thermal.
thermomètre, *s. m.* thermometer.
thermos, *s. f.* thermos.
thèse, *s. f.* thesis.
thon, *s. m.* tunny.
tien, -enne, *poss. adj.* yours.
tiers, tierce, *adj.* third; — *s.m.* third party.
tige, *s. f.* stem, stalk.
tigre, *s. m.* tiger.
tigresse, *s. f.* tigress.
timbre, *s. m.* bell; sound; (postage-)stamp.
timbre-poste, *s. m.* postage-stamp.
timide, *adj.* timid, shy.
timidité, *s. f.* timidity.
tir, *s.m.* shooting.
tirage, *s.f.* draught, pull(ing); impression; issue.
tire-bouchon *s. m.* corkscrew.
tirer, *v. a. & n.* draw, pull, drag; extract; derive; fire, shoot; print.
tiroir, *s.m.* drawer.
tison, *s.m.* brand.
tisonnier, *s.m.* poker.

tisser, *v.a.* weave.
tisserand, *s.m.* weaver.
tissu, *s. m.* texture, fabric; tissue.
titre, *s. m.* title; heading; right.
titrer, *v.a.* give a title to.
toast, *s. m.* toast.
toi, *pron.* you.
toile, *s. f.* linen; cloth.
toilette, *s.f.* dress, clothes *(pl.)*; dressing-table; *faire sa* ~ dress; *cabinet de* ~ dressing-room.
toison, *s. f.* fleece.
toit, *s. m.* roof.
tolérance, *s. f.* tolerance, toleration.
tolérer, *v.a.* tolerate, bear.
tomate, *s.f.* tomato.
tombe, *s. f.* tomb, grave.
tombeau, *s. m.* tomb.
tombée, *s.f.* fall.
tomber, *v.n.* fall, fall down; tumble; decay; ~ *sur* meet, run into; *faire* ~ push down; *laisser* ~ drop.
tome, *s. m.* volume.
ton[1], ta, *poss. adj. (pl.* tes) your.
ton[2], *s. m.* tone; colour; manner.
tondeuse, *s.f.* lawn-mower.
tondre, *v.a.* shear, clip, mow.
tonnage, *s. m.* tonnage.
tonne, *s. f.* barrel, tun; ton.
tonneau, *s.m.* barrel.
tonner, *v.n.* thunder.
tonnerre, *s.m.* thunder-(bolt).
toqué, *adj.* crazy.
torche, *s. f.* torch.
torcher, *v.a.* wipe, rub.
torchon, *s.m.* duster; dish-cloth.
tordre, *v. a.* twist, wring

(out).

torpille, *s. f.* torpedo.

torrent, *s. m.* torrent.

tort, *s. m.* wrong, harm, injury; *avoir* ~ be wrong.

tortue, *s. f.* tortoise.

torture, *s. f.* torture.

torturer, *v. a.* torture.

tôt, *adv.* soon, quickly; early.

total, *adj.* total, whole.

totalement, *adv.* totally, entirely.

touchant, *prep.* about.

touche, *s. f.* touch; key; hit.

toucher, *v. n. & a.* touch; feel; strike, hit; concern; — *s. m.* touch; feeling.

touffe, *s. f.* tuft.

toujours, *adv.* always, ever; still.

toupet, *s. m.* tuft, lock.

tour[1], *s.f.* tower.

tour[2], *s.m.* turn; tour, trip; feat, trick; (turning-)lathe; revolution; ~ ~ in turns; *à son* ~ in turn; *faire le* ~ *de* go round.

tourelle, *s. f.* turret.

tourisme, *s. m.* tourism; touring; *faire du* ~ *à pied* hike.

touriste, *s. m. f.* tourist, hiker.

tourment, *s. m.* torment, torture.

tourmenter, *v. a.* torment; se ~ worry.

tournant, *adj.* turning; — *s. m.* turn(ing).

tourné, *adj.* turned; sour.

tournée, *s. f.* tour, walk; circuit.

tourner, *v. a.* turn, twist, wind; turn round; *v. n.* turn, revolve; turn out; turn sour.

tournevis, *s.m.* screwdriver.

tournoi, *s.m.* tournament.

tournure, *s.f.* shape, figure; turn; cast; appearance.

tous *see* tout.

tousser, *v.n.* cough.

tout, -e, *adj. (pl.* **tous, toutes)** all, every, any, whole, full; ~ *le monde* everybody; ~ *son possible* one's utmost; *à* ~*e force* at any cost; — *adv.* wholly, entirely; ~ *coup* suddenly; ~ *fait* thoroughly; ~ *de suite* directly; ~ *à l'heure* just now; ~ *au moins* at least; — *pron. & s.m.* everything, all; *pas du* ~ not at all.

toutefois, *adv.* yet, nevertheless, however.

tout-puissant, *adj.* almighty.

toux, *s. f.* cough.

tracas, *s. m.* bustle, stir; worry.

tracasser, *v. n. & a.* worry, bother; fuss; se ~ worry.

trace, *s. f.* trace, track; footprint.

tracer, *v. a.* trace, draw; lay out.

tracteur, *s. m.* tractor.

traction, *s.f.* traction, pull.

tradition, *s. f.* tradition.

traditionnel, -elle, *adj.* traditional.

traducteur, -trice, *s. m. f.* translator.

traduction, *s. f.* translation.

traduire*, *v. a.* translate.

trafic, *s. m.* traffic; trade, commerce.

trafiquer, *v.n.* traffic;

trade, deal.

tragédie, s. f. tragedy.

tragédien, -enne, s. m. f. tragedien.

tragique, adj. tragic.

trahir, v. a. betray; deceive, mislead.

trahison, s. f. treason, treachery.

train, s.m. pace, rate; train; ~ couloir corridor-train; ~ direct through train; ~ de marchandises goods train.

traîne, s.f. train (of a dress).

traîneau, s. m. sledge.

traîner, v.a. drag, draw; lead (to); delay; v.n. drag; lie about; lag behind.

train-poste, s.m mail-train.

traire*, v.a. milk.

trait, s.m. arrow; dart; flash; line; trait, feature.

traite, s.f. journey; stretch; export; draft, bill.

traité, s. m. treaty.

traitement, s. m. treatment; usage; reception; salary.

traiter, v.a. treat, use, deal with; call; entertain.

traître, s. m. traitor; — adj. treacherous.

trajet, s.m. passage, journey, course, crossing.

tram, s.m. tram(-car).

trammer, v. a. weave; plot; devise.

tramway, s. m. tram.

tranchant, adj. sharp, keen.

tranche, s. f. slice, chop, steak.

trancher, v.a. & n.

cut; cut off; carve; break off.

tranquille, adj. quiet, calm; soyez ~! don't worry!

tranquilliser, v. a. soothe, calm; se ~ keep calm.

transaction, s. f. compromise, transaction.

transalpin, adj. transalpine.

transatlantique, adj. transatlantic; — s. f. deck-chair.

transfert, s. m. transfer.

transformation, s. f. transformation, change.

transformer, v.a. transform, convert.

transfusion, s.f. transfusion.

transistor, s. m. transistor.

transit, s.m. transit.

transition, s.f. transition.

transmettre, v. a. transmit; forward; pass on.

transmission, s. f. transmission.

transparent, adj. transparent.

transpiration, s.f. perspiration.

transpirer, v. n. perspire.

transport, s. m. transport, conveyance; enterprise de ~ forwarding agency.

transporter, v.a. transport, convey; transfer; enrapture.

trappe, s. f. trap; trap-door.

travail, s. m. (pl. -aux) work, job, employment; task; piece of work; workmanship; petits travaux odd jobs; sans ~ unemployed.

travailler, v.n. & a. work, labour; take pains.

travailleur, -euse, *s. m. f.* worker, workman, workwoman.

travers, *s. m.* breadth; *à* ~ across, through; *au* ~ *de* through; *en* ~ across.

traverse, *s.f.* traverse; obstacle; crossing.

traversée, *s.f.* crossing, passage.

traverser, *v. a.* traverse, cross, go through; run through.

trayeuse, *s. f.* milking-machine.

trébucher, *v. n.* stumble; turn the scale.

tréfle, *s. m.* clover; club *(cards)*.

treille, *s. f.* vine arbour.

treize, *adj.* & *s.m.* thirteen;

tremblant, *adj.* tembling, shaky.

tremblement, *s. m.* trembling, shaking; ~ *de terre* earthquake.

trembler, *v. n.* tremble, shake.

tremper, *v. a.* soak, wet; dip; *il est tout trempé* he is wet through.

tremplin, *s.m.* springboard.

trentaine, *s.m.* thirty.

trente, *adj.* & *s. m.* thirty; thirtieth.

très, *adv.* very, most, very much; ~ *bien* very well; all right.

trésor, *s. m.* treasure.

trésorie, *s. f.* treasury.

trésorier, *s. m.* treasurer

tresse, *s. f.* plait, tress, braid.

trêve, *s. f.* truce, rest; *faire* ~ stop, cease.

triangle, *s. m.* triangle.

tribu, *s. f.* tribe.

tribunal, *s. m.* tribunal, law-court.

tribune, *s.f.* tribune, platform; grand-stand.

tributaire, *adj.* tributary.

tricher, *v. n.* & *a.* cheat; trick (s.o. out of).

tricot, *s.m.* (knitted) jersey.

tricoter, *v. a.* & *n.* knit.

triomphant, *adj.* triumphant.

triomphe, *s. m.* triumph.

triompher, *v. n.* triumph.

triple, *adj.* triple.

tripot, *s.m.* gambling-den.

triste, *adj.* sad.

tristesse, *s. f.* sadness.

trivial, *adj.* trivial.

trois, *adj.* & *s. m.* three; third.

troisième, *adj.* & *s. m.* third.

trolley, *s.m.* trolley (-pole).

trolleybus, *s. m.* trolleybus.

trompe, *s.f.* trumpet, horn.

tromper, *v. a.* deceive, cheat, take in; **se** ~ mistake, be mistaken; be wrong; *se* ~ *de train* take the wrong train.

trompette, *s. f.* trumpet; trumpeter.

tronc, *s. m.* trunk; stock; collecting box.

trône, *s.m.* throne.

trop, *adv.* too; too much.

trophée, *s. m.* trophy.

tropical, *adj.* tropical.

tropique, *s. m.* tropic.

trot, *s. m.* trot.

trotter, *v. n.* trot.

trottoir, *s. m.* pavement; footway.

trou, *s.m.* hole; gap; opening.

trouble, *s. m.* disorder; confusion; misunderstanding; dispute; — *adj.* troubled; muddy.

troubler, *v.a.* stir up,

disturb; make muddy; muddle; confuse, perplex; upset; trouble.

troué, *s. f.* opening, gap.

trouer, *v. a.* make a hole in; pierce; bore.

troupe, *s. f.* troop, band.

troupeau, *s.m.* herd, drove; flock.

trouvaille, *s. f.* find(ing)

trouver, *v. a.* find, discover; find out; think; contrive; se ~ be, be found to be, prove; turn out, happen; *je me trouvais là* I happened to be there.

truite, *s. f.* trout.

trust, *s. m.* trust.

T.S.F., *s. f.* (*=télégraphie sans fil)* wireless (set).

tu, toi, *pron.* you.

tube, *s. m.* tube; pipe; ~ *de télévision* TV tube.

tuberculose, *s. f.* tuberculosis.

tuer, *v. a.* kill; slay.

tuile, *s. f.* tile.

tumeur, *s. f.* tumour.

tunnel, *s. m.* tunnel.

turbine, *s. f.* turbine.

turbopropulseur, *s. m.* turbo-prop aircraft.

turboréacteur, *s.m.* turbo-jet engine.

turc, turque (T.),*adj.* Turkish (language), Turk.

tuteur, -trice, *s.m.f.* guardian, trustee.

tutoyer, *v. a.* to 'thee-and thou' s. o.

tuyau, *s. m.* pipe, tube; flue; ~ *d'échappement* exhaust-pipe.

tympan, *s. m.* ear-drum.

type, *s. m.* type.

typique, *adj.* typical.

typographie, *s. f.* typography; printing.

tyran, *s. m.* tyrant.

tyrannie, *s. f.* tyranny.

tyranniser, *v. a.* tyrannize (over); oppress.

U

ulcère, *s. m.* ulcer.

ultérieur, *adj.* ulterior; further.

ultime, *adj.* ultimate, last, final.

ultra-violet-, -ette, *adj.* ulra-violet.

un, une, *art. & pron.* a, an; any, some; one; *l'~ ou l'autre* either one or the other; *ni l'~ ni l'autre* neither one; *l'~ et autre* both; ~*e fois* once; ~ *à* ~ one by one.

unanime, *adj.* unanimous.

uni, *adj.* smooth, even, level; united.

unification, *s. f.* unification.

unifier, *v. a.* unify; unite.

uniforme, *adj.* uniform.

union, *s. f.* union; agreement: match, marriage.

unique, *adj.* unique, sole, only.

uniquement, *adv.* solely, only.

unir, *v.a.* unite; level; smooth; s'~ join.

unité, *s.f.* unity; unit.

univers, *s. m.* universe.

universel, -elle, *adj.* universal; world-wide.

universitaire, *adj.* academic, university.

université, *s.f.* university.

urbain, *adj.* urban.

urgence, *s.f.* urgency; *d'~* urgent; *en cas d'~* in case of emergency.

urgent, *adj.* urgent, pressing.

uriner, *v. n. & a.* urinate.

urne, *s. f.* urn.

usage, *s. m.* use, custom;

habit, way; wear; *d'~*
usual, habitual; *en ~*
in use.

usé, *adj.* worn-out,
shabby.

user, *v. n. & a.* use, make
use of; wear out; use
up; — *s.m.* wear,
service, use; *être d'un
bon ~* wear well.

usine, *s. f.* factory, works.

ustensile, *s. m.* utensil;
implement, tool.

usuel, -elle, *adj.* usual,
customary.

usure¹, *s. f.* usury.

usure², *s. f.* wear (and
tear).

usurper, *v.a.* usurp.

utile, *adj.* useful, of use,
profitable; *être ~ ( )*
be of use.

utilisation, *s.f.* utiliza-
tion.

utiliser, *v.a.* utilize.

utilité, *s. f.* utility, use.

V

va *int.* agreed!, indeed.

vacance, *s. f.* vacancy;
(pl.), holiday(s), va-
cation; *être en ~s* be
on holiday.

vacant, *adj.* vacant.

vacarme, *s.m.* noise,
uproar.

vaccin, *s.m.* vaccine.

vacciner, *v. a.* vaccinate.

vache, *s.f.* cow.

vaciller, *v.n.* vacillate;
reel; waver.

vacuum, *s. m.* vacuum.

vagabond, *s. m.* trampe.

vague¹, *adj.* vague.

vague², *s.f.* wave.

vaillant, *adj.* valiant.

vain, *adj.* vain; empty;
en ~ in vain.

vaincre*,   *v. a. & n.*

conquer, defeat.

vainqueur, *s.m.* conquer-
or, victor; — *adj.*
conquering, victorious.

vaisseau, *s. m.* vessel;
ship.

vaisselle, *s. f.* plates and
dishes, table-service;
laver la ~ wash up the
dishes; *lavage de ~*
washing-up.

valet, *s. m.* valet; knave,
jack.

valeur, *s. f.* value, worth;
price; courage; *~s* se-
curities.

valide, *adj.* valid; able-
bodied.

validité, *s.f.* validity.

valise, *s. f.* valise, (travel-
ling-)bag; suitcase; *~
diplomatique* dispatch-
box, diplomatic bag.

vallée, *s. f.* valley.

valoir*, *v.n. & a.* be
worth, be as good as;
deserve; procure; yield.

valse, *s.f.* waltz.

vanille, *s.f.* vanilla.

vanité, *s.f.* vanity.

vaniteux, -euse, *adj.* vain,
conceited.

vanter, *v. a.* extol, cry up;
se ~ boast.

vapeur¹, *s.f.* steam;
vapour.

vapeur², *s.m.* steamer.

vaporeux, -euse, *adj.* va-
porous.

vaquer, *v. n.* be vacant.

variable, *adj.* variable,
changeable.

variante, *s.f.* variant.

variation, *s.f.* variation.

varier, *v. n. & a.* vary;
~ de ... à range
from ... to.

variété, *s. f.* variety.

vase, *s. m.* vase; vessel.

vaseline, *s. f.* vaseline.

vassal, *s. m.* vassal.

vaste, *adj.* vast; spacious.

vautour, *s. m.* vulture.

veau, *s. m.* veal; calf.

vedette, *s.f.* mounted sentinel; motor-boat; (film) star.

végétal, *s. m.* vegetable; plant.

végétation, *s. f.* vegetation.

végéter, *v. n.* vegetate.

véhémence, *s. f.* vehemence.

véhément, *adj.* vehement.

véhicule, *s. m.* vehicle.

véhiculer, *v. a.* transport.

veille, *s. f.* waking; vigil; eve.

veiller, *v. n.* sit up, keep watch; *v.a.* watch.

veine, *s. f.* vein; luck.

vélo, *s.m.* bike.

vélocité, *s.f.* velocity.

velours, *s.m.* velvet.

velouté, *adj.* velvety, soft.

velu, *adj.* hairy.

venaison, *s.f.* venison.

vendange, *s.f.* vintage, grape-harvest.

vendeur, -euse, *s. m. f.* salesman, shop assistant; saleswoman.

vendre, *v. a.* sell; *à ~* for sale.

vendredi, *s. m.* Friday; *le ~ saint* Good Friday.

vénéneux, -euse, *adj.* poisonous.

vénérable, *adj.* venerable.

vengeance, *s. f.* vengeance, revenge.

venger, *v.a.* avenge, revenge; *se ~* avenge oneself.

venin, *s.m.* poison.

venir*, *v. n.* come, arrive; grow; occur; arise; *~ de* come from; *~ à bout de* manage.

vent, *s. m.* wind; *grand ~* gale; *~ alizé* trade-wind.

vente, *s. f.* sale; auction; *en ~* for sale.

venteux, -euse, *adj.* windy.

ventilateur, *s. m.* ventilator.

ventilation, *s. f.* ventilation.

ventre, *s. m.* belly.

venue, *s.f.* coming, arrival.

ver, *s.m.* worm.

verbal, *adj.* verbal, oral.

verbe, *s.m.* verb.

verdeur, *s.f.* greenness; harshness.

verdict, *s.m.* verdict.

verdure, *s.f.* verdure; greenness.

verger, *s.m.* orchard.

vergue, *s.f.* yard.

vérification, *s.f.* verification; check(ing).

vérifier, *v.a.* verify; check; confirm.

vérité, *s.f.* truth.

vermicelle, *s.m.* vermicelli.

vernir, *v. a.* varnish; polish.

vernis, *s.m.* varnish; polish.

verre, *s.m.* glass.

verrou, *s.m.* bolt.

verrouiller, *v.a.* bolt.

vers[1], *s.m.* line; verse.

vers[2], *prep.* towards, to; about.

verser, *v. a.* pour (out) spill, upset; *v. n.* overturn.

version, *s. f.* translation; version.

vert, *adj.* green; hearty; sharp.

vertical, *adj.* vertical, upright.

vertige, *s. m.* dizziness.

vertu, *s.f.* virtue.

vessie, *s.f.* bladder.

veste, *s. f.* coat, jacket.

vestiaire, *s. m.* cloakroom.

vestibule, *s.m.* lobby, hall; *grand* ~ lounge.

veston, *s. m.* coat; *complet* ~ lounge-suit.

vêtement, *s.m.* clothes *(pl.);* ~*s de dessous* underwear, underclothes.

vétéran, *s.m.* veteran.

vétérinaire, *s. m.* veterinary surgeon, vet.

vêtir*, *v. a.* clothe, dress.

véto, *s.m.* veto.

veuf, *s.m.* widower.

veuve, *s.f.* widow.

vexer, *v. a.* vex, annoy.

via, *prep.* via.

viaduc, *s. m.* viaduct.

viande, *s. m.* meat; ~ *réfrigérée* chilled meat.

vibration, *s. f.* vibration.

vibrer, *v. n.* vibrate.

vicaire, *s.m.* curate.

vice, *s.m.* vice, evil.

vice-, *prefix* vice-.

vicieux, -euse, *adj.* vicious; faulty.

vicomte, *s. m.* viscount.

victime, *s.f.* victim.

victoire, *s.f.* victory.

victorieux, -euse, *adj.* victorious.

victuailles, *s. f. pl.* victuals.

vide, *adj.* empty; void; vacant; — *s.m.* space.

vider, *v. a.* empty; drain.

vie, *s.f.* life.

vieillard, *s.m.* old man.

vieillesse, *s.f.* old age.

vieillir, *v.n.* grow old.

vierge, *s. f.* virgin, maid.

vieux, vieil, vieille, *adj.* old.

vif, vive, *adj.* live; quick; lively; full of life; bright, vivid; fiery, ardent.

vigilant, *adj.* watchful.

vigne, *s.f.* vine; vineyard.

vignoble, *s.m.* vineyard.

vigoureux, -euse, *adj.* vigorous.

vigueur, *s.f.* vigour force.

vilain, *s. m.* villain, ca(

village, *s.m.* village.

ville, *s. f.* town, city; *hôtel de* ~ town hall.

vin, *s. m.* wine.

vinaigre, *s. m.* vinegar.

vingt, *adj.* & *s.m.* twenty; twentieth.

vingtième, *adj.* twentieth.

violation, *s.f.* violation.

violence, *s.f.* violence.

violent, *adj.* violent; excessive.

violer, *v. a.* violate, ravish.

violette, *s.f.* violet.

violon, *s.m.* violin.

violoncelle, *s. m.* (violon-) cello.

violoniste, *s. m f.* violinist.

vipère, *s.f.* viper.

virgule, *s.f.* comma; *point et* ~ semicolon.

virtuose, *s. m. f.* virtuoso.

vis, *s. f.* screw.

visa, *s.m.* visa, visé.

visage, *s. m.* face.

vis-à-vis, *prep.* opposite; facing.

viser, *v.a.* aim (at); aspire to.

viseur, *s. m.* view-finder.

visibilité, *s. f.* visibility.

visible, *adj.* visible.

vision, *s.f.* sight.

visite, *s. f.* visit; *faire* ~ *à* pay a visit to, call on.

visiter, *v. a.* visit; ~ *les curiosités* go sightseeing.

visiteur, -euse, *s. m. f.* visitor.

visser, *v. a.* screw (down, in).

visuel, -elle, *adj.* visual.

vital, *adj.* vital.

vitalité, *s.f.* vitality.

vitamine, *s. f.* vitamin.

vite, *adj.* fast; swift; — *adv.* fast, rapidly.

vitesse, *s. f.* speed; rate (of speed); gear; *à toute ~* at top speed; *boîte de ~* gear-box; *~ de croisière* cruising speed.

vitrail *s. m.* church window.

vitre, *s. f.* pane.

vitrier, *s.m.* glazier.

vivant, *adj.* alive, living; full of life; *de mon ~* in my lifetime.

vivement, *adv.* quickly, fast.

vivre*, *v. n.* live, be alive.

vocabulaire, *s. m.* vocabulary.

vocation, *s.f.* vocation, calling.

vœu, *s. m. (pl. -x)* wish, desire; vow.

vogue, *s. f.* vogue, fashion; *avoir la ~* be in vogue.

voici, *prep.* here (is); *le ~!* here he is!

voie, *s.f.* way, road; route; line, track; means, channel.

voilà, *prep.* there (is).

voile¹, *s.m.* veil.

voile², *s.f.* sail.

voiler, *v.a.* veil, cover, hide.

voilier, *s. m.* sailing-ship.

voir*, *v. a.* see; look at; view; *faire ~* show; *ne pas ~* miss.

voire, *adv.* even.

voisin, *adj.* neighbouring, adjoining, next (door).

voisinage, *s.m.* neighbourhood.

voiture, *s.f.* vehicle, conveyance; carriage; car; coach; van; wagon; *aller en ~* drive.

voiture-ambulance, *s. f.* ambulance(-car).

voix, *s. f.* voice; sound; *à haute ~* aloud.

vol¹, *s. m.* flying, flight.

vol², *s. m.* theft, robbery.

volaille, *s.f.* poultry, fowl.

volant, *s.m.* steering-wheel.

volcan, *s.m.* volcano.

volée, *s.f.* flight.

voler¹, *v. n.* fly; run at top speed.

voler², *v. a. & n.* steal, rob.

volet, *s.m.* shutter.

voleur, *s. m.* thief, robber.

volontaire, *adj.* voluntary; — *s. m. f.* volunteer.

volonté, *s. f.* will; *à ~* at will.

volontiers, *adv.* willingly.

volt, *s.m.* volt.

voltiger, *v.n.* flutter about, fly about.

volume, *s. m.* volume; bulk.

voluptueux, -euse, *adj.* voluptuous.

vomir, *v. a. & n.* vomit, be sick.

vos, *adj. poss.* your.

vote, *s. m.* vote; voting.

voter, *v. n. ~ & a.* vote.

votre, *adj.* yours.

vouer, *v. a.* vow; dedicate.

vouloir*, *v. a.* want, require, demand; *~ bien* be willing; *je voudrais + inf.* I should like to; *comme vous voulez* as you please.

vous, *pron.* you; to you.

vous-même, *pron.* yourself.

voûte, *s.f.* vault, arch.

voyage, *s.m.* journey; voyage; *bon ~!* a pleasant journey (to you)!; *partir en* ~ set off on a journey; *faire un* ~ make a journey.

voyager, *v.n.* travel, make a trip.

voyageur, -euse, *s. m. f.* traveller, passenger.

voyelle, *s.f.* vowel.

voyou, *s.m.* hooligan.

vrai, *adj.* real, true, right; *être* ~ hold (good); — *s. m.* truth; *être dans le* ~ be right.

vraiment, *adv.* truly, really; indeed.

vraisemblable, *adj.* likely, credible, probable.

vu, *prep.* considering.

vue, *s. f.* sight; vision; view; *à* ~ at sight; *en* ~ *de* with a view to; *point de* ~ point of view; *avoir la* ~ *courte* be short-sighted; *être en* ~ be in the limelight.

vulgaire, *adj.* vulgar; common; coarse.

W

wagon, *s. m.* coach, carriage, car.

wagon-lit, *s. m.* sleeping-car.

wagonnet, *s.m.* tub; truck.

wagon-poste, *s. m.* mail-van.

wagon-restaurant, *s. m.* dining-car.

water-closet, *s. m.* W. C.

water-polo, *s. m.* water-polo.

wattman, *s.m.* tram-driver.

week-end, *s.m.* week-end.

whisky, *s.m.* whisky.

X

xérès, *s. m.* sherry.

xylographie, *s. f.* xylography.

xylophages, *s.m.* *pl.* xylophages.

Y

y, *adv.* here, there; *il* ~ *a* there is, there exists; *s'* ~ *connaître* well informed.

yacht, *s. m.* yacht.

yeux *see* œil.

yogourt, yoghourt, *s. m.* yoghourt, yaourt.

yougoslave, *adj.* Yugoslav.

youyou, *s.m.* dinghy.

Z

zèbre, *s.m.* zebra.

zébrer, *v.a.* stripe.

zèle, *s.m.* zeal.

zélé, *adj.* zealous.

zénith, *s.m* zenith.

zéro, *s.m.* zero.

zézayer, *v.n.* lisp.

zigzag, *s.m.* zigzag.

zinc, *s.m.* zinc.

zone, *s.f.* zone, belt.

zoo, *s.m.* zoo.

zoologie, *s.f.* zoology.

zoologique, *adj.* zoological.

zut, *int.* ~*!* damn it!